Additional Praise for *Souls of My Brothers*

"Too often when it comes to expressing feelings from the heart, not only are we not socialized to do so, but our women do not allow us to speak of such things. Finally, a vehicle for us to talk from the heart! What we have to say will blow you away."
—Dr. Jeff Gardere

"*Souls of My Brothers* is a great thing for Black men, simply because we have not talked with one another enough. Finally we can come together and find out what are possible solutions."
—Al Goodman, from Ray, Goodman, & Brown/legendary singer and songwriter

"*Souls of My Brothers* is an opportunity for men to express themselves. We all have hopes and dreams, we all need a definite support system in order to have dreams realized."
—R.W. McQuarter, NFL football player (Chicago Bears)

Dawn Marie Daniels was an editor for eight years at Simon & Schuster, where she worked on adult nonfiction such as Iyanla Vanzant's *New York Times* bestsellers *In the Meantime* and *One Day My Soul Just Opened Up.*

Candace Sandy serves as the communications director for Congressman Gregory Meeks (D-NY). She was recently awarded the prestigious 40 Under 40 Award for her civic and professional work. Candace is a former radio advertising bureau fellow, and continues to produce for television and radio. She works with the U.S. Department of Justice Weed and Seed program in east New York. Dawn and Candace have also been honored with the 2002 Amazing Woman Award and the Golden Pen Award for their literary effort.

SOULS OF
MY BROTHERS

Black Men Break Their Silence,
Tell Their Truths,
and Heal Our Spirits

Edited and written by

DAWN MARIE DANIELS
AND CANDACE SANDY

With a Foreword by Isaac Hayes

A PLUME BOOK

PLUME
Published by the Penguin Group
Penguin Group (USA) Inc., 375 Hudson Street, New York, New York 10014, U.S.A.
Penguin Books Ltd, 80 Strand, London WC2R 0RL, England
Penguin Books Australia Ltd, 250 Camberwell Road, Camberwell, Victoria 3124, Australia
Penguin Books Canada Ltd, 10 Alcorn Avenue, Toronto, Ontario, Canada M4V 3B2
Penguin Books India (P) Ltd, 11 Community Centre, Panchsheel Park, New Delhi – 110 017, India
Penguin Books (N.Z.) Ltd, Cnr Rosedale and Airborne Roads, Albany, Auckland 1310, New Zealand
Penguin Books (South Africa) (Pty) Ltd, 24 Sturdee Avenue, Rosebank, Johannesburg 2196, South Africa

Penguin Books Ltd, Registered Offices: 80 Strand, London WC2R 0RL, England

First published by Plume, a member of Penguin Group (USA) Inc.

First Printing, September 2003
3 5 7 9 10 8 6 4 2

℗ REGISTERED TRADEMARK—MARCA REGISTRADA

LIBRARY OF CONGRESS CATALOGING-IN-PUBLICATION DATA
Daniels, Dawn Marie.
Souls of my brothers : Black men break their silence, tell their truths, and heal our spirits / written and edited by Dawn Marie Daniels and Candace Sandy ; with a foreword by Isaac Hayes.
p. cm.
ISBN 0-452-28460-0
1. African American men—Social conditions. 2. African American men—Psychology.
3. African American men—Biography. 4. Conduct of life—United States.
5. Spirituality—United States. 6. African Americans—Social conditions—1975–
7. African Americans—Civil rights. I. Sandy, Candace. II. Title.
E185.86.D356 2003
305.896'073—dc21   2003046744

Printed in the United States of America
Set in Janson Text

We dedicate this book to God because He shows us each and every day, regardless of the obstacles, through Him *everything* is and will continue to be possible.

CONTENTS

FOREWORD

Issac Hayes changed the way black men look at themselves.
—John Singleton

I never knew poverty, because I had nothing else to compare my life to. I grew up on a farm in Covington, Tennessee, about thirty miles north of Memphis. We raised and made our own food. I remember catching chickens, milking the cows, slaughtering hogs, churning butter, picking cotton, getting water from a well and then boiling it.

My mother died when I was a year and a half, and my older half sister and I went to live with my grandparents. We lived across the road from a church and a school, so I used to go over and sit in the schoolhouse. By the time I was six, I already had a third-grade education.

That's when my grandparents decided to move to the city. We packed everything up and moved to Memphis—and what a culture shock that was.

I was almost seven, and it was the first time I was seeing a supermarket or living in housing that was so close to a neighbor. At school, the officials at the Klondike Elementary School said that education in rural areas was inferior, so they put me back in the first grade, even though I was already reading my uncles' books.

I stayed for three grades at Klondike, and then my grandfather's health began to fail. He was working in a tomato factory, but he got sick so we moved again. Several times, in fact! But finally we settled in Manassas, and I began attending the Manassas High School. Those were hard times. I would go to school hungry and come back hungry. We were living below the welfare state. Sometimes I worked in the school cafeteria just to get a free lunch token. It was that bad.

But I was growing up, and suddenly I began realizing that I didn't look like the other boys in the school. I was raggedy, and there were holes in my shoes and patches on my clothes. So in humiliation, I began hanging out at street corners instead of going to school. After six weeks, the school officials came to see my grandmother and tell her I wasn't going to school. She had no idea, and the look she gave me said it all.

So I went back, with hand-me-down help. In those years, I did anything I could. I mowed lawns; cleaned shoes; washed cars; delivered coal; pulled groceries in a wagon; poured cement and cleaned mortar off bricks; worked as a stock boy; picked soy, peaches, and strawberries; and chopped cotton in the fields of Arkansas. We got two dollars and fifty cents per every hundred pounds of cotton we picked and three dollars a day for chopping.

During all this I entered a music talent contest and I won. Suddenly I was popular. My dreams of becoming a doctor went through the window. That's when I knew I was going to be a musician, so I changed my classes and began taking band lessons and vocal music classes.

I began doing lead vocals with Calvin Valentine and the Swing Cats, a blues band. I then became a part of a gospel group called the Morning Stars and later two doo-wop groups, the Teen Tones & the Ambassadors and the Missiles. Several times during that period we went to audition at Stax-Volt Records, but each time we were turned down. Upon graduation, I copped several global music scholarships and was up there giving a speech with the valedictorian.

After high school, I continued playing at clubs. Sidney Kurke, my friend, played with the group. Sidney would play the keyboard while I sang, but suddenly Sidney went to the air force. I was all alone, not knowing what to do when Sidney's sister stepped in and asked me if I would play the keyboard at a nightclub. I was stricken with fear because I didn't know how to play as well as Sidney. Sure I'd played some notes, but I went ahead and accepted the gig. Then the band started playing, and they were awful. But with the party going and the drinks flowing, no one seemed to mind. That soon became a steady job until I joined up with Floyd Newman. He was a staff musician at Stax Records. We played from 9 P.M. to 4 A.M. five to six nights a week. I was growing and learning, and when Floyd began recording, the owner of the label, who had heard me play, offered me a job as a keyboard player for Stax.

My first session was with Otis Redding. There I was, again afraid, but Otis had a great personality. I learned so much from watching him. Soon after, I met David Porter. We used to be rivals in high school, but we decided to team up as Hayes-Porter and began writing and producing lyrics for Stax. We were writing for Rufus Thomas, Carla Thomas, Sam and Dave and the Emotions and producing the Soul Children and Johnnie Taylor, and we even wrote something for Otis. There was "Something Wrong with My Baby," "Hold On, I'm Coming," and "Soul Man."

In 1967, I decided to return to singing and recorded my first album, called *Presenting Isaac Hayes*, with sidemen Donald "Duck" Dunn on bass and Al Jackson on drums, and me on piano. It sold a bit, and I got some acclaim but not much.

Still Stax's executive vice president urged me to do a cut on an album they were working on called *Hot Buttered Soul*. I sang "Walk On By," and I was stunned at the ovation it got. The album became a hit; suddenly I was a star.

But I never forgot the struggle. Like the challenges of all Black men in America, it was a tumultuous one, fighting against insurmountable odds but still having the will to survive. All through the adversities, Black men have remained loyal to this country.

In the South, I remember marching around lunch counters and living in fear because white children threw eggs at Blacks and crosses were being burnt on our lawns. I was scared, but I did it anyway because we wanted changes in our communities.

What bothered me most was the lack of recognition of who Blacks in America are as a people or what we had earned and deserved. Then there were the lies and the persuasion to believe those lies, the denial of opportunities and how we so easily forgot our history.

We owe so much to Dr. Martin Luther King Jr., who helped shake things up and make drastic changes. Because of him and other heroes like Frederick Douglass, Marcus Garvey, Malcolm X, Congressman Adam Clayton Powell Jr., and so many other Black leaders in our history, we as a people started to realize we are important, that Black is beautiful.

When Dr. King was killed, I snapped. For an entire year I couldn't write. I became bitter and angry. That's when I began mobilizing. We formed a group called the Black Knights and began the fight against job discrimination and police brutality. We took our fight to city hall and met with the mayor and the police commissioner of Memphis.

I remember thinking that if Dr. King gave his life for us, the least I could do is to keep the fight going. I got involved in voter registration and politics, helping former Congressman Harold Ford Sr. to win his seat in the House.

In 1978, I went to South Africa for the first time. It was during the height of apartheid, and the institution was a total shock to me. Initially, I had a negative attitude about going. I told the producers that I would not play to segregated audiences, and they agreed. When I got to South Africa, I was appalled and angry to see the way Blacks were treated. I spent a month in that country and it was horrific, especially the way Black South Africans were banned from entering certain places like hotels. Of course, I ignored those rules and took the band in with me always, forcing them to shut down the hotels. But I was always in their faces about it.

So began my sojourn into Africa. I went back in 1980 to Sierra Leone as an observer of an Organization of African Unity (OAU) conference. In 1992, I traveled to Ghana to work with Dionne Warwick. That's where I had a life-changing experience. We were visiting the slaves' dungeons, and I was standing there, listening to the guide, when suddenly I got this weird feeling. It was like my ancestors were talking to me and they were saying, "Welcome home. Our life is now complete."

I came back to the United States and launched a series of speaking tours and expos. It was after one such engagement that a woman from Queens, New York, called me up to say she had heard one of my speeches and had told her father about me. She said that her family wanted to honor me with the title of King. I was stunned. The lady turned out to be Princess Aci Ochansey of the province of Ada in the southeastern part of Ghana. She was studying here in the United States, but we traveled back to Ghana in December 1992, and they performed the ceremony that declared me a king of development. I was bestowed the name Nene Ketey Ochansey. *Nene* means "king" and *Ketey* means "brave warrior." *Ochansey* is the family name that means "I do as I say."

Ever since 1992, I've traveled back to Ghana several times each year. In 2000, I built a school there to help children train in technology. Princess Aci moved back to help run the school. Today, we're vigorously helping in the fight against HIV/AIDS and spreading literacy throughout the area. I intend to continue taking development projects there.

One day I hope to be remembered as a Black man who made a contribution to his people and one who is proud of his history. That is why this book, *Souls of My Brothers*, is so important. It documents and reveals the true feelings of Black men. There are usually a lot of misconceptions about us, and this collection of essays gives us an opportunity to communicate our real selves. We are a decent people and we want the world to know that. More especially, we want our kids to know that, so they can cast aside all the negative thoughts and stereotypes. For too long we've been denied an education of our history and ourselves. We need to teach the kids where they came from and that black is not inferior, but beautiful.

—ISAAC HAYES

Isaac Hayes's *ongoing career includes turns as an artist, songwriter, session man, film author, composer, radio host, and actor. He is also involved in humanitarian*

concerns as a bona fide African king! He is the international spokesman for the Ap-
plied Scholastics World Literacy Crusade International. The Isaac Hayes Founda-
tion also partners with other nonprofit organizations to support global causes that
serve the needs of the community. Hayes has turned his love of food and music
toward opening restaurants, the first in his beloved Memphis.

ACKNOWLEDGMENTS

We would like to thank every single man who wrote an essay or joined us in a roundtable, pulled up a chair, and shared his life with us. We appreciate your candor and most of all your love.

So many people stepped up and made it possible for this book to happen. They saw our vision and understood that Black men have been suffering for too long. Special thanks to the team who made it happen.

Extraordinary thanks to the team who pulled and stretched for us: Karu F. Daniels, Dr. Jarraylne Agee, Curtis Taylor, Melvenia Guye, Dolly Turner, Jacqueline Rowe, Barbara Hamilton, Sit Back and Relax concierge Akinah H. Rahmaan, Laura Ciocia, Kim Fuller, Selena Johnson, Ursula Miller of Ugoddess Entertainment, Traci Humprey, Carla Alleyne, Jade Hill, Yami Hamilton, Imar Hutchins, Cheryl Gentry, and Andrea Fairweather—you guys are amazing.

Special thanks to Tanya McKinnon of the Mary Evans Agency and the Plume Family: Trena Keating, Laura Blumenthal, and Brant Janeway—you are true treasures, and we really appreciate you.

To Calvin Hunter, you are extraordinary. To all of the contributors to *Souls of My Sisters:* Your continued love and support has been a true blessing. With extra gratitude and love for going the distance: Ilyasah Shabazz, Maria Davis, Patti Webster, Pastor Patricia Webster, Jessica McLean Ricketts, Phyllis Beech, Kia Skrine, Lonai Mosely, Darnelle McCullough, Jerry Lucas, Pamm Malveaux, Deborah Williams, Cheryl Procter, LaJoyce Brookshire, Dolly Turner, Hazel Dukes, Dr. Jan Burt, Karen Taylor, and honorary Soul Sister Dawn Cotter Jenkins, who started the first Souls of My Sisters Book Club and Nicole Wild, our Soul Sister from Australia. Terrie Williams, Sandra St. Victor, Ivy Simmons, Felicia Middlebrooks, Kimberly S. Varner, Reverend Patricia Webster, Vivian Scott Chew, Nefatiti

Brooks, Kathy Starks Dow, Melody Guy, LisaRaye, Victoria Clark, Pamela Shine, Lorraine Barrett, Angela Kenney, Marsha Bowen, Lorraine Robertson, Eneida Martino-Laguerra, Michelle L. Buckley, Melissa E. Brooks and Jill Merritt.

To the African American Publicity Collective: Gwendolyn Quinn and Marlynn Synder formed a group of five hundred publicists nationally and in Canada who communicate and share resources. Their group gave this book flight and we truly appreciate them: Tammy Warren, Miatta David, Tonya Peyton, Rhonda Jones, Tiaka Hurst, Robyn Ryland-Saunders, Gill Robertson, and photographer Ronnie Wright, Hillary Beard, Carletta Hurt (who worked it out for us in Atlanta), Lynn Allen Jeter. All we have to say is hire these people.

Edna Sims Brunce, Elsa Lathan, Fay Bailey, Greg King, Irene Gandy, Joyce Andrews, Lauren Summers, Lauren Summers, Lea Byrd, Lelani Clark, Leslie Short, Margot Jordan, Renee Foster, Yvette Hayward, JackieOMedia, Octavia Dosier, Dawn Marie Gray, Morena Lamonthe, BiBi Green, Pamela Smith, Ruthie Atkins-Robinson, Simeon Hankerson, Rachel Lewis, Kim LaReid's office.

While creating this book, we traveled via some wonderful airlines to many locations and met some very nice people who encouraged us along our journey, including the Sheraton Bal Habour in Florida (Alice, you are amazing), The Palms in Miami Beach (Gunthram, we appreciate you), Jamaica Airlines, Sunset Beach and Resort, Andrian and James of the Wyndham Belage on Sunset in Los Angeles (thank you, Chetera Collins), and the Cape Codder Resort in Cape Cod. Special thanks to Jamaica Airlines. We would also like to thank Keith Clinkscale, Russell Simmons, Gary Hardwick, Andre Kyle Henry, Treach, Demelte Guidry, Derryl Speers, Burgess.

Thanks Mike Valdez, the best Web designer in the world, at fastnickel.com, and his associates, Carlos Rojas and Damian Bennett at DBCreative.

Dawn Marie Daniels

I want to thank God, who has truly blessed me. This effort is born of my love for God and all that He does for His children. The lessons I have learned and continue to learn from Him are my joy and fulfillment.

First, I want to thank all the special men in my life. My father, Henry Daniels, who has inspired me and loves me unconditionally. My sons, Mark and Martin, who I am so proud of. I'm honored to be their mother. You make my life so much brighter and full. To my brothers, Danny, Darryl, and David, although we all live in different places, my love for you is always near.

Monsignor Wallace Harris, Father Eddie Cipot, and Deacon Rodney of the Saint Charles Borromeo family, I want to thank you for your inspirational words that are always warmly mixed with wisdom and wit. Pastor Wyatt T. Walker and Pastor Greg Jones of the Canaan Baptist Church Family, whose words inspired by God have always been what I needed to hear when I needed to hear it. Pastor Joel Limerick, your comforting words and encouragement will always be cherished. To all the St. Aloysius family for their love and support. The work you do in our community is priceless.

To Michael Knight, thanks for being a friend. I have always believed in your dreams even when you didn't. I am proud of you and all that you have accomplished. Imar Hutchins, thank you for your friendship, support and legal advice. I couldn't begin to say how much it's been worth. To John Watson, I'm so glad you are back in my life; it's like you never left. To Melvin Taylor, thanks for being my buddy, adviser, and friend. Walter Hutchins, thank you for your support, patience, and wisdom. My "cousin" Karu Daniels, thanks for your talent, humor, and wisdom. To my friend in faith, Chattman Johnson, for your kind words and advice.

To George Jackson and Kenny Greene, who are with God putting on some beautiful productions, we miss you.

Now for the women in my life. Mom, you are a wonderful woman who inspires me to be my best—thank you. Mom Pat, you are like a second mother to me—I love you! My grandmothers, Margaret Georke, Jesse Young, Emily McClain, and Rose Lee, thank you for being the strong, beautiful, and intelligent women you have always been. To my sisters, Alicia and Kim, I am proud of the women you have become.

To Candace Sandy, my soul sister who is always there for me even when I can't be there for myself, I love you and cherish our friendship. I look forward to continuing to support your dreams and goals.

To my sister friends Lavonne Hall, Christine Saunders, Maria Davis, Melody Guy, Erica Heyward, Allison Poole, Alice Harmon, Karla Draffen, Carolyn Hall, and Tonya Pope, you are the most wonderful women, and my life is enriched and so much better for our friendships. My mentors, Mary Bannister, Marilyn Abraham, Sheila Curry, and Becky Cabaza, thanks for paving the way for me and passing on your wisdom. Tina Winston-Lucas, you are an angel from God, and I truly appreciate you. My wonderful friends Bella and Dana Gibbs, who always make me feel special. My intelligent, talented and beautiful goddaughter, Tory Cheyenne Jackson, you are going to move mountains and change the course of history—I love you.

Little Miss Jhanna Davis, you possess a light within you that shines so bright and will only be brighter as you get older.

Candace Sandy

First and foremost, I would like to thank God, who has been the source for all and for whom I work humbly to accomplish my purpose. I was tested while writing this book, and the power of family is more important to me more than ever. My parents, Patricia and Carlton Samuel, who have turned into my best friends, my brothers Sheldon and Sherwin and my sister Saundra, who showed me that love has to be unconditional. To my aunts Geraldine (Amu), Helen, Jennifer, Henetta, Joni, Pat, Lisa Fraley, Ollie Gables, Joan Brathwaite. My uncles are the ultimate soul brothers, Uncle Vernell (Vush), Wendell, Trevor, Frank (Uncle Timmie) Fraley, Uncle Arnold. To my godmother, Cyrilla LaBorde—I see myself in you. To my cousins, Jackie, Ann, Paula, Chatarra, Brent, Jodelle, Natalie, Terrence, Trevon, Donica, Danica, Franklin, Elijah, and Langston, and all of my nieces and nephews Crystal, Nicole, Taylor, Carlos. My godchildren Mark Daniels, Channel Skyers, Martin Daniels, Naiomi Ligon, and Alyssa Ragin—all I can say is *wow!* Gary and Amy Krakow, thank you.

Dawn Daniels, I have been blessed with God positioning you in my life to teach me lessons and create a plan so that I can be better equipped to handle my purpose. You are a Soul Sister, and you will always have my love and support in fulfilling your dreams. It has been a very humbling experience, and thank you for joining me on my journey through life.

Every woman should be as lucky as I have have been with the people in my life who are just amazing. I have found best friends in men since I was about fourteen. They have taught me so much that I feel like I see the world in Technicolor—Kirk Vanzie, Al Ragin, Darren Miller, my very best friends Melvin Taylor, J.C. Callendar, Glenn Toby, Conely Van Reil, Calvin Nelson, David Johnson, Joseph Fulmore Jr., Leo Gatewood, Nick Williams, Clifford Lazarre.

My two best friends since the fourth grade and very special women, Maggie Goring and Cristy Colon, you both inspire me to be and do more. To Vera Gaskin, Ovella Bilal, Elisabeth Jackson and Ma, Allison Moore, and Paquita Hazel—may God continue to bless all of you, and thank you. Ty Young of Music Business Consultants, you have shown me how business is done. To Maribel Ng and her amazing support from the women at Maribel's Salon.

Patty Williams, Michelle Burns, Alithia Alleyne-Ligon, Joye Foust,

Royal Bayaan, Natasha Gilbert, Stephanie, Noreen Farmer, Jackie Williams, Marsha Steadman, James Goring, Jose Guerrero, Tevera Asbury, Larry Dunlap, Jennifer Pottheiser, Tiffany Ragin, Tanya Holland-Mcpherson and family, Nadia Suilman and Christine Notaro'al, Donna Karan and the Donna Karan family, Stacey Cummings, Miyoshi and Quinton Brawaithe, and Carol Gibson. Special thanks for their unyielding support: Tevera Asbury, Larry Dunlap, Melissa Mann-Jones, Patrick Henry Bass, Norman McCullough, Carol Green, fellow writers Renee Cummings, Merle English, Warren Woodberry, Dan Hendricks, Shams Tarek, Pat Adams, Mitch Abrahamson, Courtney Dench, Denise Cherry, Jim Harney, Tara Wright, and Jacque Reid. Jeanne Marie Denslow of the Ritz Carlton, Lloyd Headley, Cheryl Edrghodaro, Patrick Wilson, Dr. Fran Cook, Tracy Walker of the Londell McMillan and Partners, Chamberlain Peterside, Lynn Gonzalez, Jerry, and Chris Washington. I am very grateful to the Christian Cultural Center located at 1220 Flatlands Avenue, Brooklyn, New York and the Reverend A. R. Bernard and first lady Karen Bernard for a tremendous wealth of spiritual nourishment.

To Congressman Meeks and his wife and contributor to *Souls of My Sisters* Simone Marie Meeks, and to Patrick Jenkins, Jameel Johnson, Ida Smith, Mike Mckay, Pat Fisher, Jacqueline Pinkney, Irleen Nelson, Arlene, Bob Simmons, Ed Williams, Anthony Hill, Jennifer Stewart Marc Meealy, and my former collegues Faith Balckurne, Pyria Dayanda, Mrs. Johnson, Veronica Beckford, Nicole Collins—we know that you are with the angels. United States Department of Justice Weed and Seed program and Help USA staff, including Jeannette Ruffins, Mary O'Donoghue, Eze Van Buckely, Rick Capobianco, Michael Kneis, James Tillman, Dennis Taylor, Dedra Grant Wade, Felicia Little John, Sharon Fennimore, Ola and Jennifer, Nancy Thomas, Tamara Harris, Roslyn Payne, and Sabrina. To City Councilwoman Tracy L. Boyland and her staff.

To James Steele, Glendry Michelle, and Jon Hill.

INTRODUCTION

We began this endeavor humble at heart. Truly we didn't know how it would change our lives, perspectives, and views of Black men. We were already in awe of the men in our lives, young and old, but traveling across country and sitting with men we didn't know, hearing their thoughts on everything from money and politics to survival, family, and everything else in between made us realize just how fascinating and inspiring they all truly are. The men we sat with opened up their hearts, bared their souls, and gave us a piece of themselves that we will cherish forever.

We never thought it was a coincidence that when we decided that our next book would be about Black men, issues with the men in our lives cropped up. We experienced all kinds of things with the men we love and trust, be it our brothers, fathers, sons, boyfriends, or friends. It had nothing to do with our writing the book; it was more a shift in ourselves that produced shifts in our relationships. We were learning new things about men in general and began to apply that knowledge to the way we communicated with the men in our lives. We saw a significant difference in our relationships. The things we learned and the information we received helped us immensely in our personal relationships. The changes that were occurring gave us even more resolve to listen to Black men and to hear their views on myriad subjects and to get a better understanding of them and our relationship to them in the world.

In the past, we were frequently asked if *Souls of My Sisters* was a malebashing book. We always replied that we had to start with who we were first and get right with ourselves as Black women. *Souls of My Brothers* is about our continued journey towards understanding the hurt, pain, hopes, dreams, sacrifices, achievements, and the collective healing of Black men. We all need to know that their joy as well as their pain is ours to share and the need to begin the healing process is more important now than ever before if we want to save our families.

Whenever and wherever we did readings from *Souls of My Sisters*, whether it was in a bookstore, living room, a university, or at a special event, men in the audience would express their desire to tell their stories. "What about us?" or "We have something to say, too!" would inevitably come from a brother or two in the audience. At one particular event, the men in the audience could not hold back their feelings any longer, and you could feel their frustration filling the room.

The interesting thing was, after the book signings, the men would pull us aside and confide in us. It wasn't that we didn't invite them to participate; it was just that they didn't feel comfortable bringing up their personal issues in a public forum where the majority of attendees were Black women. We heard from a big, burly, successful contractor who had been physically abused by his wife for ten years. Or the polished young Wall Street executive whose mother killed his father because he was physically abusing her. Some of the men were raised in foster care, while others were coping with the loss of love, self-identity, and self-esteem. Some had deferred their dreams because of what society dictated. Others felt unsupported or destined to fail. There were also men who were eager and happy to raise their children, and others who followed their dreams and inspired us.

What Do You Know About Black Men?

When we shared with men that we were in the process of writing and producing this book, the skeptical response would always be, "What do *you* know about Black men?"

The answer was, "We don't know a great deal about Black men, but we love them, and since we have a deep desire to progress as a race, we need to learn as much as we can." We wanted to be accurate and fair in giving voices to men from all across the country, with different experiences and backgrounds. We distributed several hundred surveys across the nation and conducted several focus groups and roundtables from New York to Los Angeles, San Francisco to Miami, and anywhere else we could go. These roundtables took place in living rooms, boardrooms, barbershops, and hotels. The roundtables helped to shape the book and gave us insight to the hopes, dreams, opinions, motivations, and thoughts of Black men of all ages.

There were many things we learned about Black men while conducting our roundtables. The first (and we think, most important) thing we realized was that the men were grateful to have an open forum in which to talk. Many of them said they had never experienced being in a group of such diverse men and being able to talk about their feelings and the issues on their minds. We must explain that when we conducted the roundtables, there were very few and in some cases no women allowed other than ourselves. When women did attend the roundtables, they weren't allowed to speak until after the session was over. You may be asking yourself, "Why can women attend, but not speak?" We felt it was important that the men in attendance feel free to express themselves without being attacked or judged. This format allowed the women in the group to just sit back and truly absorb the powerful revelations. The female participants thanked us at the end because they felt that they received precious information that they had never before heard, especially in that way. After these sessions, many of the men also explained to us that they had never been in a room where women were present and men were able to speak freely, without being interrupted, and express their true thoughts or feelings.

We also observed that the men felt a collective sense of powerlessness to change the world around them. Almost all the men we met talked about change. They had a deep burning desire to change the conditions of our society. Whether it was to create better schools and programs for the children in their communities, to see laws designed to protect rather than hinder the lives of Black people, or to secure a financial future for the Black community, they wanted to become agents for change, but didn't know how. We met men who were making vast contributions to society, but were still frustrated because they know there's more to do and more people needed to do it. Others felt that their solitary efforts weren't enough to produce mass change and were almost discouraged to start or to even continue.

A unanimous thought from all Black men we spoke with across the country was that they're tired of hearing negative things about themselves. There is a wave amongst black men who are sick and tired, tired and sick of being stereotyped. They want to learn from one another, be accepted, be given advice, and be mentored. They want to raise their children. They want to be responsible, and if they've achieved success, they are looking for peace. They want to leave a legacy and grow closer with Black women. They want to be understood and to communicate with one another and everyone around them. They want the women in their lives to listen and support their dreams, holding back judgment and criticism. If they never read another negative statistic, hear another negative story, or see another negative media depiction, it will be too soon. They were ready to hear good things about themselves and other Black men. They were concerned about positivity and wanted to reject or change any negativity around their lives.

It wasn't that they wanted to deny the existence of anything negative that had to do with Black men. They were just tired of the negative not being balanced with positive. They wanted more positive images that they could be proud of and point to as an example of who they really are on the whole.

Road Rules

We have what we call road rules for the journey you are about to embark on while reading this book. They are the same things we tell people when they come to our signings, workshops, and conferences. When you open the cover and turn the pages of this book, leave behind any preconceived notions or judgments you might have. There are no judgments, blame, or admonishments when reading the stories of these men. Part of what keeps us all from communicating openly with one another are all the judgments we carry into our interactions and relationships. Once you take judgment out of the equation, you can get to know, relate to, and learn from others. We all have a story to tell that can enhance or change the course of someone's life; it's all in the telling of that story and the receiving of what is being relayed unfettered by your own biases. The men in this book were courageous enough to share an intimate piece of themselves with you. There is no better gift than someone revealing a piece of his soul's journey to help you enhance your understanding of yourself so just be open enough to receive the message that is there for you.

It is no coincidence that you picked up this book. A man reading this book should realize that there are other men out there who are experiencing or have experienced the same things you may be going through. Learn from their experiences, and reflect on your choices and decisions for your own personal journey. A woman reading this book should be patient and absorb what these men are *really* saying. Learn to do what we did—just listen. Hear the stories these men have to tell, and let their truths heal your soul and help you to gain a better understanding of the Black men in your life.

How You Can Benefit from This Book

Your Soul's Journey

In listening to Black men, in developing this book, and in reading personal and spiritual stories by Black men, we realized that they are on a lifelong journey. While we are all on a journey, the Black man's journey is unique because his struggle is inclusive of a variety of challenges particular to his manhood. His individual soul's journey will lead to a collective peace among Black men and ultimately throughout the collective Black community. If there was anything we did learn from the thousands of Black men to whom we've spoken, met, and given readings, it's that their journey is a spiritual one that can be navigated only by God and enhanced only by another Black man. There are a multitude of young Black men in need of guidance, security, mentoring, friendship, support, camaraderie, and love from other Black men. While the journey for each Black man is an individual one, it bears similarities to that of others. Each chapter of this book represents a part of the journey Black men are on or have traveled in their lives. Be it a personal journey to self or God or a journey toward inner peace and justice.

Each chapter of the book concludes with a section we call "Your Soul's Journey." Here you will find a biblical quotation that speaks to the truths that underlie the chapter. We will also summarize and bring closure to our thoughts from the chapter's introduction and offer exercises and tips you can use in your life to expand your spirit by means of the stories that your brothers have shared.

Soul Source

Every journey has a starting point. Where and when you begin your personal journey to self-discovery is unique to you as an individual. Some people begin the journey early in youth when they decide what they're going to "be" when they grow up. Others start their journey in college, unfettered by their parent's reign. And still others begin their personal journey later, when they are in need of a change from the routine their lives have become. The one thing that you need to know once you embark on your soul's journey is the source from which you are traveling. Once you tap into your "Soul Source" and acknowledge the origins of your life experiences that complete who you are, you become empowered to begin the process of change. And so begins the journey for you.

As you read this book, we urge you to grab a spiral notebook or pad that will become what we call your Soul Source. This notebook will house the source of your thoughts and innermost feelings while you experience the stories told by Black men. We will assist you in reviewing your Soul Source by giving you questions to ask yourself after each chapter. The questions will lead you on an introspective journey, ultimately bringing you closer to communication with the divine truth buried inside you.

The Ultimate Solution?

If you are looking for the ultimate solution to your problems, you will not find it in this book. Our goal was to create a fertile atmosphere for spiritual awakening in which you will be able to understand yourself and learn to create a better way to communicate with yourself and others.

For all the women who decided that this book would reveal a better understanding of the men in their lives—we applaud you for joining us on this journey. Together we will listen, reserve judgment, believe, and see and feel where the hurt begins and where power is stifled—as well as where moments of greatness are achieved and where purpose is formed.

Souls of My Brothers is a genuine reflection of the everyday lives of Black men from all walks of life, told through their *original* first-person narratives. Some contributors are powerful politicians, famous celebrities, and architects of history. Others are the husbands next door, the educators in your child's school, bus drivers, everyday heroes, and even criminals.

When Black men break their silence and begin to talk one another, when they open their hearts to themselves and to others, when they begin to confront their collective demons, they will begin to heal themselves, their souls, and their world. Black men's stories are not just a birthright, but also a legacy to be shared and passed on to fathers, brothers, sons, wives, daughters, the community, and the globe. Collectively we can heal our spirits so that we can continue to be, as our ancestors were, the intellectual, mighty, strong, and prosperous people we have always been.

You may not want to read this book from cover to cover. Or you may want to jump from chapter to chapter based on the challenges, issues, or triumphs you may be experiencing in your life. Keep these stories with you, and read through them as you feel comfortable, and when you are ready to hear the truth from your soul, we will be waiting.

CHAPTER 1

IN THE EYES OF SOCIETY,
I CRY, "WHO AM I?"

When I discover who I am, I'll be free.
—Ralph Ellison

While the journey to self is a universal one, the Black man's journey is a lot rockier, more uphill, and more difficult than most. Any Black man knows that—because for him, it's not a story to be read from in a book; it's something that he lives every day. Whether it's women clutching their purses when you walk up behind them; or just not getting a call back for a job that you knew you were qualified for; or standing out in the rain and not being able to catch a cab while everybody else seems to be catching one with ease; or getting pulled over for some routine police harassment—regardless of your accomplishments—the reminders are simply there every day, and we don't have to tell you about them. Sometimes the act of *being* is just enough to cause a commotion.

When you look in the mirror, whose reflection do you see? A friend of ours, Brian, was on the city bus one day, and he noticed a dark-skinned brother wearing a tight knit cap on the bus, lurking just out of his sight behind him. Out of the corner of Brian's eye, he could see the guy just sitting there, and in his mind our friend thought the guy seemed to be up to no good; but Brian really couldn't get a good look at him. It seemed like the guy was leering at him and moving around like he was trying to check him out. Brian was on the bus for a while, and the guy just sat there for the duration of the ride. Brian kept trying to see him in his peripheral vision, but he still couldn't get a good look, and he didn't want to turn all the way around, because he didn't want to start something. He had enough and was getting nervous because the guy might really be up to something. As the bus was finally getting close to his stop, Brian turned around to get a good look at the guy. When he turned around he found that there was actually no menacing guy behind him, but rather he had been seeing his own reflection in the mirrored glass of the bus reflected off the window. Brian was all alone—the only passenger on the bus.

So just like the White lady who clutches her purse when you walk up behind her, brothers, too, are programmed and taught to be afraid, not just of other Black men, but even to be afraid of themselves. We are all products of the same socialization. We all watched the same television programs growing up. We went to the same kinds of schools and studied the same kinds of curricula. We all were indoctrinated with the same images by the media of brothers as criminals, drug dealers, thugs, con men, pimps, and crackheads. The script was implanted firmly into our minds early, and now as adults we're just reading our lines off it like seasoned actors.

Black men have listened to the opinions and lies of others. You fall into this trap only because you don't know the whole and beautiful truth of who Black men really are.

Black women need not act like they're any better than the brothers. They've fallen into the trap of blaming all Black men for the actions of one or simply jumping on a girlfriend's "he did me wrong" bandwagon.

How do you finish the sentence, "All Black men are —————"? Stop playing games and falling into the traps that have been set before us. How about filling in that sentence with, "All Black men are *beautiful, intelligent beings*." Any way you slice it, we can't be all that mad about the way others perceive Black men unless Black men are individually and collectively clear on how they perceive themselves.

In actuality, Black men are conditioned to perform a laundry list of tasks throughout life and to please an enormous amount of people. They are never really given the opportunity to just *be*.

The journey to self-discovery is the first step toward true freedom that anyone can take. To know thyself is to have an understanding of you that no one can alter. Realizing you have the power not to be moved by other people's words or images of you is one of the most freeing experiences in life. You have the ability to say, "This is who I am," not as an excuse, but as a statement of positive affirmation. You need not accept what is handed to you, because you know that you have created your own space in the universe to be who you truly are to yourself and everyone you meet.

We've been told so many lies about Black men that sometimes we don't know what to believe. Intimidating or intimidated, they may not always appear to others or themselves as they wish, but there is strength in the truth of what they see and how we see them through their eyes. The stories in this section are reflections on how Black men perceive themselves and sometimes how others influence those perceptions.

A Culture's Cancer

Kevin Greene

It was late afternoon. My mother was frightened, but she refused to shed a tear while dialing the police as the banging continued against the steel door. Banging so powerful that the door seemed to fold. I thought for sure it would come down on me. An unfriendly lump found a home in my throat as my fragile, shaken little body trembled under the falling chipped paint breaking free from its hinges. "Let me in this fuckin' house!" a masculine voice in rage shouted repeatedly, accented with a pain I'll never forget. I couldn't have been more than five years old, and already I was looking death in the face.

That steel door was the property of a housing project where my family and I lived. The project was Brevoort Houses, located in a section of Brooklyn, New York, now undergoing a face-lift called "gentrification." But when I was coming up, it was the hood that spilled so much blood that great rap stars such as Jay-Z, the late Notorious B.I.G., and Fabolous were granted instant street credibility worldwide simply because that's where they're from. That hood is Bed-Stuy, a place most natives call the belly of the beast and the place where I was what many call a ghetto celebrity. They called me "Spice." From corner to corner, house to house, project to project, everyone knew my many identities, "the playa," "the barber," "the hustler," "the actor." But only a handful knew the wrongs I'd done. Fewer knew the heavy regrets that refused to leave my mind, and no one knew my pain. Bed-Stuy contributed to the making of the person I came to be. But the absence of the man who was trying to kick down the steel door contributed to who I am far more than my environment could have ever done. That man was my father.

I have no memory of him, his personality, or even his face. As far as I'm concerned, we've never met, but I have no hard feelings. According to my mother, he was a gentleman raised with impeccable manners—romantic, strong, righteous, intelligent, a true artist, and a soldier of the U.S. Marines—whose vibe was blue blooded. "He was so fine. Without question, the best man I ever had. He was perfect," my mother would say. She never uttered one negative word about him, and I ached to fill his shoes. They were childhood friends who fell in love. But my mother wouldn't leave my grandmother, who wouldn't leave New York, because she wanted to be near her other children, my aunts and uncles. So for love, my father quit the military and moved in. But the civilian world didn't embrace him. Years of layoffs and rejection drove him to depression as his Harlem-based brother, a heroin dealer, relentlessly tempted him with financial relief through the business. Eventually he weakened and took the bait. Soon after, a vortex of guilt sucked him deeper into his depression, deep enough for him to try the drug himself. It was that late afternoon he came home crazed, trying to tear down the door. That murky memory is all I have of my father. I never saw him again.

The years that followed, I found myself frequently witnessing the roundtable discussions, women comparing their "men ain't shit" stories. These were my most impressionable years, and even though my mother never took part in the venting wars, I always found myself in the mirror holding back tears, hating my unavoidable destiny. I would grow to be a monster, one of those lying motherfuckers who was good for nothing but dick and dough. Before I knew it, I was a young adult who kept his hands dirty. I would forget about Christ and profit in sin. A full-time hustler and part-time dreamer in hot pursuit of an acting career was who I'd become. My silver screen dreams and neighborhood fame as a barber were worn on my sleeve, but the part of me called "stick-up kid" and "drug dealer" was a secret and kept as far away from home as possible. My adoration for my family was too great to shit where I ate. But the streets talked, and enough lip led the police to my mother's door. And knowing I was guilty as all hell she sat with me through a case that could've taken ten to twenty years of my life.

I kept my friendships with high-status ballers and dealers across the country, but chose to change my hustle, which included a dramatic cut in pay. My new hustle was women with money. If they couldn't be used, they were useless. I could almost hear my subconscious mind calling all the shots as I moved in for the kill. The roundtable taught me well, and its definition of a man was something I would master. I had the finest, the smartest, and the richest on my arm. There were times when I outshone celebrities in clubs. At will, I could personify the bad boy women loved to hate. Life was good, but I never lost sight of the fact that the money I was spending wasn't my own, which kept me focused on my dream. One day while working on the set of Fox's TV show *New York Undercover*, I met the beautiful daughter of a vice president of a major corporation. My intention of course was to squeeze her like all the others, but when I met her father, it was love at first sight. I was starstruck in his presence. He embodied all the qualities of my mother's description of a perfect man. Suddenly that ache to fill my father's shoes returned.

Looking back on it, I don't think I ever really loved the girl, but the bull-shit stopped, and I fell in love with her world. The world I'm talking about had nothing to do with money. It was the world of an African-American family that included a father—trust me, there is a difference. My joy was so overwhelming that I confused it with love and treated her with nothing but respect. I was loyal, kind, considerate, and didn't want a dime. I spent some of my happiest times with her and was for the first time content with life. But that didn't last long. She left me while carrying another man's seed. Broke it off weeks before our engagement party, which was being planned by her parents, who had accepted me with open arms. I was devastated, but the blow that floored me wasn't the fact that I would no longer see her. Living without her wasn't something that would require any strength. It wasn't the end of the Caribbean vacations or the spontaneous trips to Vegas. The drug game gave me those things long before I met her. And it wasn't the fact that I had to return to the projects and part with the duplex in Park Slope and the place in Florida either. Starting over was something I did best. So what was it that hurt me so much, you ask? Her father—I loved him as my own, and I didn't want to lose him.

Time spent with him was short, but the revelation that came with it could touch the sky. I've done things on the streets I will always regret and never tell. I feared no man and I'm by far one of the strongest I know, but when sitting with him I found myself silly and gullible. I was a completely different person, stuck on humble and in awe of a king. He talked to me about everything from his militant role in the civil rights movement to his fear of God to his respect for women. I was a sponge and soaked up more than just his words. I studied his gestures, his posture, and his confidence. I watched how he handled the waiter, his family, his friends, and confrontation. Unknowingly he exposed me to the fact that I was ill-equipped in almost every area of my being. The revelation that slapped me cold in the face was that I was not a man. That reality was the source of pain that no one knew of. The amazing part of it all was that I didn't know of it either. And that pain I suffered for most of my life was in the form of unexplained inadequacies. I had issues that I couldn't put my finger on, let alone understand. I was too strong in most areas and not strong enough in all the rest. To me, being human meant walking a tightrope, and my balance wasn't worth shit. I can remember hanging with the fellas and always feeling like they were a step ahead of me in every way. And with women, the few relationships I did take seriously, I was severely insecure or became totally dominating. I needed answers badly and was clueless as to what the questions were.

I've made many changes since then and like to think I have most of it figured out. But I don't believe a day goes by that I don't think about what it was like to live in darkness. Had I been raised by a loving positive father whom I idolized and confided in, I would've been a different person coming up regardless of my environment. My self-worth would've been above dealing drugs. My respect for women would not have allowed me to use them. And my many other choices would've been made after a completely different kind of thinking process. Yes, losing my ex's father was tough, but the lesson learned was an indisputable fact: No boy should ever be raised without his father!

Imagine a girl raised without her mother—or any woman, for that matter. She has a good father but doesn't get the opportunity to mimic the behavior of a woman. "There is no woman in the house." She never gets the direction of a woman on how to sit, dress, or walk. How to wear her hair, how to play with girls, how to deal with boys. There's no explanation or education about her changing body from a person who has been there and done that. There's no veteran of puppy love there to relate to her first heartache. She never experiences the interaction of the adult female mind, its perspective, its way of thinking, deciding, objecting. She misses out on the secrets of a woman, isn't blessed to recognize a woman's power or witness it in use. With all that in mind, imagine the void that would form in that growing girl's being. Ask yourself, what kind of woman would she turn out to be? Whatever lacking dysfunctional description you might come up with is more than likely the mirrored reality of what most of our brothers are forced to become. Bottom line, no boy can grow to be a man without observing and experiencing one.

Today I'm an actor and filmmaker, and am moving closer by the day to becoming what I witnessed—a man, doing it as a single parent determined to break the cycle. This is possible because I keep God first and pray for guidance every morning. I suffered for nearly a decade for my sins, paid through the nose for the wrong I've done, but in the end it was a new beginning that wouldn't happen without growth. I still walk the streets of Bed-Stuy where I maintain ghetto celebrity status and get nothing but love and respect. The thugs salute me for the bad I've done yesterday and the young admire me for the good I do today. This is bittersweet, but it's good that I have their attention while working to achieve male wholeness. Regrettably, my time spent with them is often saddened by hundreds of reflections of my former self. I see brothers, six through sixty, suffering severely from the transparent unidentifiable wounds I call "fatherlessness" and they have absolutely no idea that they're in pain. This is a cancer eating away an entire culture. The only cure is responsibility.

Kevin Greene, *a talented actor, screenwriter and filmmaker, wrote, codirected, and performed in the dramatization for* Gangstresses, *a controversial docudrama that featured Mary J. Blige, Lil' Kim, and Tupac Shakur. He also coproduced and performed in* For Tha Good Times, *a popular independent film directed by Shawn Baker. Now, as CEO of GreeneWorks Inc., an independent film company, he's developing several literary properties intended for theatrical release.*

Purpose . . .

Howard Hewett

At one point or another in all of our lives we ask certain questions, like, What is all this (life) about? What is my purpose? Some of us find our purpose in life before others. Some, unfortunately, never find it. Interesting huh? I mean when you think about that, you wonder how someone would go through a complete life and never truly grasp what he or she was put here to do.

See, I believe that we all have a specific, special, wonderful, and individual purpose—a reason for existing in God's complete plan. From the second He breathed His breath of Spirit and life into man and created him in His image, we were meant to live forever! We weren't meant to experience pain, sorrow, hard times, or even death! Our women were never supposed to experience pain in childbirth. Man was never meant to deal in this land "by the sweat of his brow." But along with that Spirit of life, He also gave us *freedom of choice!*

Think about it, the purpose of all mankind was interrupted, altered through the choice of one man! So how important do you think your choices in and for your life are? Many times we hinder the search for our purpose with the choices we make—the things, people, and elements we sometimes haphazardly let into our lives. Our immediate "space" around us is precious, and should be protected at all costs. Things in that space should be motivating. People allowed there should be encouraging, and the element should be one of peace, learning, and always taking us closer to our purpose—our spirituality—closer to God!

The Libra in me always wants to balance things out and say, "Well, that's easier said than done." But isn't that what this life's about, striving for perfection in an imperfect world? So I refuse to let that be my crutch and my cop-out! I want all that He has for me right here, right now! I want to be blessed with and fulfilled in my purpose so I can be a blessing to someone else.

Singing has been my purpose since I was a child. My mother was a gospel promoter working with such acts as the Staple Singers and Shirley

Caesar. My dad was a mailman, and he played the sax. My mom formed a family gospel group, which included my sisters as the background singers and me as lead. The group was called the Hewitt Singers. We opened up for my mom's gospel shows.

When I was fourteen, I decided I wanted to branch out from my gospel roots and started singing R & B music. A lot of people from the gospel community were upset by my transition to R & B music, but my mother stood by me and supported me. She told people, "My son is a good son. My son loves the Lord. I support him fully."

At the age of nineteen, I decided to leave my hometown of Akron, Ohio, and move to California to pursue my singing career. I performed at Maverick Flats, which was the party place back in the 1970s. Great R & B singers and funk groups all performed at Maverick Flats. I met John and Alonzo Daniels and formed Beverly Hills, a showcase group.

I was in search of my self and purpose. I traveled and lived in Europe for a year and a half. I read books like *As a Man Thinketh*, searching for greater understanding. When I returned from Europe, I began working with a producer at Motown when I got a call from the group Shalamar and was offered the position of lead singer. We were a top charting group with several hit songs and traveled all over the world. We were truly blessed, but I never let the fame go to my head. I always had a strong spiritual faith, and it kept me from getting too far out there.

My strong faith in God has allowed me to pursue and continue to fulfill my purpose without compromising my belief in Him. Every album that I do has at least one song dedicated to God, and I have had the honor of doing a complete inspirational project. I have always represented my faith in God as an R & B artist that praises the Lord. I sing about love and romance, *not* sex. I am so grateful to the Lord for this awesome career and for my talent. It was His gift to give me, and I intend to use it to honor Him forever.

I've learned that "finding yourself" means finding your spiritual base. Knowing that God loves a sinner, but hates the sin is one of the most important lessons of self-acceptance people can learn. Every day you get up is another opportunity to get it right. There will come a time when believing in yourself is not enough. No matter what you do in life, there will be peaks and valleys in your career and in your life. You need something to keep you on a level plane. Get a spiritual base underneath you, something to keep you humble and to keep your feet on solid ground. Spirit will keep you lifted up; never give up on your aspirations. Don't take yourself out of the game—that's the number one sure way never to achieve.

Howard Hewitt *is a prolific singer, songwriter, and producer. According to one* Rolling Stone *writer, he is the premier vocalist in the post–Marvin Gaye era of romantic pop. Like Gaye, Hewett soars to new heights and seduces his audience. It is no wonder he's responsible for selling some ten million records; his voice is irresistible.*

From Bad Time to My Time
Reggie Hatchett

My timing has always been terrible. When I was a child, my body grew so fast that my coordination had a hard time keeping up. I've always been that friend who seemed to call as soon as you would get comfortable in bed or that brother who approached a girl a few days after she got out of a year-long relationship. I wish I had a dollar for every time I heard, "It's just a bad time." Based on what I've been told, I had bad timing even before I got to this world. I was conceived at a bad time and born at a worse time. My mother was not prepared to have another child. On top of not being married, her mental state had taken a turn toward destruction. She began to abuse her body with drugs and alcohol. Had it not been for my father's begging and pleading, I would have never been born. I wish I could have told him thank you for allowing me to exist outside the womb, but unfortunately he died several weeks after I was born. It always bothered me that the man who made me never got the chance to make me a man.

My father had always been the only person able to talk to my extremely stubborn mother. So when he passed, that pushed her over the edge she had been flirting with for so long. If you mix drugs and alcohol with the responsibility of a newborn baby, minus the only person who brought sanity to your mind, you have a formula for disaster. This obviously was a cause for concern for our family. My great-grandmother (whom I refer to as my grandmother) had been a caretaker of almost every generation in my family. She raised my mother and her siblings. She knew better than anyone else that my mother wasn't fit to raise a healthy baby. So she took it upon herself to take me under her roof and make sure I received all the love and attention I needed.

My grandmother already had custody of my older sister and brother. So all of us were together in my grandmother and grandfather's house. Even though I had my biological siblings in my life, I've always felt alone. I had a different father than they did, and it was clear to me that I was different.

I remember when I was about four years old, my grandmother would always tell her church friends, "Y'all better watch out for that boy, he's a special child!" It would make me feel so good to hear her words of approval, because I didn't receive many. I had a cousin who was the same age as I was, but everyone in my family favored him. He was light skinned, attractive, he could dance, and was very athletic. In other words, he was everything I wasn't. I remember at family gatherings everyone would marvel at how handsome he was and they would put his karate trophies on display. I, on the other hand, was just a passing thought. I remember hearing my sister tell my cousin that she wished he were her brother. Those words cut me so deep that it wasn't until years later that I was able even to speak of that incident.

Because my grandmother began to notice the difference made between me and my cousin, she tightened her grip on me. My world consisted of me and my grandparents. I must admit I was sheltered and I didn't know much about anything other than church. This actually widened the gap between me and the rest of the family. No one else in my family went to church consistently, so this made me seem like an outcast. I was spending every day within arm's length of my grandparents (who were born in 1914 and 1917 respectively). This is why everyone who knows me well says I have an "old soul." Most of my character traits come from my grandfather. I guess it seems okay now coming from a young adult, but I've had this same personality since I was about eight or nine. This was a gift that was cleverly disguised as a curse. I remember wishing I didn't have to go to church all the time, but it was this upbringing that gave me the very deep spiritual roots that have gotten me to this point in my life. My relationship with God, which was established on those Sunday mornings when I was forced to go to church, is the only reason I was able to get through all the hardships life has dealt me. And there are a lot of them.

A dysfunctional family, the death of friends, an HIV-positive mother, all these things tore away at the core of my soul. But the hardest thing I've gone through is the slow deterioration of my grandparents' health. I was used to my grandparents being strong and lively all my life. So I was devastated when my grandfather had his second stroke. It left him without the full use of the right side of his body, but what was most troubling was the damage done to his spirit. He has always been an extremely proud and dignified man. So the fact that he needs assistance with his everyday tasks makes him feel bad. I can understand his position. As I mentioned earlier, he and I are practically the same person. So I've learned by watching him throughout my life that you have to pull inspiration from the bad things that will occur in your life.

I managed to make myself an exceptional basketball player during my adolescence. Specifically because of one person, my friend Troy. He was a great basketball player himself, so we had common interests. But Troy had an alliance with the streets that led us to drift apart. I went to college, and he was getting deeper and deeper into the street life. When Troy was shot, that scared me, but it also reassured me that I was doing the right thing by not living that way. A few years later Troy was arrested and convicted of a crime he did not commit. He was sentenced to sixty years in prison. This really hurt me because despite his destructive traits, I knew that Troy is a good person with a big heart. Jail is no place for someone whose spirit is so vibrant. But the Lord works in mysterious ways, and this was a blessing in disguise. I was having a conversation with Troy and I was complaining about basketball. I was mad at the world because basketball had been taken away from me. This was my only form of self-actualization and I was told that I could not play after I transferred schools. Troy changed my outlook on everything by telling me that he was glad to be in jail. He said he was aware that he had lived very wickedly and if he hadn't been incarcerated, he would probably be dead. Jail was God's way of making him listen and change his life. He has now accepted Jesus as his personal savior and has taken it upon himself to inform as many people as he can of the healing power found in God. All I could say was, "Wow!" This was a lesson to me. If he could take a situation like being jailed for sixty years and turn it into a positive thing, then I could do the same with the minor problems I faced.

I had to dig deep within myself to find who I was and what I was supposed to do without basketball. I thought I was just plain ol' Reggie Hatchett, a six-foot-five-inch, 225-pound Black male. But a long look in the mirror helped me realize that I was much more than that. I am a collection of my life experiences; I am a survivor of the Bowles Park Housing Project; I am the direct descendant of a slave who persevered the Middle Passage. I'm proud of all that I have accomplished, but I know that I have much more to do. I am aware of the sacrifices that were made in order for me to be here; I owe those who paved the way. I know blood was shed so I could live, I know people were hanged to ensure I would be considered a man instead of three fifths of a human being. I am glad to be considered a menace. I enjoy the fact that I bring fear to the hearts of those who do not want me to achieve. I'm aware that I come from a long line of heroes. That is why I deserve the best, because I come from the best. I am the son of Louis Farrakhan, the nephew of Muhammad Ali and Malcolm X, the grandson of Nat Turner, the great-grandson of Frank and Mary Hatchett, and a direct member of the bloodline that produced Jesus Christ and Imhotep. That is who and what Reggie Michael Hatchett is.

My purpose on this planet is to lead my people, the hip-hop community, to move toward change. I realized that I was an extremely effective communicator with a passion for my people and my culture. Every talent I have,

Destination: Success

Busta Rhymes

My father was a wise, hardworking man who took care of our family. I respected what he had to say. For the most part, I followed the rules that he had set for our house. And even when my father said to me that I needed to learn a trade, I followed his wisdom there, too. I would dress like my dad and get ready for my day as an electrical contractor. My father had a theory that if you had a trade, that would be one thing that no man could ever take away from you. You own a trade, and you can be sure to always find a place in the world because people will need you for that. But it didn't take me long to recognize that my dad's wisdom was fine if you were looking to work a job all your life. I would come home countless nights having worked at manual labor. After looking at my hands that were callused and cut up, I knew that my destiny was not the pursuit of a job but the pursuit of a dream.

I figured that there had to be an easier way. I didn't mind working hard, but working hard at something that I didn't love was difficult for me to accept. I could never be okay with the idea that I was supposed to spend most of my waking hours doing something that I didn't love. I started to think of what I wanted to do. I just knew that it didn't have to be this way. I didn't have anyone else to look at who would tell me that my thoughts were on the right track. I didn't have any confirmation that I could do something in life that I found fun. All I had was faith that there had to be an alternative, there had to be another way to live my life. So I decided to follow my dream, wherever that took me. Even though I didn't know how it was going to turn out, I knew that I had to stay far away from the worst-case scenario and wish for the best.

I don't believe in coincidence. I wasn't born Busta Rhymes, but I know that I was predestined to become a part of the hip-hop game. When I got started, I didn't know—and no one else did either—how far this whole thing could go. I was just carrying out the script that was prewritten for me. At that time, I was in it for the fun; hip-hop was pure, and my pursuit of it was all about my love of the music. As a fan of the music, I just knew I had to be a part of it, so I did whatever I could do to be in the game. I did talent shows, contests, and lip-synching. I didn't have a master plan, but I knew I had to apply myself in ways to secure the result that I was looking for.

When I was twelve, my parents moved our family to Long Island. I couldn't see how I was going to meet up with my music destiny way out in Long Island. At that time, things were happening in the five boroughs. That's where hip-hop music was really starting to take off. However, I was far outside of the boroughs when I began rapping in contests and eventually met MC Charlie Brown. We were only in junior high school, but we got together as often as we could and worked hard at perfecting our flow. I felt a little discouraged. There was little chance that our talent was going to get heard all the way out in Long Island. It wasn't long before I found out that meeting your destiny means being in the right place at the right time. I didn't have to travel to the Bronx or Brooklyn; my destiny came to meet me. Through a talent show in Hempstead, Long Island, we got the opportunity to meet Chuck D from Public Enemy. The five minutes that we were given to show our talent turned into a lifetime of opportunity for all of us. It wasn't long before we began recording at Public Enemy's studios on Long Island as the Leaders of the New School.

Even before all the success that would come in ways that I couldn't imagine, I was having fun. There would be times later when there would be concern about whether or not a record would go platinum and how much money was generated from sales. But for me to be a part of the hip-hop game was living a dream. It was work but not the kind of work that I had experienced while doing manual labor. If this was a daily grind, I met each day looking forward to all the hours I was going to put into my music. I didn't worry about the money and all that. In the beginning, if you really didn't have nothing, you couldn't miss what you didn't have.

Because of my experience of growing up with hip-hop, it has always been important to me to surround myself with people who have always been a part of the dream with me. Most of the members of my Flip Mode Squad are cats who I grew up with. My family is very much involved with my life, and the same principles of working hard still apply. My parents are proud of me and my brother. Family members are always looking out for my well-being. I'm proud to say that people who care about me protect me, surround me. I make sure that each day, before I rest my head, I secure an opportunity to make sure that music will continue to feed the family that has always loved and supported me. My philosophy is that success is a journey and not a destination. That journey has helped me to reach heights that I could never have imagined when I started, and I trust that it will continue to take me to ever higher heights.

Busta Rhymes has been heralded as a hip-hop chameleon and has sold millions of records worldwide. Amid all the extraneous activities, Busta still found time to successfully engineer his own record company, Flipmode Entertainment. The tireless entrepreneur has also unveiled his own clothing line, Bushi, which is influencing streetwear in the same way Busta's early records infiltrated the hip-hop scene. He continues to fulfill his destiny in music and movies.

Sunday

Terrance Dean

I remember being a young boy who was bitter and angry toward his mother because her plight was too heavy a burden—caring for me, my two younger brothers, and little sister. I despised my mother because she died from the AIDS virus and because she gave birth to my baby brother, who became infected with the same virus and lost his life at the age of two. I despised my mother because our family was split up and we were living amongst relatives who had large families of their own. I despised my mother and family because my other and only living brother was placed in a group home, sexually molested, and he himself died from the AIDS virus at age nineteen. That left me and my sister alone in the world. The two of us holding on to each other for dear life, and I was too afraid to let anyone get close to me because all I could do was ask myself, "God, why have you forsaken me?"

I grew up in the church. My relatives made sure of that. Every Sunday from 5:00 A.M. until 10:00 P.M., we were in church. I learned how to speak tongues, "get" the Holy Ghost, sing in the choir, become an usher, and be a part of the youth ministry. So I came to know God very early, and we had this special relationship. He would talk to me, and I would talk to Him. I knew that I would get answers to my many questions, like why I was born into the family I had. I wanted to know what God's secret plan was and how come everyone else's family appeared sane and happy.

My mother died when I was a junior in college at Fisk University. I remember visiting my mother during the winter break from school. I had stopped in to visit and stay a few nights with her. I knew my mother had the AIDS virus, and I had grown old enough to begin loving and appreciating her. As the trip came to an end, I packed my bags and began to prepare for my return to school. As I was leaving and walking out the door, my mother called to me. I stopped at the door, turned to hear her voice and for the first time, my mother gently said, "I love you." I replied back "I love you, too," and I walked out the door, crying uncontrollably because I knew that would be the last time I would see her alive.

No one had prepared me for death, especially my mother's. I knew from my experiences in church that only God could answer my questions and cries. I knew that if I prayed and talked with God, everything would work out just fine. I felt comfort and love when I prayed and talked with God. I felt the easiness of life and understood why things moved and happened in God's time and not mine. I began asking God to use me to show others that if we rely upon His Spirit, we can create and have any life we choose.

God answered and began moving me in the direction of nurturing environments. God brought forth teachers, preachers, and many lessons on my path, arming me with tools to be a soldier and vessel for Spirit and His work.

I graduated from college and went on to have a successful career in film and television. I got my start at the world's most prestigious news network, CNN. After interning with CNN for over six months, I began working in film production with noted directors and celebrities. I had the opportunity to work with Spike Lee, Rob Reiner, Anjelica Huston, George Cosmatos, and Keenan Ivory Wayans. I had carved out a great working résumé and impressive reputation for myself. I realized that I had finally made it. I had overcome what so many thought I would not. I had developed an attitude of self-appreciation because in spite of all I endured, I had made it! I cared only about myself and making it in the world. I had to be successful because I had something to prove to everyone.

Then one day I got a call while I was in New York, working on a film project. It was my grandmother, who called to tell me about my brother who had contracted the AIDS virus. It was such a blow to me that I knew I would not be able to handle it. This was my brother whom I'd grown up with and loved so dearly. This was my brother who I fought with over simple little things, as many brothers do. The younger brother who annoyed me with so many questions because he wanted to be like his big brother. I could not understand why another person I loved would be claimed by the AIDS virus. This was not fair.

I spoke with my brother many times during his illness, and each time after our conversations I would break down and cry. It was too much for me to lose another life. My brother called me one Friday evening, and we were discussing his coming to visit and possibly live with me in New York. It was getting late, and he told me that he would call me the next day. We told each other we loved one another and hung up the phone. The next day I received a phone call from my cousin; she was calling to tell me that my brother had died that afternoon. My grandmother and two aunts were with him when he died.

I was extremely upset, angry, hurt, bitter, and confused. I cried unto God for His Love and Spirit to be so upon me that I would be able to hear His voice in the midst of a hurricane. I cried for knowledge, wisdom, and understanding. I cried for clarity and peace. I cried and cried until there was nothing else for me to cry about.

I dived back into my work, not wanting to think about anything or anyone. I realized I had to strive even harder and become even more successful. I chose to travel on film projects and to keep moving from city to city because I wanted to run away from the pain I was hoarding. I wanted to escape and be in the fantasy world of illusion that television and film creates for society. I hid in this world and was able to escape only so briefly when I was jolted to reality.

I heard God's voice while I was working in production at MTV Networks. His gentle voice asked if I was tired of running and ready to do His work. He asked me if I was ready to heal and ready to let go of the pain I was holding on to. He asked if I was ready to be blessed beyond measure and to see the fullness of what He had in store for me. Then God laid out his plan for me step-by-step. He told me not to become weary or fearful— He would provide for me and take care of me. He told me that I was no longer alone in the world and that He would allow me to have many brothers and many mothers in His name.

True to His word, God called on me to create Men's Empowerment. This organization was created to help transform, empower, and inspire all men of color regardless, of creed, class, or sexuality. I realized that there were many other men in the world who were afraid and were holding on to anger, hurt, and pain as I had done. The organization has more than three hundred men of color actively involved with the group. Each month we come together to share our obstacles, downfalls, triumphs, victories, and our dreams. I have seen many transformations happen in men while participating in Men's Empowerment. These men have reclaimed and are rebuilding their lives one day at a time with God's guidance and Spirit. The organization has been blessed to have many men come in and share their own stories.

Who I am now is a man committed to transforming the lives of men of color for their families, communities, and their own lives. I am committed to not losing another brother and another mother. Instead of holding on to asking God why He has forsaken me, all I can ask now is, "Can I get a witness to His power and glory?"

Terrance Dean is the creator and founder of Men's Empowerment, Inc., The Education Source, and The Children's Reading Circle. Dean is also the author of the best-selling book Be Empowered: 30 Days of Meditation for Men of Color. *A native of Detroit, he now lives in New York City and can be contacted via e-mail at mensempowerment@aol.com.*

Lessons in the Mirror

Gil L. Robertson IV

People often look at my world and conjure up what they think they see without looking into my world with 20/20 vision. As one of the nation's premiere journalists covering arts, entertainment, and lifestyles, I recognize that the appetite for fluff and stuff is almost insatiable. I have, however, managed to keep a realistic perspective on my world and, more important, on my responsibility to those with whom I share that space.

Contrary to the often-androgynous character most people think pervades the Arts and entertainment world, sisters and brothers think, act, and react differently to reading themselves. In fact, sisters have always been in the forefront of reading us—literally, sometimes—if only for the fact that they think they have the most invested and, consequently, the most to lose with respect to our liberation, elevation, and survival. As it is our liberation, elevation, and survival at stake, I submit to you that it is ours to squander or prevail, and we must act with the reverence and respect it rightfully commands. There is a time and place for everything. It is long overdue, and there is no time and place like the present! We need to encourage support and endorse Black men to look toward liberation as a measure of self-evaluation!

Amen! I have said it. Self-evaluation. How do we get there? I really don't know yet, but I am certain of where to begin. We must look at who we are, know who we are, and self-define who we are. The mirror seems like the most likely place to begin to search for who you are, or at least for what you look like. Look at yourself in the mirror throughout every aspect of your life: See what kind of father you are or have been to your children. What kind of brother or uncle have you been? What kind of husband or son have you been? It all starts in the mirror. It is an ongoing process.

Today, if asked to describe myself, I immediately use these words: *Confident, somewhat introverted, fairly disciplined, in control, very honest, very strategic, very focused*. I used the words I see in the mirror; but then, perhaps I hadn't looked long enough or often enough. I did not initially use words like *compassionate, loyal*, and *happy* or the like; I did not say things like *emotive, sentimental, gracious*, or *affectionate*; I even omitted *friendly, sociable*, and *expressive.* I am all those things, and when primed for the description, I realize that they are the softer adjectives—not at all characteristic of how most men describe themselves—but at one point or another in their lives, we clearly want to be seen in those terms.

Oddly enough, the "mirror" theory is not new. It was not conceived in the ivory towers of France, Germany, or Harvard. Many great things have emanated from those walls—however, the "mirror" theory has been a downhome tactic for as long as any of us can remember. Our parents got it from their parents, who got it from their aunts and uncles and grandparents, who got it from those who loved and looked after them. It is perhaps one of the most recognized verbal chides Black folks have in their repertoire of expressions of disapproval.

It makes me think about how well served I was by my mother's oft directive, "Go look in the mirror, and take a good look at yourself!" She has no idea how she may have saved my life. She has no idea how she singlehandedly gave me the key to my own self-evaluation—a talent and a skill I now offer to the other brothas out there. It is priceless. I know it is priceless because I had a relatively happy childhood. No, in fact, I had a great childhood. I like nice things and really know how to enjoy a nice time. I am still a relatively happy guy satisfied with both my work and my life. In my business world, I am motivated by loyalty, honesty, and propriety—and I can be driven! In the infamous tortoise and hare fable, I am without question the tortoise! But, I am on a constant mission in the mirror.

My childhood days—while every bit the happy-go-lucky, unfocused, cheery time of youth—were the foundation for my adult survival. My normal patterns of mayhem and mischief led to the requisite reprimand to which many children have become accustomed.

When I was naughty as a child, my parents would sometimes make me stand in front of a mirror to take a "good look at myself." Then they would have me ask myself why I had done whatever it was I did to get in trouble. Huh? At the time, I thought they both were nuts! I mean what sense did it make for me to ask myself about what I had done wrong?

Well, today, I understand completely what their exercise in discipline was all about. It was meant to teach me that it was up to me to recognize and be accountable for the negative behavior that I engaged in. On some unconscious level, it also made me understand that such behavior is symptomatic of an individual who is not connected with self.

In my adult life, I have come to rely upon and greatly value my parent's insistence that I remain true to and thus accountable to myself for my actions. Of course, they both knew that my identity as a Black man would provide me with an interesting life road to travel, filled with many challenges and surprises that I would need to face and overcome. So beginning when we were very young, my parents encouraged my brother and me to know ourselves—hence their question, "Do you like the person that you see when you look in the mirror?"

From professional to personal, Black men are often placed in environments that can potentially thwart our spirit and identity, but what my lessons in the mirror have taught me is that you can't let those demons consume or cast a shadow upon your life. My lessons in the mirror were the first step in developing a relationship with myself, and that connection of "self" has fortified my character and given me self-respect and inner value.

Unfortunately, too often when I take a look at other Black men, I see far too many embracing identities that reflect a life disconnected from itself. The signs are there for everyone to see:

> *A man isn't connected when he abandons his responsibilities to himself, his family, and his friends.*
> *A man isn't connected when he dishonors his name with lies.*
> *A man isn't connected when he succumbs to fears about his abilities and self-worth and replaces them with arrogance and hyperbole.*
> *A man isn't connected when his self-worth is based on the validation of others.*
> *A man isn't connected when he doesn't have the grace to accept his own limitations and vulnerabilities.*
> *A man isn't connected when he lacks empathy for his fellow man.*
> *A man isn't connected when he lacks the confidence, wisdom, and drive to reach for his goals.*
> *When a man isn't connected, his life is out of focus, and thus, he is left susceptible to disaster.*

Far too many brothas are making their way through life not being plugged in. They are disconnected from themselves, and it shows. As we become entrenched in this new millennium, I have a dream that Black men will learn to reconnect with their spirits inside.

Nobody can take away from you your beliefs, values, and respect, which is why every morning before I take on the outside world I take a silent moment just for myself to take a look at the man staring back at me in that mirror, and I revitalize my soul with the knowledge that I can respect, love, and honor the person that I see inside. It's all good for me because I know that I have to answer to that face in the mirror.

Gil L. Robertson IV *travels the world as a writer, contributing editor, and media specialist for the arts and entertainment industry and resides in Los Angeles, California.*

Your Soul's Journey

. . . the Lord seeth not as man seeth; for man looketh on the
outward appearance, but the Lord looketh on the heart.
—I Samuel 16:7

No matter how society may look at you or perceive you, the Lord sees you in a different light. He sees what's most important—what's in your heart and soul. God has made us all special and unique, but most important, in His image.

These men have been able to begin to embark on their personal inward journeys. It wasn't easy for them to truly look at themselves in light of some of the personal trials they have faced and challenges put forth by society, but they were able to begin to heal from these experiences. You can, too! That's the beautiful thing about writing. You can release your demons by putting them in black-and-white.

We would like to share with you an exercise that we found helpful in being able to look at ourselves and each other and find the qualities we would like to change or enhance about ourselves.

Looking into Your Soul

When you look into your soul, you come face-to-face with many different people—your best friend, worst enemy, counselor, commiserator, fantasy, worst nightmare, and many other people who seem to pop up at the most appropriate and inappropriate times. It's hard to decide who to trust when you can't even trust yourself: Do you trust what you see? What you feel? Or neither? Sometimes we feel abandoned when we truly look at ourselves: abandoned by people, dreams, and most important, time. The trick with looking into your soul is being able to take in the view and still know that there is something there that runs deeper than what you see on the surface.

It's time to look into your soul. No matter where you are in your healing or in your denial, let's take the time to look into your true self. The first thing you need to do is look at the person who is closest to you. What do you like most about them? Is it their smile? The way they think? The calm, peaceful manner in which they live their lives? However significant or small the quality may be, write it down on a piece of paper. Then turn the piece of paper over and write down the qualities that annoy you about this person. The way they grind their teeth when they're asleep. Their sarcastic jokes. Or their sloppy environment. Whatever it may be, write that down.

Take a separate piece of paper, and examine your own good qualities. Be honest. Don't leave anything out, big or small. On the opposite side of the page, write down all your shortcomings. Don't be too hard on yourself; just be honest. Finally, take both lists and examine them side by side. Compare your good qualities with those of your closest companion. Are there things on their list that you would like to incorporate into your personality? Take the time to write down the qualities on your companion's list that you would like to emulate, and do the reverse for the bad qualities you would like to repel. Take the time to write down a sentence or two about how you are going to incorporate the good qualities in your life and how you are actively going to improve or repel the bad. You will now have a clearer image of who you are and who you're working to become. Rev. A. R. Bernard, senior pastor and founder of the Christian Cultural Center in Brooklyn, New York, said it best, "You cannot walk this journey called life without constantly running into yourself."

Soul Source

When we say, "In the Eyes of Society I Cry, 'Who Am I?' " it is a way of us stopping and looking at who Black men truly are in spite of what society would have us believe. True self-acceptance is an internal achievement, and it comes from being at peace with yourself, your mission in life, and the love of a higher power. If you are struggling with low self-esteem, you will always worry about mistakes made and opportunities lost. Let it go! Each lesson learned only brings you closer to your purpose.

- Do you regret the mistakes you think you have made, or do you look at them as life lessons? Why or why not?
- Are you harboring any ill will for someone you think has done you wrong or abandoned you?
- Do you encompass these virtues in your own life?
- Are you comfortable with who you are? Or do you float through life dealing with problems without taking one moment to nurture yourself?
- Can you honestly look in your own soul and truly say you like what you see?

CHAPTER 2

CAN I GET A WITNESS?

*A man must be at home somewhere
before he can feel at home everywhere.*
—Howard Thurman

The traditional view of the church when it came to Black men was that they were preachers, deacons, or bishops—or they were forced to go to services by their mothers or dragged there by their wives. It has been made to appear that spirituality for Black men in general arose only in a time of crisis or loss, or in the face of tragedy.

One brother told us that most of the Black males you'll find in church are being dragged there by some woman—either their mothers if they're young or their wives if they're grown—or they're at the end of the line and they're trying to squeeze their way into heaven at the last minute. An unofficial look at the Black church certainly seems to bear this out. You find churches full of women, but the question remains, "Where are the Black men?" Or more specifically, "Why aren't they in church?"

A lot of Black men we've spoken to feel like church is talking about "pie in the sky when you die," and they're more focused on what's going on in their everyday lives, in the here and now. We met a reverend who told us that he goes out in the streets and talks to young Black men in "their language." He explains what God can do for them now. He told us that he couldn't just wait for them to come to his church when a friend of theirs died; he had to go to them, reach them where they were.

Don't get us wrong—it's not that Black men don't feel as though they have a spiritual connection; many brothers do. But how and when we build that connection with God affects the way we seek out the guidance we need to become closer to Him.

Going to church gives you a chance to learn about God, but you must decide to make a personal journey to God, Allah, Jehovah, Buddha, Jah, or whatever you call the higher power you accept. Growing to know that there is a single higher power greater than yourself, as a Black man, can help to lessen your personal load and bring comfort to you in your every-day life.

Black men have many faiths and varied roads to their spiritual growth, and they put the myth to rest that they don't have faith. In this section men put their faith in God into words and express their feelings for the Creator. They express how God has helped them rise to unbelievable heights and provided an undeniable source of support, comfort, and energy to help them fulfill their purpose in life and begin the journey to their destiny and most of all to inner peace. The stories of triumph and faith in this section will lift your consciousness to greater heights and help to set your own spirit free.

How to Hear from God

Donald Hilliard Jr.

You can sleep on a broken mattress for so long that you think it's normal to wake up with an aching back. Dr. Becker, a professor I had at Princeton Theological Seminary, talked about two kinds of suffering: needless suffering and meaningful suffering. When we insist on doing things our way without involving God, we often end up in a mess, and that's needless suffering. Meaningful suffering take place during the process of God molding us to make us into vessels for His use. Meaningful suffering will work for your good. Meaningful suffering will ultimately lift you to another level of self-awareness and resurrection.

Spirituality is an integral part of every man's life, and Church is still a central place to hear from God. God is still God. He remains constant, caring and concerned. His Word provides for the comfort we so desperately need in these days and times. "The Lord is my light and my salvation; whom shall I fear? the Lord is the strength of my life; of whom shall I be afraid?" (Psalms 27:1)

God is our refuge, strength, and hope. Yes, this life-giving, soul-stirring truth. Indeed, we need direction today and in the days ahead. Our president and legislature need direction. The police and fire departments need direction. Preachers and prophets need direction. Priests and rabbis need direction. We all need the Lord's wisdom, guidance, and directive hand. When I thought of this, it was too painful for me; until I went into the sanctuary of God; then I understood their end.

There is a passage in the Psalms where David was expressing his frustration at seeing the wicked prosper and go unpunished. It was only when he went into the sanctuary, the Church, and focused on God that he was able to understand that ultimately, we will reap what we sow. God is our comfort. Many of us are beginning to press our way into His presence because we need to be calmed by the comfort that only the Holy Spirit can give us. As David did, we need a word of comfort in the midst of our confusion. We are too often surrounded by negativity. The Church provides this Word. God is concerned about our complete selves: mind, body, and soul. The Lord we serve can speak to our faith, finances, and families. The good news of the gospel is that Jesus Christ saves. This salvation is complete. When our mind-set is changed, it affects the direction that we take. The gospel empowers us to be what God intended for us to be. He desires to speak with us individually. He desires to speak with the nation. There are many things about God that we will never understand, but we should know that He is sovereign and ultimately in control even when the issues of life suggests that He is not. "Speak to my heart Lord, and tell me what I am supposed to do." Help me to walk by faith, and to step over bitterness and anxiety.

Of course, God's concerns reach beyond this nation. God's sovereignty spans Russia, Angola, Japan, Jerusalem, as well as Harlem. He is God in Los Angeles, and at the same time, He is God in Anchorage, Alaska, and San Antonio, Texas. He speaks to all of us, and we must learn to listen to what He has to say. God uses various things to bring us to Himself and to humble us before Him. He uses broken marriages, messed-up love affairs, broken hearts, lost jobs, and even loneliness. We may not even remember what it was, but God used something to draw every one of us to Himself. In order to hear God, you must seek His face. The God we serve is attentive, caring, and concerned.

As we pray, and open His Word, we begin to see what God has to reveal about Himself, His universe, and our future. We read that wonderful passage in Jeremiah 29:11: "I know the plans I have for you say the Lord, to give you a future and a hope, not to harm you."

We need to seek His revelation, His will, His peace, His comfort, His joy, and above all, His face. "If my people who are called by my name should go hear." I am a firm believer in the power of prayer and the community of faith that we know as a church. We should press our way regularly to the house of God to be fed spiritual food. More than "things," we need God. He alone can satisfy the hunger in every soul. It is there that we also worship and offer our thanks and our service to the God who provides for us. The church should offer care, comfort, correction, and construction. As well, relevant churches should provide protection to the vulnerable ones of the next generation. If there are children without fathers in a church, it becomes the responsibility of every man in that church to provide a positive role model for those children. Today's church should be a safe harbor for all God's children, helping them to rebuild the walls of their own families.

Giving thanks to God is a good place to begin as we seek to humble ourselves and understand what He is saying to us. In order to meet the myriad needs in our communities, we must hide the Word of God deep within our hearts as we read in Psalms 119:11–16. Right now is a good time to thank God that you are alive. Here's a simple prayer for you to say:

Lord, help me to understand Your will for my life. Help me not to forget that You placed me here at this season for a purpose. Help me to seek Your face daily as You order the steps in my life. Lord plant me in a house where I can grow, where I can hear Your Word for my life continually, in Jesus Christ's name I pray. Amen.

Take some time to talk with God. . . . He hears! Take some time to hear from God. . . . God speaks! Do not forsake the fellowshiping with the people of God. Go to church. Allow this living God, Jesus Christ, to build you so that you will be a builder of walls of safety for our children, families, and communities. Let God bring out your potential, because the keys to greatness and purpose are in your hands.

Donald Hilliard Jr. is the senior pastor of the Cathedral International in Perth Amboy, New Jersey, one church in three locations. He is the founder and CEO of the Cathedral Community Development Corporation (CDC), which is the umbrella organization of many of the church's economic and outreach endeavors. Dr. Hilliard is the presiding bishop and founder of the covenant Ecumenical Fellowship and Cathedral Assemblies, Inc. In this role, Bishop Hilliard serves as the spiritual adviser and mentor for several pastors and churches across the United States. He is the author of Faith in the Face of Fear, Somebody Say Yes, Stop the Funeral, *and* Safe Harbor Begins at Home.

Take a Little Time for Little League

William Hunter

As a member of the Syracuse University Board of Trustees, former Miami Dolphin and Washington Redskin, law school graduate, student of theology, professional sports attorney, and current executive director of the National Basketball Players Association, I have seen athletics and athletes from every tangent at every level of play. I know the game in ways and from perspectives few can claim. I have had a booming law practice, served as captain of the football team at Syracuse, and have achieved much recognition and a myriad of commendations in my day. However, none has brought quite the same excitement, boyish grin, and warm feelings in my heart as the day I was inducted into the Williamsport, Pennsylvania, Little League Hall of Fame! Along with Kevin Kostner and George Brett, William Hunter's name was added to the Hall of Fame roster, and I was elated.

It has been a long time since my Little League days of 1955; however, I am convinced that many things have not changed. Team sports, at an early age, still function as a "basket" full of life's lessons. Our young girls and boys benefit greatly from the camaraderie, discipline, and participation of team sports. Most important, and as evidenced by the nation's willingness to invest in the Police Athletic League and other types of after-school athletic programs, all these programs help to keep children safe from the ills of idle minds.

The Little League experience helped to serve as a local social meeting point. How many times have family, friends, neighbors, and schoolmates extended a lunch hour or skipped the Saturday errands to attend a game? While my friends and I had to walk sometimes two or three miles to get to a game, we knew that there would be someone there to watch as we played. It gave me drive and fortitude on the court: and perseverance and speed on the diamond. Whatever the activity, folks there to cheer me on meant the game was great-win or lose. The support I received for my organized sports play carried over into my parenting days. My wife and I never missed the opportunity to attend a sporting event for our three children, sometimes flying all the way across the country just to be there.

The Little League experience, YMCA basketball, midget league football, and the like filled a void in the recreational and personality development of many children and now I see where we, particularly those in the sports industry, must fill a void in the world of youth organized sports. In the case of young Black athletes, there is no dearth of Black professional athletes to watch from afar. The locker rooms of the National Football League, Major League Baseball, National Hockey League, and National Basketball Association provide ample ground for spectator sporting. I am hoping that we can take that a step further.

We must support and acknowledge those professional athletes who go beyond the old adage: "Come watch me work" but rather have had the courage and the compassion to get close enough to work with the kids, and there are many of them. Almost every professional sports league has an academic component to their public outreach program. For me, personally, athletics and academics have always gone hand in hand: My success as a student had to supersede above all. Whether I played professional sports for ten years or ten minutes—as injuries and fate have dealt many in sports—I was set for life with my studies. While many things have not changed, some have. The number of children living in single-parent homes has dramatically increased and most often those homes are female-headed households. The number of young children turning to neighborhood street corners and worset will continue to increase unless and until we fill the void of their after-school time—the "before parents reach home" hours. Organized sports activity is not the household activity it once was for many children. Perhaps it never was for some sectors of society, and we can and have to change that. We can make the maturity of team sport a part of the social development of our young athletes. We can make the maturity of team spirit a part of the social development of our young athletes. We can provide more than visions of money, mansions, and mayhem, but instead show them slices of sportsmanship, security, and high standards. I am often reminded about the many mentoring, Big Brother–type programs that exist: 100 Black Men or Concerned Black Men and other meritorious groups exist out there that provide leadership and support to many young children on the fringes of neighborhoods, schools, and other institutions that unfortunately are not quite living up to their challenge. We must support and encourage the work of these groups and commend the men and women who have devoted their time and resources to our greatest national treasure: our children. This is the kind of human capital contributions that will speak to who we turn out tomorrow as our leaders in sports, politics, science, education, and diplomacy. You know what I mean: My grandmother used to say to me, "Garbage in, garbage out." If we do not make a credible investment in our children we will not get a credible return.

I recognize, support, encourage, and participate in the promotion and enhancement of organized sports because in almost all instances it builds character. Perhaps we can use the Little League–type experience to aid in the installation of an internal moral compass. Many of our young megastars veer far off course with their huge salaries, constant exposure, and lack of grounding. To try to teach sportsmanship, poise, and propriety to a youngster worth $100 million can be quite an undertaking. To make it part of a young organized sports player's character, attitude, and development is quite another manageable and desirable task. It will pay off in the long run. We can avoid some of the mishaps if we invest early. I worry when I see young athletes plastered on the front page of newspapers for behavior that's unsportsmanlike, in bad taste, and downright illegal. I cringe when trial after trial of our superstars reveal prurient and intimate details of their off-the-court behavior. I say a quiet prayer each time drinking and driving wreaks havoc on the lives of our players and their family members. Let's face it, whether professional sports players involve themselves with youths' organized sports or not, they will influence those youths' behavior as sports men and women. I am proposing that we maintain a hands-on approach at the point of impact rather than stand off at a distance. I see it work splendidly from where I sit, and I am campaigning for a universal approach to having responsible adults impact the lives of growing children.

While I realize that it is unfair to heap "role model" credentials on young men and women who have barely absorbed their own success, that is the way it is. I have heard many players bemoan the fact that they just want to play ball and not be "anybody's role model." I have heard a convincing case made by other athletes for parents to provide the role model for their own children and not pass it on to the more famous and yet inaccessible. These are good points, by the way, and I concede that they highlight the unfairness of the role model dilemma. I submit to you, however, that fairness is a most sought after—albeit rarely experienced—quality of the work world, and it is no different for a superstar athlete. The very public and high-profile arena is the professional player's work environment, and one of the occupational hazards of the job is the fame, celebrity status, and fishbowl existence that pervades the sports industry.

A player's behavior, lifestyle, and transportation all become a real part of the industry and a model for some of those fans and supporters. In a recent interview a former NBA megastar (and current half-billion-dollar businessman) probably summed it up best when he cautioned the young and restless nouveau superstars that owners are looking for players to whom they can pay megabucks: They must get lots of statistics and cause no headaches. We can shape the skill and the attitudes of young athletes early from the plat-

form of Little League and other organized youth sports. We can help to ensure that they embrace their studies as well as their athletic strengths.

From an economic perspective, the bad-boy image has tremendous cost
consequences. If athletes turn off viewers because of their behavior, they
turn down the public's appetite for their performance; if they turn off viewers, they turn away the sponsors from their time slots, etc. (and we all know
that the "etc." is the key to this threatened action) and the rest is history. It
is important that youngsters understand the economic reality of their behavior early in life. It is not rocket science that you pack the playground
with performance and skill.

It is important to remember that a successful sports career is a privilege
not enjoyed by many. In spite of what could be a career as short as five years
or as long as twenty-five years, I long to see the day when the desire to give
back at a level where significant impact is evident. I must give credit where
credit is due and make my point clear. As executive director of the National
Basketball Players Association, I know for a fact that many players devote
hours, resources, and personnel to the Little League effort in this country
and abroad. With the ranks of professional sports reaching global stature,
athletes have become a part of the hometown (or home country) fabric.
They lend their well-known names to all sorts of kid-targeted events, and I
commend them for it. I support it and I want us all to take a lesson from
those efforts.

You needn't be a sports superstar to touch the life of a young pitcher who
had no idea that he was swinging his arm all wrong, or a batter who needs
only to position that right foot properly to get maximum force behind the
mound, or that young female basketball player who cannot figure out why
the shot won't fall from the top of the key only to learn that the top of the
key is really not the shot but that closer to the basket is her range. Equally
important is that you needn't be a millionaire to suggest to a student that he
may want to go to the library today instead of to the gym because passing
that math midterm is more important. My wife and I were staples in the
athletic development of our three children. As a unit we gave their academic
studies the attention and commitment they so richly deserved. It paid off. I
do not claim to be a research scientist, but I am willing to bet that those days
and evenings on the courts, in the library, and together at home helped to
shape their development in many ways. It kept them healthy, busy, and
competitive.

Yes, I made the Little League Hall of Fame. I admit that humility and
hard work have led to my achievements in the legal arena. I have managed
the negotiations on behalf of some of the highest-paid individuals in the
world. On a daily basis I am thankful for my life experiences. With friends

and family in abundance to wish me well, I enjoy comfort, security, and efficacy in everything I strive to do. To some my induction may pale next to other accomplishments in life; but I am *so* proud of having made the Little League Hall of Fame. While it may not be the sole cause of my success, it is clearly a solid and significant part of the foundation upon which all of my other life's successes are built. Let's at least offer that same support to the development and advancement of our future leaders.

William Hunter is the current executive director of the National Basketball Players Association.

My Trust in God

Chattman Johnson

In 1975, I set a twenty-five-year goal based on God and a plan of action. When I set my plan in motion, I was a sophomore in college, and I was failing the majority of my classes. The recession had hit, and my life was changed because of love. Besides my grades being on the border of rejection, there seemed to be little room for the possibility of receiving support from my school or other sources (such as government, grants, loans). To make matters worse, when I arrived home that summer, my mother was having a nervous breakdown and going in and out of the hospital. My two younger brothers were in control of the house, and since our mother was away, they had all their friends who wanted to get away from their homes living in ours. It was if our home was a safe haven for all the children in the neighborhood. Well, I came home from college to find the house in ruin and my brothers enjoying the good life of living without supervision. My probability of returning to school was looking abysmal. But, there was one bright spot during this whole situation, and that was my faith in God. Without my faith and taking certain risks, I could not have made it and would not be talking about it today.

My faith was developed during my earlier years when I was in high school and my family was going through financial, marital, and health problems. One of those faith-strengthening times was as a high school sophomore. Again I was failing all my classes but one and was given an ultimatum: bring my average up to an eighty-five in all my classes—or leave. So I turned to the only person I thought could help me, and that was God. Well, without making it into a long story, God pulled me through with a course of action, and a belief that all things are possible with Him. With my eyes focused on God and what I would call a simple plan of action, I set out to finish high school and go off to college. I don't have to tell you I succeeded even though the school did not believe I could do it. They even made a special effort to inform me that no one had ever met the conditions of their ultimatum. This made me want to succeed even more. I had set my goals beyond high school, to college. When I completed my last year, I not only met their conditions, but I was also accepted into a highly recognized Black institution of learning. I was happy to see the astonishment on the administrator's faces before graduation when my name was placed in the glass case with the other top students who had applied to college and been accepted. I proved them all wrong by doing two things: believing in a higher being, and believing in myself. From that time on, I have always spelled *faith* as R-I-S-K, and *risk* as F-A-I-T-H.

The hardest thing in meeting and setting my goal was verbally expressing it to family and friends. People would always ask me, How do you set a twenty-five-year plan, and I would tell them, "With God." Their second question would be, What are you expecting at the end of your twenty-five-year goal? I would tell them to "Work because I want to, and not because I have to."

It is unfortunate when a person you admire—a mentor, a family member, a friend, or just a successful entrepreneur—asks you what your goals are, and you tell them, but they can't see your dream or criticize your thoughts. All anyone wants to do is make something of themselves. Unfortunately, it doesn't necessarily work out that way. I have always thought I was doing just what I had been taught to do, reaching for the stars. But sometimes I think when people inquire about your goals, they are really creating obstacles for you because they can't understand your vision. We must recognize that the only limitations we truly have are the ones we place on ourselves. We want to blame society for our setbacks and limitations but, as Michael Jackson said, we need to "look at the man in the mirror." No matter what others may say or do, what will be is always up to me.

I have questioned God every step of the way from my point of view, and I have wondered why He has never left me. The only answer I can come up with is having a mustard seed of faith, and taking the risk to believe in Him and myself by pushing forward even when I questioned whether or not I could do what I was up against. I believe our actions are our mustard seed of faith. That's why I spell *faith* and *risk* the way I do. I have asked God to help me through school, to help me find a job, for multimillion-dollar contracts, good health, and countless other things. I can say without any hesitation, he has never forsaken me—not once. Now, I have completed my plan and I have accomplished everything I expected with only two items left. The first is to write my story, and the second is to work because I want to and not because I have to. I am confident that these goals will also occur in the near future.

If you remember anything, remember that God's plans are not like your plans, and even though you may reach certain goals, there is a time for everything. When I look at the last two goals I have set for myself to accomplish, I recognize I will reach them in God's time, no matter how close they may be to my schedule.

God knows what we want before we ask, and it is up to us to ask and it shall be given, as the Word says. God has never asked me for anything except his love, and that I place no false or any other god before him. He has never asked me for the things that I come to Him for. My requests of Him are mine and never His. God never lies, and His word never comes back untrue. Knowing this, I can expect to receive what I ask for out of my mouth if I trust in God and believe in the following statement, "Now, Faith is the substance of things hoped for and the evidence of things unseen."

When I set my goal of twenty-five years, I was using my human insight to determine what length of time it would take to accomplish my goals. I trusted in God that He would guide and carry me along my journey when I could not see or walk using my human ability to get through the hard times of my life. God has come through for me when I asked Him to do so in His time, which is my time when I walk by faith and not by sight. The only time I have to worry about God coming in His divine time is when I become fearful and walk by sight, but when I walk by faith, I don't have to worry about God's time because God's time is when I need Him.

The two goals that were not completed were never seen as a deadline, only as goals with a bigger picture in mind. The bigger picture was I would write the book as near the end of the twenty-five-year plan as possible, recognizing that in putting the book together this would also take time, and as long as I did not quit in my efforts to write and publish the book, I am still on time. The second goal to work because I want to and not because I have to is a faith issue, and I trust and believe that when I am ready for this blessing I will receive it and I am not worried about *when* it happens but rather *that* it happens. It is important to understand that my goal to work because I want to and not because I have to is only a means to an end, not my ultimate goal in life. However, this will occur because my actions during the twenty-five-year plan have set it in motion and I have asked my God for this blessing to come forth. To sum this all up, I am presently in a position to accomplish this goal, making my efforts during the twenty-five year plan worthwhile, and God is right on time.

With God I am everything, without Him I am nothing!

Chattman Johnson is the owner and founder of Johnson Management Group CFC, Inc. and CJ Realty and Development, an all-encompassing real estate and financial management company located in Dunwoody, Georgia. He is one of less than fifty Black certified commercial investment managers (CCIM) domestically and internationally. He is the father of Chattman Johnson III and is currently writing a motivational book inspiring individuals dealing with the challenges of life.

The Myth

Terry English

Historic events and research have informed us that conditions, circumstances, and environment have the power to manipulate, influence, and shape the way we think, act, and feel about ourselves and how people feel about us. Unequal treatment and laws coupled with negative images transform a once "mighty man" into a careless, self-centered, insensitive, unmotivated, self-aggravated, indignant, and ignorant human specimen in society. This is not a reflection on all Black men, but is the view for many in America's a majority community. No one really wants you as a neighbor, an employee, an employer, or a husband. Black men are the subjects that help create what has been known as "White Laws."

This image was created to enslave and control the minds of many Black men, and today this negativity is taken as fashionable. Look at the alleged affects of rap music. Does the negativity being propagated today about Muslims surprise you? The same psychological warfare that was used to destroy the Black man's dignity is being used against the Muslim.

Why do Muslim men get a bad rap? In short, because many of them are Black men or men of color.

As a young Black man who grew up in a single-parent household in the ghetto of Brooklyn with few Black male role models, I find that my soul is challenged by the negative rhetoric associated with Black and Muslim men in the media, in our community, and most of all by Black women. These men are their fathers, brothers, sons, and husbands. In fact, many of the people we admire today came out of this very misunderstood faith, such as Elijah Muhammad, Malcolm X, Muhammad Ali, Minister Louis Farrakhan, Kenny Gamble, and H. Rap Brown a.k.a. Imam El-Amin, to name a few.

Initially, I had very little drive to speak about what I believe is on the souls of many of our brothers. But after reading Sura 53, section 3, from the Qur'an, that "Allah's power manifested in destruction of falsehood," I realized the need to speak for the many voiceless black men who struggle with the myths and falsehoods about Islam and Black men:

They are all ex-criminal offenders who accepted Islam in prison!

They are all drug addicted!

They are all unemployed or have low incomes and sell incense and oils!

They are all womanizers and engage in polygamy as a matter of routine!

They all treat their women as inferior and make them walk behind them!

They all engage in domestic violence with their wives!

They all worship a man name Muhammad!

They all make their women wear clothes that cover every part of their bodies, including their faces and hands!

They are all filled with violence and hate!

Last, but certainly not least, they are all *suicide bombers!*

All of the above statements are unequivocally false. But to hear false statements espoused from some media outlets and to watch Black people agree with this rhetoric really suggest that we know less about our history than was feared and really diminishes the role of our Black elders in the fight for freedom, justice, and equality. Allow history to remind us that when Africans were brought to these shores in bondage, they were Muslims, and in more recent history, one of the most intriguing Black social reform movements of the twentieth-century was called the Nation of Islam.

Today, Islam has brought many adherents peace, guidance, and a love for self and others—and most of all, it has taught many the power of God. This knowledge of the power of God has required me to respond to the above-mentioned falsehoods categorically:

The prison industrial system is not only full of Muslims, but it's also full of Black men—over one million of them. I have never been there, and a man who you and I admire, Malcolm X, has—so Islam served its purpose to turn people to the submission of God.

Recent statistics suggest that close to eighty million Americans have tried some form of illicit drugs, which further suggest that some of them may be from every faith known to man. It's not about the drug use or abuse; it's about the drive to fight your addiction through determination and willpower. We can believe that when billions of dollars are spent on drug rehabilitation programs, the message is that those who have abused can stop the abuse if they believe.

Recent statistics suggest that close to 5 percent of Americans and 10 percent of African Americans are unemployed. Contrary to popular belief, many Muslims (like Muhammad Ali, Kenny Gamble, and myself) are financially stable and have secured a good future for their children while being successful, legitimate businessmen. But let's keep in mind that those of us who sell incense and oils are doing for *self*. There are big corporations, such as the Body Shop, that have created a multimillion-dollar industry from selling products such as oils and fragrances.

Recent statistics suggest that 50 percent of all marriages in America end in divorce, many as a result of the husband's infidelity; furthermore, 70 percent of Black children are born into single-headed households. These data suggest that the values of marriage and sex in America are under trial. We all need to begin to take this very sacred union more seriously. I am sure some of those 50 percent are from all faiths. All faith-based Scriptures sanction polygamy under certain conditions (that is, widows, orphans, and so forth), but the Holy Qur'an urges the man that if he knows best, he should take the hand of only one. "This is more proper that you may not do injustice." (Sura 4, section 1) It does the women and children a great injustice when you don't marry, and when you take on more than one woman. God has blessed me with the hand of the woman in my life, and I will strive to be as just to her as humanly possible.

Do your own informal survey. Have you ever seen Muslim women walking behind their men in day-to-day outings? My wife walks beside me and even has more formal education than I. As her protector, I may enter the home first or some other places just as precautions to make sure my family is safe and secure—that's the duty of a Muslim man. Muslim women enjoy every political and social freedom as any other women, and I believe that these freedoms can be improved in every walk of life.

Statistics suggest that domestic violence is so pervasive in America that there are national campaigns to stop violence inflicted upon women. Islam is a religion of peace, one of freedom, justice, and equality. It goes totally against the values of Islam to hit your wife. That doesn't make her free. Give her justice and treat her equally. The thought of even associating with any man who would inflict violence onto women pains my soul.

Muslims worship Allah (God), but they *praise* Muhammad for his prophecies like the Christians *praise* Jesus for his. Enough said.

All faiths encourage their women to dress modestly. There is no compulsory dress in Islam, and many Muslim women are corporate executives, wearing clothes to fit the part. My wife has an assortment of clothes, and her wardrobe is of her choice. She has enough respect for herself to pick her attire, which varies from business suits to evening gowns, all of which I gladly pay for, and head coverings are worn at her discretion.

Statistics suggest that violence and crime are so prevalent in America that the prison industrial system is becoming increasingly privatized, reflecting the amount of profit associated with it. The several million Americans in prison are not all Muslims. Again, those in prison for violence and crime come from all religions and races. Islam is a peaceful, loving religion that teaches us to respect those in authority and obey the laws of the land. Those in prison who profess Islam did not do the crime because they are Muslim (if they did do it); they did it because they are criminals.

Emile Durkheim wrote a book called *Suicide*. His theory suggests that suicide is so pervasive that it warrants a thorough investigation into causality. He argues that suicide may look like a highly individual and personal phenomenon, but in reality is explicable through the social structure. Reasons for suicide range from depression to despair. Islam, however, teaches that trials are a part of life, and to consider suicide as a way of addressing despair is not an option. GOD shows no mercy for those who take their lives. Suicide or suicide bombers are evidence of a clinical act of depression or a rejection of faith, and instead of criticizing, we should work to cure issues related to mental illness and nihilism.

The falsehoods created to deter the interest in Islam only make many people more curious to seek knowledge. This curiosity has exposed many to knowledge, wisdom, and understanding that they never had before. We should not allow negative propaganda to manipulate us to the point that it prejudices us against any group—as it has prejudiced people against us. We should continue to hold individuals accountable for their actions and not condemn any race, or religion for the wrongdoings of a few. For the most part, people are good—or else you and I would not even be able to walk down the street without incident. Let's keep that in mind and continue to strive to set good examples for our families, people, and society.

As a child who attended Catholic school and a little later went to a historic Black college and served in the military, I knew nothing of Jim Crow, little about slavery and civil rights, and even less about being a man, father, and husband. Today, I teach, I love, I give, I employ, and I say proudly I am Black, I am proud, and I am at peace.

While attending Catholic school from the fourth grade on, I really never had a full understanding or belief in much of what was being taught to me about Christianity. I think this occurred because often I had questions that I felt were inadequately answered. In addition, I never saw where I—me, *Terry*—really fit in. "Where am I in the scheme of things?"

A few years ago, when I was not really in the best frame of mind but was searching for answers and truth, I met a brother selling the *Final Call* newspaper. Upon reading the paper and doing a little research on my own, I became extremely curious about Islam and the life of Malcolm X. I lived to study, read, and learn more about this so-called Islam—such a strange religion, but one that felt so right.

It was rather sudden that I decided to attend Muhammad Mosque #7-C, where I experienced a life-changing event. I sat, saw, and could not believe what I was hearing and feeling. The message was clear. I understood, I was awakened, and I was reborn. The minister, Minister Kevin Muhammad, was teaching, and it was like I was the only one in the room and he was directing and probing my every thought. It was unbelievable. To me it was a calling. It was what I had been missing for all my life. I then decided to involve myself and to dedicate myself to Islam.

I believe my wife is amazing because she works just as hard as I do! My wife is simply the best thing to ever happen to me. The feeling of being with someone in faith first, as friends, and also as lovers is the best thing in the world. As we say in the mosque, "The brothers of Islam will kill concrete for our wives." My wife, Elisa for short, is the reason I am able to do the things that I do that have continued to make my family successful.

Terry English is thirty-two years old and the CEO of Prime Protective Systems Inc., one of the leading security guard firms in New York City, employing approximately 150 licensed security professionals. He has been recognized for hiring people from the inner-city community and received the Borough President's Award and numerous leadership awards from various political and community organizations. Married with two children, he is currently developing a youth basketball league.

Father's Day

Cliff Lazarre

There they go again. The butterflies in my stomach must be well into round twelve of a heavyweight bout. As I make my way toward the classroom door on Jell-O–like legs, my heart begins racing faster than the Indianapolis 500. The anxiety I endured in the second grade years ago is still fresh in my memory today. My class was on a field trip, and I could not attend because I forgot my parental slip at home. So for that school day, I had to be placed in a different class. A class in which I did not know any of the students. And if that was not tough enough, it was the Friday before Father's Day, and the class had an art assignment. Each student was asked to make a Father's Day card.

It was one of those cut-and-paste kinds of tasks. The classroom was filled with students working at a feverish pace as each child customized his or her own cards. Some students drew pictures of their dads while others wrote letters expressing how much their fathers meant to them. I participated in this assignment even though I desperately did not want to. I did not know it at the time, but the card I eventually made would be a reflection of myself in years to come. I drew a card that had a shirt accessorized with a colorful tie. It said Happy Father's Day in several different colors made possible by Crayola. On the outside, it was very decorative; however, on the inside of the card, many things remained absent.

You see, I lost my father when I was six years old. Even though I was very young when he passed away, I understood that I would not ever see him again in his physical form. This was very difficult to accept, and I had a hard time doing so. However, I did not let anyone know this. My mother just lost someone she loved dearly and was left to raise two sons on her own. We had to be strong for one another; therefore, as much as it hurt, I refused to reveal to anyone the pain and sadness I was experiencing inside. My mother had enough to worry about, and I felt that my sorrow would only bring her an unnecessary burden. As the years passed, the pain and resentment increased. I often found myself in my high school years asking myself why would God take my father away from me at such an early age. Didn't God know that I needed my dad in my life? Who was going to teach me how to drive? Who was going to teach me how to shave this newly sprouted facial hair? No disrespect to my brother, Ronald, but these activities are usually reserved for father and son. Hence, I began to distance myself from many people in my life. I did not want to get too close to anyone for fear of losing them and knowing that they could never be my father.

Although I was upset at God for dealing me this unwanted card in my life, my faith in Him remained. I am a strong believer in the saying "Everything happens for a reason." And as angry and confused as I was at the time, I would always ask God for some sort of guidance to help me better understand the cards He dealt me. And instead of pushing people away from me who had good intentions, I promised Him that I would now begin to embrace them. And in doing so, the clouds of uncertainty began to give way to rays of light that reflected hope and understanding.

One of the things that I always asked of God in my prayers was for Him to continuously place positive adult African-American male figures in my life. I've always felt that life was like a staircase. Each step within the staircase can represent different things. A step can be a set of goals that one sets out to achieve. A step can be a series of obstacles that are placed in our path to success. For me, my series of steps were the different people I would encounter in life and the lessons they would eventually teach me in order for me to make it to the next level. Whether that next level was educational, work related, or spiritual, whenever I felt that I had a step missing in my staircase to understanding, somehow I always had a substitute that was always available. Whether it was my friend Asa Allyne, who does construction for a living, teaching me the importance of a solid foundation in any relationship. Or my friend Doug Watts, who is a professional songwriter, teaching me the different avenues to express oneself. And last but not least, my friend Alan Glover, who is a media consultant, teaching me the different ways to view the obvious. I have always had someone to fill in the possible void in my staircase.

I draw strength from their lessons in helping me cope with the loss of a loved one. No longer do I ask myself, Why is this? or Why has this happened to me? Instead I ask what can I learn from this situation that I have been presented with. And in doing so, I learn a lot more about myself. Although my father physically departed from my life some seventeen-plus years ago, I still feel his presence today. I know that he and God will continue to send positive people in my life in order to guide me in the right direction. And I also know that, no matter how difficult it may be, it is up to me to open up to share my experiences.

Clifford Lazarre is a business student at Pace University. Still in his early twenties, he has traveled the world, organizing live music events.

Love Is

Timothy D. Jones

No one has ever seen God; but if we love one another, God lives in us and his love is made complete in us. —1 John 4:12

I considered myself to be a good and fair person. I always did my best not to initiate ill feelings toward people; but I also never wanted to be taken advantage of. I did my best not to carry hate in my heart, because I knew that would end up hurting me more than the person I hated. Yet, I came to realize that, in some instances, I wasn't a very forgiving person. These situations involved my sentiments toward my father.

My father had always been a very inconsistent presence in my life. After a painful 1991 reunion between him, my brothers, and me, I vowed that the next time I saw him, he wouldn't know I was there because he would be dead and I would be paying my respects. When I expressed my feelings to my mother, she understood, but warned me to make sure that I was not harboring any hate toward him in my heart, because that would be bad for my spirit. With this is mind, I simply became numb to my father's presence and lived my life as if he did not exist. After all, I had other men in my life who were positive and embraced me as a son. I figured I was better off without him, anyway!

Fast-forward a few years to November 8, 1995. It was my dad's birthday, and I was in my room, writing poetry while listening to "Stairway to Heaven" by the O'Jays. I began to think about my dad, the fact that it was his birthday, and I thought that even if I wanted to call him for some strange reason I couldn't because I didn't have his number. Thinking about my dad on that day brought on various emotions that all hit me hard in an instant. I felt as if the shell I'd built around my heart were being peeled back and I could see the vibrant pain that had been covered was still there. I began to think about the moments in my life that happened without my dad, and I began to cry. I tried to stop the tears, but that was useless. With the song playing in the background, I rose from my table where I had been writing and began to talk out loud to God and to my dad because, at that moment, I was upset with both of them. I was upset at my dad and at God for doing this to me. Here's how the conversation went:

I don't understand why I feel this way. I can't believe I'm crying thinking about someone who is not thinking about me. Dad, why am I missing you? You don't deserve to be missed. No, not for a second do you deserve to be missed by me! You probably didn't even think about me on my birthday, and I'm sitting here crying because I can't wish you happy birthday on yours. Lord, what is wrong with me? Why I am caring for someone who has done me so wrong? I feel like a punk because I am playing myself by getting emotional about a man who I haven't seen or heard from in years. What would he think if he could see my tears? *What would he think if he could see my tears! Me crying for my father is like watering the ground without first planting a seed, and expecting something to grow. There is no seed of love in my heart for my father, so all I'm creating is mud. I am a man who has made it this far without him, so, Lord, please take this pain away so I can continue on without him. My heart says that I miss him, and that I want him, but that is crazy because he has done nothing for me. So, why in the world would I still want him? He doesn't want me, because he is living his life fine. It was me who came to see him in 1991 and got the cold shoulder. So why, Lord, why are you doing this to me? Take away this pain from me, and let this moment pass.* Lord set me free from the thoughts of my father, *and please let my love flow to those who deserve it and who will give it back!*

I stopped speaking and began to focus on the song, which was at the part that says "step by step"—the part of the song that is talking about taking steps toward heaven and being with God.

In my silence, God spoke to me:

Do you understand that you are asking me to take away love? You want me to take away the same type of love that I have for you and my people. For all my people have fallen short of deserving my love, and I give love to them that is everlasting. When did you decide that you had a choice in deciding who and how you should love? Do you think that my love for you is merit based? My favor, perhaps, but my love, never! I stand with my hands stretched out to a people that I died for, and yet I feel the winds of time across my palm because they refuse to hold on to me and if they came to me in this moment, I would love them as if they'd never left me. How else will a people see my love unless they see it in those that they can see who profess my name? You loving your father is worshiping and bringing honor to my name. So do this in honor of me, and I, too, shall honor you! Until you love your father and stretch out your hand to him, neither one of you will ever be free. The walk of the righteous is not steps taken but rather earned when they are steps taken in love and service. For one day when you have a child, what example will you be if you cannot love the one who you call father.

Until that point in my life, I felt that I was doing well as a human being, no thanks to my father not being around. I also felt that, since I was grown, he couldn't hurt me anymore. My mother had always been a rock in my life, so I convinced myself that I really had no ill effects from the dysfunctional relationship that I had with my dad. I was never more wrong about anything in my life. I never knew what a healthy relationship between a man and woman was, because my dad wasn't there to show me. I was blessed to have four older brothers, but I had to pick and choose pieces of them to come up with a definition of manhood. Consequently, I dealt with the pressure of having to prove my manhood through the conquest of women because I felt my dad believed that I would grow up to be gay since I was so close to my mother. One of the worst parts of dealing with this was that I was never able to talk to anyone about it while I was going through my late teens and twenties, because I didn't know then what I know about myself now. When everyone tells you that you are okay, after a while you believe it. But it also gets to a point where you begin to hide your pain because no one gives you room to acknowledge it.

So there I was, a shambles, but still believing that I was the man because, through all my up and downs, I still had the symbols of my security and self-esteem around—women. Women filled voids in me that I didn't believe existed. These voids were there partially because of the lack of a relationship with my dad. My lowest point, which led to my emancipation, came when my security blanket was taken away from me. I had to finally see me for myself, and I didn't like what I saw. I was living as my father had, without even realizing it. I was carrying his unmarked baggage and had actually put my clothes in it and labeled the baggage as my own.

With nowhere to turn and feeling like the prodigal son, I went to my true father, Jesus Christ. I repented and pleaded for a plan for my life and the wisdom to be able to know that it was Jesus speaking, not me fooling myself. It was at that point that I let go of all the baggage, because I had nothing to hold on to. I let Jesus become the center of my life. That is when Love 101 began, and I have been studying the course ever since.

I gave up practicing accounting and am now the director of the Teen Program at Martha's Table, a community-based organization in Washington, D.C. The Lord took me from a top-floor office in downtown Washington, D.C., and placed me in the fields of a struggling neighborhood to tend to his harvest. I have been doing his work for almost seven years now, and he has lifted me to heights that, in my former life, I didn't realize were possible. I've come to realize that Jesus is a love that cannot be measured, because it is as infinite as his power. When I think it can't get any better, it does. When I think I am worthy, I repent, because I am not, nor will I ever be. This lesson has given me the strength to begin to truly love.

When I look at my life now, all I see is love. I see love in my struggle to show God's love to my teens through everything that I do. I see love when I enter the Lord's house to fellowship, worship, and give Him praise with my family. When I look at my family, I see Jesus. As He pulled me out of the darkness, dusted me off, and began to teach me about true love, He blessed me with a family of my own to grow with. My wife is someone I met in high school. We were in the same homeroom for four years, and became like sister and brother because her maiden name was *Jones* also. When I went to our ten-year class reunion in hopes of continuing my quest for women, the Lord put Vanessa in my path, and my life has never been the same. At the time of the reunion, she had a five-year-old daughter named Jasmine. The reunion was held on August 23, 1996. We were married on August 22, 1998.

The message the Lord spoke to me on that day while I was crying out to him about my father was brought to fruition on July 8, 1999. It was my birthday, and on that morning, my wife gave birth to our first child together. After all that I had done to fall so short, God's love, mercy, and favor were still upon me. He saw fit to bless my wife and me with a son, Isaiah Jeremiah Ezra Jones. I've cried many times since the birth of Isaiah. When he was born, my prayer was that he would bring my entire family back together. As a teenager without my father, I always prayed for a son so that I could have the father-son relationship that I never had. I promised to love my son the way he was supposed to be loved. At the time, I didn't realize that without Jesus in my life, I wasn't ready to love myself, let alone a son. But in God's timing, everything works to bring glory and honor to him.

I now define my manhood by my walk for Jesus. Jesus is everything. He is the measurement, and the Word of God is my instruction book of life. Through the love of Jesus, I can see that my father was a victim of his own circumstances, and he had his own baggage that he hadn't healed from. I know what love is now and am reunited with my father. I have forgiven him because Jesus has forgiven me. I love my father because Jesus loves me. I now speak to my father and attempt to be a comfort for him because Jesus has comforted me. My dad is sixty-one years old now and raising a fifteen-year-old son. Jesus has given him the opportunity to get it right with this son, the way He has given me the opportunity with my son. Now, sometimes my dad even calls me to ask advice because I work with teenagers. I talk to him about my family, and I know that he is happy to finally have a grandson. There's no greater testimony than love; and there's no greater gift because that is what Jesus is—*love!*

This piece is dedicated to Jesus; my father, Howard Jones Sr., and my son, Isaiah!

Honey and Ladybug, *I love you!*

Timothy D. Jones is the director of the Teen Program at Martha's Table, a prominent nonprofit organization in Washington, D.C. Timothy is also the founder of Beat of Life, a company dedicated to utilizing hip-hop as an educational tool. Beat of Life is currently developing a hip-hop–based sociology CD and workbook for grades eight through twelve.

Your Soul's Journey

He came as a witness to testify concerning that light, so that
through him all men might believe.   —John 1:7

There's profound comfort in knowing that there is a power greater than yourself. When you feel the weight of the world on your shoulders and you don't know where to go or who to turn to and it all seems like it's on you, what do you do? Do you suck it up and say, "I have no choice but to bear this load alone," or do you call on your higher spiritual source?

Your spiritual source gives you the fuel to make it to the various destinations of purpose and peace. Tapping in to this power through prayer provides a base of strength. When you call on your Higher Power, no matter how you refer to it by name, it will answer. Through a renewed mission, you will be given the capacity for sensitivity, understanding, and volunteerism. You will be comforted with the knowledge that the Higher Power you observe will put all that you need within your path and begin to remove all the fear and doubt that have plagued your soul.

Soul Source

Do you have a relationship with your Higher Power? Before answering the questions in your spiritual journey, you must know what path you're on. Think carefully and even pray or meditate on your answers to the following questions for clarity.

- Do you pray or meditate? If so, how often?
- How do you feel about your Higher Power?
- Do you only call on Spirit when you're in trouble or do you give thanks every day for the goodness in your life?
- Are you sharing goodwill throughout your life?
- Are you senistive to what God says through others?
- What do you want from a spiritual relationship with a Higher Power, and why?

CHAPTER 3

MY BROTHER'S KEEPER

We are inevitably our brothers' keepers because we are our brothers'
brothers. Whatever affects one directly affects all indirectly.
—Martin Luther King Jr.

Slavery. Reconstruction. Segregation. The civil rights movement. The Black power movement. The Million Man March. Brotherhood is in our blood. It is what Black men have relied on to get them through various points in history. Our greatest movements were built on the foundation of brotherhood. Brotherhood is a special bond that can't be broken or altered by the pressures of society.

Brotherhood is something that Black men seem to have an innate yearning for—whether they find it in the barbershop, on the football team, in the fraternity, on the street corner, in a gang, or in prison. But society isn't really comfortable with the idea of Black men coming together in tight-knit groups, so informal and spontaneous brotherhoods end up being unrecognized, underground, and often outright illegal.

You'll almost never see a group of positive young Black men on TV or in the news. Good news about Black men just doesn't seem to be popular. You won't hear about a Black fraternity that organized to provide scholarships for Black kids or a group of Black investment bankers who broke away from their Wall Street firms to start their own private equity funds. It's as if these things don't exist or never happened.

There was an American Express commercial several years ago when the Internet was just becoming a household word that showed four clean-cut brothers in expensive suits talking over dinner at a five-star restaurant about whether or not it was safe to buy golf clubs with their credit cards over the Internet. The commercial had no punch line, but was shocking in and of itself. No matter who you are, it made you realize that you simply had never seen such a collection of guys before in your life. Is it because such guys don't exist? Or is it because guys like that might show younger brothers there are men out there like this and you can be a part of a brotherhood such as this one, too, if you so choose.

Black men have life choices other than those summed up by Biggie Smalls's immortal words: "Either you're slingin' crack rock or you got a wicked jump shot." Even Biggie realized he had more choices and exercised them, but more important, he brought his boys with him for the ride.

There's nothing stronger between Black men than the bond of friendship. These long-lasting and undying alliances form the basis for a strong and powerful brotherhood. There's a respect that they hold dear and a knowledge of the boundaries that cannot be crossed.

Black men who have discovered that they are their brothers' keepers have begun their journey toward trusting each other and relying on each other, enjoying camaraderie, and showing loyalty and mutual respect for their fellow brothers. They have learned that there are other Black men out there who are in their corner and who share the same concerns, feelings, and goals. The love these men demonstrate for each other will give you a greater understanding of the bonds that they have forged with one another.

Address Your Issues before They Address You
Mychal Sledge

Am I my brothers' keeper? He asked again, Am I my brothers' keeper?

No, I am my brother. Do not let the facts fool you. I, your brother, did make black belt at the early age of fifteen in Japanese Shotokan and jiujitsu. The facts are true; I, your brother, am the winner of five consecutive national championships. I am listed in five World Almanacs. Do not let that fool you. Not even this brother winning two gold medals in the Pan-American Games should be able to deceive you, or making the United States karate team on the first try and remaining on the team for five years.

No my brothers, please believe that:

I am you.

And, you are me.

For so long I was misinformed by the misinformed. I could not see. I was in the dark of true understanding. I believed the misinformation of others who had no clue, that they had no clue, that they were misinformed. They told me things like "Real men don't cry." "Be true to the game, and the game will be true to you." "It's a poor rat with only one hole to crawl in." All lies I almost died for. Only when I turned on the light was I able to see. Truly see, of course not by sight, but by faith. My experience in the lifestyle was blinded by the darkness; I could not see it was Almighty God who had brought me through. I was fast asleep until that inner light shone in. Today I fear no man, creature, or beast. I fear only God.

God was present when I encountered the deepest struggle of my life. During my days and nights, I lived in fear. He was there when I was shot and left for dead. He was there when I was shanked in the Men's House of Detention (you may know it as the "Tombs") at seventeen years old. This is a prison, built underground in New York City. God was there every time I stood in front of the judge, every time the case was dismissed; he was there in the deep, dark places I traveled to around the world. He was there when I was growing up in the Drew Hamilton Projects in Harlem, New York.

There but for the grace of God go I. After several spiritual awakenings and personal atonement, did I realize I am just like my brothers? Be he young or be he old. Today in the reflection of my past experience, I appreciate not being part of the conscious dead. I am no longer sleeping at the light switch. I am you, my brother. Fear would not allow me to turn on the lights. No longer do I let fear, resentment, or anger rule my life. Fear is so dangerous, oh brother of mine. It has placed me in a catatonic state; it has robbed me of life and dignity.

As a result of fear, I could not inherit the King's kingdom and live more abundantly. Fear has always ruled my life—a fear that has been prevalent and crippling. A fear that became my most familiar state of mind and being. A fear of the unknown, but most of all, a fear of me—afraid to stand alone or simply stand for something real.

I have held on to this resentment toward my father for thirty-nine years. It has had a direct effect on every brother (and especially every sister) that I have ever met—my brothers in school, in the street, and most of all in the ring.

Every time I stepped into the ring to fight, I saw my father, and I had to win at all costs. And guess what—I won every time! I kicked butt and took names, championship after championship. As my mother would say, "Take no tea for the fever and no BC for the headache." If I was in France or Japan, I saw him in the ring, in South America, his was the face of my opponent. The mind is so powerful. I believed and lived a simple phrase I once heard. "If you feed a thought and feed a thought, whether positive or negative, it becomes an action." No one ever asked why I always won regardless of the weight class I fought in. No one ever asked why I defeated full-grown men when I was only sixteen. No one wondered what was I thinking when I entered the open weight (unlimited) class, with men weighing hundreds of pounds more than I did.

If they only knew—could see my soul. If they only knew the pain I carried. I was so angry. My process was always the same. I became angry, and then anger would segue to madness, and madness to rage. Being blinded by rage is dangerous for me. I always got the same results, inside or outside the ring: police, violence, destruction. It was impossible to have a healthy relationship with anyone or share intimacy on a deep level.

I always heard the same two words from women all my life. *"Get out!"*

I had been trapped in a body and controlled by a mind that really did not give a damn! This was bondage. This was worse than doing a life bid in any maximum-security prison. How could I help my brother if I was still in bondage?

I had a "father" in my house, whom I called Dad. I love him today with all my heart for so many reasons. However, my biological father was not there for me, and the impact was devastating. I hated the way my real father was revealed to me. A fly-lip cousin told me all about him when I was eleven. I asked my mother; she thought I knew. She cried; I got angry. I knew this wasn't a subject I could talk to her about. I felt I couldn't trust her anymore. Therefore, how could I possibly trust any other woman? I love my mother so much today. Her guidance, wisdom, and teachings will always live in my life and my children's lives. She taught me what God is by her love.

Try to understand: There were no baseball games, no Christmas gifts, no birthday presents, nothing from my biological father. He came to my high school graduation and I asked where he'd been. Of course, his answer was not good enough. I look so much like him; now I understand why I never liked the way I look. It was hard to see what others saw. People tell me I'm handsome—yeah, a cutie. But I couldn't see it. Sometimes I still don't see it. I no longer wonder why I suffered, really suffered, with self-esteem issues.

I remember this almost as if it were yesterday. My manager called me and asked where I wanted to go to training. We had to train annually. It was that time of year. He had never given me a choice before. I was thirty-nine then. Wow, that was six years ago. He began naming states and cities—so many choices—where training was being held. Los Angeles, Chicago, Miami, Seattle . . . Seattle? I was choked up and told him I had to go there. He said fine without a clue that my biological father lived there. I hung up the phone and cried. I knew it was time. Time for me to see him as the man I had become. A man he had never known.

I was even angrier than before. I had heard, again from a fly-lip cousin, that he'd raped my mother and this was how I was conceived. I waited until the very last minute to call, to let him know I was coming. Actually, my wife forced me to call. He asked if I wanted him to pick me up; I said no. I told him that my company limo was going to pick me up. She elbowed me, almost knocking me off the bed. I stopped lying and told him it would be nice if he could pick me up. I had always been able to get in touch with him by phone. I had simply chosen not to. It had been twenty-two years, and I was not sure how this would go. I remember telling my wife to get some bail money ready, just in case.

I refused to let anger, resentment, or fear stop me from dealing with this one. It was important that I did not act like a thug or a gangster. It was important that I came back with some truths. It was the longest plane ride of my life. I had traveled to the Far East, but this seemed longer. On the plane, I prayed. I kept thinking about the commandment "Honor thy mother and thy father." I do not know why this stayed in my head. When I arrived, he was there waiting. A fine black man who looked remarkably like me. He told me I looked good; I said he did, as well. We drove to my hotel, and he accompanied me to my room. I gave him pictures of his grandchildren, my children, and we talked. I told him that I needed to tell him something. He became very quiet. I said, "I'm sorry." He asked, "For what?" I told him, "For not being a good son." You see, from the age of seventeen to the age of thirty-nine, I'd been responsible for not contacting him and for staying away. He cried, and so did I. We hugged—a first. I came back to New York feeling a hundred pounds lighter, with the answers I needed. I left so much in Seattle, excess baggage I had carried so long. By forgiving him, I was able to start my healing process and find freedom from the bondage of self.

We Can Be So Spiritual but Serve No Earthly Good

Prior to this meeting, I had begun searching for a better understanding of God. I searched in houses of faith—from mosques to temples to various denominations of churches. I even remember chanting, *"Nomyo horenga kyo."* I competed around the world and studied the world's religions. I studied the Holy Bible and the Holy Qur'an and the Torah. I learned so much from my investigation and my search. There are many rules; from the Hadith to the Commandments—they all say the same thing. I learned that all these religions and denominations and faiths led to the same thing. Almighty God. He is called by many different names—Jehovah, Jai, Messiah, Allah. The key is to call Him.

What I learned was that the spirit of God is in me. So simple, yet so profound. Just call Him and watch Him appear and work in your life—He works in mine. I have tried to heal in many ways and have not been able to accomplish this without first asking God to come into my life and allowing Him to take control. I had to surrender. I remember over and over again going back to the original prayer. *Oh, God please help me!* Sometimes whispering it, which was actually a scream for help, most of the time crying out as loud as I could. Sometimes in the bathroom or in the bullpen, or in the hospital. God was always on time. I have a truckload of evidence to prove that He is real and alive. I challenge anyone to do this. Just call Him. Go ahead say it, "God please help me. Please help me heal." Love God with all your heart, and love your brother in just the same way.

Now let us go there. God is love. Love is not a misunderstanding between two fools. Love does not hurt or bring harm to others or yourself. I no longer carry guns, am a gang member, get smoked up, or stay drunk. I had to let go of all the self-destructive patterns that I had become used to. This was a quick way to the grave.

Love is not obsessive or compulsive behavior.

How can I love God so much, obsessively, and not love my brother likewise? How can I be so holy and see my brother hungry when I walk outside that house of faith? How can I cherish Him and not help my little brothers or treat my fellow man without any compassion? Sometimes I can be so spiritual and be of no earthly good. How can I love God so much and not love my sisters? How can I continue to disrespect them or myself? I can no longer call them outside of their name, or mistreat them. I can no longer be verbally abusive or physically abusive. I can't even be emotionally abusive to my sisters or brothers if I call myself my brother or his keeper at times. Am I perfect? Far from it! I practice these newfound principles in my life on a daily basis. Some days I fall short and I come back strong the next day. I make amends as soon as possible. I can no longer blame others for my mistakes.

Many Are Called: Only a Few Answer the Call

The life I live today is not my own. It is about serving and giving back. I have taken so much from so many. Now it is about showing someone else how to change and make a difference. The cycle continues from one brother to the next. We don't have to be the next statistic. We do not have to keep filling up the prisons. We do not have to continue killing each other over nonexistent virtue. We are not the victims anymore; we are now the volunteers. I have harmed myself in such a way, that if the next man had attempted these acts, I surely would have taken his ass out.

I have been selected and resurrected from the living dead. I've been snatched, unnaturally, from the gates of a living hell. Pulled from the junkies and winos fire barrel on the street corners. I've been given yet another opportunity to rewrite my eulogy. Prior to my healing process, my tombstone would have read, "Here lies a bum with a lot of images, who had died on hard image time." Only after getting to the exact nature of my wrongs did I begin to heal. This process continues as I continue my journey.

I have an opportunity to live again, to step up to the plate and to be a real man. I know that I have a responsibility to my brothers and yes, my sisters. A charge, a command, if you will, from Almighty God to help another child of God from going down that same path of self-destruction, a path that I was on and didn't even know it. I didn't know that my rightful position in life is to call on God. I must call on Him not just when things are bad, but also when things are going great. I did not know how to be submissive. I did not know how to surrender to the high cost of low living, a price I had repeatedly tried to pay for with my life and those of others. I was emotionally and physically abusive. Like many of my brothers, I suffered from an inability to communicate. Even though I am a college graduate, I could not say, "You hurt my feelings." I would rather purge the hurt physically. I had conditioned myself to do so, with the help of society.

I cannot run from my real responsibilities in life anymore. My family is my heartbeat. I have six daughters and two sons. They are all my children. They do not all have my blood running in their veins, but they are my children. They are not my adopted kids or my stepchildren. They are my children! They teach me so much about life and love. Most of all, they teach me about forgiveness.

I will never be the father to them that my biological father was to me. Instead, I rather show them what James Lewis Sledge has taught me about being a man, a father, and a dad. James never—and I mean *never*—treated me like stepchild or an adopted child. He never called me a stepson or introduced me to anyone as his stepson or his adopted child. Even to this day. He was a man who worked hard every day and went to church every Sunday. He taught me to pray. Every night I would see this old man get on his knees, like a child, and pray. Every day I would see this man go to work, for over thirty years. He was also an usher in the Mount Nebo Baptist Church in Harlem for over thirty years. At some point, he and my mom decided to retire and move to South Carolina. I never saw him hit my mother or verbally abuse her. He led by example. He is now eighty-two and very sick. Every chance I get, I go and sit by his feet. I thank him and tell him how much I love him. I always let him know just how much he has taught me.

To Whom Much Is Given, Much Is Required

The birth of the Sledge Group, Inc., is the essence of being my brothers' keeper. We are operating in the heart of the village of Harlem, New York—the same streets where I grew up. Our vision is to open up in every major inner city in the United States.

The Sledge Group, Inc., is a community-based nonprofit organization that my wife and I founded. I am the chief executive officer. We provide myriad social services, including youth development, mentoring programs, HIV awareness, substance abuse awareness, and many others issues that address our communities. We are serving the underserved.

We are beginning with youth, ages thirteen to eighteen years old. We have a few that are nine and ten years old, because I do not want to lose them in those precious years of their lives. I know that they may not make it to age thirteen. There are Bloods, Crips, and Latin Kings and Queens among our youth. I want all the kids that no one else wants to work with.

We have youth who are required to attend; they are mandated by the criminal and family court system. Many are not required to attend, but often come back, after they finish probation.

Our village is not raising our children. The system is raising them. The public education system is failing our children, and our children are being labeled with all types of learning disabilities. The gangs are pulling them in at age eight and nine. The family element is the worst it has ever been. I am tired of just complaining about the problems. I am doing something about it. I remember James Sledge teaching me that I cannot complain about anything if I am not doing anything to change it.

I need help from my brothers. I ask them to come spend an hour with us. Mentor one of the young brothers. Come share with them your experience and your hope. If you are too busy, then send us a donation to keep the work going. Our mission statement is about transforming the minds of today's youth from believing that they are inferior in any way. We work to rid them of conscious or unconscious acceptance of inferiority. We teach the truth through education and life experience. Once you've been informed, you cannot say you don't know any longer. We give them the tools, knowledge, and wisdom to think and make a change in their community and in their lives. We are empowering and raising the consciousness of the young brothers and sisters that come through our doors. We have a Parents Support Group and tutoring for all participants. There is no fee. It is required that the parents attend the Parents Support Group and the youth must attend tutoring. We have slowed down the processes that have indoctrinated a campaign to divide and control our communities.

I have formed bonds with many of my brothers in the community that want this cycle to end. Some are from the clergy, some are street hustlers, and others are teachers, lawyers, and judges. Our bonds are as tight as our words and the life we bring to these words. It is about turning on the light switch and reaching back and pulling the other brother up. It's only through His grace and mercy and unmerited favor that I've had the courage to apply the action to what I believe in. Keeping my brothers safe. Keeping my brothers out of harm's way. This has touched my heart; God has brought my dead cousins' children to our programs. I never knew of these children. I have children of dealers and hustlers; I once ran the streets with their parents and shared a lifestyle with them. Children of friends I knew who are now incarcerated. Yes, many days and nights I am my brothers' keeper. God keeps us all. I know that I am just a humble servant. A vehicle that God has been using to do what is just.

The most powerful tool in the hands of the oppressor is the mind of the oppressed.

We teach the children about principles and preserving community values and life. I give Almighty God all the praise, glory, and honor for what others see as my success. I teach all on this spiritual path I call life, "that your opinion of me is not my reality." I will no longer allow you or others to validate or define my life. I have found a spiritual peace of new understanding for God, my brothers, and my community.

I am my brother.

And you are me.

Our inner souls, our pain, our struggles, make this so.

Mychal Sledge is the CEO and founder of the Sledge Group, a community-based nonprofit organization dedicated to empowering "at risk" youth through education and life experiences. He is in the process of writing a book and developing My Brother's Keeper *workshops. To learn more about the Sledge Group or volunteer your time as a mentor in the New York City area, visit www.Sledgegroup.com.*

Always with Me

Leo Gatewood

My brother was a hustler. I guess in a sense, we all were. He, my mother, and I survived as best we could, given the circumstances. My mother was a soul singer who, like too many of her peers, never truly reaped the fruits of her labor. Even when she had plenty of work and a record deal, things weren't great. However, when my mother's career and marriage to my father came to a soul-shattering halt, the three of us were on our own. At the time, I was very young and had not truly become accustomed to any sort of lifestyle. I was about four, and as long as I had my bike and my mother, I could make it. Unfortunately, my brother was never the same again. To be sure, losing your father through separation is traumatic enough. But being backstage at the Apollo with the Temptations one minute and homeless the next—well, that's just a little too much for the average adult, let alone ten-year-old. Now I am not making any excuses for my brother or his current situation. I am actually not sure that an excuse needs to be made for my brother's current predicament any more than one needs to be made for mine. I am a firm believer and sometimes a follower of the tenet that, it is not the situation but one's reaction to it that determines its true effect. To offer an excuse in his behalf would in some way imply judgment. Yet, I am unable and unwilling to judge my brother's reaction to our situation. First of all, he has already suffered judgment. Second, I am not sure that his reaction would not have been my reaction had he not come first. So here it goes.

Growing up, I looked up to my brother as most little brothers do. Given our six-year age difference, it's surprising that we were close at all. But we were. I followed him everywhere that I could, welcome or not. Sometimes with my mother insisting, he would reluctantly allow me to tag along. My mother put family over all else, and in her opinion, there wasn't anywhere that he had any business being that I couldn't be. Great for me, and not so great for him. I think my mother hoped that my presence would somehow keep him out of trouble. It didn't. When he and our cousin snatched pocketbooks, I was there to get the change. If a fight broke out, I was there and a lot of times I was part of the reason for it. When we fell on hard times, my mom vowed that we would never live in the projects, and we didn't. Yet there are people in all of the projects around town that will swear to you that my brother grew up there. That's where his friends were, that's where he hustled, and that's where he made a name for himself—meaning, I didn't have to. Now, don't be confused. Someone else's name can get you only so far. I was tried at times and always represented. Still, by the time I got to high school, the lines were drawn. I was the good kid, the good student, too good for the street. The irony of this is I was the one truly in love with the fast life. I admired the hustlers and pimps from afar, and I loved to fight. I really had all the ingredients for street success, in my opinion. The problem was that besides the fact that I was somewhat untouchable as Todd's good little brother, I got to see exactly what I would have to go through as my brother lived the life.

I remember the first time that my brother went to prison. I was crushed. He got only six months, but you would have thought that he got sixty years. I couldn't eat for weeks. I remember asking myself how he could be so stupid. Amazing how I equated stupidity with his sentence and not all his previous activity. I wish that I could say that it was at that moment I decided that his life was not for me. As I mentioned, other folks had already decided that, so I didn't have to. My mother was the most important decision maker. She had other plans for me. The fact that my brother's friends had begun to get killed and that he was now in prison made her job quite a bit easier than it might have been. Unfortunately, that was not the last time that Todd went away, or the longest time. I remember going to church with my brother and mother years later and "testifying" how thankful I was that God had allowed me to be promoted to captain in the army. My brother, ever the comedian, stood up right behind me and thanked God for both my promotion and his recent parole. I often think back on that moment and wonder if he realized how truly linked those two occurrences are. I believe them to be mutually inclusive. No prison for him, no West Point for me. I shudder to think how things might have turned out if he had been purely successful out there. Or what might have happened if he had ever invited me to join him, but he never did. I was privileged to have all my curiosity satisfied through him. I never had to stick my toe in the water; his life showed me that it was plenty cold. I learned from him that friends are far and few and that death is only cool on TV, so I never had to hurt to find out. I was free to do other things.

In 1996, my brother was sentenced to thirty years in federal prison. He escaped the habitual criminal sentence of life by the grace of God. Through prayer, good behavior, letters, and phone calls, he may soon see his sentence reduced. Regardless, he has spent way too much of his life behind bars. We speak three to four times a week. He is my backbone now that my mother has taken some much-needed rest with the Lord. He has always been my inspiration, even when he was doing wrong. I came to New York for restitution, redemption, and recognition. To reclaim as much of what was stolen from our mother as I possibly can. My brother is my virtually invisible but ever-present keeper of my resolve. My mother, Judy Clay, was a singer's singer. She was the greatest singer that a lot of the world has never known. I came to see if I could change that. My brother is here with me; in spirit. He is constantly on the phone, providing support and encouragement. Giving me advice and constantly telling me that he is "a bad man." It's funny that he still sees me as the little brother he needs to school and protect. Although I have to remind him that I'm a grown-ass man with my own children, I know that I can't complete this mission without him. That's nothing new for either of us. The new part will be upon his release. I will then have the opportunity to be to him what he has always been to me.

Leo Gatewood is Senior Director of Finance and Operations at BMG Music. Leo is integrally involved in the restructuring of the overall business to improve financial reporting, efficiency, and profitability. Prior to joining BMG Music, Leo performed consulting and analytical functions for Bad Boy Entertainment and Arista Records. Leo is also a veteran of the armed forces, having served six years in the U.S. Army as an attack helicopter pilot. He earned his bachelor of science degree in systems engineering from the United States Military Academy at West Point and his MBA from Harvard Business School. Further, he is the founder of Codyco Publishing and consults with various new artists and start-up labels and is currently developing a television movie based on the life of his mother, the legendary Judy Clay.

The Big Screen
Obba Babatunde

We are bombarded by projections that in the public eye, define every aspect of our lives. Before long, statistics, reports, and media have a great impact on our endeavors, and if we do not stop to analyze what we see and hear, we may miss the hidden ulterior motives behind the projections. All individuals who are part of humanity must carefully monitor whether they confirm preconceived notions, support statistics and reports, or define themselves by these projections. This is why I take my art and my profession very seriously. In the work that I do, I am an image projector. The characters I portray and the stories that I tell reach a potential audience all around the world. I must take responsibility for the roles that I take and create, because I am a Black man, and audiences will see my actions as an example of all Black men. I accept this challenge because my art makes a difference for those who have not yet been born and what will happen in their lives. I would like to think that many people had the forethought to consider how their actions would affect my future before I was born.

I don't say this to "big myself up" or represent myself as a leader, hero, or revolutionary, but as a man who wants to make a difference based on the experiences that I have had throughout my life. It is logical that if some people are not exposed to the varied lifestyles of my folk or if they are provided only with an unbalanced projected view, then they may develop the wrong impression of who we are. This works the same for everyone. Let's say I don't know anything about the Asian community except what I hear in school or what I have seen in the movies. If the messages I receive about this community are overwhelmingly negative, then I will be prejudiced toward the people from that community. To take this example one step further, we can use it to look at the way individuals define themselves. We know ourselves better than anyone else because we live with ourselves. If we are shown a projected image of ourselves that is negative for a long enough period of time, that is what we come to believe as truth. No matter what nationality you are, the brain behaves the same. The mind accepts the imprint it is given, even if, in principle, the individual does not agree with it. This is why what I do is so important. I represent Black men in public and present and debunk false thoughts and views of a person or people.

There is an unspoken brotherhood among people who have been subjected to the same programming and have had to fight their way on a daily journey to a place where they feel some type of power and confidence. My manager, who is a Caucasian female, was walking with me through a heavily populated mall one day. Every time I would pass a Black male or female, there would be some type of acknowledgment—a nod or a smile. After about an hour my manager asked me if I personally knew all these people. I told her no, I didn't know them. She said that she noticed that Black people usually say hello or acknowledge one another, but that White people don't speak to each other because they are White. This is reflective of a condition that I never thought about until her observation brought it to my attention. It is true, but where did it start, and how does it sustain itself? We acknowledge one another unless we make a conscious decision not to do so. I've certainly been in rooms where I have tried to catch someone's eye and they have avoided my gaze. By and large, this practice is common only in America. It's not just a Black thing, but a Black American thing. I was in Copenhagen in the late 1970s and I was trying to say hello to any Black man I saw. One started to run away from me because he thought, "Why is he saying hello to me? I don't know him." This tells me that this practice speaks to the Black American experience.

In show business, when you look at the individuals at the top of the food chain, you see that brother Denzel is at the top for the brothers, but not at the top of the entire entertainment game. We always have to continue to prove ourselves. Since there are so few parts available for Black men, the competition is stiff. Very stiff. Anyone who reaches a high position holds on to it with everything they've got because if they let it slip for an instant, it's filled by the next person in line. You have to continually prove yourself, and there is a dynamic amongst the brothers in show business—there is a joy to see a brother at the top. It's a mixed joy, though, because for every brother at the top, there is a line of brothers waiting for that opportunity. When you look at the celebrities walking in on the red carpet, it's easy to pick the brothers out. There is Wesley, Sam, and then a horde of others, predominantly with white skin, parading in. The cat on top is put into an awkward position. If I am at the top, I may delude myself that I've finally proved myself, but it's not true. The entire premise is wrong to begin with. Why do we have to constantly prove ourselves? Why don't "they" prove themselves?

Many Black men don't buy books. Maybe this is because there are no books that men are interested in reading. Yet, African Americans set the standard for the fashion, arts and entertainment, and music culture for the entire world, Africa included. Young Japanese men dreadlock their hair, wear their pants low, write graffiti, and breakdance. This isn't what being Black is really about, but it's what is projected as being cool, and others imitate Black Americans because they are cool. They have always been cool, but African Americans seldom benefit from the rewards of their coolness.

I trust and believe in my talent and craft, and I realize the necessity for solid relationships that I have with my fellow brothers in the industry. We're no different from one another. Our commitment level and steady hard work unite us, and there is no need to create a division between us over who is going to get the job. Every job comes to an end. So, I can chat and hang with Laurence Fishburne and not have to wonder about how he is going to feel about any competition between us. He is talented, and we have worked hard and achieved a certain place in our careers. I can also talk to (and I often do) the young brother in Walgreens. He asks me how I got into the entertainment business, and after I talk with him for forty-five minutes, I tell him that maybe we'll work together someday. He doesn't know how possible that may be. There are brilliant actors I watched while growing up, and within two years, I was auditioning for the same roles they were because they are Black men. They can be short, tall, someone in business for thirty years or a newcomer. So, we have to have a brotherhood, and we have one whether we want it or not.

We either need to acknowledge this brotherhood and benefit from its strengths or act like it doesn't exist, which doesn't make any sense. What I try to project and encourage are the standards of excellence. At some point there was a popular phrase, "Man, hey look, I am just trying to get paid," to which I would answer, "Well, there was full employment during slavery!" Sometimes I reach people, and sometimes I don't. The difference in time that we are born into and the circumstances of the world that we are born into shape our perceptions of what is fair and excellent from early on. For example, no one born in the last twenty-five to thirty years has ever had to get up to change the channel on the television. When I was growing up, I was the remote control. I can still hear, "Son, will you come in here and change that channel?" When you push the button on the remote control and the channel changes, there is a sense of immediate gratification. There is no use telling people stories about "When I was a boy . . . ," and expecting them to understand. With a small amount of investigation, you can find out someone's individual plane of understanding and reach out to them from their own point of reference. You need to relate the story of history to a younger brother in this modern day if you want to effect change in the future. History truly does repeat itself. Today we have more individual wealth in the black community and less collective power.

If the answer were about getting paid to effect change, we would have solved the problem. Nothing works in a vacuum. You can't lock anything down, because everything continues to evolve and change. If you go through a door and don't strike down slavery every chance you get, then you're right back in the soup. Therefore, it is very important that we keep in mind the standard of excellence that we are being measured against and responsible for protecting.

At the 2002 Oscars, Halle and Denzel were honored. The Oscar is an award presented to an actor for creative effort and a standard of excellence in a body of work. If you saw the movies and you were a brother and did not like the movies or were not happy about them winning the Oscar and did not say "Right on!" you were politically incorrect. Just because I may have an opinion that is not in agreement with someone else's does not mean that I don't have love for my brother. It means that I am entitled to my opinion. White people may say, "You people are never happy," and the attitude is "Now they will want an Oscar every year."

America has changed. It took only forty years. Our condition is always related to this brotherhood or sisterhood. When you make the movie *Waiting to Exhale*, and sisters are saying come on have a bonfire and celebrate each other, make sure you get paid, and no man is good. Now we are divided; you see your brothers don't even support your work because they believe they are being degraded. We don't have a balance.

The same thing happened with *For Colored Girls Who Have Considered Suicide/When the Rainbow Is Enuf*. In the 1970s Black men were like, "Come on!" Some men felt like that with the motion picture *Sounder*, where every Black character was portrayed as despicable. It reinforced the stereotype that Black men are basically born to be criminals and that is why the prison population is overwhelmingly Black—either we are horrible or something is wrong somewhere.

I hope that some of us will continue to communicate honestly and in doing so understand what the other is going through so that we can support one another and not feel isolated. On the set, you are generally alone in that environment, and when I realized that I was easily ticked off, I found a way to communicate when I am unhappy with what they are asking me to do. Let's take villainization and dehumanization. I can play a villain because a villain has a reason for how he thinks. However, I will not portray a character in a way that I feel will take away from the potential humanity of the individual, unless that is what the story is about. Otherwise, I will attempt to present an alternative to that image while remaining fair and true to the character.

I want Black actors and Black people not to be afraid to talk candidly with one another. There was a time when we would have a lunch once a month: Messrs. Poitier (Sidney), Brock Peters, Bernie Case, Blair Underwood, Trot Brown, and myself. We would meet at the Four Seasons and just share the multigenerations—just share, just talk about the business, our lives, and the things we have done and the things we would like to do. I would have the opportunity to hear various perspectives, and speak up because I had a chance not only to express myself, but also to express myself to people who cared about what I had to say. I received encouragement and knew that I wasn't alone in some of my experiences. So, when I go to a forum alone I can stand and dispense what I believe in as just and can be encouraged and can encourage. This type of courage comes from communication, great brothers who would have said what I did but either couldn't or didn't. So, I speak truthfully for them and the entire world without being subject to a particular slant that I am trying to project. That's what it is about: honesty, communication, establishing a brotherhood, a support system, while remaining true to your craft and realizing the power of your image.

Obba Babatunde is presently finishing production on three television specials as producer for Rubba Productions and continuing his role as the father on the hit sitcom Half & Half.

Humble Beginnings

Lonnie Holmes

As I begin to look back at my humble beginnings, I can't help thinking about how as a young man I depended on my two brothers for survival skills and guidance. They were my link to the outside world. At or about seven years of age, I developed a fondness for playing the game of chess, I remember the only thing I wanted for Christmas that year was a chess set. I looked through the blue-chip-stamp catalog to see if the chess set was available. I then tried to round up as many blue chip stamps as possible. Before the holidays came, I began to realize that I was going to come up short on the number of stamps required. For some odd reason, I continued to hope that somehow a chess set would just magically appear. There was no father in the home and it almost goes without saying that I didn't believe in Santa Claus, but I still dreamed of that chess set. On Christmas morning, my oldest brother walked in with the biggest wooden chess set I had ever seen. His gift was a long way from the small black and white plastic pieces I was used to playing with in school. Over three decades later, I still have the same chess set. It continues to remind me of my humble beginnings and the brothers who taught me how to get through.

I grew up in a family of nine struggling through just about everything imaginable. Times were hard, and everything had to be split ten ways if you count my mother. Even with dinner, no matter what was cooked, if you didn't make it home in time, then you were just out of luck. There were no hard feelings—that's just the way it was. You might have gotten mad, but you made sure that you were the first at the table for the next meal. Those experiences, along with the many lessons that I would learn from my extended family, shaped a lot of my ideas about being prepared. And I mean, being prepared for anything. One time, I wasn't so prepared when a group of guys jumped me at a bus stop. I was defenseless; there were more of them than there was of me. I told my older brother about the unfair fight, and I wanted him to rush right back to the bus stop with me. If we waited, I feared those guys would be gone. My brother told me not to worry about it and said that we would catch up with them at a later date.

It wouldn't be long before my brother's words turned out to be true. Just as he predicted, we did see those same guys again. Only this time I was at a visiting school preparing for a track meet. Here I was, in the middle of the process of preparing for the one-hundred-yard dash. I needed to have my mind on the race, but seeing those guys that jumped me took my mind off the competition. My brother had come to see me run, and it took a while for him to notice me frantically calling his name. By the time I got his attention, the guys had disappeared behind the bleachers. When my brother caught up with them, I heard him call them out by name. Apparently he knew these dudes. Always looking out for my well-being, my brother instructed me to focus on my track meet and prepare for my race. He let me know that he could handle this.

I was thinking to myself, how can I possibly run when I got to get up there in those bleachers so we can handle this situation together? I didn't want my brother to meet with the same fate as I did being outnumbered. As I started walking back to the race, all I heard was "Holmes, I'm sorry we didn't know that was your little brother." I couldn't see what they were doing because of the fact that they were behind the bleachers, but I could hear a loud thumping noise, and I had no idea what was taking place. My heart was racing, and my main concern was my brother. However, I know that he told me to run this race, and when my brother spoke, I listened. When either my oldest brother or middle brother spoke, their words were the closest thing to fatherly guidance that I would ever get, and I respected it.

I understood my brother's expectation of me to run this race despite what may be happening to him. I reluctantly listened to my track coach when he hollered for me to immediately get into the starting blocks. I still wasn't sure if I should be on that track field or in the stands. But I thought of what my brother wanted me to do, and it made me duck my head in the runner's stance and place my track shoes in the proper position. I didn't have a second to guess what those loud sounds might have been before I heard the starter pistol crack through the air. One hundred yards is not a long distance, but it seemed to me that running it took a lifetime. And in that lifetime, I was consumed by thoughts of my brotherly duties as I ran. Instinctively, as if I had no choice, I ran faster than I had ever run in my life. I wasn't trying to break a record or make a name for our school. I wasn't running for medals or recognition, I was running for my brother. I was trying to make it around that track as fast as I could so that I could be with my brother and whatever was going down.

My mind still wasn't on the race as I was the first to break through that runner's tape and keep on running past my teammates and coach, who were standing with hands raised to congratulate me. Hands slapping me fives and pats on the back rolled off my skin as I continued my harried pace down the track field and up into the stands. It never crossed my mind to stop running until I was at my brother's side. When I got there, I saw the guys who jumped me, and I looked from my brother to them and finally back to my brother in disbelief. It was those dudes who looked like they had taken the brunt of those loud thumping sounds. Before I could say anything, my brother said to me, "You don't have to worry about those guys anymore." His words fit a young man who had just handled his business with a group of guys who dared to cross the path of the brotherly bond. I never thought, not even for a second, about those guys who jumped me; my concern was then, like it is now, for my brother. The fact that my brother wanted me to run and encouraged me to excel no matter what was going on with him taught me the brotherly rule of unwavering loyalty.

It's not the ideal situation, not to have a father in the picture, but my brothers took it upon themselves to make sure that I am the man that I am today. My brothers made sure to school me—if they learned something, they taught it to me. If they went far, they expected me to go farther; that's just the way it was. But I was still, after all, the little brother, so I tried hard to fit into their shoes, or in most cases, into their fly clothes. My brothers were able to stay in style with clothes they purchased with money from their summer jobs. I was too young to buy my own clothes at the time, so I tried to wear their things. It didn't matter if the fit wasn't right—I felt smooth in those clothes every time I sneaked them out of my brothers' closet. I tried to be sneaky in my approach, but I would often miss a step in my plans to heist my brothers' fresh style. On more than one occasion, my sneakiness was discovered. Once I had taken my brother's shirt and worn it to school. I don't know why it didn't dawn on me that I would be discovered when my school pictures came back with me smiling proudly and wearing the stolen shirt. To this date, my brother will not let me forget that incident. Then there was another time I wore my brother's new Pro-Ked tennis shoes. Of course, I looked good in them and of course I got them so dirty that I tried to hide them in the closet to cover up the fact that I had had them on.

Making sure you were home to get your share of dinner, learning about brotherly devotion, and trying to live up to my brother's legacy were part of my humble beginnings. Overall, I felt like things were actually good for us in those days. That was until my oldest brother got into the street life and my middle brother enlisted in the army. Then, I was on my own, whatever I didn't get from my brothers by way of guidance, I wasn't going to get. I was about sixteen years old at the time when I developed my independence and character. I spent a lot of the time making sure my Afro was together and that I had a good supply of Brut cologne. I also started breeding tropical fish. With no one for me to model my behavior or style after, I started doing my own thing.

Even though I was just starting to make up who Lonnie the man was going to be, my older brothers still had an impact on my ideas and my life. When my middle brother came home after basic training, he played a tape of a white singer named Peter Frampton. I really thought he had lost his mind, that maybe the army had done something to his head. I soon find out that his "head" had changed. My brother began to talk about expanding his mind and opening up communications with people. He showed me pictures he had taken around the army base and encouraged me to consider life outside the comfort of our San Francisco home. I had no idea what he was talking about and still thought that the Army had done something to his head. It wasn't until I broke my leg playing football that I began to see what he meant. While in a cast for three months, I began to read things that I hadn't taken any interest in before. I read about South Africa and Apartheid, and until that point I had not recently thought about suffering in other places. I also became interested in banking and international business while I was being homeschooled. My final year of high school, I attended the School of Business and Commerce and started working at a bank on a part-time basis.

By expanding my mind, like my brother had encouraged me to do, I had enough credits after the eleventh grade to graduate early. I took his words to heart and shared my revelation by tutoring elementary school kids and then going to the Exploratorium museum to explain exhibits to visitors.

This philosophy on learning and growing helped me to get admitted to college. I had to leave my sweet, wonderful girlfriend behind when I got to school and met up with all the fine sisters who seemed to be waiting on me. My brothers' sense of style, blended with my comfortable personality, allowed me to get invited to every party on campus. I also got invited to be a part of the Kappa fraternity. One of the upperclassmen that I hung with told me how live—it was being a Kappa—and that joining that fraternity was guaranteed fun. In my mind, I was already having fun. I didn't need to be a Kappa to enhance my social life. If I was going to join a group of African-American men, that connection had to have purpose. The idea of brotherhood was set within me because of my interactions with my siblings back home. I went to the library to read up on fraternities. The first Afro-American fraternity I came across in the book was Alpha Phi Alpha Fraternity, Inc. I began to read about some of the prominent Alphas like Thurgood Marshall, Martin Luther King, and others. These were Black men that I admired. I read about some of the works Alpha men have put into uplifting the communities and other good deeds. It was important to me that I choose a fraternity that fused the two lessons that my brothers had taught me best: loyalty and excellence. I felt that Alpha Phi Alpha was based on these principles, and I grabbed the opportunity to meet with seven other men to discuss becoming an Alpha man.

About twenty-four years after deciding to become an Alpha man, I can say that I am still proud to be affiliated with the fraternity. We reach out to the community by providing food for impoverished families, football camps for inner-city youth, and scholarships for aspiring college students. I have been an Alpha for over half my life, and it continues to shape the man that I have become. But I know that the foundation for the true ideals of the brotherly bond were set by my brothers, who shaped the man that I was destined to be come.

Lonnie Holmes is a senior analyst for the San Francisco Juvenile Probation Department. He is also a managing partner for Trans-Con Investments. His goals in life are to uplift his community by his good deeds and continue to work with our misguided youth.

The Twin Handbook

Drs. Tory Z. Westbrook and Toikus Z. Westbrook

Our Mama Mae retells the story best. Of all her grandchildren, we were the only two that she had to spank. The matter was over some spilled water in her bed. Our punishment might have been otherwise dismissible, but on this particular day we managed to get on her last nerve.

"Tory, Toikus," she called to us in a tone that certainly meant business.

"I know that one of you spilled that water in my bed—which one of you did it"

Neither of us made a move. Don't ask what came over us, because we can't really recall. She said "I will whip only the one who did it. Now tell me who did it." We refused to tell on each other; it is in the twin handbook.

Mama Mae was outraged; now we weren't getting her on her last nerve, we were riding it. Neither one of us wanted to get spanked. We really wanted the water incident to be over so we could get back to our game. We were met with every child's worst nightmare: a spanking from someone who you know loves you. Even with that fear pressing on our young minds, there was no way that either of us was ratting the other out. We stood steadfast. Mama Mae threatened us, and then she offered us second chances to come clean and tell who the offender was. We never budged, and thus we sealed our own fate. We both got in trouble, and we took the spanking like men. Even though we were only four, we understood very early on that nothing breaks the bond of a twin brotherhood.

Being a twin and an African-American man has given each of us self-confidence that we aren't sure we would have had otherwise. Each of us has always had an unconditional cheering section, another person that has your back through the good and the bad times. Being in the same profession had added to unique understanding of *exactly* what the other was going through as we struggled to traverse certain hurdles. And most of all, there is an indescribable joy that we get to experience with the success of the other just like it was our own. We've shared similar goals throughout Central High School in Memphis, Howard University for undergraduate studies both as zoology majors, and then at Meharry Medical College for medical school. At each institution, people readily identify us as "the Westbrook twins."

Growing up twins has shaped our lives in ways that a lot of people don't understand. We have always entertained questions about our emotional telepathy, the twin ability to feel the other's pain from across a room. We have tolerated questions about being able to feel your twin's physical pain across a thousand miles; that does not happen with us. We once almost lost our lives together. As college freshmen, we had side-by-side dorm rooms, but fell asleep in one twin's room after a late night of studying. A fire broke out in the trash room two doors down. Known as heavy sleepers to our dorm-mates, we both slept oblivious of the smoke and alarms ringing throughout the building. Luckily a friend reentered the building to save us both by banging on the door until we awoke. Imagine that call eulogy: came in together, went out together. To this day, whenever one of has an important early-morning function, we call the other requesting a wake-up call across time zones. Our likeness of minds has manifested itself in many of the same acquisitions and achievements. We both chose medicine as a profession and drove cars of the same make, model, and color in medical school. People would often say of us that if they asked one thing of Tory and then secretly polled Toikus with the same question, the answers would be eerily identical.

Our similarities continue on into matters of love. Both of us were lucky enough to marry beautiful, independent, family-oriented women who both happen to be lawyers. Now, this was not planned, but selecting mates that shared similar background, personal achievement, and commitment to family had been a lifelong priority for both us. Once we found them, they would be best served by developing a close friendship to complement our incredible closeness. The challenge within each marital relationship was to accommodate our unique closeness while establishing the necessary "best friend" intimacy between spouses. When something great or tragic happens, we have to ignore the instinct to call our twin first and instead call our respective spouses. With the wives' conditional approval, we still serve as each other's primary source of support, inspiration, and discussion.

Nonetheless, the women we married will ask, "Did you tell your brother before you told me?" Overall, it takes a special woman to accept that someone else is that close to their husband. We were both smart enough to marry well in that area.

Being twins actually enhances our commitment to being husbands and fathers. We hold on to the ideal that family always comes first. We are both as fiercely protective of our wives and our children as we would be of our twin. Being a twin has, in many ways, primed us for the ultimate partnered relationship because we understand sharing, closeness, and unbreakable bonds. We've lived it every day of our lives.

Even though one of us lives in Connecticut and the other is now in

Louisiana, we are still as close as we have ever been. We talk every day, still share many of the same likes. Instead of Hondas, we both drive Acuras now. We both have three children, and each of us has a namesake son. With us being in different parts of the country, people don't readily identify us as the Westbrook twins anymore. Now there is a Dr. Westbrook in the East and a Dr. Westbrook in the South. We don't wake up every morning thinking of each other, but when one brother is going through something, the other is sure to keep him on his mind throughout the day. Although our individuality may be what people see now, we still have the bond of brotherhood that will be there forever.

At every Thanksgiving, Mama Mae shares with the family the hilarious end to her "twin story." Although she had to spank us both for the water incident, she didn't have to wait long to find out who the real culprit was. Mama Mae recounts that after she got done spanking us both, she walked away and heard one twin say to the other, "Don't do it again, I'm not taking no more whoopings for you!" She walked away secretly satisfied that she knew who did what. And she respected us so much that she would never ask us to divide our loyalties again. Mama Mae knew that it was true that day twenty-nine years ago and has been true every day since—if one goes down, then we both go down. It's in the twin handbook.

Dr. Tory Z. Westbrook lives in Connecticut with his wife and three children. He runs his own medical practice in East Hampton. Even though he is nearly a thousand miles away from his brother, a very close connection remains. Tory talks to his twin at least twice a day.

Dr. Toikus Z. Westbrook is the married father of three blessed children and still hopes to one day share a medical practice with his twin in their hometown of Memphis, Tennessee. In addition to practicing medicine, he is a published expert on domestic violence.

Always a Shoulder to Lean On

Corey M. Sanders

Like any other little kid, I was a pesky little brother. My older brother Gregory was way cooler and more athletic than I was. To be frank, I suffocated my brother as we grew up. We had a "tough love" relationship, because my older brother always thought that I was in competition with him. Truth is, I really wanted to be just like him. He was very influential, inspiring, and most of all *my* big brother!

Although we grew up in the same household, we shared dichotomous views and friendships. He was a street guy, and I was the schoolkid at heart. He stressed individualism. I had a difficult time grasping that, until I got older. Products of a broken marriage, my brother and I had to appreciate each other as we matured. Our father remained in the North as our family migrated to the South. Fortunately, my father never balked at his responsibility to his children. My father remained active, interested, and committed to being a part of our lives. Although he failed as a husband, he was a great father. He, however, missed the little things like doing homework with us, watching us develop and excelling athletically, and teaching us how to be men. When my mother and father got a divorce, my big brother became my father. My brother then became responsible for making sure that all the chores were done and making sure I was okay and did my homework. He would always tell me, "Do as I say and not as I do."

My brother always stressed an unyielding work ethic, respect for our mother; academics, integrity, or a swift kick in the butt would make sure everything will go all right. When I enrolled in a military college, I could not drop out because he kept me motivated, inspired. Greg left for New Jersey, and I stayed in South Carolina, when I was still in high school. He worked on Wall Street and continued his inspiration and occasionally provided financial support. When Greg left, he left me with a template for success, lessons, and goals to carry out.

In college, a new alliance of brotherhood developed in my life. I joined Omega Psi Phi Fraternity, Inc. Joining a fraternity gave me the opportunity to thrust myself into an organization replete with great minds, well-educated, positive, and socially conscious brothers. My fraternity brothers mirrored the life and relationship I had with my brother. We shared *everything*, including our families. "Lifting as we achieve" became a mantra that we embraced throughout our tenure in college. Through this unbreakable relationship, I cultivated a terrific friendship with Paul Brown, my closest friend today. I am especially honored and proud to be the godfather to his son in Atlanta. I look forward to going to Atlanta, not to party, but to spend time with my godson. Today, all of my frat brothers from my chapter are doing well professionally.

Passing the bar and graduating from college and law school were unforgettable but the greatest experience in my life was when my brother asked me to be the best man at his wedding. The odyssey from pesky little brother to best man in retrospect not only illustrated our love but a cultivated brotherhood. Along with my brother, I have a feisty and intelligent nephew, Malik. I embrace my responsibility as an uncle. I am as much a beacon in his life as his father. I accept the tremendous responsibility that an uncle has in his nephew's life. Besides the fun, games, and laughs, I am committed to transferring all the lessons, the love, and the disciple that I received from the men in my life. And when he asks for something, I ask him to read a book, write a report, and then I reward his request.

Today, I'm pouring back into the youth of my community what was poured into me. I adopt a class every year. I focus on the students pregnant with possibility, making sure they at least consider college. I try to instill in them good academic values and the value of integrity. I stress academics over athletics whenever we discuss ingredients for success. You may get into college on an athletic scholarship, but the greatest achievement from college is a degree! A college education simply affords options that may be explored in the future.

I believe in lifting as I climb, investing in people, and focusing on maintaining, fostering relationships with people. Brotherhood can be found in many places, including in church. I have learned that the most difficult part of building a home is laying the foundation. The deeper you dig, the stronger you become as a person. Bible study is an ingredient that should never be omitted in the laying and strengthening the foundation of integrity, respect, and brotherhood in my life. In closing, brotherhood is the tie that binds my relationships with brothers. Without a commitment to cultivating and maintaining our brotherhood, we would be alone in this world.

Corey M. Sanders is a prosecutor in South Carolina who volunteers his time to empower young people. He is engaged and plans to marry Dr. Renata Arrington and often visits his much admired older brother, Gregory, and his family in New Jersey.

Your Soul's Journey

And the Lord said unto Cain, Where is Abel thy brother? And he
said, I know not: Am I my brother's keeper?   —Genesis 4:9

There comes a point in your life—let's say perhaps around nine years old—when you actually choose who and what you want to be when you finally grow up. You are forced to focus on that idea because if you had a nickel for every adult who asked you the "what do you want to be when you grow up" question, you wouldn't have to worry what you were going to be because you would be rich. Let's just say you chose a lifestyle or career based on the role models that you were exposed to.

If you have been blessed to be in the company of brothers who had an opportunity to school you, whether it was in sport, school, a fraternity, church, or in a career, it made you a better human being. That person most likely saw things in you that you could not have seen in yourself and set out to cultivate those qualities. They showed you, through stories—some of which were told in jest—what to steer clear of. It feels good to be a part of a group. A strong brotherhood will give you reliable partners that allow you to be yourself, shoot the breeze, or get directions when you are lost in life. The secret to all this is your brothers sharing and providing direction to assist you with your purpose. The universe is set up in a way that sharing of knowledge is rewarded.

Sharing your knowledge is a plain and simple an exchange of power. The power to think, act, and create in a responsible way because you are equipped with the right information. You become a powerhouse—imagine a room full of Black men with this type of energy. It happened in October 1995 as men of color marched on Washington—not just a room full, but over one million strong. That sunny day, men learned collectively about why they needed to vote, how economics needed to be practiced at home with Black businesses, and how we needed to be responsible as individuals. The enthusiasm was instilled and a fire lit. Each person who went shared with other brothers about their experience, and there has been progress.

But there is room for even more growth. Are you living below your potential? Do you know any other brother who is living below his potential, not fully utilizing his talents and gifts? One of the strongest desires of human beings is the desire to be recognized and appreciated for their efforts. We all think wonderful things about others, but rarely epress them. Lift yourself up and follow your dreams, but inspire and encourage your brother to do the same, stop and talk with the young men you encounter, and share your thoughts, in the spirit of when your grand- or great-grandson attends the Ten Million Man March.

Soul Source

Brotherhood crosses blood and family lines and is inclusive of a fellowship of Black men who are united for a common cause. Creating a power source from within and getting direction and support from each other.

- Do you consider yourself to be a part of a brotherhood, formal or informal? If so, what?
- Is there anyone who you personally feel is like a spiritual brother to you?
- Do you have a supportive network of male family, friends who you can call or when you need to?
- What can you do to improve what you take from and give to the relationships with the men the other men closest to you?
- Do you wish that you had a more substantial support group of brothers/friends/family?
- What do you think of when you think of brotherhood?
- What do you feel would be ideal brotherhood?

CHAPTER 4

NO JUSTICE, NO PEACE

The secret to success is to learn to accept the impossible, to do
without the indispensable, and to bear the intolerable.
—Nelson Mandela

Blacks and Whites live in completely different worlds when it comes to the justice system, and the group most affected by this difference is Black men. A lot of brothers are wondering if the justice system in America is for everybody or for "just-us." Sometimes it sure seems like Black men are singled out for all the harassment and scrutiny the police have to offer. Whether you want to call it by it's newfangled euphemism, "racial profiling" or just good old-fashioned racism, ask just about any Black man out there, and he'll tell you stories of the inequalities of the criminal justice system, whether he's run afoul of it himself or not. The things that Black men take for granted are things that the average White person would never understand unless he or she took the time out to actually learn about how Black men are living.

It boggles the mind to hear that roughly eight out of ten black men will spend time locked up during their lifetimes; typically before the age of forty. If you think about it, that means that if ten black men under forty were selected at random, eight of them would have been incarcerated. We can't argue that this is not the case with all the civil rights violations across the country involving Black men being pulled over at random and being racially profiled. The Abner Louimas, the Patrick Dorismonds, and the Rodney Kings of the world have proved this to be so. The new revelations of widespread corruption among police officers in Los Angeles, New York, New Orleans, and other cities come as no surprise to many. Many observers have come to realize the burden that African-American males bear daily. They will have been either stopped without cause, arrested, handcuffed, searched, fingerprinted, and locked up for at least a night behind bars, shot at, or even murdered—all in the name of justice. Often leaving behind broken families, these men become depressed and even fearful for their lives. As a result,

Blacks and Whites live in completely different worlds when it comes to the justice system. Whites tend to see the justice system as an instrument of safety, while Blacks, especially Black men, view it as an instrument of oppression.

We live in a society where the type of justice you face is not determined by your crime or the extent to which your actions violate the law, but rather by the color of your skin, the size of your bank account, and the color of your victim. African-American men between the ages of fourteen and forty feel targeted, and if socioanthropologists are correct, they have felt this way for many, many years.

How many black undercover policemen have experienced the brutality of their colleagues as a result of mistaken identity? How many black executives and professionals, who shed their business suits for a relaxed weekend run in the park, are accosted, arrested, and detained because of their race and their attire? African-American tales of "mistaken identity" flood the newspapers, radio talk shows, and courtrooms. In reality, it is never a case of mistaken identity. The description is put out on the all points bulletin: the suspect is a Black male, approximately five feet ten inches, medium build, medium complexion, brown eyes, no distinguishing marks. Eighty percent of Black men fit that description. It speaks directly to the African-American family and its sense of reluctance and resistance to trust the police or the justice system. Whites see the system as just—a system to protect them, their families, and their rights. African Americans see it as a system designed to eradicate, denigrate, humiliate, incarcerate, separate, annihilate, discriminate, moderate, and reduce.

By keeping Black men down and incarcerated, the race can be controlled. In our sessions around the country, whether doctor, lawyer, or student, Black men had been profiled and treated as if they were less than human. Black men were arrested for minor infractions that made no sense, and cases were thrown out of court, but the scars were still left: low self-esteem, self-doubt, and the personal label "guilty" were branded upon them even though they were never convicted. In this section, you will read stories of Black men who fight the inherent racism of our criminal justice system from behind bars to the judge's bench.

The Gate

Robert Gay

This morning starts like most of my other days, with me behind bars. I attended college and came from a stable, supportive home. However, I made several choices in my life that cause me to spend time in prison every day. Although I am a corrections officer and not an inmate, at times, there seems that there is very little difference between my life and theirs. As they move through their day, I am following the same motions. They are the jailed, and I am part of the system that keeps them housed at the correctional facility. But we both are locked up. As an African-American man, that fact disturbs me in ways that are hard to express. Every day, I go through motions that make up the routine of their lives and mine. I often think about what brought me here. And I even start to fantasize about what it would take for me to escape.

5:50 A.M. *Check-in*—The gate swings open, I step in, it slams behind me. Guards and personnel check my belongings. I'm given chips to pick up my necessary tools that I'll use throughout the rest of the day.

6:15 A.M. *Count*—Every inmate is accounted for and cleared. I make sure that I'm always in position, always where I'm supposed to be. When I got enough seniority, I requested to be in the isolation section of the prison. The daily routine of managing relationships between Black inmates and White guards can cause anyone to question why they are here and why they do this job. It seems that support is lacking on all sides of me. When I am at work, I am an African-American man with the keys and a uniform. There are very few of us working as corrections officers in this facility. Most of the other White guards are legacies. They have worked here for some time, and they have family members who have worked here before them. They have rebel flags and gun racks in the backs of their trucks. I wonder what they think of when they see me. My presence as a Black corrections officer contrasts sharply with the sea of Black men that I come into contact with who are wearing the same state-issued clothes. When I look at the inmates, shackled and belly banded, I am relieved that although I'm in the isolation cell I don't have to be bound like that. However, I recognize that we are all bound in some way. I picked the isolation cell as my daily responsibility because it most closely fits my state of mind.

6:45, 7:15, 7:45 A.M—Every thirty minutes, a key is turned; every cell in the three-tier-by-forty-cell isolation unit that can house up to 120 inmates is secured. I'm in position, always accounted for, not looking to make any waves, just do my time and get out.

8:00 A.M. *Breakfast*—Chow is brought down and slid through the slots. Some of the inmates eat it, others leave their meals, the dullness of isolation stripping them of any appetite that they might have. Some brothers do isolation better than others. For me, being here was a choice. It's easier for me to mark time here, away from the general population. Three hundred brothers moving to recreation, another three hundred brothers moving to chow, another three hundred brothers, like me, sitting, thinking, just being still. Stillness is solace for many of the men in isolation. For others, it's the worst part of their sentence; they crave the air, the time with other inmates, the chance to watch Dallas play. For me, stillness helps the time on the clock tick faster; I'm consumed with my own thoughts: thoughts of my family, my hopes, my dreams, and the decisions that I've made.

My mother sent me to Central State University, and like many students, I thought of all the things that I had to have, and getting money was the only way to obtain those things. So I started to work—one, two, and eventually three jobs. My working left little time for school, and the inevitable happened. I was no longer a full-time student and a part time worker, I was just a worker, and college was no longer a part of the picture. I heard about working at the prison, and in a quick turn of events, I was hired and my destiny changed, no longer was I sitting in class, I was now sitting in prison.

8:30 P.M.—Transportation to minor court. Minor court is where infractions get heard out that weren't resolved by the sergeant on duty. Most brothers that I see on the inside are "innocent" by their accounts. Often, I really don't know what the inmates are in for. Brothers are quick to admit that they may be guilty of other things, but a bad rap or someone with a grudge stuck them here. I keep myself separate; I know what I have and haven't done. Somehow, the decisions I've made in my life do make me different. I can stand being called "house nigger" and "Uncle Tom" by those who look at me as if I could be in their same shoes. But I can't let what they say get to me. Just like them, I've got my time to do, so that I can get up, get out, and move on.

12:00 P.M. *Lunch*—Chow is brought down and slid through the slots. Sometimes, I'll run into a brother that I knew from the outside. A while back, I ran into a short guy who used to live with one of my good friends. He asks about James; I tell him what's new and keep it brief. What good are relationships in here? I used to think that the point of it all, the reason for me being here behind these bars, was at least to bring another brother up.

Now, I'm not so sure. There's a cycle here, and I know that somehow we are all caught up in it.

1:00 P.M. *Recreation*—Recreation is offered for one hour a day, five times a week. The guards offer. The inmates can take it or decline it. I think it's better to take the recreation, to take the shower and spend the rest of the day thinking and planning. Most of the inmates get built up in a way that guys on the outside can't even get at. I don't even try to compete. For my one hundred push-ups, there some guy who spends all day getting up to 1,200 before lights out. Getting built up is a matter of survival. The bigger you are, the more you increase the chances that it'll be someone else who gets harassed.

2:00, 2:30, 2:45 P.M.—At this time, the key has been turned almost forty times, automatic to the guards, automatic to the inmates. With the day being timed only by the activities and the turning of the keys, people have little more to do than to spread rumors. The guards about the inmates, the inmates about the guards, and every combination in between. Even I'm not immune to people's thoughts about who I am. Sometimes, a guy might check out my name and claim to have known my father. My father who has been gone longer than I've been an adult. They say they know him and some even say they know me—maybe even held me when I was a child. Even though they know things that fit, where my dad lived, what my childhood nickname was, I can't put much stock or energy into the idea of how much of what they are saying is true. Dayton's a small town, people know people, it stands to reason that even in here, there are inmates that would know me.

3:00 P.M.—I can start to feel myself getting antsy. I know that my time here is almost up. It's easier not to think about it, but somehow I can't help it. I think of my wife, who is going to school to create a better life for my family and me. She often says to me, "When I finish my degree, honey, I'm going to get you out of there." She worries, but we never discuss it, that I'm here, day after day. And each day, there's no promise that I'll make it home to her in the end. Being here makes me think of my family. I pray that they are safe; I don't want them walking in big crowds. I know what bad decisions good people can make, and then of course, I know that there are some people who are just bad. Like any father, I hope to protect my family and to provide for their future. Even if it means I have to mark my time in here.

4:00 P.M.—The gate swings open, I step out, and it slams shut behind me. I use the thirty-minute ride home to clear my mind and switch from guard to dad. I'll be seeing my family soon, and they are all that matters to me. They keep me grounded and let me know that there is a reality outside the cell. When I get home, I tell my wife, Shelly, that my day was fine. I never let her think otherwise, because I don't want her worry. My confine-ment is my own. The career that I chose to follow is part of the decisions, good and bad, that I have made. I do my job, and I do it well. I actually do care what happens to people and would love to see some of these brothers on the outside fully rehabbed. But the fact is that I have to do my job day after day. Eight straight hours of prison bound by the same routine. I have to fix my mind so that I can handle it in a way that doesn't make me crazy. While I'm in there, I think of my wife and my four children, and I think of possibilities in my future because I do have hope—it's wrapped up in them. So when I go in to work the next day, they'll be on my mind as I prepare to "do my eight so I can hit the gate."

Robert Gay *lives with his wife and four children in Dayton, Ohio. He looks for-ward to the opportunity of having an impact on people's lives before they are incar-cerated by pursuing a career in law enforcement.*

Bulletproof

Jimmy Henchmen a.k.a.
Jimmy Ace a.k.a James Rosemond

Everything happens for a reason, and my reason was I wanted to change my life. I wanted to get out of the streets, and music was my way out. I was blessed because I had people who showed me the way. In life, there are people who pass through it for certain reasons, and those of us who utilize those relationships to their maximum potential are those who benefit from them the most. My story is the same as that of many of the inner-city kids in this country who know they're doing wrong and want out; the difference is that I beat the odds by a long shot. I was introduced to the music business by two friends: David Hyatt and Peter Thomas. David had R. Kelly at the time and three other groups. I was still neck deep in the streets when David and Peter asked me if I wanted to join them in flying some industry people to Miami to throw a birthday bash for Fab Five Freddy. They knew I had thrown some successful concerts and parties in New Jersey with my brother Mario. Of course, I knew who Fab was; he was the host of *Yo MTV Raps!* so the party drew a lot of people. We flew in every publicist and editor from every rap magazine, everyone from Def Jam, and various artists from both coasts, all for free. We gave them three nights at an exclusive party Labor Day weekend. The next year they wanted to do it again and then we called it "How Can I Be Down." We still paid for it, but this time BET and MTV came to cover it. How Can I Be Down became an annual paid event that the consumer and the record industry looked forward to yearly thereafter; it was my instant ticket into the music game, a ticket out of the streets that I so longed to leave.

Once I was in, I knew I had to make good in my new life, and I met two producers who would put this whole game in perspective. Bryce Wilson, who was formerly in the Mantronics, and Mark Sparks, who had migrated from North Carolina. I started the company Henchmen and signed them on; I went on to putting the hit group Groove Theory together (Bryce & Amel) and doing my first signing with Sony/Epic Records. I put Mark with Salt 'N' Pepa, and we came up with their smash comeback hit "Shoop." I was on a roll, I had a top-ten single by my producer, and the Groove Theory single, "Tell Me" was climbing the chart rapidly—not to mention the yearly conference, How Can I Be Down. Every company wanted to do business with me so they could get leverage with both my producers and the conference. But there was something always lurking in the air about me because my friend David Hyatt from Miami had been arrested for money laundering, and so the speculations circulated. I didn't fit the rumors; however, when they looked at me, industry folks expected me to be louder than I spoke and be more flamboyant than I was. But what the industry didn't know was that I had a deep secret.

Then there was the name of my company, Henchmen. Its connotations to some people are dark because of the way it's used, but a henchman to me is a loyal companion, and that is what I am. If you look in a dictionary it may say something like "underboss," but to me, it means loyal companion. That is exactly what I am to Kedar, Barry Hankerson, Chris Lighty, Steve Rifkin, Shakim . . . I am their friend.

The industry was a good place for me, but my past in the streets of Brooklyn was catching up with me. Brooklyn was snitching on me, the streets had learned that I was a borough away, and the Feds were on my back. My whole circle had changed from the guys on the block to the guys in the industry; this was beautiful for me because I became whoever or whatever I wanted to be and I was just a borough away. The industry was a whole new world for me. I changed my name from my street name Jimmy Ace to Jimmy Henchmen because of the name of my company.

In January 1996, I flew to Los Angeles to meet with Tupac Shakur and Suge Knight regarding the so-called East Coast–West Coast war. The day before the meeting, my biggest fear for the last six years came true; while in my Beverly Hills Hotel, Federal agents along with local police surrounded the hotel and arrested me for multiple charges from gun possession and escape in New York to conspiracy to distribute and commit murder in North Carolina, and of course they found a firearm in my hotel room when they searched and arrested me along with eighteen thousand in cash. I knew whenever I was caught I would be in a lot of trouble, and I was.

I was immediately placed in solitary confinement because of the seriousness of my charges and subsequently sent to North Carolina to face the most serious charges. Because of the unfair crack laws and the United States government's reliability on informants, I was facing a life sentence with no possibility of parole. I hired Roy Black, one of the best attorneys on the East Coast, from Miami, with the help and advice of my friends in the music industry. Eighteen months later, I had beaten the case. New York immediately sent a summons for me because they exclaimed that they had a life sentence there for me also. I was a three-time loser and faced a mandatory life sentence according to their law. See, New York had it in for me because I al-legedly escaped from their notorious jail, Rikers Island, in 1993. I always thought to myself what would the odds be with the bookies that a Black man would get around two life sentences in one lifetime. I had run low on at-torney's fees, but my Henchmen office was still open, rendering its services to the music industry when it could. Many supported me because they couldn't understand why I was in so much trouble and why I was in jail for so long. I routinely called my office, and one day they told me Mike Tyson had called looking for me and left a number to call. Mike ended up hiring one of the best attorneys in New York for me, Jack Litman, and that was all I needed. I beat the case after being on Rikers Island for two long stressful years. I learned then that if most of the underprivileged youths in the inner cities had adequate representation, district attorneys would have a hard time placing felonies on young Black males. It seems as though cops arrest young Black males, at times, just so they can have a track on them through finger-printing. I thought my journey had ended with New York, but before I could walk out the door, they ushered me, handcuffed, onto a plane to face my final charges in Los Angeles for the firearm that was found in my hotel room. Of course, there was no mention of the eighteen thousand cash that was in my briefcase. By this time I befriended a manager by the name of Barry Hankerson and was burnt from the continuous battle with the courts, so I immediately took a plea. I needed to move on with my life. I understood the economics of it and the penalties. I knew it was time to let my past go, and this case was the only thing holding me up from moving forward with what I had built years before. And at sentencing in L.A., this is how it went; Barry, a mentor and a friend, had saved the day by eloquently explaining to the judge how I had changed my life around.

I come from the gutter. My music didn't pay off for the first four years, but I stuck with it, and it is finally starting to become lucrative. My past is my past, and I am really trying to let it go. I am not ashamed of it, but I am trying to move on from it. Jail helped me grow in all aspects: spiritually, emotionally, and mentally. Every wise man had some kind of solitude, some place of seclusion to get his head together. When you are in that cell and that door closes, a certain sense of reality hits a conscious person. There was just something that happened to me every time that officer came around and locked my cell and I turned around and looked at that bed and those four walls. I had a choice—I could sit on the toilet, sit on the bed, or lie on the bed. That was my reality. My journey was long, hard, and scary. I've met many good, Black, conscious brothers who will never have the opportunity that Allah has blessed me with—a lot of them because of their economic sit-uation and some because they have given up all hopes because we have turned our backs on them and forgotten them in the Black man's modern-day slavery. Wonder what would have happened to me if I didn't have a whole industry along with a Mike Tyson and a Barry Hankerson in my corner.

I have, since being out of prison, executive-produced two soundtracks (*Romeo Must Die* and *Exit Wounds*) and have helped artists of the likes of Aaliyah, Tank, Sharissa, and Wyclef, and consulted to the companies of Loud, Motown, and Blackground Records in their endeavors. Just recently I have ventured into the boxing circle and repaid Mike Tyson by putting together and negotiating the Tyson–Lewis fight in Memphis, Tennessee.

I want everyone to know that they can still follow dreams and be successful without trading in their integrity in any aspect. As long as you're alive, you can achieve anything your heart desires that is good and pure. I am thankful that the industry accepted me back—it is a blessing. Jail isn't the end—it can be a great beginning if you use the time wisely.

Jimmy Henchmen is a successful entrepreneur who continues to make his mark on the music industry.

Some Ole Nigga Shit

James Fletcher

Nigga Shit—definition: just some everyday old life, trying to make ends meet; trying to get by in society—but it's real.

A shout out to of all my old school friends reads like the *Dayton Daily News* obituary or the Lebanon pen roll call:

Gregory Grey—dead.

Lorenzo Woods—dead.

Mike Boykin—dead.

Eric Coats, Jeffrey Stokes—dead and dead.

Mike—locked up.

Chris—locked up.

Billy, DaRon, and Dusty—locked up, locked up, locked up.

A lot of the dudes I used to run with are dead, and the ones that are locked up—well, you can just go on ahead and call them gone, too. The odd thing is that after a while, after seeing so much loss, it just gets ordinary. And I'm not talking about some "bad-side-of-town Niggas ain't up to shit" kind of story. All those brothers grew up in what I called middle-class Dayton. We was right in between two projects and Dunbar High School—that's what made up the *middle* in our middle class. So, you know it coulda went either way, the whole scholastic and athletic tip or running with the Niggas that was trying to have themselves a wannabe gang. All my friends went to high school, and some of us eventually went to college, but not all of us left the streets.

There wasn't a whole lot of difference in the way we was raised. Hell, some of them Niggas was raised with me, and when I say "with me," I mean in my house. My mother took care of everybody. She was like a damn modern-day Sojourner Truth or something. She'd be the only person in the neighborhood who knew how to do taxes right or get somebody out of jail or complete a college application. If there was trouble and it required talking to some authority or some White person, my mom was called in, and she could either do "House Shoe" momma or "Ohio Belle" momma on you. Ohio Belle momma is that voice you want her to give your second-grade White teacher that's kind of cool. But House Shoe momma is what you want her to do when the assistant principal hate yo' ass and always trying to make an example out of you. Well my momma had to pull out all her moms when Billy came to live with us.

It all started with my sister's big mouth. . . .

She picked up the phone while I was talking to Ray-Ray about this dude that was locked up in the pen. The guy in jail was Billy's older brother, and I would make fun of him at school and Billy would run back and tell his brother. I guess my jokes was pretty funny because Billy's brother got pissed and was coming after me. I was in the seventh grade. My sister hollered upstairs, "Momma, Ray-Ray said that Jamie is going to get shot at school tomorrow." Her and her big-ass mouth! I was mad at my sister until the next day when my mom showed up at the school—and you know my nosy sister faked being sick so she could miss high school and come, too. Sure enough, Billy was there with his brother, who had just been released from the pen. And sure enough he had a gun and he had violated his parole and was arrested.

So this dude was really going to shoot me, a twelve-year-old kid, because of *some Ole Nigga Shit*. He was mad behind some words I said in the cafeteria, trying to be cute, some stuff that don't matter at all and certainly is not worth going back to jail for. But that's right where that dude was headed. The part that pissed my momma off was that this brother was supposedly the caretaker of Billy, so now he was left an orphan. Even though we didn't have nothing, we figured zero divided by zero still add up the same so we decided that Billy would live with us. My mom got him into Dunbar, and he became the star football player. She even helped him go to college. But then when Billy came home one summer, he got caught up and ended up doing some time for something. I'm not sure what he did time for because we lost track, but I'm betting it's probably *some Ole Nigga Shit*.

Our next houseguest was the only survivor in the Ardmore killings. DaRon came to live with us after his mom's boyfriend lost it and shot everybody in the house. He shot the mother, the grandmother, all the kids, even a baby in a crib. There is no reason to shoot a grandmamma and some kids. This guy had lost it—he probably was all mad about some bullshit. Maybe she said she didn't want to see him anymore; maybe they got in a fight over some Baby Mama Drama. Only *some Ole Nigga Shit* would cause a man to do something crazy as that—try to wipe out a whole family. He shot them all, but DaRon survived. I know that had to be some fucked-up stuff to think about, but when DaRon came to live with us (even though he was in the papers and all) didn't anybody ever mention it not once. So it was just like that: One minute you got all your people; the next minute they all gone. Here he was orphaned and really all he could do then was sit around and try to figure out what his hustle was going to be. And the reality is that it had to be a good hustle since he was only nine years old and had already been shot once behind *some Ole Nigga Shit*.

DaRon and I stayed close until I went off to college. I mean the hustle was set in him, and DaRon ended up in prison in the exact same place where the dude that wiped out his whole family is waiting to die. My mom was smart, she knew all of what was going on in Dayton, and she helped a lot of brothers come up. But she wasn't taking any chances with me. In order to make sure that I stayed away from *some Ole Nigga Shit* that might go down in Dayton, she sent me off to Alcorn State University. She flat-out vetoed any school in the state of Ohio; she recognized how easy it would be for me to shoot back to Dayton and hang with my old friends. So somehow my stuff got packed and somehow I ended up in the Deep South in late August. I got down there, and wasn't nothing in Mississippi but dirt and women. Since I don't do dirt, I did the women. But women can be trouble, too. One bayou girl put some voodoo on me and made me get scaly all over my body. But then she took back the curse when I apologized for whatever she thinks I had done. I just said sorry, but I don't know for what. Probably *some Ole Nigga Shit*.

On my summer breaks, I looked forward to coming home and running with my old friends. Except for my boy, Rabbit, who was in college like me, most of the other cats were running the same game that was being played before I left for school. But they were still my dogs, you know. I have never dropped any of my boys for stuff they do and don't do, but I had to start picking my times that I hung out with them. I mean everybody was going down for some crazy shit. This one guy, Mike, was the star basketball player, family was the pillar of society—he got locked up as a serial rapist. Another guy, Chris, was a track star went to Ohio State and I think the Olympics, too. Same thing—he got locked up on *some Ole Nigga Shit*. I'm still not sure if all of what they pinned on them is true. 'Cause I know some of these guys, and well I'm not going to say that they're all perfect, but some of the stuff they're trying to say they did don't fit with the guys that I used to know.

I think about my younger days where it was just hide and go get it. Where you had to be on your street by dark, at the light post when the light came on, and in your own front yard by eight. All the cats whose momma lived on the same street as me could have been headed for college just like me. I mean it wasn't any difference between us. Most of us had daddies at home and some of us had parents that didn't drink. I mean there was drama, but not all-the-time drama.

We were just kids playing. Some of our play was innocent and some-times not so innocent. Like the time I got bit by a Doberman pinscher and then when I got out of the ER I got a whipping because this girl said we was trying to force our way into her house which is why she sicked her dog on us. I think I was ten. Well that wasn't the only time I got bit by a Dober-man pinscher, and oddly enough, both times I was with Gregory, Glenny, and Gary. Those cats was real smooth. Their mother worked at General Motors, which was good money and she drove a Corvette, too. They had it all! My mom was cool with them, but made me watch the time I spent with them. It was right around then that my momma started in with her daily whippings for all the stuff she knew I did and all the stuff she knew I was going to do. One time, my so-called friends lured me into my own garage so that my mom could trap me and whoop me, and then she gave them each a dollar for it—the sell-outs.

Now that I think about it, maybe my momma knew something. Maybe the whippings were so that if I ever got caught up in *some Ole Nigga Shit* that I might make different decisions for my life. It's me, my wife and daughter, and the baby girl that's on the way. Now, I choose a life a lot more dull than some of my old school friends. One time I was watching the news and there was a shoot-out between the police and a local Dayton man. They made him sound like a crazy thug, but then when they said his name I was stunned—it was my old friend Gregory. He went down in a blaze of fire against the Dayton 5-0, just like a lot of my other boys. There's been too much bad stuff that now I don't even know how to feel. Don't take it wrong—Gregory was my boy, and I think of him sometimes, and it messes with my head that he died over *some Ole Nigga Shit.*

But that night, when I watched the news reporter say that he died trying to rob Shields Restaurant on Gettysburg, my real first thought was. "Shit, that *is* some good barbecue."

James Fletcher is a thirty-two-year-old commercial real estate investor. He lives in Dayton, Ohio, with his wife and their beautiful five-year-old daughter, Jasmine, and newborn daughter, Jaila.

Fighting for Our Children: A Father's Struggle

Reverend Conrad Benette Tillard
(formerly Minister Conrad Mohammed)

Many young Black men of my generation have declared that they would become better fathers, even more dedicated and ever more present than we have been in the past. What has happened is this commitment has coincided with the appearance of the first generation of exceptional professional African-American women that we see today. When I say *professional*, I mean the influx of Black women present in corporate America. There have always been Black schoolteachers, nurses, and secretaries, but unprecedented opportunities have opened up in the corporate sector for Black women. So, as the divorce rates escalate, you still have men who want to be fathers to their children. But the laws of the family court have not caught up nor have the opportunities for advancement in corporate America kept pace when it comes to Black men. Over the last thirty years, it has often been established in and out of the court system that after a breakup, the children automatically go with the mother.

Men are challenging that notion today because we understand the importance of a father in the children's life. We love our children, and we are willing to make sacrifices that our fathers couldn't make or weren't willing to make due to their circumstances. Most of our fathers did not grow up fatherless. It has not been that long since the father was not at the head of the African-American household. This phenomenon is a fairly new development and I would say that it took place largely in the 1960s and the 1970s. So, our fathers born in the forties had fathers in their lives, so they never knew the pain that it caused when they weren't there for their children.

In many instances we are trying to be there for *our* children, but our women are very knowledgeable of the laws and the courts. Unfortunately, all too many women can't resist the temptation to manipulate the courts system to there advantage. They help to play into the stereotypes that society holds on to of the Black man: crazy Black man, unconcerned Black man, and angry Black man. Often when we do wind up in court, we meet judges who are under the assumption that we are there not because we are interested in being fathers and fighting for our children, but rather we are in court fighting because either we are not over the breakup of the relationship or we are trying to do something to harm the mother. So a lot of men are suffering tremendous burdens to get their children or to have appropriate access to them.

I have friends who are doctors, attorneys, teachers, and hardworking men and who drive long distances—some even fly—every two weeks to see their children. I know one brother who flies between Chicago and Philadelphia every two weeks to see his son. These dedicated fathers are doing everything they can to be a part of their children's lives; however, the courts aren't meeting them halfway. They aren't helping to facilitate a sense of fair play, and so we are suffering because we are fighting to stay in our children's lives. Limitations are being placed on us, and I'm even experiencing this in my own life despite all that I have done as a father to my children and as a father figure to the young men in the community.

As an advocate for fatherhood, often I find myself in the presence of judges who don't know me or who have had an inaccurate picture of me drawn by an opposing counsel. Although I may be recognized and respected all over the country as a good man, I've suffered some very demeaning things from judges who have never brought my children a bowl of soup. I have stood in front of judges who have looked at me as though I were no better than a crackhead. Even though I have raised and loved my children from the time that they were born, the burden is always on me to prove that I'm concerned about them. I think that for us as Black fathers, were it not for the pain that we experienced as men knowing what it was like not to have a father, many of us would probably have walked away from the antagonisms, false charges, and manipulation of the system. Despite being degraded by the family court system, many of us are dedicated to really fight that fight and do whatever we have to do to stay in our children's lives.

You must know that we as fathers are paying a hefty price, because it takes away from our focus on our lives and our careers. It also takes away from our ability to establish new relationships. It takes an extraordinary woman to really understand the commitment of a father who is going to get his children every two weeks and every other holiday and the whole summer. In the cases of many men, I know it takes an extraordinary woman to respect their spending the kinds of resources necessary to be able to do whatever it takes to be in their children's lives. It definitely takes a special woman to understand the need to fly every week to see one's children, spending that kind of time away from one's new family.

It is often said that Black men walk away from their families, but today increasing numbers of women are making the decision that they want divorces. The judicial system is not considering that factor when censoring men in the process of child custody and divorce. The other issue is that of child support. If you are independently wealthy, child support is not a problem. But for the average father who makes an average salary, the way the child support guidelines are currently constructed can be oppressive. For example, if 33 percent of a man's income comes off the top to pay child support, he's only able to live off 70 percent of his income. Let's say you have three children and you are paying 11 percent of your salary per child. That's 33 percent. Now if you have joint visitation or frequent visitation, nothing that you spend—the thousands of dollars that you spend on the visitation (gas, tolls, clothing, airline tickets)—counts in the child support and if you buy your children necessities like school clothes, boots, or a coat, it doesn't count either. So a man can pay the 33 percent in a case where he has three children or 44 percent for four children, and yet if he buys winter boots, coats, or school clothes, none of that is calculated in terms of child support. Nor is the money spent for travel, hotels, entertainment, education, or other miscellaneous expenses that occur while you are with your children. Now if the mother is on welfare, then that makes sense, but what happens when the mother is a professional, vice president of a corporation, a doctor, or a lawyer, and the man is a laborer? Is it fair that the man is paying child support which really may be going toward paying someone's Range Rover note?

Most men find these things frustrating because we know that when it comes to the African-American community, women do just as well economically—and in the professional realm that's even more true. It places a tremendous burden on men, and in many respects—and this is not to say in all respects—we are now talking about hardworking fathers who are not independently wealthy. My ex-wife is a doctor; I'm a community-based minister and activist. In terms of earning power and salary, we knew when we got married that she would probably make more money than I would. I have friends who are lawyers and teachers, and they have married professional women, and you hear very similar horror stories. Think of the financial strain that is placed on these men. They are forced to pay their own personal monthly bills on a depleted salary all the while having to entertain their children when they do have them. Consider this; if you have your children for the whole summer, you are still paying child support that whole summer while the children are with you. To me, this is an oppressive burden.

I have decided that a large part of my ministry will address this issue. It's devastating to our communities when a father is put in a position where he has to pay eight hundred or nine hundred dollars a month in child support and he has to decide what kind of father he is going to be based on the pressure and obstacles placed on him. Ask yourself, Do I want to pay nine hundred dollars a month and never see the children because I cannot afford to do so after I pay the nine hundred dollars? Or, would I rather take the nine hundred dollars over the course of four weekends and get my kids and take them to the movies, the barbershop, a restaurant, to a play or museum to cultivate a relationship with them? But remember if you do the latter and fall behind in child support payments, they will call you a deadbeat dad and take action against you.

It's a tremendous dilemma for fathers. As I said, if you are independently wealthy, it's probably not that much of an issue, but if a man is making fifty, sixty, or even eighty thousand dollars, it can be a tremendous burden. The way the laws are structured, some states are progressive, but many of them are not. What I've constantly said to brothers is, "Don't allow those burdens to run you away from your children." Some men will say, "You know what, I can't deal with the financial burden. I'll pay my child support, but I don't have the extra money to get my kids, travel to see them, or to spend extra money on them." Some men are resentful about having to pay women money and would like to use that money to buy the children the things they need. It's a dilemma.

God has always provided for me. When my marriage broke up, my wife was a practicing physician and I was a full-time graduate student at Harvard Divinity School and at John F. Kennedy School of Government. She sued me for child support, so I had to drop out of graduate school to go back to New York to get a job. At the time we were living in Cambridge, and I had to leave because all my contacts were in New York. When I was notified that I was being sued for child support, I tried to appeal to her to allow me to finish my degrees before she did that because ultimately that was in the best interest of the children. But she would not relent. So—thank God—Percy Sutton, the great businessman and a supporter of mine, made it possible for me to get a job in a radio station in New York, which allowed me to continue to commute back and forth to graduate school, but ultimately that became too much of a burden.

I've always paid my child support. After September 11, advertising revenue was down, and my radio show was canceled. For a while, I could not pay child support. I try to book a lot of speaking engagements so I can keep up with my child support payments. I get a lot of speeches, and whenever I've fallen behind in child support, I'll book as many as possible, and my checks from the universities go directly to my ex-wife. That's fine—I never mind doing that—but one of the things I've learned in going through divorce and transition and coming out of school and trying to complete my graduate education and having child support payments is that many times fathers certainly aren't deadbeats; they are simply dead broke. And if you don't have money, you can't give it, so even when I can't meet all the child support obligations—and there are times that I have been in that dilemma—I have to ask myself, Do I take this four hundredd dollars and send it to her, or do I use it to pick up the children? Any parent knows that between the gas and tolls, the meals and movies, hair cuts, toys, books, sweaters, and jackets, you can easily spend between four hundred to five hundred dollars in a weekend.

There are times that I've paid all my child support and not paid my own rent. There are times when I've had to pay my rent and not my child support. Despite all of this, my strategy has always been to see my children and spend time with them. God has really shown me what these men are going through. I can go and do a speech and make three thousand dollars in one clip and send that to her, and that gets me out of hot water for a minute. But what about the laborer? What about the man who's on a hourly wage and is really in a very precarious financial position and cannot make an extra couple of dollars when he needs it? There is a solution, but it requires putting the children first, because when I lived with my children I didn't spend nine hundred dollars a month on them. The point is that we have to put the children first. That means that a father should never duck his financial responsibilities but sometimes the custodial parent has to understand that it is better for children to see the noncustodial parent than see his or her money if both are not available. It's better for my children to be able to spend time with me than them not seeing me at all because I can't afford to get to them. Both parents have to support each other and recognize that people are not cash machines. They are human beings.

There are times that the mother may have difficulty and the father should do more, and there are times when he can't do what he's obligated to, but in any case, you can always show support and give love. Even when the fathers can't give money, mothers shouldn't discourage them from giving love. When fathers pick their children up for the weekend, the mother may be angry because she hasn't received the money that she wants from Dad, but it's better that they see him than he be discouraged. If you can't give money at the time, you can always give love and support. And love is more valuable than money. In fact in the words of Jennifer Lopez Love don't cost a thing.

Reverend Conrad Benette Tillard (formerly Minister Conrad Mohammed), a former radio host, has dedicated his ministry to dealing with the issues of fatherhood and empowering men.

Working on My Ph.D. in Life
Michael Stoney

I felt my arm go completely numb, as if it had been separated from my body. Less than seconds later, I remember hearing *Pow! Pow!* like two firecrackers being set off as I stood on a drug-infested street in Brooklyn. I turned toward the sounds of the shots and was blinded by a muzzle flash as more shots whizzed by my head. Feeling completely defenseless, I pulled my .38-caliber handgun from my waistband, with no time to aim, and fired back at a man running and firing at me. He stopped firing and took off in another direction. My team moved in almost immediately, and I was soon in the back of a car being raced to the hospital. I remember my partner yelling and crying for me to stay awake and hang in there as sirens rang from every direction. You see, I was an undercover narcotics cop working a high-priority drug case, I was shot in my left arm and left side of my chest. The attending trauma doctor told me I was lucky to be alive, for the bullet had just missed my heart. My injuries forced my early retirement from the New York Police Department with a moderate disability pension and benefits.

I spent the next two years recovering from my physical and emotional injuries resulting from the shooting as well as contemplating my next move. Where do I go from here? Who have I become? What was my purpose in life? Why was there divine intervention? I joined the police department to fulfill a deep-rooted passion to help others and for financial stability, which I desperately needed. Now I was confused, almost like a child, and I looked to God for answers to my troubling questions. While praying and experiencing uncontrollable flashbacks of pivotal events in my life, it became overwhelmingly clear that I needed to look within myself, something I had never done before—or really wanted to do, for that matter.

It all started when my biological mother became pregnant with me at the tender age of sixteen and was placed in a convent for the duration of her pregnancy. Due to her inability to care for me, she was forced by her mother to surrender me to foster care at birth. For five years, I was cared for and loved by the only mother I had ever known, my foster mother, only to be ripped out of her arms by the court system and placed in the custody of my biological mother, who was now a drug addicted twenty-one-year-old with two more children: a complete stranger to me. I went from a stable environment to one filled with serious drug abuse, poverty, child neglect, and domestic violence. As a result of her severe drug habit, my mother became alienated from her family. She also had numerous encounters with police officers and psychiatrists. Imagine if you will, a five-year-old impressionable boy witnessing his mother going through such terrible ordeals. As I got older I wondered how my little sisters had survived those few years under such sour circumstances and what long-term effects they would have. It wasn't long before our family intervened along with the court system. After numerous unsuccessful foster home placements, my sisters, whom I had become quite fond of, and I were about to be placed in separate foster homes. Fortunately, our maternal aunt and her husband, who had seven children of their own and lived in a three-bedroom home, petitioned the court and were granted full custodial rights of my siblings and me. Although I had a roof over my head and was with my family, I still felt cheated. I missed my foster mother, who I wasn't allowed to see or talk to, and I felt sympathy for my real mother and often wondered who my father was. I also felt I was a burden to just about everyone in my life except my sisters.

After a few running away episodes, I decided to venture out on my own at the age of sixteen and in the eleventh grade, never to return. Sounds young, but I wasn't your typical sixteen-year-old and I was ready to take on mature responsibilities, or so I thought. Although the education curriculum came easy to me, juggling school, rent, and a means to eat almost caused me not to graduate on time. I survived by legal and illegal hustles, witnessing and experimenting in drugs, sex, and violence. By the age of twenty-one, I'd held twenty-one jobs and had accumulated sixteen suspensions on my license prior to ever taking a road test. Hustling and jumping from job to job, I was unable to keep an apartment for any extended period of time. At one point, I lived in my car for almost three months. My friends, after their parents' departure to work, would sneak me into their homes for a much-needed shower and a decent meal. It was obvious to me that my total lack of self-value and -worth were leading me down the road of self-destruction. My maternal aunt instantly introduced me to God upon my arrival to her home, but it wasn't until this unforgettable point in my life that I truly developed an everlasting relationship with my maker. He became my best friend, my confidant, and my salvation. I became enlightened.

God helped me in many ways, but what most stands out in my mind is that at a young age I understood that one's position could always be worse. Being exposed to the streets all my life and growing up in a society that glamorized tragedy, it wasn't hard to find others less fortunate than myself, and I became thankful for the few things that I did have. Although I had been dealt a bad hand, I realized that the best players win with the hand they've been dealt. Equally important was how to use one's winnings to help improve the lives of the meek. My constant desire to seek out the less fortunate exposed me to the people with the most character and strength. I was unable to assist them monetarily, but I listened to their struggles and their shortcomings with compassion and understanding. Like a dry sponge thirsting for water, I soaked up as much knowledge and advice from these wonderful people as they did from me. Our positive interactions validated my desire to help them, and that desire quickly turned into a passion. I used my own personal struggles as a forum to coach, mentor, and give sound advice to the troubled youth in my community. This was my passion! This made me happy and kept the focus off my own problems. But I was broke! I grew tired of not knowing where my next meal or rent payment was coming from. I wanted some sort of stability in my life. Unable to afford college tuition, I had only one legal option: to take city exams in the police, corrections, and transit department.

The valuable "Ph.D." in life and in people, which I'd acquired on the streets, propelled me in becoming a sensitive and caring police officer. Over the next few years, I would be exposed to people of all genres. I studied them as much as I possibly could. I wanted to know, good or bad, what made them who they were? What made them happy or sad? How were they motivated to do the things they did? What drove different people? The answers to these puzzling questions became some of my most valuable possessions, which saved me from many life-threatening situations I faced as a police officer and later as an undercover narcotics officer. My fearless attitude, willingness to get involved, and eagerness to help others allowed me to have a positive affect on the lives of many people. No matter how bad their situations were, I was almost always able to put a smile on their faces and to help them see the light at the end of their darkened tunnels. Ironically, this happened with even some of the criminals I locked up.

In the midst of all my glory, fate would have it that a single bullet to my arm and chest would force me to take on one of the most important studies of my life. The subject was now me: a twenty-eight-year-old retired police detective, husband, and father of two boys. Composed of all my life's experiences (good and bad, fair or unfair), knowledge, wisdom, and lessons learned, my visible instructor was me. I learned that the fabric of my character remained unchanged. I still possessed a passion for helping others in need. The difference now was that I wanted to secure financial freedom for my family. The same freedom would allow me the opportunity to help others on a larger scale, through developing and funding programs that would give those in need a new lease on life. God spared my life so that I can help spare the lives of others. The only question remaining was how to obtain financial freedom.

For the next two years, I held a couple of jobs, not necessarily for money, but for knowledge of the corporate world. I managed residential and commercial properties for a millionaire, was part owner and manager of a nightclub, and sold real estate. I learned a lot from my employers. I also utilized the Internet and the public libraries to research any unanswered questions I had about starting my own business. I would apply my street and corporate knowledge into developing a product or service that would be well received in the financial market. I teamed with an equally passionate childhood friend. This decision proved to be an instrumental part in our success. We complemented one another quite nicely. His weakness was my strength and vice versa. Building and running a successful company that would, for the first time in our lives, have our money working for us became our central focus. But what would be our company's specialty? What would make it stand out from all the other companies already in existence?

Those questions were answered late one night, during a brainstorm meeting my partner and I held in his small kitchen. Realizing the lack of variety in the men's underwear and loungewear department, we decided to fill that void by introducing a "male Victoria's Secret" emphasizing style, comfort, colors, and the fusion of different material to create a brand that the male public in large would gravitate toward. The name for this brand simply became dug (Downundergear). We created a unique logo cohesive with our brand. My partner and I sold some of our possessions, borrowed from friends and families who believed in our mission, and used whatever meager savings we had in order to come up with the capital necessary to make samples of our products. I used my connections in the music, television, and sports industries to place our samples on movie and television stars, athletes, singers, and models. Not yet in stores, our product found its way into the pages of fashion and entertainment magazines, album covers, television interviews, music videos, and celebrity events. The responses we received were overwhelming. Everyone loved our brand.

Armed with an acquired knowledge of the fashion industry, confidence, a few product samples, and an impressive press kit, my partner and I met with a potential investor whose office space was at least ten times bigger than my two-bedroom apartment. He was so taken by our presentation and our ability to successfully ease any of his concerns that he decided to invest $3 million into our company. Prior to leaving his office that fateful day, our new business investor informed us that in all his twenty-five years in the business industry, he had never seen more dedication, passion, confidence, and resourcefulness exude from two "businessmen" as he'd seen in us.

Not a day went by that I didn't work diligently to make my company a success. We spoke passionately to everyone in the fashion business that would listen and soon impressed editors from the hottest and most popular trade and consumer magazines into getting us editorials that assisted us in growing more awareness for our brand. I knew what we wanted to create, but more important, I knew what role I played. We filled positions to compliment our company and to help it grow. We were fortunate enough to be able to employ some of the kids from the neighborhood. We wanted to give back to our community.

dug is still growing, and I'm still learning. I'm confident that someday soon I will be in the financial position to do more for my people. My intentions are good. My passion to help others and to secure financial freedom for my family are still my driving force.

I speak and write about my negative childhood experiences not for sympathy but to inspire and motivate those in similar circumstances. I continue to teach what I've learned to others who come to me for advice. I make it a priority to seize every opportunity to go to schools and talk to our young, impressionable youth. My message to them is that no matter where they come from or what obstacles stand in their way, with faith, hard work, dedication, and the willingness to survive, anything is possible. I'm a testimony to that. My bad experiences in life have molded me into the individual that I am today. Those same bad experiences turned out to be blessings from above. Thank you, God!

Michael Stoney is the founder of Downundergear, commonly know as dug, a successful line of men's lingerie. dug allows men to finally have the ability to wear their favorite downtime clothing around the house, as well as venture outside in the same outfit. dug is a men's lifestyle brand of loungewear, where men can live a comfortable, stylish, and relaxing life at any time of the day. Artists such as Usher, Gwen Stefani of No Doubt, Backstreet Boys, N'Sync, Toni Braxton, 112, Q-Tip, Donell Jones, and Ja Rule are just a few of the many trendsetters found wearing dug. In addition, movie stars and athletes have sported the comfortable look of dug. For example, Leonardo DiCaprio, Tyrese, Michael Grant, Chris Webber, Steve Francis, and John Sally dig this new style. For more information, visit www.duglife.com.

The Gentleman from New York

Congressman Gregory W. Meeks

I grew up in Spanish Harlem in public housing, the oldest of four children. My dad, James Weldon Meeks, was a hardworking man and a former boxer who loved sports. He drove a cab and was a porter at the Schubert Theater. My mother, Mary McNeal, was an at-home mom who was very active in the community, including the PTA, various associations, and civic groups. I have fond memories of occasionally going with Dad to work. I would accompany him in the cab or join him at the theater. There were days that I would sit through the rehearsals. On many occasions, the actors would request that I come on opening night and sit in the front row. I was a good luck charm, and if I liked the show, it thrived. I enjoyed those days, I saw Barbra Streisand in *Funny Girl* and so many other plays.

Our kitchen table was the center of where hotbed issues were discussed and politics debated. We never ran short of topics, because the newspaper would be our source. It was at those times my parents challenged us to make a difference and encouraged us to be part of the solution. Every child is asked the inevitable questions a child would be asked, What do you want to be when you grow up? I decided that I would be a lawyer, because in order to make a difference, I would have to change the laws.

Every summer the Meekses would climb into my daddy's car and take the long road trip to the South to visit relatives in the Carolinas. We would stop at various rest areas, and the signs FOR BLACKS ONLY and FOR WHITES ONLY alarmed me. Why should we have to be a certain color to use the bathroom? On one occasion, a Southern man called my daddy a boy. He was a grown man with children, a fighter in his day. My dad retreated to avoid a confrontation, and that confirmed my resolve to be a part of the solution.

When it was time for me to attend college, my mother decided to go back to school to further her education. I went on to Adelphi University, and there I began to work alongside the Black Student Union. We protested what we thought was unfair treatment at the time. We did everything from picket lines to letters. We changed the policies that the administration may have not known affected African-American students.

I wanted to be amongst some of the best African-American minds, so I went to Howard Law School after graduating from college. While at law school, I took photos to make additional money—I didn't want to ask my parents for very much. My father came to visit me and saw that I was sleeping on a lawn chair in my friend's apartment and said simply, "This will not do." He took what money he had saved and found me a wonderful apartment under one condition, "You can't let your mother know how much this costs." The fact that my mother and father believed in me and what I wanted to accomplish made me work harder. When I became ill and my mother surprised me in Washington, D.C., she was shocked by the great digs, but happy and immediately went home and said, "We are moving. We are buying a house."

She was a woman who was determined, and the entire family moved to Far Rockaway, New York. After graduating from law school, I became an Assistant District Attorney, Compensation Judge, and after a failed campaign for City Council, I ran and won the New York Assembly race. My mother and longtime friend Josephine Johnson along with Bob Simmons helped—these were good times. I set forth and worked hard in Albany to make sure that Far Rockaway received all its just dues.

While I was enjoying a thriving career, my mother, who had excelled in her own right, died. It was one of the most tragic things that ever happened to me. Mom was our right and left hands. She was the steam that always kept the engine running. Our home would be the organization point, the hub of activity or just a place for people to come and relax. I promised her that I would be my very best, and that still holds true.

When I ran for Congress and won, it was bittersweet. My mom was not there to see how far her oldest son came to be the ninety-eighth African-American man to be a member of Congress. I saw this as an opportunity on a national level to effect change, not only for African Americans, but also for people of every race, creed, class, or color who were not empowered.

I have always trusted my instinct; with my mother's spirit as a guide, I immediately stood up as I did all my life for issues that were important to me. I cosponsored numerous laws. I was arrested on the steps of the Supreme Court along with Kweisi Mfume because we were protesting the fact that Supreme Court Clerks were not represented racially. When Amadou Diallo was shot, I was arrested two times because of protesting the treatment of a prisoner by the police. I went against then Mayor Rudolph Giuliani, especially when during his entire administration he met with Black leaders only a handful of times. I was racially profiled several times while growing up and understood how young Black men felt when they were targeted based on their race alone.

When the World Trade Center towers fell, I was overcome with grief as I found out several of my friends had perished. Still, I had to be strong for my family and the community. I traveled the world as a member of the International Relations committee and saw firsthand the situations we would have to vote for from Africa to Cuba, China to Indonesia. The world is a big place, and the scales of justice will always be unbalanced if people don't get up and say this is not what we want.

I have been blessed with so many wonderful things that I choose to pass on to young people, but the most valuable lesson I have found in my journey is that family is the center. As my own parents were the center of my strength, today my wife, children, siblings, and extended family have given me the strength to fuel the debates I have on the House floor, to create new laws and to be the best person that I can be as I make a difference in America. Things come full circle. My eldest daughter, Ebony, a freshman at Howard University, called me and asked, "Daddy, should I go to this protest?"

Congressman Gregory W. Meeks has served in the House of Representatives since 1998 for the Sixth Congressional District. The Congressman is a member of the committee on financial services, and its subcommittee on Capital Markets, Insurance, and Government Sponsored Enterprises (GSEs), as well as the subcommittee on Financial Institutions and Consumer Credit, and the subcommittee on Domestic Monetary Policy and Technology. Additionally, Meeks serves on the International Relations Committee and its subcommittee on Africa, and the subcommittee on East Asia and the Pacific. He successfully authored legislation that increased air service from New York City airports to communities in upstate New York—Albany, Buffalo, Syracuse, and Rochester. Further illustrating his leadership ability, Meeks led the largest congressional delegations ever to visit the New York Stock Exchange and the United Nations. Also believing that effectiveness in legislative bodies requires consensus as well as steady prodding, Meeks is an active member of the Congressional Black Caucus (CBC), and in 2001 became CBC Whip.

Congressman Meeks resides in Far Rockaway, Queens, with his wife Simone-Marie and his three daughters, Ebony, Aja, and Nia-Aiyana.

Your Soul's Journey

My conscience is clear, but that does not make me innocent. It is the
Lord who judges me.   —I Corinthians 4:4

Racial profiling, driving while Black, and racial discrimination in sentencing continue to evoke controversy and spark debate. Research has found that crimes by racial minorities are punished more harshly than similar crimes committed by Whites. In one of our roundtables, the group consensus was that quite often it is the Black officers who are giving Black men a hard time.

A brother's journey to justice is about not being afraid to stand up for his beliefs. As Dr. King marched for justice, we need to know that collectively we can change the course of social justice as it stands today—in countless ways, big and small. Social indicators, including employment, education, and personal circumstances, are often directives on why people choose a life of crime. There have been too many cases of Black men being profiled just because of the color of their skin. How many men have been stopped because they were driving while Black? The justice system is far from perfect, but we must learn the laws and become a part of the solution process to protect ourselves and our children,

The media is controlling us with negative stereotypes, which perpetuate the image of Black men as victims and aggressors. What is sad is that we are falling for it. We thank God for the men and women who put their lives on the line each and every day. But, just as in any other industry, there are racist officials in law enforcement who will impart their bias in a stop-and-search situation, criminal case, or lawsuit and not lose sleep when infringing on your human and civil rights.

Black men know that society is against them. You know it is wrong, but how much of your time is spent changing the situation? You cannot let your frustration take away your hope. That is why several years ago a group that included Congressman Gregory W. Meeks; Kweisi Mfume, the head of the NAACP; and several aides was arrested on the steps of the Supreme Court. They were protesting that the Supreme Court Clerks, a highly coveted position for any law student, did not represent the ethnic fabric of America. The riots in Los Angeles after the Rodney King trial acquitted the police officers of the brutal beating all of America witnessed. The rallies and outcry in New York with the Amadou Diallo shooting and the demands for racial profiling findings in New Jersey all sent a message. Yes, the solution begins with you. Being active with civic responsibilities and giving a voice by voting, writing letters, and standing up peacefully when you know of an injustice occurring. We have spoken to scores of parents who were hardworking, law-abiding citizens who just kept to themselves, and found that they had no clue about who they should call when or if their sons were arrested. Often leaving the fate of their child to the court-appointed lawyer.

We have been personal witnesses to the absolute necessity of having a plan and being prepared so you or a loved one would not be thrown in jail. That is very clear when a front-page article in one of New York's daily papers depicted more than ten men who served over ten years or more for crimes they never committed. Yes, they did sue and will be compensated, but what amount of money could pay for the loss of freedom, and the pain and suffering these men and their families have endured?

Soul Source

Control what you can, and not for one minute should you think of participating in any illegal activity, utilizing drugs, or keeping bad company. As the laws change, even knowing someone who is actively involved in a crime can land you in jail on an accessory charge. The journey to a life of balance begins when you create a life that allows you to close your eyes at night and not fear bodily harm from anyone, especially someone you know.

It doesn't matter if you have made mistakes in the past. The point is what you will do in the future. You can always turn a negative situation into a positive one if you can change your perception of the situation in your mind first. Going to jail is never a good experience, but many men say if they didn't go to jail, they probably would be dead. It's not the place your physical body is in; it is the place your spirit and mental self are in that keeps you locked up. Reuben "Hurricane" Carter was a good example of not letting a system imprison his mind although his physical body was incarcerated.

That also goes for the men in corporate America—if it is fishy, don't cosign to it, because you could be the next scapegoat. Don't be a participant in the blame game. Just take a look at the MCIs, Enrons, Tycos, and Arthur Andersens. It's not worth the pain and suffering your family will endure. Be an active participant in your life the way God intended it.

- What has been your experience with the justice system?
- What do you believe needs to be changed in regards to the justice system?
- Do you know or have a lawyer?

- Have you ever been arrested?
- Have you been targeted in a driving-while-Black incident? How did it make you feel?
- Do you know your legal rights?
- If you were accused and arrested on assault charges today, what would you do?

CHAPTER 5

A FAMILY AFFAIR

The real source of Black strength has been Black love. The sense of Blackness or Black love has, in turn, been the impetus for Black families to ensure our survival.
—Dr. Wade Nobles

The Black family is a complex one. Not necessarily built on the nuclear family model, the Black family has many different facets and faces. It's the universal family, the extended family, and then some. It's how we've survived from slavery until today. During the depression and at the countless times when things have been rough, we've survived because we were and are a universal family. That's why we call each other *brother* and *sister*. Black men and women brought strangers' children into their homes and raised them as their own. Time and time again, in times of crisis, we pull together no matter our differences and make a way. It's sad when you hear Black people say the only time they see family is at holidays or funerals. It's now more than ever that we as a people need to draw on that Black universal family to pull together.

But how do Black men view the Black family? We've all heard the lyrics "Papa was a rolling stone, everywhere he laid his hat was his home." All too often we hear the stories of the father who left or who was barely there. What about the man who stayed and why he stayed? In turn, what made the absentee father leave?

When we spoke with Black men about the Black family, many of them were terribly disturbed about the state the Black family is in today. Many men were talking about starting families and building with Black women. We heard them loud and clear. Many of them wanted the same things that many of the women we met wanted, so why do we see so many Black families separated? We had to think about this and dig deeper.

If we look back at the original structure of the American Black family, its origins began in slavery. As slaves, Black people weren't allowed the legal, emotional, and physical bond of marriage. The union of one slave to another was in secret and done by jumping the broom while their White counterparts were legally bound to each other in the eyes of God and in the eyes of the law. It didn't matter if one jumped the broom, your husband or wife could be sold to another plantation, and there was nothing that could be done about it. It created an atmosphere that required no social, emotional, or physical responsibility to one's mate. It robbed the Black man of being able to take responsibility for his family because technically they weren't *his* in the first place.

It's time we let men be men in the family structure. We've seen too many times the emasculation of the Black man in the family. Whether it be because a woman has more job opportunities and makes more money, or because she's asking herself, "What's a man going to do for me that I can't do for myself?"

We're not going to be able to get around the fact that the family is like an incubator in which the Black man grows up. It's where he learns his values, his strength, his manhood, and his power. Many questions arose about all the young men who are being raised by single mothers. Can they teach boys how to be men? The Black family isn't just the family you see when you go home and close the doors. As Tupac said, we all "got our name from a woman and our game from a woman."

The Black man's journey to family is a journey to harmony—working in tandem with your family to move forward in creating and fostering a family legacy. Here you will find all types of stories on how we cherish the very foundation that has allowed us to tell our stories today: our families.

Quite Simply—The Man

Anthony G. Boone

"**B**oy, I can hear grass grow," He said to me. The strongest Black man I ever met was also the most arrogant man I've ever met—and I loved Him for it. It rubbed off just enough to instill in me a confidence that I can do anything. Thanks to Him, I think I am invincible. "You were born to be leaders, not followers," He also said. I had no idea then what that meant. But He made me a leader without ever telling me how to lead.

There was always a signal that He was coming in our building. The front of 40-09 Tenth Street, Queensbridge Houses, Long Island City, New York, where people hung out on benches and were either smoking or drinking (and were so loud, you could hear them on the sixth floor), got quiet when He walked past them. They had a certain reverence for Him that to this day cannot be explained.

The familiar sound of the key in the lock sent my siblings and me into motion. It was my duty to get His slippers ready before He walked in the door of the housing project apartment. The house wasn't big—just three bedrooms for eight of us—but it was cozy, and it was home. The living room was the first room entered, and it was just a square. Two old couches squared off across the room from one another. The black rotary telephone sat on the stand next to the couch closest to the front door. That section of the couch was His section of the couch. As soon as He got home, that section of the couch was vacated, faster than schoolkids being let out at three o'clock. The television was on top of an old stereo in the far corner of the living room. The entertainment center, which He built, was to the left, just past the entrance into the kitchen. If He wasn't on the couch, He was in the kitchen. His chair in the kitchen was the first one at the table. No one sat in that chair. His chair was directly across from the stove. The refrigerator was to His back as He sat sideways—always sideways—in the chair.

He walked upright, with military precision, never a motion wasted, like He was still in Patton's Third Army in 1942. He served, with dignity, courage, and honor. He never talked about the war, but its impact showed on his face. When He came back and they called Him names and thought He was less than a man, He was proud to have served anyway. I think about that all the time. Men like Him helped save the free world, and they couldn't ride in the front of a bus in some states in their own country. He once told me He wouldn't give me a nickel for the experience but He wouldn't trade it for a million dollars. If He could serve, I *had* to serve. So I did.

His head was always straight ahead, but His dark, round, serious eyes, hidden behind square, black-framed glasses were always moving, observing the world around Him. He would always say, "Keep your eyes and your ears open and your mouth shut. You might learn something." I listened, and I observed. I said nothing. As directed by Him.

His scent was extremely comforting, the kind you never forget. Gillette Menthol shaving cream, Aqua Velva Ice Blue after shave, and Kool King cigarettes. He smelled like a man was supposed to smell. I wear Aqua Velva today like a warm blanket. His hands were rugged, with steel rods for fingers, from years of working in tobacco and cotton fields under a searing North Carolina sun, and from making cabinets from wood. The right pinkie was bent at a ninety-degree angle, the result of a table-saw accident. When He spoke it was direct, in your face, but not threatening. He was clear about His directions. He commanded, not asked.

His aura spoke of strength, and of courage that bordered on arrogance, yet there was a quiet, subtle humility about Him. He never let any of his children see His pain. It wasn't until He was starting to lose the fight with His own body, the cancer that overtook Him, that He let his children into his inner sanctum. He called on us like He had never had to before. Even as He faced the cancer, he remained arrogant, believing He was going to beat cancer by His sheer will. I saw Him so strong for so long, I believed Him again. And He actually did for a little while. The doctors took a look at a brain scan and told Him he should have been dead six months ago. "Well I'm still here, aren't I?" He said.

Eventually it became my turn to be strong for Him. I welcomed—no, relished—the opportunity. I stepped into the forefront again like He said, not even realizing it. That confidence, arrogance, and strength is part of me and the man I have become. As a pop song said, "His blood runs through me and He is in my soul." He remains to me, the greatest Black Man who ever lived. "*He*" is Robert Colin Boone, "*He*" is my Dad, and He was and forever will be, quite simply—the Man.

Anthony G. Boone is an occupational health and safety instructor living in San Francisco. He is a part-time freelance writer currently working on a short-story collection.

Who's the Bastard?

Jason Orr

I was a love child. My parents met while my father was stationed on a military base in Savannah, Georgia. My dad was a pilot. He runs an airline in the Caribbean now, where he's from originally.

I've been in the Caribbean alone on vacation, and something divine would always happen—like I'll be driving, and he'll just happen to be in front of me at a traffic light. I ran into him like that twice. But it happens to be two of less than six or seven encounters that I have had with my father in thirty-two years.

On one trip, I was driving behind him, and he saw me in the rearview mirror. When I realized it was him, I stuck my hand out the window. Homeboy looked back at me and took off at top speed up the hillside! I was going up the hillside, too, but I said to myself, "I'm not going to give him the pleasure of thinking I'm chasing him." Although I don't really know him innately, I know how he thinks. I told him that at one of our brief, face-to-face encounters on the island. I said to him, "Dude, intuitively, *I know you better than you think! . . . There's something about me that you fear, and aren't ready to confront!*"

Once I ran into him at a small yet popular, island beer-and-patty hangout and saw him at this little bar, where he was drinking. He looked at me, appearing to be surprised on the outside, but by looking in his eyes, I saw a coward. He looked me up and down and then looked at my dreadlocks and said, "What are ya, a Rasta?"

I said, "You got something against Rastas?"

The islanders are heavy into church, and they look down on Rastafarian culture, considering them outcasts or delinquents. I was, like, hey, don't get too occupied with how I look. Does that prevent you from having a conversation with me? Is it too much for you to have a conversation with me because I have locks? I could clearly see that that wasn't it at all; he was simply caught off guard and not ready to face one of the skeletons out of his closet, especially one that's walking around talking, spreading the *truth*. Maybe this is what he fears. To this day, he's spent half his life running from and denying the truth about having other children in the world. Is it really that bad? "Hey man, you're running from your own children." Why? They're adults now with their own lives.

On another spontaneous trip to the Caribbean, I called him. He was like, "Call me tomorrow."

When I called him again, he said, "Where are you?"

"I'm at a pay phone," I responded.

He replied, "Call me back," in a rude and uninterested, quick island dialect, but I knew what he was doing because it's a habit that, at that moment, I realized that I do myself when I'm preoccupied and mentally engaged in a project. Knowing it would be hard for me to call him back because of not having a phone, he says, "Call me back." I saw myself at that moment, and I decided I was going to be more aware of how I communicate with others. This has been a great lesson for me and one of the few things that I've learned from my father, along with forgiveness, that has helped me mature into manhood without him really knowing. Who said you can't turn bad situations into good situations?

Anyway, before he could get off the phone, I was, like, "Hey, hey, hey— Joe, look, I'm at a pay phone. Allow me the chance to tell you where I'm staying, and maybe you can come up there at six o'clock. We can have dinner."

Needless to say, we never had dinner and I didn't hear from him for another three or four years.

Once, my girlfriend in high school went down there to see her own father and was going to try to find my father, too. I shouldn't have been at all surprised when she called me from a pay phone, all out of breath, saying "Jason, your father literally ran from us!" I couldn't believe it—I thought it was a little exaggeration—but it was no exaggeration at all.

All said, I might've spoken to my father six or seven times in my entire life. The last time we talked, in early 2003, he called me out of the blue to tell me that he loves me but wasn't sure if I'm his child. What a contradiction. Out of all of his kids, I'm the only identical look-alike. In a nutshell, that's bullshit. I didn't even buy into that one. What was the real purpose of this call after five or six years? I suggested that we take a blood test, because who wants to talk to a person you don't know or really care for if you don't have to. This sixty-year-old, stubborn, and control-happy Leo doesn't like to match wits with his thirty-two-year-old, conscious, secure, intellectual, and independent Scorpio son. An obvious mismatch if we aren't both in the LIGHT. Think about it.

But truth be told, my pops, I wish him all the best anyway. I'm here now, live and glad to be alive. Both he and my mother in different ways have said, "I love you." But my question is, What are you really telling me? Love to him is just a word. And he might've said it twice out of the few times that we've had a conversation. I wonder how and why this guy who has run from the fact that I exist all my life musters up the nerve to say, "I love you." I question his method of demonstrating love. My mother, on the other hand, is *always* saying, "I love you," and she has difficulty demonstrating it, as well, because of how she was raised. I think that's a part of the old school—to use a buffer phrase to keep the peace in an apparent rebuttal. It's a phrase to keep you near and break down the argument that you just had—and yeah, it does that—but it's also very hard to feel love where there is a lack of love being demonstrated. There's that word again. It's becoming easier for me to discipline my thoughts and actions, whereas beefing with one of my parents doesn't happen, and if it does, I'm going to handle it differently in the future, in a more positive light.

Sometimes I wonder, Why do I have to think like that to keep the parent-child relationship healthy? You're my mother. Why do I have to think like that for you? You're my father. Why can't you *school* me about some of the things I'll face while growing into manhood? Why can't you sit down and let me get some of that wisdom?

It has never worked that way—ever.

Who's really the bastard here? It all makes me realize that, yes, I came through my parents, but I am different from my parents, and my purpose is revealed to me every day. I just have to be quiet enough to listen to spirit.

Jason Orr is the creator and producer of Atlanta's perennially popular FunkJazz Kafé Music & Arts Festivals. He is also a music producer and manager of talent working with a wide range of successful artists including Meshell Ndegeocello, U.K. soul legends Loose Ends, Caron Wheeler (formerly of Soul II Soul), Omar, Dionne Farris, Public Enemy, and Erykah Badu.

Second Chances

William Fletcher

"**D**ad," my daughter cried into the phone. "I'm pregnant, so now you have to move to California."

My daughter had been telling my wife and me that we needed to move. Either back home to Dayton with our other two children or out to California with her and her husband. My wife and I weren't excited about doing either. We had been living in North Carolina for the past five years. We had both lived in Dayton, Ohio, all our lives, and we had made the decision to move to Greensboro in anticipation of greener pastures and new opportunities. Where we expected great things, we were met with obstacles and a series of misfortunes that devastated us financially and personally.

A quick history of our life shows that my wife and I have not been the perfect parents. We knew that kids were supposed to have food, shelter, and love. Well, we had the love part down, but we were often deficient on providing some of the basic necessities that children need. At the time, I would blame my wife for our financial situation and the tumultuous life of being evicted from houses and getting lights cut off monthly. I hardly noticed how bad things were. My adult children can easily recall repossessed cars, empty cabinets, and toyless Christmases. It's not as easy for me to remember because for most of my children's formative years, I was drunk or on my way to getting drunk. By the time I decided to clean up my act, my children were grown. My oldest daughter was already a sophomore at Fisk University, my middle child was a senior in high school but already planning on how she'd leave Dayton, and my youngest—my son—well, he was born grown.

So, in a way, I missed some opportunities that I would pay to get back. I met with each of my kids to apologize for any hurt that my drinking had caused. They never had anything but kind words. My middle daughter told me, "Dad, you never hurt us. We hated to see you hurt yourself. But we are all fine now." Recognizing that my kids were grown, I prayed that the things that I did teach them when they were younger were helping to guide their adult lives. There is no way that you can anticipate the way your life is heading. I was sheltered from some of the pain that my children might have experienced because it was always up to my wife to fix things that were broken.

My wife, Karen, was the kind of woman whom everyone in the community used as resource. She could get you into college or out of jail in a matter of hours. She was that good. There were very few things that I would have to worry about because Karen handled it all. Well, God had other plans for our lives. In August 1999, after a series of bizarre behaviors that we would later learn were symptoms of small strokes, my wife was overtaken by a massive stroke that changed our lives. Karen lost the use of her left leg and arm, and I was immediately thrust into a role for which I was unprepared, but I did the best I could. The months ahead of us were hard. We had no family around. I would often drive to the hospital where they had her in extensive rehab, and spend the day with her. This was such a strain on me because I had to drive the fifty miles out to the hospital in Chapel Hill to see my wife and then go to my general laborer job in the evenings. It was hell, and I looked forward to the day when Karen would come home. Then I could get more rest, I thought. Well, again, things did not turn out as planned.

When my wife was discharged, she did not come home the woman that she had been. She was at the point of needing 100 percent dependent care. If I didn't feed her, she didn't eat. I had to take care of everything for her and it felt impossible for me to leave and go to work. I was eventually dismissed from my job. I didn't have the guts to call my oldest daughter, who was an attorney, and tell her. Even though she said that my job should have been protected long enough for me to care for my wife. In the beginning, I was just so ashamed that I couldn't handle it all. In fact, where I had to handle things for my wife, it became my middle daughter's responsibility to take care of things for me. I remember that she had to fly out to Greensboro, once again with check in hand to avoid the eviction proceedings and utilities disconnections that we were threatened with. In one moment when my daughter was anything but calm and understanding she hollered, "Dad, did you think things were just going to work themselves out?" I could barely reply that I had hoped that things would just work themselves out but those kinds of fairy tales weren't happening in Greensboro. From that point on she would fly from California to Greensboro, North Carolina, at least once a month. She stocked the house with groceries and not just necessities, but things that we liked to eat, too—Cherry 7UP and Orange Slices. She insisted that we both have cable and not just the basic version, but the premium version, too. On Thanksgivings and Christmases, she made sure that a complete dinner was made for us and sent directly to our house. I was starting to feel that in some small ways, maybe I had been a better father than I gave myself credit for. After all, what kind of children take care of their parents in this way if their parents were bad to begin with.

My daughter married a great guy. Bobby must share the same values as my daughter because he always sent her to take care of us and often he came himself. He'd talk to doctors, nurses, and in-home support staff. He sent medicine and gave advice over the phone. He also made sure that if he had the latest Playstation game, well then, so did I. So, when they offered to move my wife and me out to California, it seems ironic but I didn't jump at the chance. Here they were, a young couple starting their new lives. They built a house and paid almost as much for the extra room for us as we paid for our first home. But, even with all that, my wife and I could barely stand the idea of being a burden on the two people who had provided so much support to us.

We did move, though, because my daughter said that she needed us. And even though I could have done it—taken care of my wife on my own—the thought of having some kind of help was appealing to me. We packed our bags; we didn't take much. My daughter told us to bring all our pictures and throw everything else away, what we didn't have, we'd buy again. Our neighbors were ecstatic, we gave away all the things in our apartment, and it made us feel good to know how much we were contributing to the lives of others.

My wife and I had our reservations: How will this all work out? Will the kids be happy that we are there? will we be in the way? How will Bobby's parents, who live in the area, feel about us being around? It's almost unbelievable to report, but things did not turn out just as good as I expected but actually better. In fact, moving to California has far exceeded my expectations. My daughter tells people that I retired early. She created a résumé for me so that I could volunteer at the YMCA. They liked my work so much that they created a position for me doing what I love: coaching kids. But more than anything, the real dream that has become a part of my life was the fact that my daughter did need me. After forty-eight hours of labor, she delivered my first grandson. Now, I know that most people love their grandkids, but for me, Trey represents so much more than a lifeline to future generations. I am so fortunate that I get to stay home to be with my grandson. While my daughter and son-in-law go off to work, Trey and I settle into our routine that includes the Disney Channel, diced apples, and rides in his "limo" (a wagon that I bought him) through the neighborhood. Trey calls me GeeGee for Grandpa Gene, and when he wakes up in the morning, I can hear his padded feet and imagine his tiny hand dragging one of his parents to the top of the stairs, where he hollers out "Gee Gee!" in order for us to start our day.

Of course, things are different now; my daughter believes now more than ever that people have to have things that make them happy. I believed that, too, but never had the means to act on that. Now, in our house we have all of what we need and most of what we want. My relationship with my son-in-law couldn't be better, and I think my grandson thinks I'm as fantastic as I think he is. My wife has made emotional progress, but very limited physical progress since we've been out here. But there's a definite difference for both us. It was somewhat of an adjustment for us to come here. Like any mother and daughter, Karen and Jarralynne have had their things to iron out. We are all happy to be together, but who knew that it could be like this? My daughter has said that she's happy that she lived long enough to forgive her parents for all the things that she didn't have as a child. Well, I have to tell you, I'm glad that I've lived long enough to forgive myself.

William Fletcher lives in California near his daughter and son-in-law. He takes pride in raising his grandson while caring for his wife. He also works as a coach at the YMCA.

We and Us

Brian Olowude

I'm my momma's baby. I'm the youngest of her six children. I have three older brothers and two older sisters. Growing up, I could always tell when my mother was speaking to a friend of the family. Her conversation would go something like this, "The boys? They're doing fine, driving me crazy, but fine. The girls? Good. They think they're grown, but they're doing good. Brian? He's okay."

That's how it was in our house. The boys (my brothers), the girls (my sisters), and then there was me.

I'm not sure when or why it happened, but somehow I was set apart from my siblings and in some ways my entire family. Always a part of, but never really included. I knew or at least have known as long as I could remember that my brothers and sisters and I had different fathers. It was a fact, but never an issue talked about in great detail. My momma would always say, "You all came out of me, so you're all the same." It was never "This is my half brother" or "my half sister."

To me, not having a father was no different. It made sense: It's all I knew. Unlike my siblings, I never had to deal with feelings of abandonment or feeling like my father didn't love me. For as it was explained to me, my father was a Nigerian grad student who left the states to return to fight in the civil unrest of that country in the late 1960s. He never knew my mother was pregnant. And by the time my mother knew she was pregnant with me, she had received word that he was killed in the country's civil war.

From the rue, as I like to call it, I created multiple images of him. He was strong, tall, rich, and most important, an African king. Which, of course, made me an African prince. I hold my father's last name, which was always the most difficult name to pronounce in my classes; I would dread roll call. There would be Adams, Baker, Collins, Nelson . . . (Here it comes.) "Oh, Ohh, Oh . . . is there a Brian here?" They never got it right. And the kids, they only knew it sounded funny and was fodder for numerous taunts. When they would make fun of it, I would secretly think if we were in my country, they'd be bowing to me, and I'd have them stoned for such disrespect.

I began describing myself as Black, and African. It helped me explain certain things. Like, why was I so different from my siblings? Why was I darker? Why was my nose broader, why did I have hair that my sister called "naps that snapped right back"? Where my siblings were flashy and funny, I was dull and awkward; where they were popular, I was geeky. Where they were at times criminal, I was the "good one." While I wonder about all these things, I never questioned that they loved me. I just felt different. When these doubts would grow, I'd imagine my father had secretly been spared in the war and was waiting until it was safe to return to claim his heir and take me back to Africa as the African prince I was.

As I matured, these fantasies lessened, but in many ways the divisions between my siblings and me grew. When I was a preteen, my older brothers felt it was important that they teach me what it meant to be a man. I came to the conclusion that it involved them beating me up as often as possible. My sisters felt it important they teach me what it meant to be invisible, because they just largely ignored me. My family loved me; they just didn't get me.

In my family, two of my brothers have survived being shot. The other is serving a life sentence. One sister struggles to keep her head above water, and the other is lost to the haze of the streets and drugs. And then there's me. The psychologist. No, really I'm a psychologist. I don't think I ever really appreciated what I received from my family until I was forced to put my fantasy father to the test.

While in grad school, I had posted a message on an Internet message board looking for information on any member of my father's family. With this simple act, I put on the line not only the fantasy image of my father, but in many ways my image of myself, as well. Months passed until I received a phone call from someone claiming to know members of my father's family in Nigeria. He spoke four words that changed everything, "Your father is alive." Alive. Alive. Alive. That word shook my soul as never before. After a series of correspondence verifying facts and dates, I spoke with my father on my thirtieth birthday. Was he a king? Was he tall? Was he strong? Was he rich? In short, could the reality father live up to the fantasy one I had created?

As I readied myself to meet my father and my Nigerian family, I began to prepare a photo book of my mother's family. I came across an old photograph of my mother holding me on her lap. In it, she's dressed to the nines, and I'm in footed pajamas. She is gazing down at me, and I'm gazing up at her. In that one moment, the reality of what my family gave me hit me like a ton of bricks. My mother gave me my father's name, but she also gave me a sense of pride in who and what I am. She gave me love and patience. My brothers gave me safety and protection. They kept the life they lead far from me, but I never feared being hurt or harmed by anyone when my brothers' names were mentioned. My sisters gave beauty and respect. They were my pretty older sisters. They made me smile; they made me laugh. They helped me see that a woman deserved respect.

Were they perfect? No. Was I a part of them and they a part of me? Yes. Did their struggles help secure my success? Yes. Did their joys increase mine? Yes. For the first time in my life I didn't feel like it was the boys, the girls, and me. It was *we*, us. Good or bad, I wasn't separate or different. I was a member of this wonderful, dysfunctional, exciting, frustrating family.

As I boarded the plane to fly to Rome to meet my father, I did so as a man, husband, brother, doctor, and as I was in the beginning, my momma's baby.

In case you're wondering, my father was in fact very . . . *tall*.

__Brian Olowude__ is currently a correctional psychologist for the California Department of Corrections and lecturer at California State University, Fresno. He continues to work at reaffirming solutions to the issues that plague communities of color, which lie not outside the communities, but within recognition of their innate strength of heritage and resiliency.

My Hero

Curtis L. Taylor

Like so many Black men who go without recognition, my father was more of a rock than a rolling stone.

He was not ashamed to work two jobs to support his family, always came home, and almost always had enough extra to help his friends.

In short, he handled his business.

All too often, we hear stories about the father who left his family or who spent his time, money, and youth chasing women and drinking. I am sure those stories are true.

But there are also plenty of Black men who work overtime, provide for their children, and always show up. I know from experience.

As far back as I can remember, my father was always at home handling his business and playing a positive role in my life.

In our home, as in many others, there was discipline, love, and respect. Things were never perfect but always livable. The environment, attitude, and tone were set by a man always willing to go that extra mile to meet the needs of his family and close friends.

I guess my bond with my father started developing sometime during my infant years when I am told my father was quick to change a diaper, warm a bottle, and pay the bills—all the things that come with fatherhood.

I just loved him because he allowed me to reach into his pockets every Saturday to retrieve all the coins my small hands could hold. Or, how he stood me on the counter at the corner store so I could stuff my penny-candy bag.

Of course, there were the toys, piggyback rides, and hugs—the rewards of fatherhood I would later come to learn.

As I grew older, I came to respect his timing. The pats on the back and words of encouragement that always seem to come at the right moment.

I still remember the pride in his voice when introducing me as his son. His voice showed me there was something special about being a dad.

I also came to respect his consistency. Every morning without fail, he was up by 5:00 A.M., including the mornings when he came in late after hanging out with the fellas, when his back hurt, when fighting a cold. He was always up on time and off to work. He would drag me along to work during the summer months to work, watch, and learn. It wasn't until years later that I realized he wasn't telling me how to be a man but showing me.

While I hated getting up so early, I loved the drive home where he would answer every question I could throw at him under the sun.

Questions would flow about money, God, and being a father. As well as about fun stuff like girls, football, and our mutual respect for then Los Angeles Mayor Tom Bradley, Bill Cosby, Hank Aaron, Mack and Jackie Robinson. We talked about our love for writing and Richard Wright, Langston Hughes, John Steinbeck.

It was in high school when I guess I knew my dad was my hero. I think it was the time when I woke him up in the middle of the night and he drove an hour to pick me up after my truck broke down.

Upon arriving, there was no lecture, just the concern of a man trying to raise a son. He conveniently forgot that I had disobeyed his orders the day before not to drive the truck until I saved the money to fix the electrical problem that kept draining the battery.

But there were rules at work: Live up to your mistakes and responsibilities. Don't hold your head down.

It was also about this time that the doctors told us about the cancer. I was too young to understand the pain or why he never complained. I wish I knew what I know now. I would have loved him even more.

At first, it seemed the cancer was just another challenge he would take on and beat.

Things were normal.

I could always find my father watching television, tinkering with some project, or sitting on the edge of the bed, reading his Bible when I strolled in past midnight, after curfew.

No lecture, just that stern look and unspoken words of knowing. And, then we would talk, sometimes well into the morning. It was during one of those early-morning sessions that the great debate about my career began.

He wanted me to become a lawyer. I wanted to become a writer.

The back-and-forth continued for years, but I eventually won.

I still remember the pride of showing him my first, front-page story in my college newspaper.

I also remember the weak, happy, peaceful smile on his face and the feeling like he knew something I didn't as he read the story. It was the kind of peaceful look that only a rock of a father can arrive at after spending a lifetime sacrificing, providing, and raising his children as best he can.

The cancer won.

I had never seen my father give into anything; the country boy had finally failed a challenge.

Heroes don't always win.

I later become an author and award-winning journalist, keeping a promise to myself the way I was taught real men do. And, my father got his first college graduate. I knew he was up to something with that peaceful smile.

My father was no rolling stone, just a solid rock providing the cornerstone of my foundation for life.

Now, as a father, I am a pebble trying to grow into a rock foundation.

Thanks for the lessons, Dad.

Curtis L. Taylor is an award-winning City Hall reporter for New York Newsday, the nation's sixth-largest newspaper. Mr. Taylor has been nominated for journalism's highest honor, the Pulitzer Prize, as a member of Newsday's investigative team. He has received the James Aronson Award for Social Justice given annually by Hunter College, as well as awards from the New York State Associated Press Association and the National Association of Black Journalists, and the Casey Medal for Meritorious Journalism. Mr. Taylor also coauthored It's Like That: A Spiritual Memoir with Joseph "Reverend Run" Simmons of the legendary rap group Run-DMC. Mr. Taylor is the former president of the New York Association of Black Journalists.

In the Tradition

Akil Kamau

When I was a child, one of my favorite songs was "Papa Was a Rolling Stone," by the world-famous Temptations. It's funny, I remember playing that song over and over again on my little plastic record player, singing and dancing along with that infamous song. That's how deep my absentee fatherhood tradition goes, all the way deep down past the bone, to my subconscious.

See the irony of my loving that song so much is that I could kind of relate to it. I say "kind of" because, honestly I couldn't tell you whether or not my "biological" (the term of endearment used to describe the donor—I don't mean to sound hateful, I just got hate in my blood) really was a rolling stone. See, I wouldn't know that, or *him* for that matter. He wasn't in my life like that.

Not that I ever asked, but I never heard bad things—or good things for that matter—about him. But he is in me deeply, deeper than I'd like to admit. As a child, I couldn't imagine the damage being done as I played that song over and over. They say music can touch the soul, and that song surely did, it is the song of my gene pool. Innately, I gravitated towards those lyrics; selfishly (as children often are), I didn't think about the feelings my mother must have endured having to hear that song played so many times a day. That song proved to be cruel and unusual punishment for myself, and probably my mother, for crimes we never committed.

Fast forward to the present. Here I am today in the age of faxes, e-mail, two-way pagers, and so forth, and there's still no cure for the "rolling stone" gene that resides within me. I am in the tradition of many men before me and traveling along with me. But as a virus will do, that gene has mutated to fit the life and times of our generation. I (like many of my peers in the same situation) am not absent or even a "rolling stone." We are fathers, but fathers in our own casual way. We couldn't get along with our "baby mamas," or they couldn't get along with us. Whatever the case may be, so many of us are physically separated from our children.

"Casual" fatherhood suits the times. In the world of "We have overcome," Black people have greater freedom to pursue the American Dream than at any other time during our sojourn in this country. However, our pursuits have a cost: our family, something us fatherless children vowed to cherish and uphold. But what went wrong with this freedom? Where did we fail? The answers are plentiful, but so very hard to articulate.

Many of us were raised by strong mothers, grandmothers, and aunts. And in those examples, we may have gotten lost, or our signals could have gotten crossed. In many of our minds, we saw the strength of a matriarchal system as a substitute for family, as opposed to a compliment. We honored a commitment to survival and not a commitment to nuclear family building. Traditionally our nuclear family was our extended family. And that tradition is from a proud heritage, one that should continue. However, I argue that there is some detriment continuing this tradition in a country that does not honor or respect our traditions.

Traditionally, in the eyes of America, the nuclear family is mother, father, and children. Father and mother work, but at the end of the day, everyone's under the same roof. Grandparents and other extended family are people you visit on occasion, but not necessarily a part of the core family structure. However, this wasn't the tradition many of us grew up in, myself in particular.

My core family structure consisted of my grandparents and my mother, with a helpful dose from my uncles, along with various street characters who were popular in my projects. There was a strong male presence in my life, but casual due to the lack of closeness from my biological. Some may argue that at least I had positive male role models in my life. However, I will tell you that I envied my cousins and classmates who had their fathers in their homes, or at the very least *knew who their fathers were*.

So again here I stand, a father from a "broken" home, who continued the cycle, or the tradition, if you will. How do I live with myself, knowing that I've helped to perpetuate a situation which saddened me as a child and that I detested as an adult? What steps can I take to ensure that my son doesn't grow up with the same pain I grew up with? These are questions for all of us who truly seek family to honestly answer.

Some people don't believe Black men care or feel the pain over this subject; we do, it's all around us and in everything we do. It was in the music we grew up to and is in the music we create and listen to today. Biggie, Pac, Jada, X, CL, and almost every other male rapper has at least half a bar dedicated to their biological. Try listening to Jay-Z and Beenie Siegal's song "Where You Been" without feeling the pain and frustration of growing up without a father around. Once again, music touches the soul. No disrespect to the grandfathers, uncles, older brothers, and male cousins; but not having the person you supposedly look like around to play ball with or to teach you how to ride a bike are the little things that make up this adopted new tradition.

Unfortunately, there is no triumphant end to this story. As for me, well, currently I am in the middle of this war to break this new tradition; have been all my life, and probably will be in it until I expire. But be very clear, I'm a soldier rushing to the front lines of this struggle. I am back-to-back and shoulder-to-shoulder with many of my brethren. I fight constant battles and gladly struggle against the scourge of feeling, and becoming obsolete. I don't want to feel this pain any longer, nor do I wish to pass my pain on to my son. So I'm fighting the good fight against a tradition I was raised in and one I do not wish to continue or maintain. And like the Roman god Janus, I am constantly looking toward my future and at my past at the same time. My allies are my opponents—pride, ego, arrogance, freedom and independence, honor, and trying to be right. I am a father, a parent, and a Black man with a child. But unfortunately, as tradition dictates, my child is being raised by his mother as I struggle to build my place in the world.

As stated before, like most people, I don't want to feel the pain from the scars this war has inflicted on me, but more so, I don't want to enlist my son into the same struggle. Ideally, I wanted to show him a family environment different from the one in which I grew up nearly half my life. Fortunately, he was exposed to the "ideal family structure" the first four years of his life. That foundation created a bond between him and me that I can only continue to strengthen and hope doesn't dwindle away with the physical distance between us as he gets older.

I know it's still not too late for him to raise a child in a situation different from what I was raised in, but my fear is that he is now in the boot camp for this army that I've been a part of my entire life. And the sad fact is that this "new tradition" isn't really new at all; it seems to have developed into becoming the "norm."

Now I recognize the many positive attributes this struggle can build, strength and character being at the top of the list. But I don't know if that is a fair trade-off. I think I would have exchanged all the strength and character I developed over the years just to have my biological be a positive part of my life. Maybe with him there, he could have helped to develop that. I know much of my character and strength were built with the help and examples of my extended and core family—my grandmother, in particular. However, I can understand my son's pain about this situation, even if he can articulate only it in the phrase, "I want my daddy."

My struggle to "be somebody" in the world, business or otherwise, does not go without knowing that I am somebody in my son's world, whether I'm there or not. This fact is due to the bond he and I built from the first day he came out of his mother's womb. However, now I feel as though I've passed on more than just my eyes to him. Unfortunately, he will know a similar struggle because we share the same last name. To some, that may not seem like a big deal, but when you think about it, it can be either a heavy burden or a wonderful blessing. Imagine growing up in a home where everyone had the same last name except you. And the person you shared that name with was not present, not spoken about, and not seen on a regular basis. Can you imagine that? Some of us, such as myself, don't have to imagine, because we actually lived it. Fortunately, his road will not be as rough, because at least he knows me.

Tradition is a hard road, but I passed it on to my son just as easily as I passed my legal name on to him. This was not my intention—it's rarely anyone's intention to do this—however, the circumstances as they are now force me to fight the war to break this tradition. And in doing so, some battles are lost. But in the overall scheme of things, we must know that the struggle must continue and battles must, at the very least, be fought. That is our only faith as warriors in this struggle, and is what drives me never to give up.

Being in this struggle leads me to believe, sometimes, that I was destined to this life and now I've doomed my son to the same future. That is a big fear. I didn't try to end up here—none of us did—I wanted the opposite of what I was brought up in, and I was under the perception that I was well on my way there. After finally getting my head together and going to college, boy met girl, boy and girl fell in love, boy and girl had a child (no marriage), and boy and girl broke up after trying to make things work for a few years. Now here I am, right back where I started—sort of. Now the constant battles of how not to allow this situation to dwindle into a carbon copy of my life growing up is what I fight against. I don't want to be like my biological; I do not want to carry on tradition.

Who needs a father around when you have a strong mother? The answer to this question is obvious; however, this is part of my struggle against becoming obsolete, against being a "casual" father. Throughout our history, Black women have been the mothers, and mammies, to most in this country. I myself was primarily raised by my grandmother. That is not to disrespect the priceless rearing participation by my grandfather and my mother, and stepfather. But honestly I feel that some of us brothers are potentially playing ourselves out of the picture.

I see it every day, and I feel it in every way. I live it, myself, along with many of my contemporaries who have fathered children who may not need us in the day-to-day struggle to survive. They see their mothers doing it, just as I saw mine, and these are valuable examples. And they will survive, just as we did, without the help of our biological fathers. But this is far from a reality game show. Unfortunately, we are forcing ourselves, to a degree, to continue this "new tradition." And this is the legacy we must fight against.

I recognize that the importance of being strong, positive fathers in our children's lives cannot be ignored, downplayed, or misrepresented. But for myself, I believe that in the day-to-day rearing and cultivation of a family environment, we are perceived as not being needed. That is what's being sold to us. Or maybe we've just adapted to this as fact and reality. But if this is the case, how come many of us have the reaction to move away from this tradition and try to break the mold? If given a choice, I think few of us who strive to be progressive in our lives would want to embrace or continue this tradition. Because the simple fact of the matter is that we hate it and would love to destroy the mold of history. And many of us have done so.

I think it's a major mistake even to suggest that we are being forced out by our women's strength. But the tradition of a strong Black woman raising three or four children on her own, with little or no help from the father, has been the example for the better part of the past fifty years. This tradition has also been the proving ground for "daddy-less" babies to grow up to be strong, intelligent, Black adults. Of course, there have been many, many failures along the way, but that is to be expected. Now what we need to ask ourselves is has our success failed us? Have we Black men casually accepted the fact that our children are being raised securely without our help? Have we built and developed this "tradition" of ours only to have it destroy us in the long run? To have it render ourselves obsolete? I think not—I honestly do not believe things are that bleak.

However, I think this "idea" of becoming obsolete has not been addressed. Many of us find ourselves torn between "carrying on tradition," and trying to create a new future despite our past. We hated that we had to grow up without our fathers. Many of us even hate the "invisible man," the father who was not there, yet maintained a mysterious presence through photographs or even merely a last name. Many of us have desperately tried to run away from this destiny. Sometimes the run seems to be in vain. Instead of being a twenty-six-mile marathon, it is a marathon of a lifetime that seems unbeatable. It's a struggle that we almost feel we have been bred for. And as a family, a people, it seems we've easily adapted to it. But again, this is why I continue to battle and wage war against this new tradition and eradicate it from my life.

Akil Kamau is an independent publisher and author of the upcoming novel Opt Out the Game.

Only Huevoas Kiss Other Men

Shaka King

It was late summer of 1989. In two weeks, I was to start the fourth grade at PS 11, a public school just outside of my neighborhood, Bed-Stuy, Brooklyn. Clothes and supplies for the upcoming year had been purchased long in advance, so little more existed on my two-week itinerary than daily, marathon-like sessions of flies up, skelly, and kill the man with the ball.

Apparently my parents hadn't gotten the memo.

MOM: Why aren't you dressed?

ME: For what?

MOM: Stop playing games, and go take a shower. You know we're visiting two schools today.

ME: I don't feel so good. I think I might have rickets or something.

MOM: Do you want me to call your father?

As longtime employees of the New York City Board of Education, both of my parents had courtside seats to the system's downward spiral throughout the 1980s. With classroom sizes averaging a claustrophobic thirty-plus students and citywide abandonment of the music and arts departments, it was becoming increasingly clear that you got what you paid for.

Hence, I found myself seething in the backseat of the family Thunderbird en route Poly Prep, a private school located in the heart (or armpit, depending upon whom you ask) of Bay Ridge, Brooklyn. Poly Prep. It sounded like a school for guys with androgynous first names, like Francis or Lindsay. And what was this business I'd heard about a dress code? I wouldn't be able to rock my Cotlers up in this piece? Oh, hell no.

As we exited the Brooklyn-Queens Expressway, dad lowered the volume on Freddie Jackson's soulful "You Are My Lady," and ice-grilled me in the rearview mirror.

"I don't want to see no poking your lip out when we get inside. You hear me?"

I did. And I didn't—poke my lip out, that is. But in the end, my shift in attitude had little to do with the fact that my father woke up at three in the morning, five days a week to bench press four hundred pounds of steel I believed he had mined, welded, and shaped himself.

Next to Disney World, Poly Prep was the most beautiful stretch of land I'd ever laid eyes on. Its twenty-six-acre campus boasted two ponds, imported wildlife in the form of rabbits, chickens, and turtles, and a dynamite chemistry lab. (I was a nerd on the low). Sure, the place had its "minor quirks." The student body was largely white, and the boys, in their standard uniform of tweed blazers, tight jeans, and filthy hightop sneakers, resembled a bunch of mediocre stand-up comics. But by the end of the tour, my parents had to promise me control of the radio just to get me inside of the car.

That night my father entered my room and took a seat on the edge of the mattress. I could see him smiling faintly in the dark as he nodded in silence.

"What?"

He dismissed me with a frown and shake of the head. Often, when I try to figure out what emotions lie behind my father's offbeat facial affectations, he answers with another.

"So you want to go to Poly Prep?"

"Yes."

He stroked his beard and nodded some more.

"Okay."

I leapt up and clasped my arms around his neck. He returned the embrace.

It would be one of our last for years to come.

Black prep school students often struggle with issues of self image, whether relating to race, class, or both. I never had that problem. *The Spook Who Sat by the Door* was required reading in my household. Poly Prep didn't rob me of my identity so much as it robbed me of my dad.

In my excitement upon first visiting, I had failed to notice that our Ford Thunderbird was surrounded by Lex coupes, Beamers, and Benzes, the owners of which could easily afford Poly's fifteen-thousand-dollar annual tuition. Meanwhile, my parents' salaries barely covered the cost of feeding the rabbits. To supplement our household income, my father, in addition to his nine to five, worked weeknights, weekends, and weekend nights. Within two years, he dropped forty pounds in muscle, developed deep creases extending from his nose to the corners of his mouth, and was all but pleasant company. Not that my father had ever been the most amiable fellow. I remember giving him a kiss on the cheek at six years old and being informed that "only huevoas kiss other men" (pronounced we-bow.) I didn't know what an huevoa was, but the throbbing vein in the middle of his forehead let me know I hadn't been paid a compliment.

Nevertheless, my father and I had what I thought was an extremely healthy relationship early on. Every Saturday, he'd take me window-shopping with him in Midtown. If I was really lucky, he'd buy me a book or crystal for my rock collection. (Like I said, nerd on the low.) Afterward, we'd swing by Coronet's, world-renowned for its gargantuan pizza slices, and as we returned home along the FDR Drive, I'd fight "the Itis" while he lectured me on the evils of White supremacy and how the Jewish merchants on Delancey Street sold the best gabardine.

Poly Prep put an end to our weekend excursions. When my father got home from work, he'd immediately pass out on the couch, and when awake, he wasn't very talkative. I approached my teen years, that age when you start wanting to get to know your parents beyond being the people who blame you for running up the phone bill. Yet, I felt like my father and I were stuck in this awkward, almost corporate, "employer-employee" dichotomy. Our conversations consisted of the doling out of tasks, followed by a reprimand concerning their failed completion. I wanted to know what it was like growing up in Panama. Did he get in a lot of fights as a child? Where'd he hide the porno? I was forced to seek advice about girls from a bunch of kids who doused themselves in "Florida Water" and unbuttoned their shirts halfway to show off their bone structure. Maybe he was interested in talking to me about something other than why I'd gotten a C-minus in Algebra. "You sure ain't have no problem adding up all them minutes on the phone bill. I'll tell you that." But I didn't feel comfortable approaching this brooding giant from whom I'd inherited my stooped gait and proclivity toward toilet humor. Yeah, at least I had a father. But why couldn't we be friends?

In hindsight, my dad wasn't callous. He was lonely. As many friends as my mother had, I can't remember anyone outside of my family visiting my father in a purely social context before I turned sixteen. Up until that point, I was his social life. Like many Black men, far more than are given credit, he lived for his offspring. His mistake was in equating self-neglect with self-lessness.

American culture celebrates martyrdom, particularly when it relates to parenting. We extol praise upon the mother or father who works to put food on the table. But what good are they in a pine box? For years, my father was dead in that he ceased to grow. The realm of his existence was so minute, it choked him, like an oak tree in a flower pot. He needed a hobby, a friend, an interest. And I needed him to have one just as badly. Don't get me wrong; I appreciated the sacrifices my father made in order to provide me with the best education possible. But fuck Voltaire. How did I get rid of these razor bumps?

In 1995, my mother wrote a brilliant play titled *Endangered Species*, exploring the relationship between Black masculinity and violence. My mom tried to move the play, initially performed by her students, beyond her high school auditorium. After several unsuccessful attempts, my father stepped forward as executive producer, despite having no prior experience in theater whatsoever. *Endangered Species* ran in several theaters, citywide, for the next three and a half years.

As a producer, and as an artist, my father got a chance to flex muscles I don't think he knew existed; or if he did know, he was afraid to use. Along with me and my uncle, he built the set from scratch. Through that process, my father discovered an eye for design that had been present for years. (The man could always dress). In addition, our collaboration fostered a level of comfort between the two of us that had been lacking for quite some time. I can recall being backstage, laughing as one of the actors imitated my father's accent. (Think of a West African man, reared in Jamaica, who received a British education.) On the car ride home, my father railed at me for mocking "the person who'd wiped my ass," but this time his curse words came from a different place. He was hurt and unafraid to show it. That vulnerability was something my father would never have revealed to me years prior.

Through producing *Endangered Species*, my father established contacts with several artists who eventually became friends. Soon after, he began collecting art, and in recent months he's even expressed an interest in painting. With all of his growth over the years, I've had to do some, as well. Most important has been conquering my fear of the man. It helps that we're pretty even in the bench press. All right, he's got me by fifty pounds—all right, sixty-five. But to be honest, he's made being his friend pretty easy. It could be that I'm an adult now, but he's nonjudgmental, very easygoing. I love him for that. I love him for loving himself enough to be happy. But enough of this "huevoa" talk.

Shaka King is a filmmaker residing in Brooklyn, New York. His directorial debut, Stolen Moments, *won third prize in the 2002 San Francisco Black Film Festival and was selected for competition in the 2003 Pan African Film Festival. An experimental documentary,* Stolen Moments *explores the effects of global capitalism on hip-hop music. Shaka is currently at work on a screenplay titled* Strip Mall, *about the unlikely bond between a narcissistic flautist and an illiterate security guard.*

Your Soul's Journey

*And that these days should be remembered and kept throughout
every generation, every family, every province, and every city.*
—Esther 9:28

At our roundtable, we talked with men who felt they were sincerely doing their best. The consensus when it comes to the Black family is that we still have to overcome. But how can Black men overcome when they themselves are products of a cycle of families unraveling faster than ever?

Families are a mix of some of the most intelligent and talented yet illogical and unreasonable people we know. Family is where personality is developed, identity is formed, status is assigned, and values are learned. So what are the personality, identity, status, and values of today's Black father? Families provide a support system, which sustains you.

Most men that we spoke with put their dreams and hopes on deferment in order to raise their families the best way they knew how. Perhaps they were not equipped with all the information and sources. There is a new wave of young fathers. Even if the children are born outside of marriage, these fathers insist and demand that they be allowed to participate in the nurturing and development of their kids. They are fueled by not having their fathers around when they were growing up. They recognize that being a father is one of the greatest opportunities in life and are ready, willing, and able to meet the challenge of parenting.

Forgiveness is the path to peace within the family. We condition people to treat us in a certain way. If you are hurt or angry with someone in your family, express it in the best way you know how, and then let it go. You will always meet inconsiderate schmucks in this world who enjoy putting others down, and unfortunately, sometimes those folks are related to you. It is a greater release for you to forgive than it is for the person who you feel has done you wrong. On the flip side, being humble and apologizing for your inconsiderate actions allow you to move past any disagreements between you and the ones you love.

Truth is, there is no formal training done in schools concerning raising a family. And in some homes, parents are unable to provide their children with all the needed social and psychological support and development.

Children are an extension of their parents, and products of dysfunctional families have a greater tendency to emulate their parents. Once the Black man begins to look at his seed as a possibility to regenerate his lineage in a positive way, the cycle will be broken.

Soul Source

There are two things that are pleasing to a Black woman's eye: the first is a Black man with a book, and the second is a Black family, fellowshiping together. A Black family is a wonderful thing!

- How did you grow up?
- What are the two largest challenges your family has overcome?
- What is the number-one challenge your family faces now?
- What sacrifices did your parents make to raise the family?
- What would you like to do differently or the same when raising your own family?
- Can you forgive?
- What are your family's strengths and weaknesses, and what can be done to strengthen the weaknesses?
- Is your family supportive of you, and in what way?
- Does everyone communicate in your family?
- Do you pour yourself in your work and negate the needs of your family?

CHAPTER 6

SISTERS, WIVES, MOTHERS, AND DAUGHTERS

Dipped in chocolate, bronzed with elegance, enameled with grace,
toasted with beauty. My Lord, she is a Black woman!
—Yosef Ben-Jochannan

Guys often say to each other, "Women, can't live with 'em, can't live without 'em." This seems to sum up the love-hate relationship that many brothers have with their sisters. Maybe it began with Mom blaming Dad for not being around and for putting her son in the crossfire of negative words and images meant for someone who wasn't there. Or maybe he feels this way after being hurt by a string of what he considers "bad" relationships. Whatever the case, brothers instinctively know that women are their complements. As such, women have the ultimate power to make brothers feel on top of the world or at the bottom of the ocean.

It's very rare that you find a Black man who doesn't love his mother, grandmother, aunt, or matriarch who was at the helm while growing up. A Black woman who does her best to take care of the family and make sure that you have what you need to grow up to be the best person you can be. If you can come from a place of loving your mother, then that love should transcend to other Black women in your life, shouldn't it? But so often it doesn't, and Black men end up being abusive and hurtful to their sisters.

Every Black man needs a Black woman. It could be the mother who helped give him life, the grandmother who nourishes his soul with her stories and that special kind of love, the sister who had his back at all costs, the girlfriend who supports his ideas, the wife who loves him unconditionally, the daughter who adores and idolizes him, or the friend who is always his biggest cheerleader. The one thing we tend to forget is that Black men truly love Black women.

He sings tributes to her in song, "I'll always love my mama, she's my favorite girl." He writes about her lovingly in movies like *Soul Food*.

Your journey to loving a Black woman is about learning to understand and relate to the various women in your life—establishing, reinforcing, connecting, and creating lasting bonds with these women and loving them for who they are and the sacrifices, contributions, and joy they bring to your life. When the timing is right, Black men are ready to grow and build with Black women. These stories will show true love, respect, and admiration Black men have for their Black women.

Everlasting Impressions

Kenny Lattimore

This is dedicated to the mothers. The sacrificial position we as men swear we can relate to, but in reality are grateful to God that we were not the chosen vessel to give life. However we learn that the responsibility goes so far beyond creation. It extends to the mind, body, and soul of a child. At least that is the attitude my mother took in raising my older sister and me. It must have been hard finding her way and ours in a world full of swift change. I remember her fly Afro and dashiki flowing with full expression as she went off to Howard University each day—a proud Black woman. That's my momma! A young mother determined to pursue her education and somewhere along the way introduce me to myself. She was the catalyst to my imagination, my knowledge of culture, gender, and Spirit. No disrespect to my fathers, especially when I mention her teaching me about my maleness. I had two great men to pour wisdom, love, and resources into my life. But it's something about the connection between my mother and me that was essential to my becoming a man. Respecting a woman began with her example. Her way of affirming who I was and who I would become left an everlasting impression.

My parents divorced when I was two years old. But determined not to allow her personal circumstances to dictate her destiny—Mom requested that my great-grandparents step in and share some of the caretaking of my sister and me as she continued her pursuit of higher learning. I wonder till this day where her ambition was born. God just gave her a positive perspective on life that nothing could change. You might call her a dreamer or even a visionary. She believed in closing your eyes and picturing yourself doing what you loved most and believing that if you could see it in your mind, it was achievable. To her, struggle was not abnormal; it was necessary. And as with many mothers, improvising was mandatory. We lived between my grandpop's Northwest Washington, D.C., home and Mom's one-bedroom apartment on Fairmont Street near Howard. Close enough to family support, but just far enough for her to remain independent. Although extremely tenacious, her goals never upstaged us as her first priority.

Living in Washington, D.C., had its benefits. Besides the free admission to museums and Federal-sponsored children's activities throughout the year, I knew at an early age that D.C. was a cultural melting pot and a place of world attention. I saw our city on TV and in the movies all the time, but more important at age five was Mom painting the vivid impression of me as a morsel in what was called the "Chocolate City." You couldn't help but be proud of your Blackness here. There were so many people who looked like me in the city. Then there were Black businesses that we patronized and so many historic accomplishments made.

"Look over here," Mom would say, "this is the place where Martin Luther King Jr. gave his 'I Have a Dream' speech and thousands marched for civil rights." The city's very landscape was drawn by Benjamin Banneker, who by memory reproduced its complex design inspired by the city of Paris. The monuments were beautiful, but we better had been just as excited when we visited Fredrick Douglass's home museum and learned about his triumph over slavery. She used African-American history to prove that we could do great things with hard work and determination. Mom was no joke for encouraging us to be proud and appreciate every bit of our culture and Afro-centricity. And if we could see and touch success through the accomplishments of others, it would let us know that we could have the same.

One of my grandpop's favorite things to say was, "the Reverend Walter Fauntroy, a Black congressman, lives around the corner, and he always called me Dr. Lattimore." Maybe that is where my mother began to understand the power of affirmation. I don't know what was spoken into her spirit as a child, but she would fill my mind with "You are very handsome and strong, you are destined for greatness." Once I thought was kind of corny, but I will always remember her saying, "That's why I call you son, because you are so bright." How could I escape the feelings of strong potential? My earliest influences seemed to believe that I would amount to something, so I believed it, too.

Mom's take-control philosophy on life extended beyond our immediate family. After graduating from Howard, she landed a job at Lincoln University in Pennsylvania, and I remember our home becoming sort of a boarder house for African and African-American students. Her position was to uplift her people in whatever way she could. It was in Pennsylvania that lasting impressions of art were shaped in me. At six years old, I had access to the minds of young college painters, sculptors, dancers, and singers—you name it. I felt as if I were being invited to watch the birth of art, which taught me the patience of process. Mom, not knowing what I would become, exposed me to every creative vehicle imaginable. But it was something about music that compelled me most.

It was my grandpop who actually introduced me to music. There was a piano in his basement on which he frequently played and sang spirituals. But it was at home, listening to Mom sing to her favorite collection of Marvin Gaye, Aretha Franklin, and Stevie Wonder records that made me want to sing back. She had a way of allowing the experience of listening to incite her to sing along uninhibitedly, as if she had written each line. Was she reliving a moment in another place and time? Every word seemed to mean something. Perhaps that was the Spirit of respect for lyrics that was passed on to me. For our African ancestors, a song was not "just a song." It had purpose. A song celebrated life, community, and personal struggle.

The first song I remember Mom singing was Thomas A. Dorsey's "Precious Lord." She explained to me what the song was about and began her rendition. I don't know if it was the somber melody or the pain in her voice that touched me most. Although she did explain the lyric, in hindsight, I was too young to really comprehend the true meaning. But the emotional exchange still moved me to tears. She frequently made a song a personal moment like that between the two of us. She would pull me aside, caress my face, and just sang. Oh, yeah—she could really sing! It was as if she was proclaiming who I was and who I would be.

My appreciation for what she was pouring into me has grown proportionately since I became an adult. As I relisten to some of the music she shared, some of the song lyrics were like prayers for my life and future. What a revelation!

As I was coming into my teen years, gospel music became prevalent in our home, which was also accompanied by a new word, *faith!* I used to think Mom was the Black Wonder Woman undercover, but who would have thought she could find any more power than she already had. The visionary who dared us to dream and believe in what we could imagine now had a new source of strength, Jesus Christ. She made a spiritual discovery that changed our family's lives. It was easy to give Him a try because her approach was so gentle and practical, as we did not grow up consistently going to church. She did not become some kind of self-righteous tyrant who demanded us to become miraculously perfect, which was the view some folk had of becoming saved. Instead, we were taught the Bible in a very tangible way and joyfully gave our lives to the Lord, too. We joined a small church just beginning its ministry. Mom never asked us to do anything she wouldn't do with us. So when Pastor asked for volunteers for the choir, there we went, Mom, my sister, and me. I loved singing with her songs of faith, deliverance, and salvation. It felt like a progression from all that had been placed in my spirit from childhood. The messages in the music were soul stirring and life changing. "I can do all things through Christ who strengthens me" (Philippians 4:13), became a short melody of hope Mom would sing around the house. One of her favorite passages in the Bible was Hebrews 11:1, "Now faith is the substance of things hoped for, the evidence of things not seen." But surely, faith would be tested.

I remember the call came after school, at around four thirty. "Kenneth," she said, "I have news, and I don't want you to be afraid. I went to the doctor with back pains, and tests have revealed that I have a rare form of cancer." My first thoughts were purely selfish. What? I was still basking in the joy of being her child! What was going to happen to me? I just can't accept this! She was supposed to be here to see me graduate from high school, become an adult, and get married. Wait a minute—we have faith to overcome this. If anyone could heal my mother, it was the Lord. But soon I would have to put aside my adolescent way of thinking to learn an adult lesson. Everyone has a different course, and she was about to complete hers. If my faith in the Lord and all the affirmations from my earlier years meant, anything it would be proved now. It was time for me to walk in what I had been taught, realize that God's ways are above my own, and He would be the one to sustain me as I continued to pursue my dreams. I would have to be the man that I was encouraged to be without my hero. Sure, I knew I would still make mistakes, stumble, and even fall down sometimes, but that was part of the process. I was art in the hand of God being shaped in manhood.

In God's mercy, He allowed her to live three more years. She was able to see me graduate and sign my first major record deal. It's funny how my belief in myself began with my mother's belief in me. She was my biggest cheerleader, business partner, and confidante. I could not hold her forever, but I would let her know that I respected the love and lessons she gave me. My way of giving back to her was visiting the hospital, praying, singing songs of faith and hope, and letting her know how beautiful she was and would always be to me. The longer I live, the less I regret. She gave me so much substance while she lived that I understand now how complete she was. Ultimately the story of her everlasting impression will be shared with my children. And my only hope is that I am as life changing to them as my mom was to me.

Kenny Lattimore first entered the music industry at the age of fourteen, when he joined the R & B vocal group Maniquin, who recorded briefly for Epic Records in the 1980s. When that band broke up, Lattimore remained in the industry as a songwriter for artists including Glenn Jones and Jon Lucien. As a solo artist, Lattimore has a more mature, sophisticated image, though one still rooted in a traditional R & B style. Married to Chante Lattimore Moore, Kenny recently took on his most challenging role—Dad.

Perfect Planning

Robert Agee Jr., M.D.

It's every expectant father's worst nightmare, to get a call from your pregnant wife saying that something was wrong. I held out hope that everything would be all right and maybe Jarralynne was being just a little paranoid. The fact that she was having these doubts horrified me. The fact that I was in Birmingham, Alabama, and she was all the way on the East Coast paralyzed me. There was nothing that I could do but wait by the phone for the news. As I waited, of course, I prayed that it would be good news.

The events of the days leading up to the scare did not suggest that the weekend would turn out the way that it did. In fact, it seemed that good things were happening for us suddenly. I would be completing my Sports Medicine Fellowship in June, and she was completing her predoctoral internship in August. We had been trying to get pregnant for months. At the same time, we had been looking for the perfect jobs where we could be together and start a family. We had no idea, nor would it have stopped us to know, that the stress of trying to plan our lives could have such an impact on the outcome of things. Even though my wife spent Monday morning through Thursday night in Atlanta and I was in Birmingham throughout the week, that didn't stop us from going about the business of trying to conceive. The timing seemed perfect.

It was fun at first. What am I saying? It was amazing. At first.

In the beginning, we went about it with an almost casual air. After all, getting pregnant was the thing that you avoided in college and even graduate school. So conceiving a baby would simply mean that we would just stop doing the things that we did to prevent a pregnancy. But we found out soon enough that we were wrong. Getting pregnant was not as easy as picking a perfect month that fit with our life schedule. If we ever believed in God before, it was confirmed now that our steps were ordered in ways that we couldn't plan. I could study harder in medical school and get good grades. I could be more disciplined in my recreational spending and watch my account grow. But, there is nothing that a person can do that can ensure that they will certainly conceive on any given month. I can say this 'cause we tried. Boy, did we try.

As the months dragged on, the babymaking mood shifted from fun to strategy sessions. The nature of our medicine cabinet changed from vitamins and cold remedies to a whole different genre of drugstore commodities. My wife initially started buying pregnancy tests in single packages. Then she would get the kit that came two in a box. Later, she would go online and buy lab strips that had as many pregnancy tests in it as she cared to buy for $2.50 a test. She started temping and charting and planning, every month. You could tell where she was in the cycle because in the beginning there was hope, in the middle there was doubt, and by the end when the test showed only one lonely line, there was despair.

It was hard on my wife; she believed that it had to be something that she had done in the past that was keeping her from getting pregnant. And we were, after all, African American—there are very few stories about Black women and their inability to conceive. She was sad, and I was at a loss. As a physician, I was tormented by not being able to help my wife. I tried to be as helpful as possible, but even I didn't know what to do. I pulled down medical schoolbooks at her requests. I read everything that I could, but still there was no baby. I entered the profession of medicine so that I could help people. The sad irony here was that I couldn't help my wife or, for that matter, myself.

Then after months of trying to conceive, my wife really got aggressive. She joined an Internet message board of other women trying to conceive. She found some resources outside my medical journals that helped her to put an almost boot-camp tempo to our babymaking attempts. I had no problem with going along for the ride. If it required more on this day, less on this day, every other day and skip Sundays, I didn't mind. I just did it. I endured the highs and the lows with her, month after month. I made her promise that if the test was negative she wouldn't cry. She broke that promise often. Because of that, we made a pact that she would never test unless I was with her. Well, that was one promise that she broke that I didn't mind. One night she called me hysterical from Atlanta to tell me that at last, we had done it. I was going to be a father!

We were so happy that we didn't wait the politically correct twelve weeks or so to tell. We told everyone. The thought that something could go wrong didn't cross our minds. It had taken us so long to conceive this child, everything would be fine, we just knew it. My wife started to redirect our energy to raising a baby. This meant some major changes for her career. At the time, she had been interviewing for her dream job. She was great at managing people, and she was in the final stages of interviewing with a company that promised more money than she'd ever made in her life and the opportunity to have an impact on people all over the world. I was surprised, but not disappointed when she called me from New York City and told me that she had declined to go further in the interview process. She flew into New York to meet the potential employers. She told them that it was the perfect career for her, but not the perfect time. My wife asked me to call UC Berkeley on the three-way in order for her to accept an offer as a post-doctoral fellow in their counseling center. Her reason? Berkeley would be a perfect place to walk around pregnant.

Things were coming together for us in ways that we couldn't have imag-ined. I accepted a job doing Sports Medicine in the Bay Area in California, where I was raised. My parents were still there, and all our closest friends lived near by. By accepting the Berkeley position, it seemed that we had everything figured out and all we had to do was wait on the baby to come and make our family complete. Our joy in the perfect planning was short-lived when she miscarried on Easter Sunday. This was a "Gift of the Magi" turn of events, since less than forty-eight hours had passed since she had de-clined her dream job to take care of a baby that would no longer be coming two days before Christmas.

My wife was alone when the physician in the ER told her that she didn't hear a heartbeat. There was no cell phone signal in the ER room, and of course my wife cried, alone. She was in a city with one of my best friends from medical school and her best friend since junior high school, but I was all the way in Birmingham. I was originally scheduled to meet her in New York. However, a canceled flight and a series of delays due to an unexpected storm made it impossible for me to get to her in a reasonable amount of time. It had been my wife's idea that she fly home. She was alone when she flew from Hartford to Atlanta AMA (Against Medical Advice). The physi-cian said she didn't support my wife's decision to travel so soon, but she would have done the same personally.

My wife was alone as she cried through every leg of the trip, the depar-ture from Hartford, the stopover in Cincinnati, and the arrival in Atlanta. I was beside myself as I rushed to meet her. When we saw each other, we hugged, we cried, and then we fell on the bed in depressed exhaustion. The next day, we were still lying in the same position, fully clothed: coat, shoes, and all. I felt so bad that I wasn't there when she got the news. It was liter-ally an act of God that had kept my plane grounded in the first place. That fact caused both my wife and me to wonder and then worry what God had planned for us. If the plans didn't include a child, at that point, we didn't want to hear about it.

In the months following, my wife went to calculating: Maybe there was something she did wrong. Maybe she ate the wrong thing, flew on one too many flights, or forgot a prayer. She went back to her planning with a maddened passion. I recognized that she had gone too far into planning when she spent a whole Saturday alone, sitting in a sea of temping charts, trying to find out the perfect day to try to have a baby. She was horrified to learn that she had read her charts wrong and that she spent a potential ovulation day speculating on charts instead of spending time with me. At that point, she decided to switch her strategy altogether. Since we were past the time that it takes the "average" couple to conceive, she scheduled an appointment with an infertility specialist for several months into the future. Obviously what my wife knew about making babies wasn't enough for her. Now, we were calling in the experts.

I decided that the only thing left for us to do was relax until the appointment in October. I invited my wife to live life with me, in the meantime. She accompanied me on every road trip that I took; preparticipation physicals with the Cincinnati Reds at their training camp in Florida gave us a chance to slip away to Disney World. Spring training for the Seattle Mariners allowed us more time in Florida. We lived it up on South Beach in Miami. In a moment that seemed like old times, she took me up on a dare and spent the whole evening doing the South Beach "thing" in nothing but a bikini top and jeans. Definitely, not what she'd plan to do when or if she got pregnant. So she decided to enjoy it now. When the NFL called me to check out their players overseas, Jarralynne spent ten days traipsing around three different European countries with me. Of course, there was the visit to Amsterdam's red light district. Not a place that we'd be planning family excursions to in the future. It was the time of our lives, and it was fun. Fun was something that we hadn't enjoyed in a long time. I couldn't believe it— I had my wife back, and she was happy to be back. Instead of focusing on what we didn't have, we took joy in the blessings that were staring us in the face every day. To keep that spirit of fun going, I tempted my wife to one last challenge. I dared her to join me in some good old-fashioned pre-baby making fun, every night that the 2000 Olympics was on. She was all in until the tenth night when she finally yelled uncle.

As a physician, you go into the health profession to help heal people. We are problem solvers who help to make some people's worst nightmares fade and greatest dreams come true. Well, in the case of trying to conceive, I had to recognize that I'm only human and that I can do my best, but it's the powers that be that makes the final decision on our fate. So, I would never say that it was my fault that our first pregnancy ended prematurely. I also can't take credit for the fact that after my "Olympic marathon" suggestion, my wife got another positive pregnancy test. She found out that she was pregnant on the day her infertility appointment was scheduled. They say when man plans, God laughs. This time, when God laughed, he let us in on the joke. We are grateful in a way that we know we couldn't have been had we not had this experience. So now, when we laugh, we share that laughter with others, especially our new best friend, a boy that my wife insisted on naming Robert E. Agee III.

Dr. Robert Agee Jr. lives with his wife in the San Francisco Bay Area where he is a sports medicine physician at Kaiser Permanente. He has also worked as a medical consultant to NFL Europe and is a team physician for UC Berkeley. Robert's favorite job is being a dad, and his favorite day is Monday, when he takes off from work to be with his toddler son, Trey. Robert and his wife are expecting their second child.

Lessons from a Sunset
Robin D. G. Kelley

"**B**lack men love they mamas!"

Looking from the outside in, one might find that statement inconceivable in a culture where playing the dozens was as common as breathing. But the mamas of our verbal duels were usually absurd inventions, cartoon characters able to leap tall buildings or kill entire neighborhoods with their body odor. But if your mama was fat, ugly, poor, or strange in some way, the line between inventive humor and straight-up slander was not always so clear. Fights erupt only when your opponent veers a little too close to home.

My mother was an exception. Barring the chemically dependent, mine was clearly the "weirdest" mama in the neighborhood, and yet no one talked about her. Whether it was the Harlem of my early childhood or the ghetto-fabulous Southern California community of my teenage years, no kid ever snapped on my actual mama. When they did turn their verbal skills on me, my boys would barely say "your" (pronounced variously *yo'*, *ya'*, *yer'*) and before the word *mama*, as if somehow dropping the pronoun would render their jabs anonymous. We all tacitly agreed that my mama had nothing to do with the joke.

Why was she spared? First of all, my mom was superfine, especially in light of the aesthetic criteria of the day. Small framed and demure with light brown skin and long, wild hair that delicately framed a stunningly beautiful, cherubic face, she was constantly propositioned by young and old alike. Even a couple of my partners were foolish enough to hit on her. All comers went down in flames, not because my mom possessed a sharp tongue or a cold stare. On the contrary, she had the kindest, sweetest disposition imaginable. She exuded a beatific aura, a strangely divine light that chased away carnal thoughts and convinced those who stood before her that they were in the presence of a wise spirit.

Which brings me to the second reason why she escaped the underworld of the dozens: She was culturally illegible to most folk in the 'hood. She never conformed to the "Black mama" image that dominates the media—from Esther Rolle in *Good Times* to Big Mama of the film *Soul Food*. In fact, we never called her *Mama*. The soft-spoken young woman we called Mom or Mommy didn't drink, smoke, curse, say things like "Lawd Jesus" or "Hallelujah," or cook chitlins, greens in fatback, or gumbo, for that matter. A vegetarian for most of her life, she chanted and played the harmonium (a hand pumped miniature organ), spoke quietly with textbook diction, practiced meditation and yoga, wore her hair like Chaka Khan before she even came on the scene, burned incense in our tiny Harlem apartment, sometimes walked the streets barefoot, and when she could afford it, preferred to cook Indian. The resident flower child of 157th and Amsterdam, she did share one thing in common with the other mothers on our block: she was poor and single.

Born Audin Modah Reid on the island of Jamaica, she was raised by her single mother, Carmen Rodriguez, until she was sent north to live with an aunt and uncle in Queens, New York. Relatives remember her as a voracious reader, a profound thinker, and a relentless dreamer with incredible facility with a paintbrush and molding clay. Had my mother been a young White boy and had this not been the 1950s, she would have skipped a grade or two. Instead, this Jamaican immigrant—whose cruel classmates beat the patois out of her—was put back two grades. Being seventeen years old in the tenth grade was a little too much for her; she eventually dropped out of school and joined most of the other young West Indian women in the labor force.

She never ceased being an intellectual, however. My earliest memories of my mom are of her reading, writing, drawing, and creating in any medium available. My sister and I used to study her clay bust of Dr. Martin Luther King Jr., and we dug the way she repaired and painted our old toys and made furniture out of found objects. Our house overflowed with books—Grolier Encyclopedias, Time-Life science books, lots of literature and history. Before I could read well, I used to stare at *Harlem on My Mind* (from the photo exhibition of the same name) and Simone de Beauvoir's *The Second Sex*—titillated, of course, by the title and the cover illustration of a nude woman sitting on the edge of a bed, posed like Rodin's *Thinker*.

More than anything, spiritual matters happened to be my mother's main preoccupation. She might have owned miscellaneous texts about Buddhism, Taoism, and Hinduism, but I specifically remember seeing works by Paramahansa Yogananda, the founder of Self-Realization Fellowship (SRF). As a longtime (and continuing) member of SRF, my mother changed her name to Ananda Sattwa, studied Indian religions, and drew on these teachings to provide her children with important life lessons. She read the Bhaghavad Gita (sort of a Hindu version of the Bible or the Qur'an) and told us about figures like Shiva—the god who is half-man, half-woman. She explained that God was neither male nor female but a force within all living things. When I was seven, she taught my sister and me about sex, not about sin or fornication. Sex was a beautiful thing, she explained, an expression of love and equality, where two people—any people—communicate their love with their bodies and create a living art. She showed us how to meditate, to embrace the comfort of darkness and silence, to see the inner world through our Third Eye.

She taught us to help any living creature who needs it, even if that means giving up our last piece of bread. Strange, needy people always passed through our house, occasionally staying for what felt like long stretches of time. (She once helped me bring home a New York City pigeon with a broken leg in a failed effort to nurse her back to health!) She taught us to always stand apart from the crowd and befriend the misfits, to embrace the kids who stuttered, smelled bad, or had holes in their clothes. She showed us that the marvelous was free—in the patterns of a stray bird feather, in a Hudson River sunset, in the view from our fire escape, in the stories she told us or the way she sang Gershwin's "Summertime," in a curbside rainbow created by the alchemy of motor oil and water from an open hydrant.

My mom constantly practiced what she preached, and I wasn't always mature enough to understand her. I felt embarrassed by her big poncho and flower child sandals, the Nehru suit she once bought for me, or the way she would put her feet in public fountains. I'll never forget the day she got down on her hands and knees in the Metropolitan Museum so she could pray to Buddha. My sister and I were so ashamed that we momentarily considered running away. But as I grew older, I began to understand what my mother was trying to do. She wanted to raise free spirits, revolutionaries who understood that freedom is not what the majority thinks. She wanted to raise feminists, critics of patriarchy who believe gender and sexual relations can be reconstructed. She wanted to raise poets, spiritual surrealists who can see the poetic and prophetic in the richness of our daily lives. She wanted to show us a more expansive, fluid, "cosmos-politan" definition of blackness, to teach us that we are not merely inheritors of a culture but its makers, as well.

I am who I am because of my mother. She did not need a high school diploma or a husband or a switch to raise a black male intellectual committed to feminism, social justice, poetry, love, and something even more visionary than socialism. She introduced me to more profound ideas than all my professors and comrades combined. Most important, she taught me how to be a man by rejecting manhood altogether. She taught me that I did not have to model myself after my father or any man, for the beauty of humanity is in its potential for transformation, in its ability to transcend the categories that define and constrict us. We don't need to return to some old, traditional ideas about community, family, or masculinity when we possess the imagination to create new ideas, new ways of living. And as my mom continues to show me, our well of ideas should be the entire planet, if not the cosmos itself.

If my childhood homies ever did decide my mom was fair game and dropped that old school snap, "You ain't the man yo' mama was," I know exactly what my comeback would be: "You're right, but I'm damn sure trying."

Robin D. G. Kelley *is Professor of History at NYU and author of several books, most recently* Yo' Mama's DisFunktional!: Fighting the Culture Wars in Urban America *(1997). His mother, Ananda Sattwa, recently completed her bachelor's degree in Ethnic Studies from UC Berkeley and is working toward a Ph.D. in Native American religions.*

Raising Ladies
Eugene K. Myrick

I must admit I was a little naïve when I became the single parent of my twin daughters. I honestly thought, "How hard could this be?" My mom raised three sons by herself. My grandmother raised my aunts and uncles by herself and all my friends growing up came from single-parent homes. All these homes were headed by women. I don't think I'm a chauvinist, but I honestly believed that if a woman can head a household, it shouldn't be too hard for a man to do the same.

I soon learned that by being a single parent, your day starts with a list of things that you didn't have time to do the day before. On one particular Friday the thirteenth, my problems were a lot more serious than forgetting to pay the phone bill. As I stated earlier, I have twin daughters (Ayana and Zhada), one of whom (Zhada) is having a serious battle with asthma. On Wednesday, her teacher told me that she was sneezing a lot so I may want to have her checked out. When we arrived home, I immediately put my ear to Zhada's back, to see if she was wheezing. Without a stethoscope, I could hear the difficulty in her breathing. I hooked her up to the nebulizer, gave her the breathing treatment, and prayed that she would get better. I ended up giving her another breathing treatment before the night was over. On Thursday, Zhada awoke smiling and very cheerful. I thought she would be okay. But that is one of those cruel tricks that asthma plays on little children. Thursday evening, I again had to hook Zhada up to the nebulizer. I also had to increase from two to four treatments throughout the night. I again prayed that she would be okay. But the next morning, Zhada arose and said, "Daddy, I don't feel too good."

I immediately wanted to take my child to the doctor, but today was Friday. *"So what?"* you may say. The problem is, I am a New York City schoolteacher, and it's a sin for a teacher to continuously take off on a Friday or Monday. The Board of Education views this as "extending the weekend."

In order for you to fully understand my dilemma, I have to take you back one month. It was a Friday, and I waited until after school to carry Zhada to the hospital. That night, she had to be placed in the intensive care unit. We spent the weekend in the hospital. I felt bad because I wondered if it was my fault that she went to intensive care because I waited to bring her to the hospital. That Sunday evening when they released my daughter, they told me to have her in the clinic for a follow-up in the morning. I didn't care what day it was. I had to get my child to her appointment. I did. So, I missed work that Monday.

Wouldn't you know it, by the time the very next Friday came, Ayana, who hardly ever gets sick, was running a fever. I tried to call my mother, my brother, and my aunt to see if someone could sit with Ayana while I went to work. They are all usually very reliable, but on this particular Friday, no one was able to do it. I continued to try to get my sick daughter ready for school as she coughed, cried, and sneezed. Finally, I decided to take Ayana to the doctor.

That following Monday when I arrived to work, my time card wasn't in its normal slot. I went to the secretary, and she explained to me that she moved my card because the principal wanted to see me. I honestly began to think that maybe my boss wanted to speak to me concerning some of the problems I was having with my special education class, such as the student who cursed throughout class or the student who scratched my arm as I tried to prevent him from stomping on another kid. Maybe she wanted to speak to me about the student in my class who spit on a parent from the PTA. I then convinced myself that she wanted to speak to me about the student who told Ms. Grandison to "Suck his dick" and called her a "Black bitch."

When I walked into the principal's office, she asked me to take a seat. She then handed me a sheet of paper with three dates on it and walked over to a calendar. She called out the dates as I looked at them on the paper. Monday, October 18, and Friday, October 22, and a Monday that I missed back in September. She went on to give me the speech about extending the weekends. Though I heard her talking, I couldn't believe that with all that was going on in my classroom, I was being reprimanded for missing certain days of the week. I tried to explain that I had doctors' notes for the days that I took my daughters to the clinic and that I still had a few sick days in the bank. My principal continued to tell me that my sick days were to be used for me and anything else would be considered personal days, which had to be approved by her in advance. She continued to talk, and I sat there and accepted all that she had to say.

Now to bring us back to this Friday the thirteenth. I had all this on my mind as I watched Zhada attempt to eat the chicken noodle soup that I prepared for her breakfast. Ayana on the other hand, had finished eating her cereal, and she was ready to go. Today was the day that the girls were supposed to plant flowers in the success garden at school. When I told Ayana that we may have take Zhada to the hospital, she immediately burst into tears. Now what was I going to do? After a moment of thought, I called my mother, who said she could come over and sit with Zhada and give her the necessary breathing treatments that she needed and if need be, she would take her to the doctor. I immediately told Ayana the good news, and she ran over to her sister and said that she was going to plant a flower for her, too. I smiled as I watched my two ladies together.

My conscience started eating me up before I could walk out the door. For the entire workday, I worried about my little girl. On my lunch break, I ran home, and on my preparation period, I called home to make sure Zhada was okay. I then went by Ayana's classroom just to sneak a peek in on her. By the time Ayana and I arrived home, Zhada was up and about. Though she smiled and wanted to play with her sister, she still looked a little weak. I decided to take my child to the hospital. When we arrived at the hospital triage, they immediately took Zhada in and began administering medication. After three and a half hours of treatment in the emergency room, my daughter's oxygen level did not increase to the norm. The doctor informed me to be prepared to spend the night in the hospital.

At about 3:00 A.M., I looked over at Zhada, who was finally sleeping peacefully. I wondered if she would ever outgrow her asthma. I thought about Ayana, who was at home with my mother and wondered if she felt lonely. I thought about my phone bill and the cable bill that I did not have a chance to pay. I also thought about the payment on my student loan, which I have yet to get the money order for. I also wondered what was going to happen at work if my child wasn't released by Sunday or if I had to bring her back for an appointment on Monday.

As all this weighed heavy on my mind, I had to stop and say a prayer. Not just a prayer for me, but a prayer for all the single parents in the world, who are in situations similar to mine. I then said a special prayer for my mother, my grandmother, and for all my friends' mothers, who were single parents, as well. Being a man, you try to stay strong and pretend as if nothing can bother you. But at this particular moment, I felt tired, afraid, and extremely lonely. My hat goes off to the millions of strong women in this world who have and continue to raise children on their own.

Eugene K. Myrick *graduated from Thomas Jefferson High School in Brooklyn, New York. He obtained his bachelor of arts degree from Shaw University in Raleigh, North Carolina. After teaching at P.S. 174 in Brooklyn for seven years, he is currently shopping a script as well as a book.*

Can a Woman Raise a Man?

Robert Roots

When I was about twelve years old, my uncle Genghis, my father's brother, told my mother that a woman couldn't raise a man. My mother, who was divorced and had been raising four children (two boys and two girls), on her own for almost ten years in the Astoria Housing Projects in Queens, New York, with barely enough money to buy herself clothes was offended and hurt by that remark. My mother was so offended, she must have expressed her disagreement with that statement at least a dozen times in the years that followed.

Today I am thirty-five, and my mother passed away eight years ago at the age of fifty. Just like mom, I, too, have four children: three sons, Robert, Michael, and Emmanuel, and a daughter, Janara. As my boys grow older, I am conscious of making sure that I show them what is expected of a "man" and what they should expect from themselves. At the same time, I am teaching my daughter how a man should treat and respect her in addition to how she should treat and respect a man.

But the remark that had vexed my mother had also nagged at me over the years. Can a woman raise a man? If something were to happen to me, and my wife were forced to raise our sons by herself, could she teach them how to become men, or would they, as my uncle said, just be good sons but not "men." Without a doubt, there are differences in the ways men and women think, act, react, and communicate. So the next question is, having been raised by a woman, am I just a "good son" or am I a "man"? Given that, am I even capable of raising a "man"?

Having been married for more than thirteen years and being a former police officer, consultant, and entrepreneur and having served as a role model for a few school- and community-based programs, I do know this: Male and female children do need positive male role models. There is something that a "man" brings to the table that's different from a woman's contributions. Without clear male/female role distinction in a relationship, both parties experience frustration and the entire relationship suffers.

Though men and women are different, their differences complement one another and help relationships to grow. In fact, a woman's nature helps a man to become a better man, and a man's nature helps a woman to become a better woman. This is the divine design of nature, which maintains balance. But when one of the parties—in this case the male—is not performing his or her role, then the relationship is off balance.

Understanding the necessity for balance in a relationship, we must accept the idea that there must be a difference between the roles of men and women. But where does a man learn how to truly be a man, if he has never had a man to learn from? It cannot come from a woman. She can only teach from her perspective just as a man cannot teach a girl how to become a woman. Men and women are socialized differently, and this is apparent by observing children in the playground or by listening to the conversations of men and women when they are either segregated or together. Both sexes act and react very differently.

We emulate most of what we see and some of what we are taught. Because of this, even at my age, I have sought out older men to learn from. These men reflect the kind of male leadership that I seek to exhibit for my family. Their families have a reverence and respect for them of confidence, faith, and a sense of security. When I asked these men about their exceptional leadership skills they all said they had strong male role models when growing up. They observed the respectful interaction between a man and a woman, a father and child, and the man with the rest of the world. This experience or education gave them a foundation and structure by which to build their lives.

The ability for a woman to have the strength to care for a family in the absence of a man is incredible and worthy of the highest respect and admiration. Unfortunately, these women are the backbone of Black society in America when it should be men. The proliferation of single-parent households, of men not taking responsibility for their families and not stepping in to help women in need is causing role confusion, and in my opinion, is one of the main causes for the current crisis and the destruction of Black families.

Black males are beginning to look and act more like their mothers. They have gone from no earring to two earrings. And more women are saying they don't need a man to raise a child, that they can do it alone. The ones who are suffering are the children. And when the children suffer from this kind of dysfunctional thinking, society as a whole feels the consequences. If more responsible men were present in the homes, the argument for the necessity of both men and women to work together to raise a family would be evident, and we would have fewer dysfunctional families. What we are developing are strong women and weak men.

This female domination and male submissiveness in Black relationships is cited as a reason for Black men and women to purposely date outside their race. Some men have said that White women are more submissive and that Black women are overbearing and controlling. Whereas some Black women state that Black men try to be in control and they aren't letting any man control them. Because they see White men as less threatening and easier to control, they pursue White instead. These excuses should not be a prime reason for dating someone of any race. Relationships should first be about love, but when a race of people lack a clear understanding of what their roles are in a relationship, they are left confused.

This is not a new phenomenon; the Black family in America has purposely been separated and fragmented since the days of slavery. Men were stripped of their manhood, and women were forced to raise the children and act as the mouthpiece or voice for the family. After hundreds of years of being stripped of his role, the Black male has lost his role model. And in the workplace, the Black male has been forced to shut up and be submissive or lose his job. So he takes the abuse on the job in order to keep his paycheck and then vents at home furthering the struggle of having a productive respectful relationship. Like the series *Good Times*, with James Evans arguing at home about low pay, no opportunities, and no respect.

Can a woman raise a man? And am I capable of raising my sons to be men? The answer is no and yes respectively. No, a woman cannot raise a man. As much as she tries, a woman is still a woman. It is up to the father to assume his role and raise his son to be a man. And when the father is not around or is failing to show leadership, then other men in the family need to be men and act as role models. If I hadn't identified with my shortcomings sooner, then I would have failed to correct my actions and would have done an injustice to both my wife and children. Acknowledging the truth that my mother, who did an excellent job of providing for and raising her children, was still only a mother and not a mother and a father, I sought out male role models to emulate and learn from.

Thank you to my mother, Bernadette Gonzales, and countless other women for doing their best to play two roles, mom and dad. Just like a portrait of the company founder is displayed in corporate boardrooms, a photograph of these courageous and committed women should hang in the home of every child and grandchild to show respect for their dedication, love, service, and planning; for without these women, the family would have filed bankruptcy and shut down.

So can a woman raise a man? No—and she shouldn't have to, every man should take responsibility for sowing a seed in every male child's life starting today!

Robert Roots, *author of* Prepare for the Wolf, Success Secrets from *The Three Little Pigs, is a national and international motivational speaker, business consultant, and success coach. For more information, go to www.robertroots.com.*

New Fatherhood
Billy Johnson Jr.

I can hear Ebony moaning through the door, and I'm trying my best not to panic. The nurse just told me that I can't come into the delivery room until after the babies are born. Ebony had a reaction to the anesthesia, and they had to put her under, and needed to deliver the babies as soon as possible. They didn't think it would be a good idea for me to be in the room.

But I can hear her crying. My girl. My best friend. My wife. I'm her coach. I keep her calm. And I can do nothing to help ease the pain. I'm more scared than I've ever been in my life. Every negative thought crosses my mind.

What if she doesn't make it?

What if something happens to one of the babies?

Lord, please don't give me these babies without my wife.

I'm becoming irrational as I pace alongside of the delivery room trying my best to eavesdrop on the delivery room chatter. But the only thing audible is Ebony's obvious signs of discomfort.

It's a good thing that I'm by myself in the long, drab, white hallway that reminds me of the basement scene in *The Shining* because I can't turn to anyone for comfort. There's no one to acknowledge my fears.

The negative thoughts begin to come so fast that I realize that they will consume me if I let them, and I remember that Ebony wasn't supposed to make it this far—to thirty-six weeks.

When the doctor confirmed her pregnancy at eight weeks, he took an ultrasound and said that he didn't see an egg. He said that the egg could be in her fallopian tube, which would mean that the pregnancy would need to be terminated.

At ten weeks, he told us that not only was the egg comfortably nested in the wall of her uterus, there were two eggs. But one baby was twice as large as the other, and that the smaller baby in similar cases usually doesn't make it.

Ebony's morning sickness—around-the-clock sickness, rather—turned out to be a condition called hyperemesiss that got so intense between the twelfth and seventeeth weeks that she was prescribed medication and received an order to stop working until nausea, heat flashes, dizziness, and weakness subsided.

While the average mother's morning sickness subsides at sixteen weeks, Ebony's continued. Baby A was still considerably smaller than Baby B, and at twenty weeks, the doctor referred Ebony to a physician who specializes in complicated pregnancies.

There we learned that the babies were dangerously small, significantly smaller than the fiftieth percentile mark for babies at their maturation. Baby A, at some points, dropped into the lowest fifth percentile.

At twenty-five weeks, the specialist strongly suggested that Ebony stop working. He put her on moderate bed rest for two weeks, but because he was still concerned about the size of the babies, he then put her on complete bed rest, forbidding her from sitting at the computer, doing laundry, and excessive walking. He limited her to the refrigerator and rest room. He told her to lie on her side and to rest. He said the growth of the babies depended on her rest, not the amount of food she ate.

By twenty-eight weeks, we had three doctor's appointments a week. Two with the specialist. One with her regular OB-GYN. The specialist told us that if the size of the babies lagged any further, he would have Ebony deliver the same day, even though the babies were under two pounds.

But after being placed on complete bed rest and regular monitoring from the doctors, the babies began to approach the fiftieth percentile mark. One week, Baby A would be trailing behind Baby B, and the next week, they would be close to the same size.

At thirty-four weeks, exactly two weeks ago from today, both doctors were ecstatic. The specialist told Ebony that most women with her same circumstances delivered between the thirtieth and thirty-second week. She had reached a milestone. Her progress was miraculous, and she was just about "out of the woods." I told him that everyone in the world had been praying for us. He told me that the prayers had worked.

The OB-GYN was just as happy. He told Ebony that it was a blessing. And that if she could reach thirty-five weeks, the babies would be fully mature, and able to survive outside of the womb without the need of being in an incubator. I was prouder on this day, than on the day Ebony tricked me into stumbling across the pregnancy test with the two pink lines.

It was the first time that I wasn't as scared. That I felt like my babies were going to be okay. It didn't matter that Baby B was breach, and that a cesarian delivery was likely needed. Immediately after the doctor's appointments, I called Ebony's grandparents, who live sixty miles away, to tell them the good news.

And yesterday, November 27, after the OB-GYN confirmed that Baby

B was still breach, he called the hospital to schedule Ebony's cesarian for December 5. But the office had closed for the day. It was after five on Thanksgiving Eve. So he told Ebony that he'd schedule the delivery later.

As Ebony and I walked out of the doctor's office, we looked at each other and exchanged faint smiles. We didn't want to deliver the babies by appointment. We wanted to experience labor. To wake up in the middle of the night. Fumble to get our bags together. Rush to the hospital. Be admitted to emergency, and wait sixteen hours—the normal length of labor for first-time mothers—for our babies to come. But we didn't say anything. We dare not be ungrateful to God for bringing us this far.

But at 4 A.M. this morning—Thanksgiving—Ebony's contractions wake her up. There is some pain, but it is not excruciating. The contractions are three to six minutes apart. After two hours, Ebony takes a bath to see if they will stop, and they don't. At 7 A.M., I call her mother, a nurse, to get her advice. She says to call the doctor.

When I call the doctor's message service, I leave a detailed message explaining all the activities. He calls back in ten minutes, and does not ask any questions.

Take her to the hospital immediately.

Ebony and I have butterflies. I scramble to get all our bags together, while trying to videotape as much of the experience as possible. I call all our parents and tell them that this could be it.

And as soon as the doctor examines Ebony and notes that she has dilated two centimeters, he orders her to deliver immediately.

We arrive at at the hospital at 8 A.M, and at 9, they are handing me my scrubs, telling me to get ready.

Though the anesthesiologist tells us that Ebony will be awake during the delivery, and I will be by her side videotaping—just as Ebony has witnessed other mothers on TLC—the nurse now tells me that I can't come into the room just yet because there are complications, and they have put Ebony under.

The fear on my face is so apparent that the nurse gives me a hug and tells me that everything's going to be all right. The only words that come out are, "But I love her so much."

The thought of Ebony enduring any more pain is killing me. I can't do a thing. I can hear her crying and moaning through the door, and my only recourse is what has carried us to this point.

The Trinity Broadcast Network should have been there to tape this. I've never had a praise and worship session outside of the privacy of church and home. But I begin to counteract the negative thoughts with praise.

As I pace alongside of the delivery room, I extend my hands toward the walls, and thank God for blessing us with two babies. For bringing us to thirty-six weeks. For making Ebony strong. And for taking control of the delivery.

Within ten minutes, I hear a baby cry, and I instantly shed a tear. And I keep praising God. I can still hear Ebony wailing, and I pray that God eases her pain.

Then I hear a woman's voice say, "Baby B is a girl." And I laugh, hard. I am not scared anymore. I cannot believe that the big baby, the baby who ate most of the food, that was breach, that had Baby A pinned in a corner for the duration of the pregnancy was a girl.

She is no doubt her mother's child.

The delivery room door opens. And the nurse motions for me to come into the room. I follow immediately. I forget about my camcorder and digital camera. They lie under the bench in the hallway.

I enter the room, seemingly in slow motion. Ebony is hysterical. She is murmuring something inaudible. The babies are crying. Three people attend to each baby. The nurse directs me to a kicking, bronze-colored baby. But I can tell that the baby is okay. I pull away and go to Ebony's side.

Tears are running down her face, and she looks more scared than I've ever seen her look. I rest my cheek against hers and tell her that it is okay. I begin to pray for her, thanking God for this miracle, and for intervening to ease Ebony's discomfort. I tell her that we had a boy and a girl.

As she continued to weep, her mumbling becomes more clear. She is not in any physical pain.

I haven't seen them.

I haven't seen them.

I haven't seen them.

I tell the staff that she needs to see the babies.

They bring our son, Reese Alexander, over first. When Ebony sees his squirming, bronze body, that resembles her own, she calms down a bit.

Where's the girl?

Let me see the girl.

When they bring Bailey Jonee, she is amazingly calm. Her eyes are wide open, and she looks directly into Ebony's eyes. Bailey is at peace, and Ebony's demeanor changes immediately.

I start to cry.

The anesthesiologist explains that Ebony had a reaction to the epidural, and told me to go get my cameras.

Reese was born at 10:05 A.M., and weighed four pounds five ounces. Bailey was born at 10:07 and weighed four pounds twelve ounces.

Today was the first Thanksgiving that I didn't even think about the turkey, dressing, candied yams with marshmallows, cranberry sauce, Ma Dear's homemade bread, macaroni and cheese, ham, and peach cobbler.

But it is clearly the most meaningful Thanksgiving, because I've never had more to be thankful for.

Billy Johnson Jr. is a Los Angeles–based editor for Yahoo! subsidiary Launch.com. His work has appeared in Entertainment Weekly, Hollywood Reporter, Vibe, *and* The Source. *His e-mail address is BJhnsnJr@aol.com.*

The Delicate Situation

Mel Jackson

At an early age I knew that I had a drive to succeed. I was on a mission to accomplish the goals I set forth. I use to utilize the excuse that I did not have enough time for love. I didn't understand women and what I thought were emotional outbursts. One of my past girlfriends use to argue with me all the time and one day just shouted, "Are you fucking the studio?" She acted like my work was my woman. Now at thirty-two years of age, I understand that a woman needs to spend quality time with me. For a long time I focused on making money. I did not have any relationships for six or seven years. I actually grew quicker professionally than personally because I never opened up that side of me. I sacrificed my need for affection to business. In order to temper it, I had a lot of satellite women. I literally had one for all different aspects of my life. There were ones I could talk about the Bible with, play with, smoke and drink with, hang out and philosophize with.

Sometimes I just wanted to smell a woman's skin. I would set up bowling dates with women who were just friends. I would then get hugs without the commitment a relationship would bring. Maybe if I had a woman's point of view, I would have gotten to this point in my life quicker. As I achieved my goals, at the end of the day I could not forget what was really important to me. I knew that it was family, love, and a significant partnership, but what was stopping me?

I was in a situation where I needed to do some real serious soul searching. I had a wonderful friendship with a woman who I knew was just amazing. It came to the point that I did not want to get intimate with her because I didn't want to lose her friendship. I asked myself, What could be better than having someone who you could have a friendship with and make love to? Sharing my life became exciting. I began to see her argument that she really was an asset to me. It was different from talking to my guy friends and keeping up with my satellite girlfriends. I found that there was no need for me to keep up those satellite relationships, because she filled up those needs.

It was hard at first to come to terms with it because when you begin to love an articulate, independent new-millennium woman, you deal with the emotion of love and all those experiences and stereotypes that make you who you are. Love is a spiritual thing, and it takes you to another level. I started really examining the roles that men and women play. I am not a Bible thumper, but the Bible has wisdom. In a passage in the Bible, it clearly talks about a woman and a man being a team.

I had issues with sharing finances. My grandfather never spoke to my grandmother about finances. My granddad was the only male figure that I saw on a consistent basis. Growing up in a single-parent home, it caused a problem. Not having a father figure really affected the relationships I had with women. I wanted more, and although a challenge for me, I decided that marriage would be the very best thing for us.

I had an opportunity to share some of my insights with a group of women at an event and didn't want to get on a soapbox, but I did anyway.

> *It is a struggle just getting beyond the racial thing, let alone getting beyond the man-and-woman thing. It touched me a couple years ago; I was with my fiancée's sister, and I watched the whole process a woman makes as far as sacrifices. I am an actor. I played the villain in the movie* Soul Food *and the new roommate on* Living Single. *I feel humble to speak with you today. When I told my grandmother that I was speaking here today, she gave me some advice, "Don't wear cheap cologne and don't say anything stupid." There is no question that women have been climbing to positions in the presidential cabinet, not to mention Oprah and the numerous women entreprenuers hanging a shingle and open for business each and every day. If it weren't for women, I would not be here today speaking before you. I met Sharon King on a Chicago bus who then convinced me to come to L.A. and get discovered. It was Robin Reed Humes who gave me my first significant role on television. It was Yvette Lee Bowser who picked me out of three hundred people to be on a television show. Tracy Edmonds convinced Baby Face to put me in their first film* Soul Food. *It was Marguerite G. Jackson who taught me values, faith, and she also gave me life.*

Marguerite Jackson was my *mama*, CEO, and mother. What I did learn from my mother was determination. My mother had a novelty store, managed political campaigns, and she taught me how to speed-read. When she was in college, I would crawl into bed with her while she read her textbooks. It became ingrained in me. Which brings me to a very important point: While women of color are excelling in all fields of business, are we losing our wives and mothers at home?

Women have put off having children until they achieve their goals in the boardroom. That is making me nervous. If my mother thought that way, I would not be here. Men do believe that they are the bosses—but that's not entirely true. If we really understand the plan God laid out, we should work as a team and not one person being the boss. A man has certain responsibilities, but they are still equal as partners. Brothers need to understand that being a man means taking responsibility for your actions until God can grace you with the true power of love and family. As an actor, director, and producer, I am committed to working with brothers who understand how the roles we play on television and film has a huge impact on the lives of the viewers.

I performed on soap plays on radio in Chicago. There was a woman who always had the lead in all the productions. Her name was Carol Hall. Carol was a teacher who motivated me to use the leadership qualities I possessed. To be the best that I could be. A talented woman who never drank or cussed. Carol was pursuing her master's and preparing herself and building a foundation to share her life with the right man. It never happened. Lupus had taken over and she died, but not before she received her master's and they rolled her across the stage in a wheelchair. When I went to the funeral, Carol's mother was the only one sitting in the front row of the funeral home. A place designated for family. Tomorrow was never promised; she was steadily being promoted and moving up the ranks, but never had anyone to share that joy with.

Just remember—as you expand your horizons, amassing power in all fields, I hope that you do not lose sight of the anchor that makes everything make sense: family. Society somehow has trivialized all the big and small miracles. It is the biggest reason we are having a problem with our Black families. True power is the power of love and giving birth to the beautiful Black family.

With no formal training, **Mel Jackson** *was cast as the guy you love to hate, Simuel St. James in the box office hit* Soul Food. *Other films include* Deliver Us from Eva, Dancing in September, *and* Uninvited Guest. *Jackson has graced the small screen as well in such shows as* Living Single, In the House, *and* DAG. *Jackson has found time to start his own production company, Instinct Entertainment. The company's first production,* Carmin's Choice, *won the Showtime Filmmaker's Award.*

Your Soul's Journey

Who can find a virtuous woman? For her price is far above rubies. —Proverbs 31:10

Often we look for perfection in others, hoping that another individual can fulfill our every need. It's an almost romantic idealization, especially when it comes to the roles men play in the lives of the women they know. Whether it is your daughter, friend, sister, wife, mother or colleague, sometimes the roles are not clear and you may be left with the feeling, "Am I enough?"

In our community, the Black community, there is a significant undercurrent and perception of an "us versus them" sentiment among Black men about Black women and vice versa. Are we listening to one another? Is communication a tool that you use or avoid? Do we truly care about what happens to one another? Why and when did showing your emotions to the closest people in your life become something men don't do?

To incorporate any woman effectively in your life, you must do so in a way that protects or enhances her self-esteem. By the same token, you aren't a superhero who can make everything go away with a single bound or Mr. Fix-It, who fixes everything. Your role is to be honest, sincere, loving, and supportive regardless of what life brings. Standing hand in hand during the storm is the best gift you can ever bestow on another human being.

Women must take care of their inner selves to set the stage for the right man to become part of their lives or to maintain the existing relationships. Women must dismiss the need to enable and not blame current or future men for any of the baggage left by others, including the fathers who could not and did not want to be there.

Regardless, if you are a son adoring his mother, father raising a daughter, a man who has chosen a best friend as a woman, or a woman married to the best man in the world, before we truly love someone, we must love everything else about us in order to truly receive love.

Soul Source

A big part of the journey of cohesiveness is giving and forgiving. It empowers reconciliation where estrangement has prevailed. Forgiveness empowers reunion where hostility has prevailed. Forgiveness empowers our acceptance of others where nonacceptance has prevailed even for the women and men who made mistakes that have affected you.

- Are you a good listener?
- What have you learned from the women in your life?
- What women were pivotal in the growth and the development of who you have become?
- Describe the loving relationship that you have with the women in your life.
- What strengths exhibited by a women in your life have inspired you?

CHAPTER 7

THE COLOR OF MONEY

Politics doesn't control the world, money does.
—Andrew Young

Money is a tool utilized to create economic, social, and political power. Sometimes we look at foreign money in awe because it is a depiction of that society's culture, people, and the political climate. You will find currency around the world with the faces of presidents, kings, queens, princes, and the things that are important to the people of that particular nation. It wasn't too long ago that our own American currency depicted what was important to us as a young nation. In the mid- to late nineteenth century, individual states issued currency depicting slaves in cotton fields, smiling with baskets of cotton, sowing and hoeing fields, and various other plantation scenes. Can you imagine working to acquire money that depicts you in a negative light?

The rich, along with the poor, is one of the fastest growing classes in the United States. There is definitely a disparity of wealth in America. How have you perceived money in your own life? Were you raised to believe that the person with all the power won the game of life, or was that person considered evil? Did you witness friends and family members pursuing that one thing that would bring them riches and then witness them never reaching that goal?

Do you believe that money is the final destination on the road to success? For Black men who may subconsciously believe that their ethnicity and skin color have limited them, money seemed to open the door. It is perceived to bring an enormous overflow of promises, possibilities, freedom, and power. The doors were opened wide because they believed and acted as if they deserved it. It is sheer confidence, self-esteem, talents, and an open mind to business that truly open doors for you.

Some Black men put off marriage—buying property, investing, furthering their education, taking vacations, or pursuing their dreams—until they make that right deal or a certain amount of money. In other words they put off *life*, and when things do not go as planned, feelings of failure, resentment, and guilt set in; sometimes immobilizing and preventing them from trying again. Men feel that they have failed us when they try to live up to unrealistic expectations and can't.

Those expectations are often propelled by the media. Madison Avenue marketing departments tell us that the real men are having all the fun—you know, the ones with all the women, lovers, and throngs of friends—are the wealthy. But, are they really having fun? Your perception of what you believe success is, is not always someone else's.

The First, Only, and Few

When money has been attained, if not done with spiritual balance and purpose, enormous trade-offs take place. The law of the universe is that if you place something in a space previously occupied, there will be no room for what was there before. Clearing out space becomes a tremendous burden, especially since we are still part of a generation of "first," "only," and "few"—being the *first* person to go to college in your family, the *only* person to start your own business in your community, or one of the *few* African Americans in your department. When brothers have "made it," they find they end up spending a considerable amount of time attending to crises, doling out gifts, money, and sometimes even property and cars to family and friends who act as if they are owed something. They negate the hard work, sacrifice, and planning that went into your achievements and look to you as if you are an ATM. We have spoken with several sports figures who said that after being drafted and signing huge contracts, the jubilation one would expect is quickly replaced by telephone calls saying "Don't forget about me since you made it big," "When are you going to buy me that house?" and "I need a loan." One player told us, "It is the loneliest time I have ever experienced where I have nowhere to turn and I am just looking for a way to escape."

Some men put off attaining wealth by sabotaging themselves because they believe they do not deserve to be wealthy. Or perhaps, he had a mild experience when things were going well and that same exact moment everyone seems to turn against him. And if they truly haven't, he begins to suspect that they will. It is the phenomenon that new words are created every couple of years as people become successful and experience probably the worst experience of their lives: It is called "hating," "crabs-in-a-barrel mentality," "jealousy," and "envy." It is done to you by people who sometimes are your friends and family, who will stab you in the back and turn their back on you because you have done the one thing that they have not been able to do. Make a plan, work hard, stick to it, focus, and most of all, stay determined to succeed. These qualities, when combined with talent, breed success.

It is pumped into our heads that fancy cars, homes, jewelry, and clothing should be very important to us. It is a level of status that we seek to acquire. Earlier generations of African Americans may have felt tied to their community affiliation and the constraints of ghetto life. With a world that promoted individualistic identity, assimilation, and sometimes a need to get away from the people you believe held your spirit down, people have created their own identity through the process of acquiring things. This nation's culture promotes individualism and assimilation; it stimulates the urge to move away from your roots. Many have used the acquisition of material things as a means of gaining a new identity, or a way of setting themselves apart from their surroundings.

With songs like "Hood Rich," "Money, Power and Respect," movies like *Paid in Full* and *All about the Benjamins*, the same industry that exploits this notion produces some of the wealthiest African-American men in the country. Just as African Americans were promised forty acres and a mule after slavery but were left with sharecropping, the music and entertainment industry, as music entrepreneur Charles Huggins puts it, "is the largest sharecropping industry in the country." At the end of the day, you can only truly gain wealth through ownership. The question remains, Do we really own anything?

Robert T. Kiyosaki in *Rich Dad, Poor Dad* tells it best. "Money represents infinite possibilities, and when it is replaced with *stuff*, there is a bitter sense of regret. Money is less satisfying because for some, it is the loss of its power." Society has two interests to promote at best: one of which is economic, and the other is cultivating the talent to make money. African Americans seem to be steered only toward being fleeced for the economic spectrum of this ideal; but we are willing participants. We live in a cosumeristic society, and African Americans spend more money than any other ethnicity in America. We outspend an clothing, alcohol, and cigarettes. Money, a financial instrument, is marketed for us to believe that it has magical powers. Russell Simmons said at an Urban Campfire event for young people that Congressman Gregory W. Meeks was hosting, "I know many artists who were focused on just making money, worked hard to attain it, only once they had it they became instantly depressed."

You Are Being Targeted

Research and marketing departments are designed specifically on how to chart and target how you spend your money. Advertising agencies spend billions of dollars selling you a lifestyle suggesting that you will be accepted and adored if only you had this type of car, watch, suit, clothing, and so forth. One business owner stated in *Shopping for Identity: The Marketing of Ethnicity*, by Marilyn Halter, "How can you ignore these ethnic streams of revenue? You can't. The color of money is green, and you get it whatever skin tone has got it." Or putting it slightly differently, another commentator writes, "Black Is Beautiful—especially if you're black and have some green."

We have issues with money and the importance that it places on our own lives. Today people are requesting to see a credit report before contemplating marriage or membership in a union. As one television commercial states in an advertisement for computers of the future, "Are you ready?" We have some way to go in closing the disparity in wealth and society's unhealthy perception of wealth, but the goal is absolutely reachable. The men in this chapter (from financial powerhouses to everyday working men) will share their thoughts on education, money, debt, saving, street successes, and climbing the corporate ladder. They show you their secrets—what worked and what didn't. Learning from our brothers can helps us figure out exactly what to do to get to our own place and space of financial freedom.

What I'm Really Worth

Jim Jackson

If I died today and people remembered me only for being a professional basketball player, then I would not have reached my full potential as a man. What's important to me is more than just the talents that I showcase on the court. As a Black man who is motivated to see our people grow, I feel like I have a lot to offer to my community. I have ideas that people who are close to me have always known were there. However, the vast majority of society that sees me in the warm-ups and carrying a ball never gets to see my thinking side. The general public never sees the introspective work that I do that causes me to want to be a better man and educate others as I go. Being in the public eye has been my blessing and sometimes my curse. As I'm a professional athlete, people have always seen my face, but until now no one has every really heard my voice.

In both games, the game of basketball and the game of life, I've learned that people judge me by their perceptions. Unfortunately, those perceptions are based largely on filtered information that the public is fed, and rarely are they my own words and feelings. As a professional athlete, I recognize that I'm going to be judged by how well I perform at my job, and I look forward to that challenge. However, I am more than the ball that I dribble. If you want to know how I measure myself, I look at how many lives I've touched and whether or not I can look at my face in the mirror at the end of the day and feel confident with the decisions that I have made. I realize that there is a system that I have to work within to meet some of my own personal goals. The trick is that I've had to make sure that I work that system and not let it work me.

I came into professional basketball on what felt like a bad business note. As the fourth pick in the 1992 NBA draft, what should have been one of the most exciting times of my life ended up being the most frustrating. I had to swallow my disappointment in not being offered a contract consistent with my worth and make a decision about what I should do. Any profession has a market value, and the NBA is no different. The exceptions are that you are dealing with a seven-figure salary instead of a six- or five-figure salary. I turned to my parents and hometown mentors who knew Jim Jackson long before my face had ever been broadcast. I valued the opinions of Pete Culp, Calvin Lawshe, and Ed Scrutchins, who knew my work as a player but also understood my value as an educated Black man. I also relied on Anthony Ross, who has been my best friend since kindergarten, for his wisdom and opinions because he understands me better than anyone.

I respected their opinions, and it was important to me to keep them close at a time where people might have considered my hold out selfish. I asserted my position as a man and insisted that I be paid my fair market value for the job I was being asked to do. Because of the strenuous negotiation process, I missed fifty-four out of eighty-two games my rookie year before I was finally offered a fair salary. People think that it is an honor to play professionally, and I definitely consider it a blessing. However, no one would ever expect a man in any other profession to accept a penny less than what he was worth. I didn't have any money before I played in the NBA, and I figured I can't miss what I didn't have. It became more important for me to maintain my position because of the principle of the matter. Even though the average person could only see the symptoms of what was going on, I recognized it as a larger issue. If I'd just let it go, it would have affected the brother who came up behind me. Once the smoke cleared, I started to see that people understood what my struggle was because they could also identify with a man's desire to feel adequately compensated for his work.

That move may have haunted me, but I would never take it back. I'm actually proud of a lot of decisions I've made that on the outside seem a bit controversial, but internally these were decisions that had to be made in order to state what kind of man I was evolving into. I feel like living through adversity is what has helped me to learn and grow. Adversity has been what's motivated me to read more, ask more questions to try to understand new things, and to challenge myself to think. And most important, living through change and difficult times has caused me to refuse the position of remaining visible but mute. People rarely get to understand the depths of what I have to say unless I actually get out there and say it. In the NBA, however, there is little room for athletes who offer opinions. We've seen the casualties of lost players who have made statements contrary to what the public opinion might be. To be pigeonholed as athletic and nothing else reduces my power as an intelligent man. I've heard it said from people within the system that upon speaking to me, they find that I am very articulate and intelligent for a basketball player. They may find that as a compliment, but I consider it a slap in the face to a Black man's intelligence.

I know that historically the system has not been set up for a Black man to make it. It's hard to function in a system that is overbearing and not designed for your survival. In my role, I've found myself having opportunities where things have been made a little bit easier for me because of what I do. But, I never kid myself, and I never forget that everyone doesn't have those same doors opened as widely, if it all. I use my wealth to create more for my people. I often hear the question of why I haven't opened a nightclub. The misconception of a professional athlete is that as soon as we get paid, we want to open a nightclub.

However, I feel like I have a responsibility to bring new kinds jobs to our community, not just those in entertainment. I read about my heroes who use their position to advance the Black communities. Leaders like Malcolm X, ex-professional athletes such as Muhammad Ali and Magic Johnson, or business professionals such as the founder of BET and now NBA team owner Robert Johnson are among those who have inspired me to act. It could have been just as easy for me to think of myself only as a professional basketball player. However, I feel that I have more to offer to the world. I have refused to fall into the trap of playing the role where it seems that I don't have a mind and all I have is the ball. I'm making plans now for the day when playing ball isn't my day job. When that day comes, I want to meet it head-on using my other talents that make up all of the man that I am. And that will be my measure of what I'm really worth.

Jim Jackson is an eleven-year veteran of the NBA. His long-term plan is to devote his time to his Toledo-based residential and commercial development business, JAJ Development Company, and to Adaris Engineering Firm, both of which fall under a parent company called The JAJ Company. He is married to Shawnee Jackson and has one son, Traevon.

Turning Wisdom into Money
Perry M. Mallory

If you had a choice between a one-time gift of $1 million or $100,000, once a year for the rest of your life, which would you choose? Most people that I have asked would choose the $1 million. Your response would reflect your current mind-set regarding money.

I grew up in Camden, New Jersey, and didn't think I was poor. I believed that poverty meant you had to be homeless and hungry to be classified as poor. Later in life, I discovered that poverty is a curse upon our mental life first that later manifests itself in the physical arena with little to no personal possessions, belongings, or money. There are nations throughout the world that have more natural resources than our nation, yet they live in abject poverty. There are people every day who die like paupers, and yet thousands of dollars are ascribed to their names. How can this be the case? These are examples of where the mind-sets of people are tarnished. The curse is an impoverished mind-set. Growing up, as late as college days, I remember committing certain acts that indicated that I, too, was ensnared by this evil force against my mind.

I remember putting water in my shampoo and ketchup bottles to "make it last forever." I never can forget about the empty mayonnaise jar in which we used to put water and the useless remnants of soap bars in order to create a "born again" bar of soap. Why didn't I know that squeezing those tubes of toothpaste until my thumb pierced the emptied tube was a sign that I had a real situation going on between my two ears?

I swear to you that I could afford another bottle of shampoo or ketchup, or bar of soap. That wasn't the issue. My mind was poor; therefore, I lived poor. Many of these occurrences were taking place while I was in college and later while I worked with a major pharmaceutical company making good money with a company car. The Bible tells us, "As a man thinketh, so is he." I submit to you that wherever you are right now in your life is a direct indication of your former thoughts or your thoughts right now.

Money has been around since the story of creation. In fact, some of the major components found in the Garden of Eden are linked to money. Therefore, we must understand that money was never a by-product of man's toils in the beginning but instead was an integral tool of the initial overall plan of God for man. So why is there such a great disproportion in the distribution of money among countries, races, and even genders? Why do the rich in life seem to keep getting richer? Why is it that the poorer appear to keep getting poorer? And why is it that the middle classes find themselves daily trying not to make the one wrong move that could have them reclassified as "poor?" Are men really worth more than their female counterparts? Are industrialized nations really more deserving of wealth than third-world nations?

One reason the previous scenarios seem so real is because most of the time, money is something learned and taught at home or informally in society. Most of the time, money is not taught in school. Therefore, it is easy for an unlearned, poor parent to teach a child very little about being "financially literate." So what can a poor person teach about money?

In fact, every day we witness people with great access to large sums of money who remain void of financial literacy. Most of us as Afro-American males do not come from affluent backgrounds. Therefore, we lack many of the necessary firm financial values that make us eligible to reap higher-end financial rewards and returns. However, the greater crime is that we don't rally together to instill these strong financial values into one another and into our families. We lack the checks and balances of accountability in our culture and therefore are guilty of many of the common practices of lack, debt, poor credit ratings, bankruptcy, and the like.

Many other cultures become a challenge to us in the model that they set to instill firm financial values into each other. Even the typical West Indies immigrant that comes to live in the States is a tutor in this area. Often they rally together to pool their accommodations and resources until every participant receives sufficient impartation of the principles and is not only ready to practice what has been learned, but also ready to teach others the same principles.

In comparison, in the Afro-American culture in the States, it is far too common that we find ourselves buried up to our necks in debt before we start our families and reach the childbearing age. Then without our control, we instill this same lifestyle in our children and we continue the vicious cycle in our family line that was transferred from our parents and ancestry. Brothers, we have to stop this deadly cycle in our generation. We have the potential to be the "Josephs" (pioneers) in our heritage. Let us commit to not only getting out of debt, but also to living debt-free.

Having been through college myself, my observation is that money is not taught in school as a curriculum. In school, the focus is primarily on scholastic aptitude and on the development of professional skills, but nothing on the development of everyday financial skills. This is why you may find a double-degreed accountant or doctor who still struggles financially because of an elementary-level education on finances.

Many nations around the world are in severe national debt because of governmental representatives who make monumental financial decisions with little or no education or training on the subject of money.

Now I also insist upon balance in this matter. I am not in support of just anyone with a little bit of money teaching others on money. I am, however, a great supporter of those who teach money from a biblical perspective. I believe it makes sense to study and teach from a manual written by agents of the Creator of all money, God.

As with anything else in life, I have greater trust in the manufacturer of a thing, than in close representative. Even though two manufacturers may produce German-made automobiles, I don't feel as comfortable having a BMW mechanic work on my Mercedes Benz when I need answers. God manufactures the money, so my interest is, "What does He say about it?"

For those that may feel that money and the Bible or money and God just don't mix, let me quote (and paraphrase) a couple of comments that were recorded in the Bible from God's mind.

"Money answers all things." (Ecclesiastes 10:19)

"Out of everything in life, I wish that you may prosper." (III John 2)

"The love of money is the root of all evil." (I Timothy 6:10)

The issue of money, wealth, and riches is by far the greatest topic (with the most references) covered throughout the Bible.

Money is power. Knowledge is power. But what happens when you are not privy to knowledge? You perish! As Black men, we don't rank as the least worthy to obtain wealth. We no longer lack formal education. But I believe that the knowledge to obtain wealth has been largely withheld from us.

Our culture has been enslaved by a welfare mentality—a mentality that promotes sustenance by the provisions of others. By lesser access to the world's knowledge of financial literacy, how can Black men scale the walls of injustice and denial and rank among those with plenty? Gain the knowledge of the Creator of the thing (money) itself.

Many of our role models are plagued with the same problems. Often, the celebrities (such as rappers, musicians, actors, and sports figures) that we idolize are experiencing massive debt themselves. Entertainment's glamorization of money has worsened our financial situation and has assisted in digging deeper ditches for our culture. As we strive to mimic the images that we see on the popular music videos of our day, we fail to understand that most of the clothes worn and automobiles driven on the big screen are borrowed.

Look what the richest man of all times says about wisdom and money. Keep in mind that when I use the word *wisdom*, I'm not talking about a sage or an elder. Wisdom is the ability to properly use obtained knowledge:

"Wisdom is as good as an inheritance, yes, more excellent it is for those [the living] who see the sun. For wisdom is a defense even as money is a defense, but the excellency of knowledge is that wisdom shields and preserves the life of him who has it." (Ecclesiastes 7:11–12 AMP)

No matter your race, no matter your nationality, the playing field is even. We need more knowledge concerning money. We also need, simultaneously, more wisdom (the ability to properly appropriate the knowledge obtained) concerning money. And most important, we need to be instructed by the right source.

These are some suggestions to begin to convert wisdom into money:

Find books or a church that teaches financial principles from the Holy Bible. Dare to apply the principles. Black man, God has given you the creativity. You have the talent to do just about anything. You have the potential. You have the drive. Now get the knowledge! Press in for the understanding. Pray for wisdom, and nothing will be withheld from you.

Start denying yourself today to build a dynasty for tomorrow. This takes discipline. Ask yourself this important question: "Where are you?" Not geographically, but in your life. What's your maturity level? What's your realized after-tax income? What can you really afford? Not what do you have money to buy right now, but what can you *really* afford? Are you completely out of debt? *"Where are you?"* In other words, at the end of the day, was getting the fur coat or the Mercedes Benz worth it when you don't have anything to eat? Or do you have your Benz but are house poor?

We need wisdom. Godly wisdom.

By the way, regarding the opening question: I would choose $100,000 a year, and with wisdom I would create millions out of it.

Remember this:

"The beginning of wisdom is: get wisdom (skillful and godly wisdom)! [For skillful and godly wisdom is the principal thing.] And with all you have gotten, get understanding [discernment, comprehension, and interpretation]." (Proverbs 4:7)

Perry M. Mallory was born in Philadelphia in 1960. He grew up an honor student in Camden, New Jersey. Perry graduated with a B.S. degree in biology/premedicine from Lincoln, University in Oxford, Pennsylvania. He has worked for corporate America for fourteen years. He now works for a leading Fortune 500 company as a solutions account manager. Perry is an associate pastor, author, publisher, inventor, teacher, motivational speaker, and counselor. His passion is teaching biblical financial principles. He also owns a thriving Christian publishing company. He is happy married to Sharon D. Mallory. They have two children, Natan and Nia.

Prosperity Will Come!
Glenn Toby

When I came home from school one day to our apartment in Brooklyn, we found all our clothes and furniture on the sidewalk. I found my toys, books, and clothing scattered on the ground. My mother, an office administrator for New York State Employees' Pension Division, had recently lost her job. She was fired because she would not support a report that was made against a fellow employer. She was terminated without pay as a result of not joining in their plan.

I remember following my mother up the stairs to witness an eviction notice on our door. She tried to unlock the door, and to our surprise, it wouldn't open. This made no sense to me because my mother open locked doors all my life, and to me these doors were larger than life.

Mom went to several meetings and hearings and even met with an arbitration board to try to get her paycheck. They were forced to pay her back pay and a small severance amount. They held all her pension money and would not give her a good reference for future employment. Can you imagine, the State Employees' Pension Division held back my mother's pension! Mom called the landlord, and they agreed to make an arrangement for her to pay the rent on a later date, but then he had a change of heart, and we were evicted.

My brother and I were without a stable home for the next eight years of our lives. We lived in homeless shelters and stayed with relatives. When my mother requested help, she was told to apply for welfare and was offered foster care for us and a shelter for herself. She refused because she didn't want us to be separated. She didn't want our spirits to be divided. Mom refused to compromise, refused to sell her body, and did not turn to drugs or partner with a man for her own convenience. My mother always put us first, and has always been there for us in every regard. I thank God to this day that my grandmother was following us and trying to assist us in every way possible. She refused to bow to the systematic controls and sabotage even when my mother went to the unemployment department and was denied any unemployment insurance due to the comments that her supervisor reported.

As a family, we cushioned the blows of life by praying, laughing, and protecting each other, which meant dealing with the truth and accepting the horrible situation we were in. For many years, I had prayed and asked God to allow me a permanent place to live, to not allow me to remain hungry. When most kids asked for toys for Christmas, I asked for my mother to recover from her illness. I pondered on all the events and activities that we participated in long before we had lost our home. Even at that young age, I cherished the time, knowing that it was so valuable.

We always had faith that one day things would get better. The only thing I ever wanted was a home, a bed, and a steady meal. We did have a home in every place we ever went or stayed temporarily. We were never homeless, just without a house. But the pressure became so overwhelming for my mother, she suffered a severe nervous breakdown and was hospitalized for long periods of time. When she was in the hospital, we were sent to stay with relatives. When my mother was first taken from us, it seemed like I had died inside. I could not focus or concentrate. I had never given up on my mother, but I was prepared to live without her in the event that I lost her in some manner. When we visited her, it was a great time for us. My brother and I really started healing when she told us not to give up. And we didn't.

Today, my brother is an entrepreneur, and my sister is a computer information systems specialist. My mother is healed and well. I am a real estate developer, business consultant, and manager, with an immense background in the music industry as an artist and manager. I was a member of the team that managed LL Cool J. I was known as rapper Sweety G in my teen years, then left rap and got into business marketing. I did not sell drugs, but I hustled like everyone else and did what I could to get ahead. Instead, I sold business equipment and machines, and then began selling and trading stocks and bonds. I always had friends that sold drugs or were involved in the drug game. I do not want to sound like I am putting them down. I think many drug dealers are geniuses and just do not have a product to sell. I understand people do what they must to survive, and I only pray for them to have a better product to sell. I was not a hustler, but I hustled, and America hustles. I do not want to be elitist or condemn anyone; I just want to offer solutions. Currently, I manage eleven NFL players and consult Don King.

Now how did I go from bouncing among social agencies to being worth several zeros behind that first digit? I never lost touch with the fact that I or anyone is only a rent or mortgage payment away from becoming homeless. After I won each race, I still saw the next finish line ahead of me and always skipped the winner's circle. I never lost the homeless mentality. No matter how successful I was, I would always tell myself, "You are homeless! You have nothing! Save everything!" I lived frugally, pretending that I was still in a rooming house, always keeping my things neatly lined up and clean. Whenever money came, I paid myself first, saving 50 percent of everything I made. Everyone should pay themselves first and save no less than 25 percent if they have cash flow problems or can't really make ends meet. When my money started growing, I kept telling myself that I was in an economic war. And I lived like I was in an economic holocaust. I put my money into mutual funds, and it grew because I never touched it.

Even to this day, as far as I'm concerned, I'm homeless. Now, I do have a house, but I'll always feel like I'm homeless until I go to be with God. I appreciate the basics, the basic three meals a day. Nothing satisfies my thirst for life more than receiving the basics. I started with nothing but concept and vision, and that is what made me creative and resourceful. I do not want having money to cause me to lose that edge. I always believed it is not just important to win the race, but also to run it well and make every stride between the first step and the last step over the finish line count equally. When it comes to finances, control is important. You must create a revenue stream and consolidate your debts. Control what's coming in, and filter what's going out. If you stay rooted in God, prosperity will come. I'm a firm believer in living in Hope and Faith. Hope is desire accompanied by expectation, and Faith is the substance of things hoped for. Hope keeps us believing in the tomorrows, that tomorrow will be a better day, and Faith puts it all in God's hands. My motto, "This can't fail me, because God is involved." Make that your motto, too, trust me, it won't lead you wrong.

Glenn Toby is the president and CEO of a firm that specializes in business management and marketing for high-profile entertainers and professional athletes. He is also the founder and president of the Book Bank, an organization that provides books and storytime to inner-city children.

Driven by the Dream

Bryan "Baby" Williams

Growing up in New Orleans with my brother Ronald "Slim" Williams is where the music started. More or less, it was probably a death in my family and losing a lot of my homies to the street life and the penitentiary. It was enough to make a nigga be like, fuck, let me try something new. It gets old doing the same shit for so long, so a nigga just jumped in music and tried that shit. I feel like anything I put my heart and mind to, I can accomplish. I knew I could do it with music, too. I put my faith in God toward whatever I do, and I knew when I got involved with music, I would be successful in it.

I mean, before I made money I learned how to get money—you know we lost a lot before we made a lot of money. Our first two years were down hill. It was all normal shit; when you start a business, there's a down before an up. So we went through the ups and downs; the not having it then not getting it; then breaking even and then making a few dollars on a small level. We knew how to flow with the downs because we came from a family of sacrifices. A nigga learned how to share even if it was a loaf of bread. It was like twenty of us, we had to split that bitch so we knew how to sacrifice with the sweet and the sour. Good or bad, that was a part of life. That's why the wealth shit a nigga know, how to budget a nigga know; how to put up and how to spend a nigga know, ya know?

We kept our same little method from the beginning. It was first, it worked, and it came easy to all of us, so we ain't really change. Right now today, we're still doing the things we did back then, just on a bigger scale. So a nigga ain't really change nothing—we just staying one way, and the only way we know how to do it is the ghetto way. We ain't changing shit.

We was hand to hand with the shit. P. and a whole bunch of us started off hand to hand, and as time grew, it got big—and before we knew it, it got too big for independent distribution. We were shipping like 150,000 units per project, and we were putting out an album a month. I had to sign because I was moving too many units. But we saw what it was doing and how it was growing. This shit is like stocks: It goes up and down. We saw everything that goes with this music shit. When we got to do a deal with a company, we were seven years out as an independent. I had read up and studied the game. I studied niggas in my line of work. I studied Russell, Eazy E, Suge Knight, Puffy, and P. I studied them because for me to be what I wanted to be, I would have to be faced with the same obstacles that they were already facing. I studied the game because I was going to walk that path, but just try to make better decisions when the time came.

As an independent before I signed with Universal, we were generating about two or three million a year. I came in the game with Universal already a millionaire from independent money. Nobody has been independent as long as us. I've been with Universal for five years, and I'm going on thirteen years with this shit.

I didn't come in the game as a hurting artist or hurting company. I was already, to me, successful. I was established, I made two or three million a year easy, we were doing that. So when I went into the situation, I was still watching and studying the game. I wasn't letting them take nothing from me. Me and them niggas, Fresh, Wayne, and Slim, worked so hard, so I wasn't trying to give up half of nothing, and Universal wasn't giving me a lot of money. I didn't care about the money. I knew we could sell records— I just wanted more of a back end because without it it's a waste. I make eighty and you make twenty—we'll never probably see another deal like that in the industry. I mean right now times are fucked up and I still make a lot of money, more than an average company. I love where I'm at; we have a good relationship, and I wouldn't want to be anywhere else. I mean I don't think any label—and I mean especially right now that the industry is so fucked up—is going to do any more legendary deals and shit. If it's not done now, it's going to be hard to get them motherfuckers to do shit.

I'll tell any motherfucker, anybody, always have God first, dog. Without God, I can't see it. You know what I'm saying, I don't see life without God. Second, put it in your heart and mind. Set goals for yourself because without a goal, you ain't got no aim, and if you have no aim, what the fuck are you focusing on. You've got to put it in your heart and mind and work at it every day. Sometimes it may look like you're not getting there, but if you set it in your mind and heart, this road you got to walk will become clear. You've got to walk this yellow brick road so every day you wake up, you got to work toward it to get closer and closer to your goal and aim. So sometimes it might not look good—it might even look fucked up because some days I used to be like, *fuck*, but I never stopped. I always worked and I always had my faith and belief that I'm going to get to where I'm trying to get. But if for some reason you do get whatever it is you have aimed for, never stop setting goals. When you reach one, reach for another. Keep reaching your goals and then you'll have something to wake up and struggle and strive for every day. Keep setting higher goals, 'cause a nigga got to have a goal and an aim—then you got something to focus on.

Basically that's it. Just work hard, stay focused, and stay away from the drugs and all the other plagues out there. It's already a fucked-up world we live in, so we got to duck the dumb shit, get with the good shit, and say fuck the bullshit and *always* have God first.

What I learned is this is how I look at all this shit here. We were born to die. You live to cry 'cause you suffer, but it's cool tho' 'cause you can make it be whatever you want it to be, so the reality of it is that it is what it is. I'll tell any nigga you not gonna live this life twice. That's why I'm gonna do what I want to do. I'm gonna buy jewelry, play with these broads, whatever I'm gonna do I'm gonna do it. I'm not gonna be here twice, but I'm also sacrificing for my family, making sure they're good, but I'm gonna do me. You not gonna live twice, so you might as well live this motherfucker like you want to with the guidelines of respecting God. 'Cause God is always first.

Bryan "Baby" Williams gained national notoriety when Cash Money Records inked a multimillion-dollar, unprecedented deal with Universal Records, igniting the Cash Money Millionaires' explosion into stardom. The industry was not ready for the empire that would shape, mold, and perfect the signature sound that is now known as the Dirty South. Playing a significant role as a triumphant entrepreneur, a creative musical innovator, and a confident performer, Baby a.k.a. #1 Stunna has helped craft multiple gold albums with various Cash Money artists and amassed three platinum albums as a member of both the Hot Boys and rap duo the Big Tymers. The #1 Stunna is now pursuing a solo career with an album, Birdman.

The Bottom Line
David King

I grew up in a row house in Philly, a three-bedroom row house with five children. My two older siblings were much older than my younger brothers and me, and I was the oldest of the last three. Our next-door neighbors had three boys, too, and our summers were filled with baseball, basketball and most of all, adventure. My father was a police officer who was extremely disciplined. You could set your watch to that 5:00 P.M. train that came from the city depositing my dad at the station. Within seven or so minutes, you could see him coming over the hill. That was a signal that whatever chores weren't done, you were in trouble. While growing up, I saw little of my mother during the week. God blesses her—Mom worked twelve-hour shifts and still went to graduate school to pursue her Ph.D. She was clearly the breadwinner, as my dad made twenty thousand dollars on a police officer's salary. But Dad loved what he did; in addition, it gave him the flexibility to be at home with us to manage homework and put us in line when we needed it. Ours was a loving home, filled with patience and security, structure and discipline. While other kids' parents were getting divorced, my parents remain together, married forty-seven years.

Every morning we ate oatmeal, grits, or cereal. Every evening it was the usual rice, vegetables, and some type of meat. Friday was fish night; my dad was a big fisherman. Our freezer was stocked with trout, whiting, and perch that he caught, and we would enjoy fish every Friday. Our family was run on pure organization. Clothes were bought in bulk three times a year: the beginning of the school year, Christmas, and the end of the school year. Every morning, my dad would neatly line up our coins for the day on the kitchen counter.

I went to private school and excelled in sports. Each morning, I took a ninety-minute train ride to a very prestigious prep school. There were only four blacks in the school, and I was at the top of my class. After that experience, I wanted to see what it would be like going to school with African Americans. I applied to Howard University, and when I arrived on campus it was a taste of freedom. I was finally on my own, ready to experience life. One of my buddies said, "You will never see so many beautiful women concentrated in one place in your life." He was 100 percent correct; I jumped in headfirst and dated every beautiful woman that I could for the first three years. I was amazed at the caliber of people at school, each person was at the top of their class. Brothers and sisters from all across the country had very rich and diverse backgrounds. In my last year, in order to graduate, I had to complete twenty-three credits. True to the discipline that I was raised with, I pushed myself to the limit and finished. My stringent schedule included going to the library every day from three to six P.M., and I held a part-time job.

After graduation, I was well sought after, and I ventured out into the work force with an eagerness to succeed. I excelled, quickly relocating and climbing up the ranks. I found my niche in commercial real estate management and development and knew that I wanted to reclaim some of the camaraderie and togetherness I felt with my Black brothers and sisters in college. I began to specialize in turning around failing condominium developments. I came in with great ideas and a plan that would increase property value by 40 percent and create curb appeal, something every homeowner desired. I raised the maintenance fee probably the equivalent of between 10 to 25 percent annually, and you could have sworn that I committed a crime. First I would argue with them—no beg them—to see the value of what I was trying to accomplish. Then I realized that they needed to be educated and to show them how this would increase their investment tenfold. I didn't want to believe the stereotype that Black people did not want to put money in their property. It paid off because a few owners decided to move on and reaped large financial gains once they sold their property.

In business I had to meet another challenge. In my twenties, I managed a team of over fifty people and was responsible for the bottom line and efficiency. I hoped that I got workers willing to work as hard as possible to get the job done, but that was rarely the case. In reality, you have people who have problems, addictions, emotional difficulties, debt, and crises. I tried to be sensitive but I was focused on the bottom line. The Black women that I worked with were looking for leadership in a father or brother figure sort of way. Personally, I wanted to just get the work done, which caused a lot of dissatifaction within the ranks. I was a perfectionist and expected everyone to be like me, which just does not happen.

It was weird—I was learning from the development company how to build wealth, how to aggressively go after a deal, and how to maximize an investment potential not to mention the art of the deal. However, I also had to be the big-brother guy who should be compassionate enough to listen to my staff's issues and problems. I had to develop balance if I wanted to remain successful. But was I going to give up responsibility of my feelings and emotions to people who have proved to be irresponsible and careless with their own well-being?

I wouldn't do it. My feeling was "that's tough." Just get over it—hey, there is money to be made. But things have a way of seeping into your personal life regardless of how disciplined you are. Like the fact that I've been engaged twice. I must admit I have this idealized way of looking at how my wife could and should be. Maybe it's because I pride myself in being the best that I could be, so she should be the best she can be, right? I went from one extreme to the next with the first engagement. I was with a young lady who could stretch a penny for a month. My second engagement was with someone who could not even begin to have a notion about balancing her checkbook. What attracted me to her was her intellect. We could communicate on so many levels, and that was sexy.

I pride myself in being a good partner, I don't live beyond my means, and I don't desire keeping up with the Joneses. If this was going to work, we had to get her in shape financially and physically. I have another pet peeve. I can't deal with women who are not physically fit. There is nobility in putting yourself last, and I definitely do not subscribe to that. I work out six times a week, and I am still the same weight since high school. I encouraged my ex-fiancée to eat healthier, and we developed an exercise program for her. I reconstructed the entire money thing. I put her on a budget and got everything back on track. She excelled in her career and became absolutely stunning. Again, the discipline and commitment are constant factors in my life; I commuted each and every weekend to Michigan to see her.

I was looking for a job so that I could relocate, and one weekend I came home and there were roses in the house that I did not give her. I was mentally exhausted, and I didn't even try to fight it. I just went to bed. We tried to reconcile, but she found someone else and it just did not work. I was devastated and still it hurts to this day. I spent a tremendous amount of money, and I felt she just didn't appreciate all the hard work and commitment that I laid out.

I am forty years old now, and what I have learned is money is, just as financial security is, important to everyone—it is also just as important that you share your time and be compassionate to what people are going through. You definitely can't fix people's issues, but whether you are in a working or love relationship people want to know that you understand them and most of all they just want you to listen. I have a more open-door policy than I ever had before. I extend a hand in nurturing the staff at the office to be the best that they can be. One of the greatest things I have gained from these experiences is that I began to create harmony by exercising compassion—but the bottom line remains, you must be proactive and focused to be successful.

David King *is a real estate and asset manager in Washington, D.C., and is currently writing a series of books on men, women, and money.*

Faith, Planning, and Action

Justin Kennedy

Faith, planning, and action have meanings that, if put together, can unlock the doorway to prosperity. Many who have sought their perfect health, wealth, and fulfillment have journeyed long to find the true desires of their heart. It is the belief in lack that blocks our vision and fearless faith that opens our eyes.

As an entertainment attorney and business consultant, I have had the honor of working closely with some of our world's greatest talents, people with amazing accomplishments and interests, whose faith and action have inspired us all. In the search for my own purpose, I began my quest for prosperity in the legal profession. It wasn't until I took a leap of faith and formed my own company that I began to understand how true prosperity is attained. As much as I had hoped to teach my clients, I was taught in equal measure about the world and myself.

Faith

All great ideas are brought to manifestation by first taking a leap of faith. Faith is fear turned upside down. Many people are afraid to express who they are and share their ideas. Many of us come from troubled past and abusive households filled with fear of lack, worry, and anxiety. These feelings can rub their way into a person's being without them knowing it, and can become a part of their personality. Belief in lack and limitation is the stuff that failure is made of. If we look deeply at ourselves and find these feelings, it is easy to conclude that we must change the conditioning of our mind. Fearless faith comes from the accomplishment of a dream or idea. Faith grows and continues to expand to the extent that you repeat the process.

As an attorney, I found it very hard to believe that I would someday have a magical work, giving magical service and receiving magical pay. Of course, it was something I dreamed about, but I couldn't see the road to accomplishment. One day, all of this changed.

A new client came to the law firm that I was working at to see me specifically. I will call him Peter. Although this was not my first client and I was already representing famous artists, it was the first time I felt that someone truly believed in me as a person and not because of some propaganda spread by industry gossip. After meeting with Peter and discussing his ideas for his company, Peter immediately gave me a three-thousand-dollar retainer for my services. Even though the retainer was small in comparison to what I was then earning at the firm, I quite my job the very same day, and the Kenendy Firm was formed with only a three-thousand-dollar investment and my newfound fearless faith.

It wasn't the money that inspired me. I felt the validation that comes when someone truly believes in who you are and not just in what you can do for them. This situation taught me that there is a supply for every demand, and if Peter believed in my purpose, others would, as well.

Today, many clients have come to me for business advice. Serving them has been as difficult as it has been rewarding. Often, the very people who have the most faith in themselves or their ideas generally don't believe that they need guidance.

I am reminded a singer I once represented whom we will call Cleo. Cleo came to me wanting to be a worldwide superstar singing in both Spanish and English. Although she came to me without a marketable demo or character and really could not sing or dance at all, Cleo had energy! Cleo was driven, confident, and had a work ethic that inspires me to this day. I watched her reconstruct her mind, body, and talents over a short period of time, and she grew to the point where the possibilities of her worldwide appeal drew very near.

Once Cleo confronted and overcame her fears, however, she became impatient for success. Her impatience made her choose to ignore the necessity of strategic planning and focus. Cleo, instead, chose to fly before her wings had grown, and her career seems to have fallen.

Faith alone is dead! Faith is merely a starting place on one's journey to success and prosperity. Although Cleo found her faith, she didn't learn how to use this new power.

True faith looks to learn from every situation, to grow and easily change from experience to experience without ego and judgment. Faith understands that there is a supply for every demand and waits patiently for completion. Without the balancing of strategic planning and focused action, you will fall often.

Planning

Prosperity doesn't come from money; it comes from individuals who follow the disciplines of money. Believe it or not, patience, relaxation, discipline, and order in your mind, body, and affairs bring forth your perfect plans and accomplishments.

Many of us have suffered from some kind abuse and are still finding our way back to mental freedom. There is no prosperity without the balancing of mind, body, and affairs.

If you turn on the television, you are easily seduced by entertainment's notion of prosperity and lured by ideals that symbolize great achievement. But in fact, most of what you see is an illusion of prosperity clocked by corporate marketing and publicity schemes. This has been one of the most difficult teaching points of my career, because our society is so brainwashed by these corporate machines. In fact, the companies themselves believe their own propaganda. Sadly, many famous individuals are living very unfulfilled lives. The truth is that the entertainment business is a hustle from check to check, and there is really no glamour in that.

One of my clients, whom I will call Martin, continues to succeed in the entertainment industry and has done so with out much balance at all. Martin has a very creative mind, good heart, and solid work ethic. Like most of my clients, his ego continues to block him from his heart's true desires. Through the practice of balance, your mind is able to relax. It is through a relaxed state that our perfect ideas and perfect plans are born. All of Martin's ideas are wonderful and shine with possibility. However, an idea without manifestation is also dead.

Martin's business is built on talent instead of talent and focus. Although he has achieved national recognition, Martin still searches for the feelings that come from well-planned actions. Because of the accomplishments of his ego, he is reluctant to change.

Relaxation, order, and planning are a practice that we must work hard to maintain equally. By disciplining yourself to do these things and working as hard at them as you would at your other tasks, you will find success, satisfaction, health, true wealth, and harmony. Faith and ideas are like children. They need protection and direction. Because each person is unique, this direction must come from the intuition found in an individual's calmest mind. In this state, the perfect plans are created. I learned from Cleo that it is very important to build a strong business foundation before you expand. Your foundation is your seed of life. It must include your perfect health, happiness, interest, joys, and fulfillment. What you stand for should be chosen wisely.

Every great work, and every big accomplishment has been brought into manifestation through holding to a perfect well-planned vision. This may seem simple enough, but many people still look at work as something they have to do, instead of something they enjoy doing. Faith in action is a vibratory force that attracts its own. A successful business is like a successful marriage. It must be built on truth, commitment, responsibility, communication, and work. No matter how great an idea my clients may have, their plans rarely come to completion unless they are 110 percent committed to the idea.

In Martin's case, he used his creative talents to become a jack-of-all-trades instead of becoming a master at one trade first. Creativity, combined with focused planning, can accomplish anything.

Action

Completion comes from our faith in action. Doing the work necessary for growth without fear of failure is the best medicine for success. I once represented a record label owner whom I will call Rich. Rich had no shortage of money, and I can assure you, that is a godsend in any industry. Although Rich had money, neither he nor anyone on his team wanted to commit to the business. The entire executive team wanted to travel and live the superstar lifestyle, but when it came time to handle business, all cell phones were off. In the business of music, the music and carefree lifestyle are selling points, not the business itself. Without a commitment to growing your business, there will be no success in business. Just as money can't buy love, money does not ensure success. People ensure success.

As an associate at a well-known entertainment law firm, I had the honor to work closely with some of the industry's greatest minds. As a new attorney, I was afforded the opportunity to represent royalty and superstars in the very beginning of my career. One project in particular proved to be a lesson I will carry with me for the rest of my life.

The office was retained to put together a benefit album. I was excited about the experience and the mission of the client. I soon learned, however, that the entertainment community was not as interested as I was, and over the next nine months, my job was to beg and persuade people to get involved. Needless to say, I began to lose faith in the viability of the project and could not understand why the firm didn't just tell the client that it could not be done.

It took over a year, but the album was completed with well-known artists who donated their time and talents. What I learned during this process was never to give up, never lose faith in what you truly believe, and your work (active faith) will accomplish any goal you can dream. The person who achieves success has a fixed idea of success and works until completion. Act as if you expect success, and prepare for it immediately.

Sometimes action does means to change your plans completely. As our interests change, our need to satisfy our new interests inspires us to create fresh opportunities for wealth. Those who understand this principle invest their time, plans, and actions to expanding new territories. As we are non-resistant to the changes of the world, we can easily see opportunity and take action. Taking the time to patently look at the world as a creation in progress and setting your plans to add its beauty will bring the fulfillment of all your greatest desires in perfect ways. To resist the growing changes in who you are is to resist the truth about who we really are.

One of my clients, whom I'll call Chris, always wanted to own a thriving recording studio. Chris worked very diligently, invested his time and money into the creation of his studio. As he was on his way, Chris began to set his sights to more profitable ventures and realized that he really didn't want to be in the studio business—he really just wanted to own his own studio. At the same time, the studio recording industry was rapidly changing. More and more people were benefiting from the ease and affordability of this digital technology, and more and more home studios were being built. As the recording studio industry was becoming more competitive, Chris decided to hold on to the idea of running a recording studio business, but his true focus was on new opportunities.

Being stuck in the middle of old unfinished idea and an immediate opportunities can sometimes make our choices difficult. But remember, money moves with the interest of the people, not necessarily with your personal interest. If Chris followed the immediate opportunity for prosperity, prosperity would be his immediately.

Change is movement toward completion. Completion is the result of your faith, planning, and action. There are no opportunities in the past. There are no opportunities in the future. Our opportunity is now!

Justin Kennedy is an attorney in New York who has gained expertise in the entertainment industry and has personally represented many companies, artists, and foundations.

Your Soul's Journey

For wisdom is a defence, and money is a defence: but the excellency
of knowledge is, that wisdom giveth life to them that have it.
—Ecclesiastes 7:12

If you don't believe you have a choice, you set yourself up to fail. We are fed so much negativity that we don't know it is ingrained in our souls. How could you listen to negative messages in music, television, movies, or in public—whether you're Black or not—and not have some it rub off on you. We are sponges. Fast money can happen overnight, but from whence it came it shall go. Whether you earn a modest salary or six figures a year, you must believe that you deserve to grow and be prosperous. This idea is the first step to maintaining and establishing wealth. Take a good look at your financial life. You are a sum total of your habits, and your wealth is created based on your ability to believe that you deserve it.

What hurts the Black race is the idealized American dream. We are taught to accumulate all the material things we want. The American dream is focused on individualism and not on the collective. Fortunes have been built on monthly interest rates and the finance charges that accumulate when luxury supersedes necessity. Some of us were never taught about ownership, entrepreneurship, or investments. Our parents may have been the first to achieve middle-class status and were preoccupied with having a roof over our heads and making ends meet. Some of us still use the catchphrases that we grew up listening to and wear them like badges of honor although we are making significant salaries, phrases like "surviving," "maintaining," "keeping your head above water," "making it any way that you can." If your mind believes that you are barely surviving, then your money matters will reflect that prophecy. Clearly we haven't progressed in our minds as our prosperity has grown.

Soul Source

Your journey to financial freedom starts by developing an understanding of money and how it works and has worked for others. All of this is in an effort to work toward wealth building, entrepreneurship, financial freedom, and stability.

How much would you pay for what you already have? We never truly understand the value of the things that we have in our life that money could never truly buy: happiness, peace, or the knowledge and wisdom that you have accumulated over the years. Guess what? If you are not a master at money, you have mastered something else that is of great value to the masses.

The road to prosperity includes a humble approach at reeducating yourself on money matters. You are never too old to be a student, and every student has lots more or something new to learn. Set life goals, and have your money work for you to give flight to your dreams. Work with a professional adviser, have adequate insurance, file an updated will, invest, and get rid of rainy days by being prepared. The source of success begins today with you. Believe, and master the possibilities!

- What does your financial future look like?
- What are your financial goals?
- What are your two-year financial goals?
- What are your five-year financial goals?
- Do you own property?
- What are your assets?
- How much debt do you have?
- What is your strategy to accomplish your goals within your time frame?
- How can you ensure that your wealth can be passed on to the next generation?

CHAPTER 8

POWER AND RESPECT

A race without authority and power is a race without respect.
—Marcus Garvey

Power is a high, and respect is a must.

Feelings of powerlessness may be at the root of many of the problems facing the Black man. Power is such an amorphous word. On one hand, it seems so hard to attain—and on the other, we all possess it. As Black men get older, power becomes more important to them. The power they possess or don't possess over their environment becomes a critical part of their social makeup. Power coupled with their infinite struggle for respect can lead a Black man down many roads. Power is taught through example. One can exert their power over a situation in a positive manner with respect, or one can exert their power in a negative way with a lack of respect. That's what make movies about the Mafia so attractive to Black men. There's an organization of power with the implicit rule that it be met with respect. If the respect is lacking, there is immediate and swift punishment: "I made him an offer he couldn't refuse. Either his brains or his signature will be on that contract." (*The Godfather*)

Power doesn't need to be overt, but it needs to be consistent. So many people confuse money with power. With very little formal education and orphaned at the age of nine, Fredrick McKinley Jones taught himself electronics and auto mechanics. When he came back from World War I, he moved to Hallock, Minnesota, where he built the first radio station transmitter in Hallock and a soundtrack device for motion pictures. His inventions got the attention of Joseph Numero, the owner of a movie equipment company, Cinema Supplies, who then hired him in 1930. Years later, Joseph Numero and Fredrick Jones formed the U.S. Thermo Control Company to market and manufacture a mobile refrigeration unit Jones designed. Jones's mobile refrigeration unit changed the face of the food industry by making it possible to ship meat, dairy products, fruits, and vegetables across the country without the food spoiling. The mobile refrigeration unit was also vital during World War II with the transporting of blood and medicine.

Now that is power and respect. Fredrick McKinley Jones gained the *respect* of a White man in a time when Black and White business alliances were rare. His inventions were so innovative and *powerful* that they changed the course of the produce and meat industries as well as the medical industry and how men were medically treated in World War II.

The journey to inner power and self-respect is growing to understand a true sense of power and how to utilize it to help others, recognizing the need for self-respect and respecting others, and knowing how power and respect work hand in hand.

Black men have come a long way from sharecroppers and cooks to the entertainment moguls and CEOs of their own corporations. Black men have made great strides in their lives and have set many a standard for our younger generations to follow. Some powerful brothers told us what power and respect mean to them. Whether it's on the streets or in the boardrooms, we heard how power and respect play an important role in the lives of every Black man.

Power Is . . .

Michael Ajakwe Jr.

Power is knowing you can take your job and shove it and still be okay; power is being able to motivate people to fight for something outside themselves; power is trusting in God for real; power is a smiling six-nine point guard who likes to share; power is two Black girls from Compton beating the hell out of racism with their tennis rackets; power is every time a Black "tiger" enters a golf tournament; power is a lightning-quick, dancing poet giving up his heavyweight title for nothing more than principle; power is Motown music and knowing the genius behind it was a Black man; power is being able to walk away from the deal; power is Denzel in any scene from any film with anybody; power is the ability to say no and mean it; power is the ability to say yes and mean it; power is taking care of your family; power is being able to pay your bills every month and still have money left over; power is believing in what others can't see; power is taking the long way home instead of the shortcut; power is giving; power is clean money; power is caring about someone besides your family; power is what Oprah's got; power is not selling drugs to your community; power is knowing the law; power is knowing how to read and write; power is listening to Marvin Gaye's "What's Going On" album over and over and over again; power is being able to articulate how you feel without pulling out a gun; power is knowing who you are; power is never raising your hand to your woman no matter what comes out of her mouth; power is never leaving your family, no matter how hard it gets; power is going to college; power is getting a job; power is owning property or anything that appreciates, like the Beatles catalog; power is never turning your back on your homies but never letting them bring you down; power is a Black woman with a nice ass in some tight jeans; power is doing the right thing; power is being able to tell the forest from the truth; power is being a good listener; power is taking every win with a grain of salt and every loss in stride; power is never giving up; power is having the courage to speak up, even if it kills you; power is putting on a condom before you put it in; power is an alley-oop pass from Kobe to Shaq; power is using it only when you have to; power is not forgetting where you came from; power is Denise Williams opening her mouth to sing—anything; power is not burning down your own neighborhood because you're mad; power is a good homemaker; power is waking up every day; power is good health; power is overcoming despite poor heath; power is when you can't be bought; power is not being afraid to die for the right cause; power is talking to your kids instead of beating them; power is not hitting on your wife's girlfriend no matter how fine she is; power is not putting down your man even if it is his fault; power is nature and all its wonders; power is surviving the Middle Passage; power is setting a good example for the next generation; power is loving yourself; power is having your own; power is respect.

Michael Ajakwe Jr. *became the first Black playwright published in the twenty-first century with the release of* Company Policy *(Pipedream Press, February 2000). His other book,* South Central Stories *(Pipedream Press, 2001), is a collection of one-act plays. He has written for TV shows like* Martin, Sister Sister, Soul Food, The Brothers Garcia, The Parkers, Moesha, Entertainment Tonight *and* Talk Soup. *He's won two NAACP Theater Awards, for Playwriting and Producing, and also an Emmy. Mike was hired by Artisan Pictures to write* Crips, *a motion picture about the life of L.A. Crips street gang cofounder-turned-hip-hop-producer Mike Concepcion. The film is being produced by* Rush Hour *and* Red Dragon *director Bret Ratner and rap icon Russell Simmons.*

A Call to Heal

Dr. Sampson Davis

As one of six children, I grew up surrounded by the crime, poverty, and hopelessness of Newark, New Jersey. My parents divorced when I was thirteen, and my mother, faced with the task of raising the six of us, was forced to go on welfare. Any aspirations that I had were shaped by my imagination because I had no tangible images after which to model myself.

Like many children, when I asked for guidance—no, *screamed* for guidance—no one was there to hear my plea, except the streets. Mainstream laws don't apply to the inner city. The inner city is like a third-world country. The streets were there, and I fell victim to certain "patterns" necessary for survival. Not just basics for survival, like food and clothes, but respect. I even had a stint in juvenile detention. Believe it or not, on the streets was where I had opportunities to control my destiny and flex my leadership qualities. If hustlin' was what I had to do to survive, I was going to be the best hustler on the block. Two things I always believed in were controlling my destiny and being the best at whatever I did. Those same "homies" that I hung with on the corner are now either dead or incarcerated. Many of them now realize their mistakes. Thank God I was blessed with the insight to realize that I could not live this life forever. I knew that I would not grow old on the streets. How many hustlers do you see retiring as millionaires at age thirty or even thirty-five? It's a life of hard knocks and quick money, but not longevity.

I never had intentions of attending college, let alone becoming a physician but I remained loyal to the pact I had made with two of my best friends. The growth I experienced during my freshman year as a biology major was exponential. We even formed a group named Ujamaa, where we mentored and tutored grammar-school students. We were our own fraternity. One thing I realized was that from early on, God taught me how to accept failure, poverty, and being unloved. Now, crazy as it sounds, I had to learn how to succeed and accept good fortune. This was new to me. When times got rough at school, when the work seemed to be overwhelming and I felt as if I couldn't take anymore, my motivating factor was that I had nothing to go home to. I did not have wealthy parents or parents who were physicians as many of my peers did. I did not have the ideal support system at home that so many people take for granted. I had myself, my desire to control my destiny, and to be the best I could.

Now, as an attending ER physician and director of community health at Newark Beth Israel Hospital, I have the opportunity to be the tangible image for kids to model themselves after, an image that I did not have when I was younger. God has given me the opportunity to touch people, to motivate students, and to reach teens who are screaming for help, just as I was. I want kids to know that education is "hot," the "in-thing," the same way the latest sneakers or jeans are. I want to create a fad. I want them to get excited about education and excelling in whatever they set out to achieve. I want kids to know that education saved and improved the quality of my life and can do the same for them. We have to show the younger generation this, but in a way that is comprehensible and interesting to them. This is the purpose of the Three Doctors Foundation.

The Three Doctors Foundation puts a face on education and health. It allows me and my two friends, Drs. George Jenkins and Rameck Hunt, to motivate kids without "preaching" to them. That's one of the reasons why I didn't listen to many adults when I was growing up. Either they sounded as if they were "preaching" or I picked up the vibe that they weren't genuinely concerned. When we attend book signings, we draw hundreds of people. Sometimes the line is out the door! Parents write letters and send e-mails about how inspiring our book is and that they themselves decided to continue their education. Or sometimes they tell me that they saw their own child in the pages of our book. What unifies us all is that the struggles in life are real and it's always a good feeling to know that you are not alone and that someone was once where you were and made it. I have been blessed with the valuable commodity of peace since giving myself to others. I don't mean being taken advantage of, but giving my time, my positive energy, and sharing my story.

There are many valuable lessons that I have learned along this journey, my life. I had to learn how to balance mainstream America and the inner city. I learned how to become a chameleon because although I was no longer involved with the streets, I wanted to keep my street credibility. I learned to overcome interpretations of interactions. That is, I learned that when someone looked at me, it wasn't because they had "beef" with me. They were just looking. Last, but not least, I learned that in order to be "large" and make a worldwide impression, we sometimes have to affiliate with others unlike ourselves without a fear of losing ourselves because, after all, we are all just people.

Education is a foundation. We need to be educated in order not to be taken advantage of. I want kids to know that getting good grades is cool and nothing to be ashamed of, but something to be celebrated. I want kids to say that they want to be like "the three doctors" the same way they want to "be like Mike." What the Williams sisters and Tiger Woods have done for sports, what P. Diddy and Russell Simmons have done for music, I want to do for education.

I still reside in Newark, New Jersey, and I have to wear different hats every day. On my way to work, I travel through "war zones." At the hospital, I am a respected physician who can hang with the best and brightest of them all. I sometimes treat a patient with a stroke, and five minutes later I am treating a teenage boy who was shot two blocks away from where I live. This is how my reality stays balanced.

If I had to create a motto that defines my life it would be "Dedication, determination, and discipline." The dedication to stay focused on your goals, the determination to overcome all obstacles, and the discipline to sacrifice what it takes to achieve your destiny.

Dr. Sampson Davis *is a practicing physician at Newark Beth Israel Medical Center. He's the best-selling author of* The Pact.

Charting Success

Antonio "L.A." Reid

I grew up wanting to be James Brown.

I was born and raised in Cincinnati, Ohio, in a single-parent home, where my mom provided unconditional love and support. I began my music career by playing drums with various local bands. I was influenced by a diverse range of artists whose music spanned genres from pop and rock to jazz and soul—Miles Davis, Sly Stone, the Beatles, Led Zeppelin, and of course, the legend himself, James Brown.

I became a member of the Deele in 1980. Kenny "Babyface" Edmonds and I found that we had a special musical bond, and we went on to collaborate as songwriters and producers for a range of artists including veteran soul crew the Whispers, Bobby Brown, Karyn White, Pebbles, After 7, Paula Abdul, and Whitney Houston.

Discovering an artist with that special something is a feeling I cannot describe. Some people have the presence, others have the talent, but when combined it is absolute magic. The feeling I get from discovering talent is second only to the feeling that I had when my children were born.

Together, Kenny and I discovered amazing talent, won three Grammy Awards and numerous Producer of the Year and Songwriter of the Year Awards, and had thirty-three number-one singles. We took our partnership to the next level when we decided to start our own record company, LaFace Records.

Within ten years, we were able to develop artists like Toni Braxton, whose forty million albums and singles sold and six Grammy Awards have made her one of the most successful female artists in modern music. And Outkast, which is the most innovative hip-hop band in the world today. And Usher, whose talent and drive have made him an international superstar. And TLC, which is the most successful girl group in history. We were also able to develop younger producers such as Dallas Austin and Organized Noise.

When it was announced that I was named president and CEO of Arista Records two years ago, I felt that it was an incredible opportunity for someone like me—someone who had grown up in the ranks, first as a performer, then a producer, and later as cofounder of a music label.

I prepared myself and enrolled in a twelve-week Advanced Management Program at the Harvard Business School. The program, designed for senior-level executives, was a crash course in contemporary management principles. I was the only music business professional among the group of CEOs and COOs, who represented a variety of business disciplines from around the world.

The media and some of my peers were counting me out before I even got in the race. Before I could even set up shop, the criticism was swirling. Many thought that my stint would be very brief and that I could not live up to Clive Davis's accomplishments or fill his shoes. Clive Davis is a bona fide legend, and instead of trying to fill his shoes, I set out to chart my own course.

I dived into my work and challenged myself to accomplish what others were saying was impossible. I had to take a look inside, and identify and pursue my ideas of happiness and success. I love music, I love creating it, and my passion was my career. This was an incredible opportunity, and I planned to take full advantage of it.

It was not easy, but the focus and long hours that my team and I put in have begun to pay off. We have had incredible success the past two years with artists such as Dido, Pink, Carlos Santana, and Avril Lavigne, as well as all the artists who came from LaFace with me. A belief in God, and the lessons I have learned along my journey have taught me that it is not easy charting your place in life, but the rewards of hard work and faith are wonderful.

Antonio "L.A." Reid is the president and CEO of Arista Records. He maintains the Arista legacy in which he has played such a key role during the past eleven years. He continues to inspire and nurture today's top artists, just as he did at LaFace Records, the groundbreaking Atlanta-based recording company (owned by BMG Entertainment and distributed by Arista) that he founded with partner Kenneth "Babyface" Edmonds in 1989.

Academics . . .

David Maurrasse, Ph.D.

My favorite part of being an academic is the flexible schedule. Some might say, "What a shallow thought." No matter, it's my life. Certainly I work within a hierarchy in academia, but my flexible schedule sometimes lulls me into believing that I control my own destiny. Don't get me wrong, politics in higher education may be worse than corporate politics, or even politics themselves, but when you can work at home some days, and come to campus on others, and stay away from campus for about four months out of the year, you can have the time to collect your sanity.

Something about academia is not as insulting as some other fields, since we are given the latitude to determine our topics for research and writing. But just when an academic thinks he or she can coast, the "peers" come along to remind everyone of just how tricky the world of higher education can be. Who are these peers? Friends? Coworkers? Well, they're the ones who study what you study in your field. On one level, having your future determined by your peers sounds, looks, and smells like justice. But what if these peers are jealous? What if they expect you to be just like them in order to advance? I forget the precise figure, but the number of Black tenured professors is something like 2 percent of all tenured faculty; I think almost 90 percent of tenured professors are White. So, basically, peers are White, unless one solely focuses on Black studies.

Sometimes I wonder if I will ever have to stop proving myself. But it has become painfully clear that any professional Black woman or man is in the perpetual position of reminding supervisors, employees, and students of credentials that would be considered superior for Whites, and demonstrating that we can do our jobs and do them well. Being a professor, especially a young athletic-looking one, takes me out of the role that mainstream society has envisioned for a Black man. One day I will actually be who someone thinks I am in an airport. I guess every day is Halloween for me. I can recall the day when I was in my undergraduate dormitory at the University of Michigan. I stepped into the elevator. Two young White men were on board. One of them asked, "Are you on the football team?" I replied, "No, I'm just a regular student here." He said, "Are you sure?"

I love football, but I am not a football player. I, however, can be a football player every day. I think I've been a basketball player more often. I don't think that I resemble many people, but I am not sure if that matters. "Haven't I seen you on TV?" Well, maybe someday. But today, you probably did not see me on TV on the court or on the field. For some whites, it is so hard to imagine Black people stepping out of their media-shaped idea of who a non-poor Black person should be. Black athletes and entertainers are often celebrated by many Whites, but it is harder for them to celebrate Black professionals whose lives center on primarily mental pursuits. After all, the pursuits are to be left to Whites—thinking, management, decision making, ownership, policy making, medical research, and on. This is not to suggest that athletics and entertainment do not involve thinking (they obviously do), but when someone thinks of a profession for "smart" people one envisions particular roles—roles that are not intended for Black folks.

This perception adds a few more bricks to the towering wall before any Black person's path to some form of professional success, only adding to the pressure that comes with challenging course work or training. The pressure to exceed expectations sometimes makes me want not just to achieve, but to shatter any task before me. Because shattering the criteria (for me) means shattering the perception (of Black people in general), it means breaking out of the box. It still amazes me how quickly, with limited information, people can place someone else in a box. It often takes a lot of effort to get out of that box. If you're Black, you have to get way out of that box—be a star. Why is it that in order to become a Black professional, one must be a star? It's not that we should strive for mediocrity, but the persistence of discrimination has led to widespread White mediocrity in our various professions. Whites who exceed the requirements of their training are fast tracked. You've seen them, whizzing by you, even when their work isn't as good as yours.

There's a dehumanizing quality to our professional pursuits. In our efforts to succeed and dispel myths of Black inferiority, we can become distant and limited. We can devote too much time to work, and not enough time to relations with others and community service. I can recall leaving behind a number of my artistic interests while in graduate school. I was so focused on finishing my dissertation and proving that I could get a Ph.D., that I lost some of myself in the process.

When I was teaching a number of Black undergrads in my first academic position at Yale University, I was struck by how many of them went to law school. Maybe a couple of them went on to business school. Those who went on other paths tended to do so after they tried law school or a corporate career path. For some of us, it is so important to make money and support our families, as well as gain "respectable" careers, that we limit ourselves. I remember my mother's reaction when I told her that I was heading to graduate school instead of professional school. It seemed a waste to her, at least until she realized that I was getting a Ph.D. and teaching at Ivy League universities. But I have watched some Whites take on some really compelling careers. Absent the pressure to be the first or among the first college graduates in a family, and the various dynamics that affect the goals of young Black men and women, one can think more freely and explore more widely. My undergraduate years did that for me, but I wonder what I might end up being if I had more time, and I did not have very many pressures—maybe a sommelier, I don't know.

Ever hear of divide and conquer? If so few Black people reach particular levels of professional advancement, then some of us are leaving others behind. Therefore, we are competing among ourselves for a few slots. Of course, this is the case for everyone. But these realities are magnified for people of color. Sometimes I wonder if our competition with each other might be too intense, and whether or not a more collective effort to increase the number of slots might be the best use of our time. If we are not organized around some unified strategy, then who will hold institutions accountable when we are not sufficiently represented? When conditions make our lives difficult?

Everything I have stated so far is focused on the experiences of the more privileged sectors of the Black community. If we want to talk about power and respect, professional and wealthier members of the community must take some responsibility for those who are not so fortunate. Legalized barriers, which prevented Black clerks and nurses and teachers from becoming managers, doctors, and professors were removed in the not-so-distant past. Undoubtedly, discrimination was not eliminated, but opportunities opened up for some; some of us could move out of the 'hood, and get higher paying jobs. This demographic shift created a chasm within the Black community that had not been seen in the United States. Therefore, if my individual pursuit of power and respect does not coincide with a collective goal for the Black community, then I am really enriching only myself. How to incorporate social responsibility into career goals is a continual challenge for all Black students and professionals. Indeed, it is important for others. But one of the things that I have noticed about being Black is that, unlike in the case of most Whites, anything I do is measured against some community-wide goal. This is something we live with every day. It is yet another dimension of pressure, but, in my case, one that is very welcomed.

I could go on, as there's just too much to say about power and respect, but let me just leave you with a few ideas—sort of like a survival guide:

Know the rules of the game, but don't follow all of the rules.

Always think about your next gig.

Avoid premature celebrations.

Plan, plan, plan.

Know your strengths and weaknesses.

Know your friends (from those who are not your friends).

Salute those who determine your destiny (more people than you might think).

Challenge those same people. (They'll never respect you if you don't.)

Treat as many people as possible like royalty.

Organize your supporters. (Some aspects of life are like political campaigns.)

Always support your community.

Constantly pursue knowledge.

Be good at what you do, even if you don't like it.

Never go away until you have to.

Stay "on" as much as possible, wherever you may be.

Make yourself indispensable.

Be prepared to remake yourself.

David Maurrasse Ph.D. *is a consultant, lecturer, and social commentator whose primary position is as an assistant professor in the School of International and Public Affairs and the Urban Planning Program at Columbia University. However, he wears several other hats. He is the president and CEO of DJM & Associates, a consulting firm dealing with nonprofit management and philanthropy. He is also the author of* Beyond the Campus *and the soon-to-be published* Listening to Harlem *and* A Future for Everyone.

A Measure of Success
Kojo Bentil

First and foremost, family is the foundation upon which our society is built. I am originally from Ghana, West Africa, and family is very important to us there. I think the importance of family is a fundamental principle that can be transferred anywhere and exists in most cultures. So before anything else, if you have a sound family, to me that is a more accurate measure of success than your amassed wealth or career status. I do think quality of life is very important. I am also an ambitious guy. I appreciate the fact that being successful in your career and being able to build wealth are directly associated with family. I can create an environment where my family can reap the benefits of my hard work, and that is very, very important.

You know what is more important? The happiness and well-being of my wife and children will result in me being happier. Luckily, I work with a boss who is pretty understanding, and that makes the difference. I don't know that I have a specific formula, but I try to get up pretty early in the morning. I wake up with my children at 6:00 A.M. so that I can get some "our" time. It is all about time management—getting as much as you can into one day's time even if it is forty-five minutes fixing them breakfast, talking, and getting them ready for school. I try to get home at least two to three times a week before they go to bed. On the weekends is when I spend most of my time with the children. I spend all day with them unless there is some other obligation to be out. That is where I get my balance. During the day, I focus on what I do pretty much undisturbed with an occasional check in for five minutes with my wife, Ingrid, and the children.

Other principles that I try to live by are trust and loyalty. Trust and loyalty are what matter in every relationship in life. Love, to me, is an emotional reaction that you almost can't control; it will come and well up inside you just because you are a human being. Trust and loyalty are things that you work at and, you have to make a conscious decision day in and day out to demonstrate and practice trust. I work in the entertainment industry, and in this business, your personal integrity is frequently tested, whether it's by the lure of an affair or a one-night stand or by someone proposing a lucrative but shady business deal. The real issue is, do you breach that trust and take that chance even if you are discreet about it? I couldn't live with my-self, because I couldn't live a lie and pretend that nothing ever happened. As far as I'm concerned, if someone I trust did that to me, the entire relation-ship would be undermined. In my view, the issue of trust is a zero-sum game. There is no halfway disloyal—you either are loyal or you aren't. This is the philosophy that Ingrid and I are teaching our children. The ramifica-tions of deception typically result in a never-ending slippery slope. I think of how I would feel if I encounter a situation where I discover that I am being deceived by a person who I thought was a compadre or loyal ally. The feeling of betrayal could be devastating.

Even in business, there are various times that I hear from other people who suggest shady deals and offer to "take care" of me on the back end. Simply put, I don't have a price. It is about personal integrity. Once you play the game of deception and deceit, you can never know how it ends. Once you tell that lie, you are going to keep lying to cover it up. It is not a good way to do business, because then you end up on the same slippery slope. There's no trying to cut corners in business or in life, because there is no substitute for hard work. People talk about being lucky and being at the right place at the right time, but it is also being prepared as a result of the hard work so that you can take advantage of the opportunities that come your way. It's important to have a plan and direction, but you must be flex-ible enough to take advantage of unexpected opportunities.

Solid relationships are what led me to the music industry. Kedar Massenburg and I were law school colleagues. We met in 1988 when we were both students at the University of North Carolina at Chapel Hill. He was a first-year student and just came into the law school, and I was a second-year student. We met in the hallway of the library and just started talking. During that first conversation, we both connected and knew that we had to work on something together in the future. I told him that my plan after I graduated was to work for a major New York City law firm and after that I planned on doing something on my own, using what I learned at the firm. I always knew that I did not want to work for someone for my whole career. We stayed very close, and when I graduated I ended up with a job with a major New York law firm, and Kedar came out and went straight into the music business. He always knew that's where he wanted to go after law school—whether it was as a manager, industry lawyer, or label head, he was going to work within the music industry. I spent almost six years at the firm where I was a well-respected associate in a firm with two hundred lawyers. In my first two years at the firm, I was the only Black lawyer. The education that I got learning about business and how business gets done was at the firm, which represented many *Fortune* 500 companies.

I made some key contacts and consider my experience there as my own personal training day.

I was well regarded at the firm and even considered that I may stick it out and try to make partner, but I had a five-year plan (that lasted almost six years). I decided against the partnership route because the firm did not encourage young lawyers to go out and develop client relationships, which are the lifeblood of firms and companies in the service business. You need new blood to develop relationships so that you can retain this business long term. Whenever I tried to develop new relationships and bring in new clients, I was told that client development was the domain of partners or more senior associates.

At the same time, my conversations with Kedar were ongoing. In 1995, he was planning something big, and he approached me about the idea of finally having the opportunity to work together. I had to think about my readiness and flexibility. Was I prepared to make a move? At the same time, an opportunity came up with one of the firm's clients, a major pharmaceutical company, to come in and be an in-house lawyer.

A decision had to be made. I had to look at my life and determine exactly what it is I was striving for. It is a precious thing that very few get their hands on—the golden ring. As a lawyer, you strive to be the client. You have a much more manageable day as far as hours. You are working within a major corporation. You get a very good compensation package and the opportunity for advancement is mind blowing. Many CEOs, presidents, and senior executives of major corporations went through corporate legal departments. It was so ironic—I got an offer from my firm at the same time Kedar came to me. I had to trust my instincts, and my instincts said to go with Kedar. The trust between us was genuine. He believed in me, and I believed in him. And being best friends was simply the icing on the cake. I also knew we are competitive enough that if he became successful, it would burn my ass. He would never let me forget it. I just knew he would call me form some island he owned and say, "How does it feel humping for somebody?" That is kind of the lighter side of it. Finally, I just said to myself, "You know what, I have to take this opportunity, because if I don't, I'll be looking back over my shoulder always."

I had to take the chance with Kedar. If I didn't succeed—which was not part of the equation, but if on the off chance that I did not succeed—I still had my law degree. I had a great career I established for myself, and a great name in my circle. I am a member of the Bar of the State of New York and a member of the Federal Bar in the Southern District of New York. Those are the two tough places to be admitted in the bar. I knew I would be fine no matter what. At the time, my wife was pregnant with our first child, we were in the process of buying our first home, and she was saying, Are you sure you want to do this? "Are you going to have coverage? Health benefits? Is this going to be a steady check?" All those questions had to be considered at the end of the day. I love my wife, Ingrid. She asked those questions, but in the end she said, "Whatever you are going to do, I am going to support you 110 percent. We are not going to look back, because I trust you to do the right thing."

I took the chance, and here we sit eight years later. It has been a great ride. The first two years we went to a start-up company—a small boutique label that had $26 million in sales. We developed that for two to three years. After a few years, the partner in the venture reached out to us to run a legendary label—Motown. Unfortunately, it required us to move back to working for somebody instead of being entrepreneurs, which can be a tremendous amount of fun. But, that is, again, about being flexible. Our first reaction was we don't know if we want to do that, to go in-house, but we looked at the big picture and the opportunity. Berry Gordy's formula was what Kedar based his company on originally. What better challenge to take—to try to revive that legendary label so that it is once again legendary in today's contemporary market. We took the challenge, and as my wife said, we aren't looking back.

Most people think there's a duality that exists between the business person they are and the person they are when they are at home with their family. I see no duality. The same integrity, flexibility, and readiness need to exist for you in both places. You can't be a dishonest, manipulative monster at work and not have it translate to your home life. Recognizing that your family is your backbone and that it is important to rely on the stability, love, and support of your family is what's important. Nurturing your family is the most important thing you can do. True success begins and ends at home.

Kojo Bentil is the senior vice president for operations and business development and manages the daily business operations of the Motown Record Company. Mr. Bentil develops strategies to cross-promote the Motown brand and Motown recording artists. He and his lovely wife, Ingrid, have three beautiful children.

The Power of Influence

Smokey D. Fontaine

I am an only child who was born in London to an African-American woman and a British father. Both of my parents are also only children, so growing up my family consisted of my parents and my two grandmothers. Both of my grandfathers passed away before I was born and I never knew any aunts or uncles. My mother is from New York, and when I was seven, the family left London for the city and I spent my childhood on the Upper West Side of Manhattan. My parents work together as documentary film-makers, and we moved to the States for the filming of *I Heard it Through the Grapevine*, a documentary my folks did with the writer James Baldwin. The film took the better part of three years and my mother and I have never moved back to England. I have been writing since elementary school. Poetry, at first, then short stories, often with all kinds of strange and futuristic details. Writing was an escape for me, a place where I could explore worlds different from my own.

In school I loved creative writing because it allowed me to express my feelings and showcase my talent in a place where, all too often, I wasn't taken seriously. See, Smokey is my given birth name, but teachers never believed me when I introduced myself. They couldn't believe that Smokey wasn't a nickname, and often threatened to suspend me if they checked my school records and discovered what they thought had to be a lie. Now, after years of working in the entertainment industry, my name has served me well because it's so memorable and pretty damn cool. But it took me a long time to be able to carry the name Smokey without any embarrassment.

After graduating from Wesleyan University, where a love for essay writing grew, I went to teach sixth-grade English in Baltimore, Maryland. Teaching was one of the most challenging experiences I ever had, but also the most empowering, because it gave me the opportunity to be truly influential. There is nothing like standing in front of a room filled with thirty twelve- and thirteen-year-olds who, whether they admit it or not, are desperate to learn and be taught about life.

One of the most striking things I saw while teaching was how meaningful hip-hop music was to my students. It influenced every aspect of their lives, from how they spoke and the clothes they wore, to what they believed and how they behaved. It was like they lived through it. And it was everywhere: on TV at home, on the radios outside, in their headphones all the other hours of the day. For better or worse, hip-hop was clearly the primary way that these kids were being socialized and I often asked myself, "How do I compete with that? How can their parents, first, or me, their teacher, ever conteract something so influential?" It was then that I began to think perhaps if I wrote about this music and culture, a culture I, too, felt was a huge part of my life, maybe I could make a difference in that area. Maybe I could impact the way we enjoyed and understood what we were all consuming so ravenously.

In 1995, I took a chance on my dream of becoming a music journalist and after fulfilling my two-year commitment to Teach For America, I came back to New York City. Three months later, I couldn't believe my luck when I landed an internship with Scott Poulson-Bryant—a writer who had a column I read all the time in *Spin* magazine called "Dreaming America." He was also one of the founding editors of *Vibe*. I remember screaming out loud in my apartment the day he called and asked me to be his intern. I didn't even care that I would be working for free, I was just so excited to have found an opportunity to get in the game and make my dream a reality.

My time as an intern with Scott at *Vibe* was truly a learning experience. I quickly realized that I had idealized many things and learned that everything is not always as it seems. Having just graduated from college, I held idealistic views about the staff, who they would be, and how they would handle their business. I thought I would be in a hotbed of African-American creativity, working with a team, striving for a meaningful mission. There were many gifted writers and editors there, but the politics of the business interfered with many things and our work enviornment was affected every day. As a result, I've become slightly cynical about the entertainment and publishing business and make sure to temper my expectations so I don't become awestruck and then ultimately disappointed by people and things. It's my way of protecting myself and trying to remain productive in whatever environment I find myself.

The most valuable aspect of my *Vibe* experience was that I formed a wonderful friendship and mentor relationship with Scott, and he taught me my first lessons about being a professional writer. The first thing he said was not to be one. "Smokey, you don't want to be just a writer; you want to be an editor. Editors have power over the words on the page, and they write the checks. Writers don't." That was advice I ran with and, since I also loved the process of editing, looked for a way to start my editorial career. It came by helping launch the U.S. version of a British hip-hop and fashion magazine called *Trace*. After forming a relationship with the publisher, who liked my writing and the hustle I was doing for the magazine all around New York, I became *Trace*'s U.S. editor and worked hard to find the magazine a distribution deal in the States that would establish it as a presence on the newsstand. It was a fabulous magazine with interesting commentary about pop culture and music, and when we relaunched *Trace* in 1997 with Mariah Carey on the cover asking "How Can I Be Down?," I considered it an attempt at doing "a better *Vibe*."

Trace was a blessing for me because I found my own voice in the midst of building the magazine. I worked on my editing skills and wrote stories about everyone from Mary J. Blige to Lenny Kravitz and the Notorious B.I.G. I began to establish an identity in the music industry, and artists and executives began to trust my talent and integrity so much that one month for a cover story, Sean "Puffy" Combs agreed for me to spend an entire week with him. I asked Puff to let me be "a fly on the wall" and just watch him do what he does. I made arrangements for a photographer to shadow him as well. My week with him was fascinating. It was after Biggie had passed away and Puff was preparing to do his "I'll Be Missing You" tribute to him on the American Muisc Awards. In that seven days, Puff took me everywhere. We were in the studio, in the rehearsal hall, in meeting after meeting, on the basketball court—wherever his day's business took him. I titled the article "The Hottest Working Man in Show Business." Now Puffy's only concern during the whole process was the photographs: "Don't have me looking fucked up on the cover," he warned me and I assured him that this "reportage" style would work just fine. Well, my heart sank the morning I was in my art director's office in London and opened the box of contact sheets. We had nothing. I almost shrank to the floor. The only cover possibility we had was Puff wearing a T-shirt and shorts while talking on his cell phone. He was getting ready to play ball at the time, standing outside his fancy gym at Chelsea Piers in New York. Later, I felt the image did capture what Puff was about, a man always taking care of business, but it also did exactly what Puff asked not to happen: It caught him with his hair messed up.

My goal for *Trace* was for it to be a nationally distributed magazine with popular stars and engaging articles, one that people all over the country couldn't wait to read. After a while, though, it became clear that my vision was different from that of the publisher's. He wanted more of a small niche fashion magazine devoted to African-American couture. I liked what he wanted to do, but my vision was bigger and grander.

After working at *Trace* for almost three years, one day *The Source* called, and I joined their staff as music editor. This was where I found a relationship with the rapper DMX. At the time, he hated the media, but after our first meeting, we somehow formed a unique relationship. Whenever I interviewed him, we'd end up having deep conversations about everything from the plight of young black children to the struggles he fought in his own head. Over the years, I wrote all three cover features X gave *The Source* and realized that he had more of a story than could ever be captured in a magazine article. We decided together to write a book, and once publisher HarperCollins came on board, *E.A.R.L.: The Autobiography of DMX* was born.

Ralph Ellison writes in *Invisible Man* about being unseen as a Black man in American society and how damaging it is to allow yourself to feel emotionally and intellectually limited. Many young brothers are faced with this dilemma every day. They have a limited view of their place in the world, and their identity is based upon only the few things they have experienced. The challenge with my students in Baltimore was to get them to think about things other than what was directly in front of them. Many of them lived only a few blocks away from Baltimore's Inner Harbor, a beautiful downtown entertainment and shopping district, where there were many wonderful things to explore, but most of them had never been there. It wasn't that they didn't want to go, it was more that they didn't even know going to the Inner Harbor was something to want to do. As kids, that's not their fault, but many times, even as adults, we tend to feel safe in our space, no matter how small or unfulfilling it is, because it's what's familiar to us. It's what we know.

But we have to conquer this fear of stepping outside of the box because many opportunities to expand our way of thinking will remain elusive until we go out and grab them.

Through my career, I've learned that you can learn something from everyone. That is why I am a big supporter of mentoring, whether as part of an official Big Brother or Big Sister program or just privately in your own home or workplace. I am very thankful that Scott was there to guide me and show me the ropes of my profession.

The impact of hip-hop on popular culture is immeasurable. I believe it has touched more people than any genre of music before it. Hip-hop artists of all kinds can now use their talents to bring them to places they once thought unattainable. And once you capture that hip-hop passion, you can achieve whatever you focus your mind on. I am a product of that philosophy and I believe in that power.

Three months ago, my wife and I celebrated the birth of our first child, Sofia. Now I feel my life has become a big cliché because I'm always telling people, "Becoming a father is the best thing that's ever happened to me."

But it's true. When a child comes into your life, parenting goes to the top of your priority list and everything else becomes a distant second. A baby looks to you to teach them everything about the world. They're sponges who absorb every word, every behavior, every image you put in front of them. There is no bigger influence, and I am in awe of the challenge.

Looking back at my life so far, it's clear that I've found it rewarding to take the high road, the road less traveled. I find myself constantly striving to find things to motivate, excite, and teach me. I like to push and explore and try new things. I also work to really care about and take responsibility for everything I put out there—to my friends, my audience, and my family. My choices haven't always been easy, but the reward is that much sweeter.

Smokey D. Fontaine *is the author of* E.A.R.L.: The Autobiography of DMX *and coauthor of* What's Your Hi-Fi Q? *He has written extensively about the entire spectrum of hip-hop and rhythm and blues for more than a decade. He lives in New York.*

Your Soul's Journey

Withhold not good from them to whom it is due, when it is in the power of thine hand to do it.   —Proverbs 3:27

The perception of choosing a business partner or business service because it is White-owned and therefore "better" is a horrible mistake and a setback to Black professionals. A publicist who went on to become major news herself once said that "Black rappers and musicians prefer White publicists." This is, of course, after they become successful. This infuriated so many Black publicists nationally who work with musicians sometimes in the beginning stages of their career. The fact was, after their clients "made it," there was a mass exodus to White publicists.

Gwendolyn Quinn of GQ Media and fellow brother Marlynn Synder, along with some heavyweights across the country, built the African American Publicity Collective. Over five hundred publicists talk to one another daily if not weekly across the United States and Canada. They share resources, help one another selflessly with projects including this book. Now that's power!

True power is taking defeat or challenge and turning it to a life lesson or an opportunity. The ability to be truly powerful is to create positive change for yourself and in turn help to create for others. Your journey to inner power and self-respect is growing to understand a true sense of power and how to utilize it to help others. Recognizing the need for self-respect and respecting others is an opportunity to create alliances with one another. We all need to know how power and respect work hand-in-hand to grow as a people.

Soul Source

Giving people the opportunity to enhance themselves mentally, culturally, economically, and spiritually is the most powerful and respectful thing you can offer someone.

- What is power to you?
- Do you think you have the power to change things in your life that you don't like?
- Do you provide honest and sincere appreciation?
- Do you point to other people's mistakes?
- Do you make other people feel important?
- Do you talk about your own mistakes first before criticizing others?

CHAPTER 9

LOVE, SEX, AND ROMANCE

The Black experience is 360 degrees. Love and sex are probably two
of them, but there are 358 more.
—Gil Scott-Heron

Sexual desire is the most powerful of human desires, and love is the most
powerful of human emotions. To fully understand Black men, we must
look at their sexuality as well as their ability to express love in partnership.
What do Black men want from their women? What are they giving, and
what are they seeking in return?

At our roundtable, we met men who earnestly did their best in relationships. Some men never had the opportunity to witness a healthy loving relationship between a man and a woman in their homes. Often their ideas on
relationships came from television. If you really think about it, we all look
for the ideal individual and have hopes and dreams beyond what we have
witnessed in our own lives. Where did those ideas come from?

Men as well as women have preconceived notions on what they want in
a relationship: a combination of the way mom cooked or took charge, a submissive partner for comfort's sake, security, carnal satisfaction, or companionship. The problem is that Black men sometimes may not express exactly
what they want to their partner because they don't even know what they are
truly looking for.

Black men are sensitive loving creatures that are just as afraid and fearful about the power of love, sex, and romance—they are not supermen.
They experience low self-esteem, hang-ups and bad habits they want to
change but may not have the ability, training, or foresight to do so. Before
you tell them what their issues are, they already know, yet don't have the
know-how to make the necessary adjustments. They have to compete with
the fact that the perception is all Black men have unusually large members
and must always outdo the last sexual encounter, sometimes never relaxing
to truly enjoy himself. One man at our Atlanta roundtable described what
he believed to be true. "Men," he said, "are like an apple pie—they a have a

hard exterior, but when you get inside, and sometimes you've got to work to get inside, it is soft and wonderful." But most of the men we talked to were frustrated and angry and uncertain what role they should take in a relationship. Many of them felt unsupported and not listened to. They feel that they are judged in reference to how much money they have. They experience loss just as women do, but they won't let you know it. One thing's for sure: they wanted everyone to know that they cannot take the place of our fathers. They can't read minds, and they don't truly know what you want.

The lack of totally understanding who you truly are and what you want turns a wonderful romance, steamy sex, and great conversation into one huge mess. It becomes a car without a navigational system, directions, or gas. It all adds up to that feeling of being lost and stranded. Where do we go from here?

Love, romance, and sex can drive men to heights of superachievement. Love serves as a safety valve and ensures balance, poise, and constructive effort.

Sex and love have been misunderstood throughout the ages. Sexual desire is the most powerful of human emotions. When driven by this desire, men develop keenness of imagination, courage, willpower, and persistence. So strong and compelling is the desire for sexual contact that men freely run the risk of life and reputation to indulge in it.

Researcher and author Napoleon Hill brought this concept to life in his book, *Think and Grow Rich*, that men of great achievement are men with highly developed sexual natures: men who have learned the art of sex transmutation. Switching the mind from thoughts of physical expression to thoughts of some other nature. When harnessed and redirected, it can become a powerful creative force in literature, art, or in other professions or callings—including, of course, the accumulation of riches. Some men who have accumulated great fortunes and achieved outstanding recognition in literature, art, industry, architecture, and other professions were motivated by the influence of a woman. That influence can be derived from mother, wife, sister, lover, or friend.

There are an increasing number of men who understand the true power of love, sex, and romance—that they are exchanges of energy. As they get older and wiser, men refrain from having sex immediately and opt to get to know their partner first. On the other side, some men also will have sex with multiple partners, letting each individual believe the relationship is monogamous. Often they maneuver to shield manhood or ego. Sometimes if he has a woman he truly cares about, he wants to be one step ahead of the hurt just in case it is on the horizon. They don't understand that the number one reason a woman loses respect for a man is that he doesn't keep his word.

With all that is happening in a Black man's life, such as pressure, stress, and prejudice, it is sometimes hard to extend love for someone else if the love and esteem are not there for themselves. Your journey to love is understanding and maintaining self-love and knowing it will beget the true love you can develop for another human being. Establishing a union with a mate should not be based on fairy tales or falsehoods, but on a solid foundation from which you can together work and grow as a team. These stories show why men make the choices that they do, and give you an inside look at how they hurt. We hope that their experiences will help you to shape a better relationship.

Smoke Screens

Lenny Green

With the allure of smoke-and-mirror images often discussed and promised by brothers to sisters, it still amazes me that brothers are surprised when sisters refuse to remain in the picture long enough to see these so-called images materialize. We, as brothers, have a tendency, all too often, to give sweet ear candy to the sisters we think very little of. At the same time, we lure them in with great fantasies and hopeless dreams of a meaningful relationship, knowing deep down inside we can't fulfill that order. Now that's not to say we don't want to be in a relationship, we are simply afraid of keeping it real. Oh, didn't you know, keeping it real, to us means commitment, responsibility, emotional support and sometimes even love, which inevitably we feel will lead to the one thing that controls the soft spot in all our souls, the fear of rejection.

My observation came to me when I was a little boy. It was in my house; I lived it. My mother, my first image of womanhood, woman-ness, and womanly love, fell victim to a brother with these identical character traits. He was a man who portrayed himself to be one way but ended up being another. He filled her mind with hopes and dreams, which he had no intentions of living up to, with her by his side. He ended up being a run in the hay and a burden of responsibilities. His relationship with my mother did show me how some men very often will play on women's emotional state. Needless to say, my mother endured this type of pain for many years, so her effort to teach me how to really interact with women became one of her main focuses.

The sad thing is that in today's society, there's a whole generation of relationships that are built on false images and smoke screens, and it's highly accepted by so many women. Simply put, if you're not the brother driving the hottest whip (car), or making big paper (money), most women are not even checking for you. You see, we've grown to accept that the character of the person is not important; it's simply what can you do for me—self-gratification. Ironically, men are choosing their ladies under the same measures of false pretenses, she's "fine as wine," her booty looks so good, and so on. Don't get me wrong; choosing someone who looks good or who is motivated and successful is not a bad thing; however, it shouldn't be the *only* things we get caught up on.

Brothers choose certain partners based on their needs, wants, and desires, often the things they have lacked in life. And again, wanting some things may not be a bad thing, but time and experience have shown us that *greed* often takes over our minds, and physical desires eventually lead to destruction. Instead of choosing one or two partners, we choose twenty or more at the same time for different reasons, promising them things beyond our reach, temporary need, and sometimes even our understanding. We're leading our women down a road of hopelessness, low self-esteem, and depression when all they are looking for is to have a little more from us as men.

I'm not an advocate of misusing, abusing, and causing emotional and psychological turmoil in our women. I'm one of those brothers who enjoys keeping it real. Sadly, I report this often doesn't have many women knocking at my door, and that's cool, too, because I'm not a department store wanting and waiting for just anybody to come in. Trust me, I've had my share of being taken advantage of and even abused, and I'm thankful and happy of life's various adventures, for they have matured me over the years. I've been able to become more aware of certain women and their intentions in the earlier stages of us getting to know one another. This is not to say that I or any man can't be tricked or persuaded by other means, but I try to stay aware. We, as men, fall short when it comes to holding our ground at the sight of a beautiful woman's sensual and sexual persuasion. In the world of radio and entertainment, temptation walks by every five minutes, so the waters are always being tested.

I assume whoever feels they have satisfied their personal desires with no care in the world of the other person's feelings may feel a sense of being in control of the situation. Control is a very interesting power that many wish to have; men generally have a tendency to desire control, and in turn, women have a tendency to appreciate men who take control and take charge. To the ladies, I say be careful, for this is where abuse can slip in for the wrong person; the person who doesn't have an interest at all in your well-being.

Our visual senses play a big part in the lives of men—we are attracted to women who look good—and ladies know that. That's why they bring out their best representative every chance they get. Two lessons of life I've grown to appreciate are, "All that glitters is not gold" and "You can't judge a book by its cover," but more and more often, men forget about those rules and just go with the flow. I know I have.

I remember this one young lady who caught my attention one night while I was hanging out with one of my boys in New York. She was very attractive, she had an interest in modeling, she was five feet six and around 120 pounds, very shapely, and had a great personality. At the time when we met, she was involved with someone, so I knew from jump, nothing could happen. I'm just not one of those brothers who will pursue a woman if I clearly know there is someone else in her life.

Don't get me wrong—I'll get tempted like the next man, but I look at the bigger picture. So after that first night, our paths crossed on a few other occasions at social gatherings, and needless to say, over the course of time we became friends. As time passed, her relationship with the other brother started to fall apart, he got hooked on drugs, and that took her on an emotional roller coaster so bad that she went into a state of depression and moved from the New York area to her mother's home, in Maryland. A couple of years had gone by, we had been out of touch with each other due to her moving back home and me moving ahead in my radio career. Then one day at a social event, there she was—we literally bumped into one another. We had a great time, caught up on old times, and planned on getting together as quickly as possible. When we did get together, I was working in radio in Connecticut, and ironically she had family in Connecticut. We started dating shortly after. She was the first woman I ever saw in a thong, I didn't even know what they were at the time. I was falling in love—the question was, Was I falling in love with the woman or with her beauty? We were engaged within a year, even though she was still living in Maryland. At the time I was working for a little urban radio station making little to no money with no benefits. I knew I couldn't jump the broom working at that station. However, we set a date to be married anyway because I didn't want to chance losing her. I kept her abreast of my hopeful career moves, but things weren't looking promising, so I went to her and suggested we push the date back just until I got another job in radio. That's when she started to change. Communication went from little to none, she wasn't calling me as much as I would call her, and she was starting to keep in contact with her ex-boyfriend, the one who put her in a state of depression. As a matter of fact, she ended up staying at his house overnight in New York on a weekend when one of her girlfriends was getting married, telling me it wasn't any big deal and to understand. Well, to make a long traumatic story short, she ended up getting married while we were still engaged. This was truly a heart-breaking turn of events that I've never had closure with.

I realized we're put through lessons in life to make us stronger and hopefully wiser. The outcome of that situation didn't turn me sour toward women or relationships or both; it simply made me realize that I needed to learn more about myself. I'm still learning, and it's a wonderful journey.

That was also my first time having to deal with celibacy. In the entertainment industry, fast sex runs rampant at the drop of a dime, but I was never a man who just jumped from woman to woman. I've had my fair share of relationships, and I haven't been afraid of commitment, both long and short—but dealing with celibacy was something at first I clearly didn't want to face. Most men don't like to deal with it, so as a way of running they prefer to start jumping from woman to woman. Looking to satisfy that quick fix, some booty; that's all it is, with no emotional ties and clearly no commitment. More often than not, these quick fixes turn into one-night stands that just satisfy the need for the moment. When men do that, we are at a risk of continuing to help perpetuate dysfunctional views of men and the stereotype phrases become louder and louder: "All men are dogs," "They're all liars," "Men are good for nothing," "I don't need a man if I have to put up with nonsense."

The question that I leave you with, then becomes, What perception does man have of himself and woman seeing how, my brothers, woman is the other half of man? The brother whose upbringing has been without knowing the true essence of what love really is and what it really feels like, is *lost*. Lost from his mind, body, and soul, his individuality is tainted with foggy images of what he thinks women are, and with his lack of understanding, his knowledge is limited. He never understands what a woman really is, a gift from God for us to love.

Lenny Green is the host of "Kissing after Dark" on 98.7 KISS-FM, a radio station in New York City.

Open Your Eyes

Eric Roberson

I can pray for your dreams
Even if that means
That if all of your dreams come true
That I will not be with you forever
If I have to understand
That it's not in God's plans
For us to hold hands
Across untraveled lands together
I don't want to lose you
But you don't smile like you used to

Open your eyes to see the future
Is open like my arms to you
I'm not too blind to see
You're no longer happy
So if I have to walk away to say I love you
Then that's what I'll do

I can see it in your eyes
You can no longer disguise
That something is wrong
And the feelings are gone from this venture
Those warm kisses you gave
They now feel like winter days
And snowflakes are fun
But they melt when sun shines on them
I don't want to lose you
But you don't smile like you used to
And my arms no longer soothe you
And my words no longer move you

Open your eyes to see the future
Is open like my arms to you
I'm not too blind to see
You're no longer happy
So if I have to walk away to say I love you
Then that's what I'll do

Eric Roberson *is a singer's singer. He has worked with numerous artists from Musiq, Jill Scott, and Will Downing to 112, Malik Pendleton, and Kenny Latti- more. In addition to having a publishing deal with EMI Music Publishing, Eric runs the Blue Room, a fully equipped forty-eight-track recording studio in Franklin Park, New Jersey. He is currently recording his major label debut album. You can visit with him at www.blueerrosoul.com.*

The Power of Pussy

Kheven Lee LaGrone

I had spent weeks looking for the book. I couldn't find it in the local African-American bookstore. When I called White bookstores and asked for the book, the sales clerks hung up on me—even though I prefaced my request with the statement that the title might be offensive. One day, I saw a book vendor at the Berkeley flea market. I discreetly searched the table for the book. The vendor, an African-American woman, asked me what book was I looking for. Based on my experiences the past few weeks, I had decided if I didn't see the book on the table, I wasn't going to ask for it. She kept pressuring to help me. If she didn't have the book, she offered, she could order it for me. I told her that the title was a bit offensive. "I'm a fifty-year old woman," she told me, "I've seen and heard everything." She looked at me and waited.

Reluctantly, I told her, *"In Search of Good Pussy."*

"What?" She was obviously offended.

"In Search of Good Pussy," I answered.

She rolled her eyes and turned her back, grumbling, "I wouldn't bother with such trash."

"Have you ever heard of the book?" I asked defensively.

"No, but the title says it all," she growled.

The album *Rufus Featuring Chaka Khan* came out in the 1970s. On the back cover, Chaka flashed her sassy toothpaste smile seductively while wearing feathers in her untamed hair, a skimpy fur bra, and tight animal-skin pants. Her legs were spread *wide* across a bloodred, lip-shaped sofa. The background was hot pink. "Look at her." My sisters and girl cousins frowned. "She's so nasty. You can see the lips [of her pussy]."

My boy cousins loved it.

Boys and girls have different experiences with their genitals. While girls may be told "Don't let boys touch down there" or that "it" was dirty, boys had pissing contests and bragged about how big they were. In Oakland in the 1980s, I remember it was popular for young African-American men hanging on the corners to grab their crotches. It was a fad. Even the androgynous Michael Jackson seemed to have felt the need to similarly advertise his "manhood." A crotch-grab became one of his signature moves.

Around the same time, I remember sitting at the kitchen table with two women when one of them started rubbing the table and said, "I love it when a man takes his hand and rubs my big fat pussy." The other woman covered her face in shame. I found out later, they didn't like each other. The one woman had intentionally made that statement to offend the other "prissy" woman. She knew the other woman had always considered her to be vulgar.

The Black phallus has been mythologized. We grow up hearing that it has been envied and vilified. It is reputedly more powerful than other phalluses. In the early 1900s, when African-American men were being lynched, their genitalia were the focus. The penis was cut off and stuffed in the victims' mouths or kept as a prize. In the 1970s, some African-American writers and intellectuals "theorized" that it is the one power the Black man has in America, and that the White man is jealous. Even today, we often hear of Black men investing their whole personality and self-worth in their phalluses.

Yet this empowered Black male sexuality does not have to be restricted to the phallus. I've heard same-gender-loving male friends talk about "b.p." or "boy pussy." They brag about it. They "own it" even when giving it up. It is a position of power, the bestowing of pleasure. One man referred to his "boy pussy" as the Black man's kryptonite.

One of the most assertive and self-centered men I know brags about being "total pussy" in bed. He likes pretty young men because he can control them. Obviously, he exercises the power of pussy.

So when an African-American man, same-gender-loving or not, talks about pussy, it may not be vulgar or disrespectful. For some, it may be an appreciation of the power of pussy. In all the talk about the power of the penis, it is forgotten that it is the pussy, or a simulation of it, that gets it hard and useful. Even in prison, where the low man on the totem pole is the one who "gives up the pussy," inmates have fought over that pussy.

So when I asked for the book *In Search of Good Pussy*, the book vendor and I were speaking different languages.

Kheven Lee LaGrone is coediting with Delroy Constantine-Simms the upcoming Taboo or Not Taboo? *His writing has appeared in* Journal of African American Men, Media Ethics, To the Quick, San Francisco Chronicle, San Francisco Bay View, San Francsico Review of Books *and* River Crossings. *Kheven's interview of Michael Eric Dyson appeared in his book* Open Mike. *He also had a column titled "Afrocentrically Yours" in* SBC *and* Whazzup! *Kheven's installation art has been exhibited in Oakland and noted in the* Oakland Tribune.

Rhapsody in Two

T-Money

It takes just a few events that transpire early in life to help shape a man. Such experiences emerge more than others like matters of the heart. And in some cases, it can leave long-term impressions on your character. Often we hear the term "matters of the heart," and we think of soppy, weepy, teary-eyed females. We don't always give brothers the benefit of space for matters of the heart. While I would not use words like *weepy*, *soppy*, or *teary-eyed* to describe a hallmark event of my youth, I would definitely refer to my experience as meaningful, emotive, everlasting, and life changing.

This saga-turned-drama starts out in a quiet, clean, upper-middle-working class, neighborhood east of New York City. Let's just say when you mix youth, popularity, hormones, and ego, you have the makings of a three-year roller-coaster ride where the landing was anything but smooth, and the emotional impact can still be felt today.

I was the local football star and DJ at Westbury High School. I had my eyes on a young woman who was everything I could ever have wanted in a girlfriend. She was fine; she was smart; she had the right look and everything. There was one problem: She refused to pay me any mind. I felt like she behaved that way because she was from the uppity crew, and that she was out of reach—hailing from the side of town that I never frequented. Look, I was not a Casanova, but being a DJ and a football star determined my crowd. Yet this lady was not interested in the "pulse of popularity." She was indifferent, and this put her into an entirely different category in my eyes. She was fine and desirable and clearly different from the women who clamored for my attention—chicks who stayed out all hours of the night to be part of the in-crowd posse. This was not her thing.

Then I learned that the "opposites attract theory" actually did not apply to my situation at all. I found out that she wasn't uppity and from the other side of town, but actually lived down the street from me and was my cousin's female hangout buddy, as well. The typical contrast and contradiction between the proverbial "jock and the prima donna" was not to be. Through the friendship with my cousin, I seized the opportunity to have a casual conversation with, let's call her "Princess," and eventually a date came into fruition. In no time, other opportunities to be together presented themselves, and I took the openings to spend as much time with her as I could.

I had a great last year of high school as a superstar football player and DJ, and I had a big, big crush on this girl. I was like Superman and she had me weak like kryptonite. Then on a starlit August night, just before leaving to go away to school, I asked her to be mine, and she said "No!" In shock and disbelief, I turned to walk away and she called me back and said, "Let's give it a try!" The next five to seven months with her were a dream come true; it was everything I wanted it to be. She was more than just virginlike; she was a virgin. And for some time, that was a very endearing quality to me. But then I had to apply the pressure. I had needs.

So here's where the saga turns into a developing drama. I was frustrated and in haste. I'll blame it on the youthful hormones. I befriended a young sister that happened to attend the same school as Princess. This young sister was able to provide all my emotional, physical, and social needs. Now to make this even more dramatic, this newfound confidante lived on the same block, too! Our relationship developed with all the attachments, intimacy, and frequent sneaking around. We hung out together, cooked, cleaned, and partied together. I took it as far as she would let me, and she fully understood that Princess should never get wind of this.

This went on throughout the summer and into the fall. And for me the relationship with, let's call her "Sister Sister," was all about sex. But unfortunately, Sister Sister was falling in love. She would confront me, and I would have to ease my way out of the situation, telling her, "I love you, too, but my girl and I are having some problems!" My excuses didn't really hold up, and Sister Sister's best friend's family was tight with Princess's family. Everyone suspected something, but for some time no one confronted anyone. Sister Sister and Princess felt as though if neither were approached, neither need complain.

So it continued, and as time evolved, I was sleeping with both young ladies. I was involved in the families of both, buying presents, celebrating holidays and birthdays with both. I was treating both with tenderness and the attention they both expected and felt they deserved. I was lying to both, and my closest friends were telling me that I lost my mind. They knew that eventually I was going to be confronted. Not to mention the cost of this extravaganza was unfathomable: jewelry, perfume, dates, and the like. Also around this time, Princess is away at school and Sister Sister was all up in my mix, getting closer and closer.

People started talking, and the "arrangement" survived several breakups and fallouts on both sides. Then words started to be exchanged.

"I saw you shoveling her mom's snow! Why? Are you sleeping with her?"

"Nah," I would reply, "she lives across the street, you know how it is!"

"Well, why," she would ask, "is your car parked in front of her house the day she came home from school?"

"Boo," I answered, "I just put my car there because I couldn't find a space." Long before Shaggy canonized the excuse, I was simply saying, "Babe, in spite of what you saw, it wasn't me."

The reality was that they both loved me. And I acknowledge and concede that my behavior was damaging and caused me a lot of guilt and remorse throughout my emotional development. This triangle had a permanent, indelible, and undeniable influence on my current relationship behavior as well as the integrity in the caliber of advice given and asked of friends, colleagues, and family. I hurt both of them, and I ultimately hurt myself.

Finally, after several more breakups, lies, and makeups, things came to a head. Princess and I got together—one last time. She ended it. Sister Sister left ten days later. I was without the both of them for years. I didn't realize until it was over that both of these women made up my emotional, physical, and mental profile. I pretended that I didn't care, but I really did. I wished that I could stop feeling so bad about the way I treated these two valuable, lovable, and sincere women. Their only mistake was that they loved me and tried hard to please me. Granted, they did not look at me very hard or else they would have discovered long before the three-year circus was over that my behavior did not warrant their commitment and devotion. We all found ourselves in a cycle of negativity.

I never told Princess I was sorry, but how could I? I never told the truth, so therefore I could never apologize for something I could never admit. Sister Sister always felt like she was my girlfriend, even though in my mind that title was ever vacillating. There were too many contradictions. I knew that it was not right to do what I did to them. I was playing with them, hurting, and emotionally affecting them in ways we all could not see.

Today, I know that we cannot define ourselves, or our roles in relationships, by some artificial and unimportant measure of social advantages. I am responsible for the impact. I am responsible for the pain and compassionate treatment of my friends, lovers, and others. I am no longer oblivious of my personal responsibility.

DJ T-Money has always had a significant impact on hip-hop culture. As a member of Original Concept, T-Money signed to Def Jam Records, where they released one of hip-hop's most sampled records, Pump That Bass. *In addition, T-Money co-hosted MTV's first hip-hop show,* Yo! MTV Raps. *Since then, T-Money has appeared in numerous movies, including* Juice *and* Who's the Man? *while continuing to work on various music projects. T-Money has a bachelor of fine arts degree from New York Institute.*

Trying to Go There

Vanthony Bryant

I remember back in January of 1996 (two years before I was married), I was struggling with my true identity. On one side, I was this young man who was struggling with my own moral values and the way of the world. I had always wondered why those who had little to no morality seemed to always have the most interesting lives. I would sit at work and listen to the "weekend after" stories of some of my coworkers—how this person slept with that person, how this person went to the club and had gotten all these phone numbers, and all kinds of things like that. I would silently listen and compare my humble weekend with theirs and would wonder, "Is this what my life has come to? Why have I put so many restraints on myself to the point where my life is stagnant?" I mean, I was single at the time, so what was stopping me from going out there and obtaining that same excitement? I figured my social résumé was too tame for a woman's liking.

I don't care what some of these females out there say about finding a "good man." There is always that yearning inside that calls for that "thug," "rough-neck," or someone who had (or has) a colorful lifestyle. At that time, I could see where they were coming from. I thought that a woman wanted a man that will give them a regular dose of excitement and adventure without the drama, and my personality was lacking both. So, I started hanging out at clubs, trying to be seen and to get my name out there. I started talking to all kinds of women, those I was compatible with and those I was not. It did not surprise me one bit, while all of this was going on, I started to feel so unlike *me*. I used to sit up at night and ask God, "Why can't I be like everyone else? It looks to me like everybody else is enjoying life, and here I sit at home trying to be Mr. Good Guy." But, all that changed in mid-February of that same year.

I was on the expressway, coming home from work one evening, and there was this attractive young woman looking at me with the cutest smile. I found it flattering but didn't think much of it until I decided to ask her to pull over on the next exit. She smiled that much more and agreed to pull to the side. I followed her to an Exxon gas station, where I got out of my car and approached her. She seemed very happy that I asked her to stop, a little too happy, if you ask me, but that didn't matter to me at the time. Her name was Lannette, and she seemed to be the type of woman I could really get into, but during our conversation, I noticed she was wearing a wedding ring and furthermore there were two baby seats in the car. "Married with children? Great! Boy when I pick 'em, I sure can pick 'em."

She asked me, "Will me being married and having two little girls be a problem for us being friends?" I immediately saw this as that golden opportunity to build that social résumé I was talking about. "Nope! Not a problem for me if it's not for you." We exchanged numbers, and she told me that she would call me first. Little did I know I would be getting more than I bargained for.

Three days later, I get a phone call from Lannette, and she is asking me if she could stop by my place. I told her that it wasn't a problem but when she arrived, to my surprise she had her two children with her. We all sat around talking, watching movies, and having a wonderfully harmless time, but the atmosphere changed drastically after the children fell asleep. I put them in my bedroom and I shut the door behind me. I came back to the living room, and I cracked open a couple of wine coolers. There we were the two of us sitting on my living room floor talking more intimately and listening to jazz music in the background.

She was telling me in great detail the circumstances of her marriage, about how her husband wasn't doing the things that made her feel like a woman, how she felt like she was doing everything and he would just sit on his ass all day and how her husband didn't understand her needs. I felt compassion for her situation, and I asked her if there was anything I could do to help her. At that moment, I saw tears in her eyes and she responded by saying, "Just to have you listen to me is all I need." And she leaned over and gave me a sincere hug. I thought that was innocent enough until she pulled away and kissed me and then physical attraction took over and as they say, "one thing led to another." It was sad to say, but I knew the evening was going to lead to that moment, and a little piece of me wanted it to happen just for the sake of having a "married woman" as a résumé builder.

After that moment, there were many other encounters with Lannette. At first, it was the kind of excitement I was looking for. I was just like everybody else, but this quest took a mental toll on me when I was planning to go home to visit my family one Saturday afternoon (I lived in Atlanta and my parents lived just outside of Macon) and Lannette called to see what I was up to. When I told her my plans, she asked if she could come along. She said, "I'll just take off my wedding ring, and you can introduce me as just a friend." That was fine with me until we got there. As soon as I stepped through the door, I felt this overwhelming sense of shame, humiliation, and disgust with myself as I introduced Lannette to my parents and my brother as, "my friend." My mother could tell something about Lannette and I was not right and that we were up to no good, and I could read it all over her face. I could swear my father felt something, too. He just kept looking at me with this sly grin and sinister giggle.

I felt that I had to take a walk just to get out of my parents' sight. Lannette came along with me, and she knew I was bothered and tried to get me to talk about it. As I began to talk to her, I noticed that we were acting like a couple. At that point, the floodgates opened. I knew I genuinely cared about her. Even through all this stuff we were caught up in. I can say that we were friends. It wasn't about sex all the time. There were many occasions where we did nothing but talk, but at that moment I realized that this was not the life for me.

It was stupid of me to try to conform to this kind of life. I was committing adultery in the eyes of God, and if I continued to go this route, I would be contributing to the demise of a family. In essence, the ride was fun while it lasted, but it was time for me to get off. It was an eye-opener for me to come to terms with who I am and that the reason why I could not be like "everyone else" was because God had his hand on me and he would not allow me to go that route. It became clear to me that I was trying to be rebellious, but the spirit kept making me aware that I will not be the person I had set out to be, and I just stopped fighting against my true nature.

Vanthony Bryant is a thirty-one-year-old African-American male born in Dublin and raised in Jeffersonville, Georgia. He currently lives in Lithonia, Georgia, with his wife of five years, Trina Bryant, and two sons, Zion and Zaire, ages three and one.

Punany Preferences
Meshaq Black

The topic of interracial dating is such a heavy and at times emotional subject, I almost chose not even to bring it up for discussion. As a Black man with dark skin and long dreadlocks, I have been called everything from confused by my thirteen-year-old son to completely lost by my Black female friends and former companions. I respect their opinions and points of view. However, when conceding to their perspectives I can't help but shoot holes through the entire notion of there being separate "races" to begin with. I taught myself a long time ago that there is but one race called human beings. That's it. We might have different ethnic backgrounds and come from different cultures with different tongues and whatnot. But we are all human. Of course, American history is filled with endless accounts of what fear of the Black man caused the so-called White man to commit, atrocities that would enrage even the most docile brotha were he fully exposed to that barbarity. That isn't why I am writing this.

Follow this line of thinking, if you will. There are all sorts of dogs. There are breeds upon breeds of them. When a female dog is in heat, there are dogs lined up to serve her. There are many different colored horses. Does a brown horse stop to think that he ain't gonna stud that pretty white one in heat? With humans it's basically the same when all ideas and notions of how things are supposed to be and whom one is supposed to "stick" with are removed. Call it free will. And I'll exercise my will freely.

I like to date women of all different backgrounds. Even White ones. Is that a crime? Is it confusion? Is it a form of escapism? Is it being a sellout? If so, why? Because all my life I've always asked, "Why not?" I am thirty-seven years old. When I was my son's age, going to the same middle school he attends, I was attracted to girls who were Black, White, Central American, Asian, Middle Eastern, and so on. That has not changed. What has changed in the last twenty-five years is the acceptance through hip-hop of the intermingling of the different ethnic groups both socially and intimately. Back then it wasn't necessarily socially acceptable, whereas today is isn't so strange to see a young Black male with any type of female within the full spectrum of both background and hue.

When I was my son's age, a song called "Rapper's Delight" came out and went to number one on the airwaves. Hip-hop was official, and in the years to come, everyone would eventually join the party. I remember girls telling me, "I like you only as a friend," as if it were a broken record. Later in high school, things loosened up and the girls started being nicer. But I learned quick that the rest of society wasn't as forward thinking as I. In the generation I came up in, there were varying degrees of hostility coming at me from all different angles. Every woman in my family wasn't too thrilled about me dating women who weren't Black. Especially if the girl was White. I was an outcast of sorts, and it wasn't much better in the outside world. I was called Oreo and wannabe White boy. I imagine playing on the varsity tennis squad only added to the antagonism. It didn't and still doesn't matter what they said and did, because I didn't care what they thought. As a senior, I was nominated for both Class Flirt and won for Class Couple. How about that? My girlfriend was Jewish.

As a man, I was married to a beautiful Black woman of Creole descent. We had a beautiful son together. Let me back up. I came around to what we call knowledge of self and started growing dreadlocks. I met the mother of my son, and we got together for seven years. It didn't work out, and we have since separated. To her, my dreadlocks are not a cultural statement but a hairstyle. She also feels that there is a large contingent of Black women who are sick and tired of brothas like me who turn their backs on Black women. In her opinion, there is no Rasta movement in America because, "Brothas with dreads are too busy getting jocked by Asian women. It used to be White girls!" My retort to that is why is it the very same brothas that are being complained about can be all up in the club with their homies and many of the very same sistahs wouldn't even notice him. All of a sudden, when he's with another woman who happens not to be Black, he becomes Public Enemy Number One.

Truth be told, I grew dreadlocks for two reasons. One, my hair is very nappy, and it used to really hurt to try to run a comb or Afro pick through it. Second, I have this deep-seated hostility toward the elder females in my family from childhood. I can remember vividly the first time my little sister had a straightening comb put on her head. I was about eight years old, and she was five. My mother, grandmother, and great-grandmother were all in the room, heating up the comb. I remember them telling her to sit very still and not to move. Then I could smell the most terrible scent of hair burning, a smell I would come to get used to while growing up. I ran into the room and asked them all, "Why do you straighten your hair? Do you want to be White?" My grandmother smacked me in my mouth, my mother scolded me for "being negative and so damn critical," and my great-grandmother sent me out of the room. I was forever scarred for asking an innocent question out of concern they were hurting my little sis. Whatever their reasons were for scalding themselves was no reason to subject her to the same torture. Or so I thought. Same goes for getting haircuts and combing my hair growing up. Dreadful in a word. Painful as a description.

Do I prefer non-Black women? No. Do I like natural Black women? Definitely. Beauty, intelligence, class, and grace are colorblind last time I checked. I am rather proud that I am able to attract such a wide range of culture, ethnicity, and femininity from fellow citizens of the world. The dreadlocks may be part of the attraction. But I would sincerely cut off my locks the day my mother, grandmother, sister, or aunt starts growing them. My mission would be complete. I will have proved beyond a doubt that with time and patience, the Black woman can have long and flowing hair just like every other type of woman under the sun with "straight or wavy" hair.

This much I will admit to. I would argue that hip-hop has done more to open the floodgates of love that knows no boundaries than any hairstyle ever could. Look at it like this: In the past twenty-five years, you have an art-form that has surpassed all other forms of music and lifestyle. That 90 percent of the artists are Black males and 90 percent of the audience are non-Black people is a powerful fact in and of itself. On the cultural landscape, in an era where the best tennis and golf players are Black and the best rapper is White, things done changed. But love, my friends, is here to stay. Thanks to hip-hop, the future looks very colorful indeed.

Meshaq Blaq is the founder and publishing editor of Kronick *magazine. Dubbed the world's greatest free 'zine, this West Coast bimonthly music and lifestyle magazine is ten years strong and in a constant state of growth and flux. Meshaq is also the single parent of a teenage son. Meshaq's goals and objectives include meeting as many women from as many different cultures as humanly possible, making sure his son grows to become a positive and productive citizen of the world, and distributing a million free* Kronick *magazines by 2005.*

Your Soul's Journey

*A new commandment I give unto you, That ye love one another; as
I have loved you, that ye also love one another.* —John: 13:34

We've talked to several men about their love relationships. We find that their concerns are very similar to those of the women we meet. The lack of communication between mates seems to be a big factor in the tension in love relationships between Black men and women. We all want what we want from each other, but we tend to think we're going to get it without saying what *it* is. Do you think that you are going to be able to establish a relationship with someone who doesn't possess the qualities and values that are important to you? Do you even know what values are important to you? If you can't identify within yourself what it is that you want to share with someone else, how are you going to recognize that person when you meet him or her?

Soul Source

Compassion creates intimacy in a relationship. If you are a woman or partner reading this book, you may feel dismayed and downright upset about the communication between the both of you. Take a few days, and really think about the person you have become. Chances are everything that you do not like about your partner is what you absolutely hate about yourself. Your partner is a mirror image of you or a composition of your mother and last two partners. Consider the source–before fixing your relationship, take a look at what needs to be healed within you. A shift in how you relate with an individual creates a change in how they relate with you.

- What type of relationship did your parents have?
- What religious beliefs may have directed you on love, relationships, and sex?
- Do you feel that you measure up?
- Does your partner compare you with other sexual partners?
- What are your sexual fantasies?
- Do you believe that your partner is unfaithful?
- Do you masturbate frequently?
- What are your ideas of good relationships?
- Do you have love in your life?
- Are you mourning the loss of a past relationship?
- Have you ever been in love?
- What can you do to improve receiving and giving love?

CHAPTER 10

ANOTHER SLICE OF LIFE

*Everybody's journey is individual. If you fall in love with a boy, you
fall in love with a boy. The fact that many Americans consider it a
disease says more about them than it does about homosexuality.*
—James A. Baldwin

Until as recently as the 1980s men who slept with men were relegated
to a secretive underground community. Today, there is an open community of Black men who are considered gay or bisexual. Although proud
and strong, for these men being Black and being gay sometimes still is one
of the hardest pills to swallow. Even in the twenty-first century, it seems that
if you are wealthy and have a considerably high-profile personality, it is perfectly acceptable for you to say publicly, "Yes, I'm gay, and this is what I do."
Otherwise, the snickering behind the doors, in addition to not being included in certain circles with heterosexual men, still prevails for Black gay
men. Quite often women are more accepting to gay men than heterosexual
men are.

Black gay men are up against straight Black women, who are well educated, loving individuals looking for a man who is independent and similar
to them. Unfortunately, many of those men are Black gay men. So, there is
a fight to deflect the advance that, while well intended, is always disappointing for the women who either think they can turn a man around or just
ignore that he's gay.

There is a population of men who served time in the penitentiary and
jails who participated in what they considered institutional homosexuality
and don't consider themselves gay. One man served time in jail and had sex
with and washed the underwear of a more aggressive and larger prisoner,
basically for protection and companionship. When he was released from
prison, another former inmate came into the neighborhood and told everyone about the man's sexual exploits with the larger and aggressive inmate.
The guy ended up murdering him because he was ashamed of his relationship in prison and ended up going right back to jail, but this time for life.

Dealing with other gay men can be a challenge whether you consider yourself a brother on the DL (down low), bisexual, fem, and the list goes on, and on. These are titles bestowed upon you by you, and whether you are out of the closest or in the closet. Whether you are a top, bottom, or versatile. How freaky can you be? Whom can you trust with your sexual preferences and whom can't you trust?

Mostly, when you are attracted to another Black gay man, it's usually a staring match, until someone breaks the ice, then getting through the other stuff is the challenge. No one really wants to be *real* with the real hard-to-ask questions. There are myriad issues that Black gay men run away from, such as why Black gay men don't have businesses like White gay men do, or buy homes, or make the right investments.

Some Black gay men would prefer simply to know where's the next club, or who has the best body. It seems more impressive to look good. In addition, to some Black gay couples are on the low, and would rather have multiple partners, in groups or casual sex, than commit to someone for a lifetime and not look back—forgetting that they need and desire a companion who loves them for them. Just as in heterosexual relationships, it takes a certain level of maturity and love of self in order to have a balanced relationship.

The stories in this chapter explore the varied sexual relationships that Black men have with each other, from the loud and proud to the undercover lovers. Perhaps we can learn to be accepting and to know that these brothers want to be equally loved and respected regardless of their sexual preference.

Circle Theory

Jamaica Carter

Growing up, I knew that I liked boys. I really didn't understand what gay was, but I knew to keep whatever it was a secret. Growing up, I never got teased, although I knew I was different. I never got in trouble. When we all played hide and seek, I remember always running and hiding where the boys were and never the girls. Sometimes the conversation or debate comes up saying, "You can't be born gay," but I know different. I was not taught to like boys and never molested as a child. But I remember being attracted to them at an early age. I was one of those blessed people who grew up in a nurturing environment filled with church and good times with my childhood firends.

I excelled in school, and when I ventured out to stake my claim on the world, my grandmother, who raised me, gave me a warning. She said, "If you gonna be gay, you be the best mothafuckin' faggot you can be, always be at the top of your game." She went on to say, "You are a Black man first, and your sexuality comes second." I took my grandmother's advice and never made my sexuality an issue, a debate point, or a conversation piece. I was Jamaica Carter, the hardworking individual who wanted to learn and master what was put in front of him. My sexuality was second or third, and I toiled at my craft first in the field of accounting and then in the entertainment industry as a business manager. Although my colleagues would utilize other things to try justifying why they would be angry, I knew the fact that I had taken my granny's advice and landed high positions in corporate America with conservatives where homosexuality is *not* welcomed or talked about angered their asses. Like the fact that I did not possess a college degree when I was promoted or received larger raises than they did.

As I got older and worked deeper into the entertainment industry, I was priviledged to work alongside celebrities. I have had several of the male celebrities say, and what I believe to be the biggest compliment, "You break the stereotype of what we think of fags," or "Most people who don't fuck with fags would fuck with you." I always try to be a voice for gays because we are talented. We are UPS delivery men, accountants, parents, executives, vice presidents, real estate agents, and make up at least fifty percent of the religion in the churches in the African-American community, and I don't give a damn what any religious leader has to say about it. It is only our sexuality that makes us different. We are not all the ones you see acting like clowns who are on *Ricki Lake*, *Jenny Jones*, and *Jerry Springer*. You can best believe this: *If the shit is running smooth and correct, there is a punk on board that made damn sure of it.* It is a known fact that we are perfectionists as well as creative and talented. Until I die, I will make sure that gays and lesbians get their props.

Just like some rappers or rock stars want you to know who they are and not be judged and stereotyped, gays want you to know that they are good men, with talent and common sense and we should appreciate them. We want the straight community to know the same thing. I have never watched a talk show where a gay person is shown in a positive light.

I am blessed, and the hundreds of people that I have included in my "circle of life" accept me, and my sexuality it is not a problem for them. I love my life and would never change it for the world. Every *true, sin-free Christian* (and I do mean true and sin-free) that disagrees with my behavioral pattern or my sexual preference should just pray for my lost soul and go own with their life and not spend so much time judging me. My God will change me and fix me *when he is ready and not before.* The God I serve has blessed me with a job, financial stability, happiness, and health; my blessings don't come form any evil spirits. Occasionally I'll meet folks, and during the conversation we discuss sexuality. I can't stand it when people try to force religion in my face and dictate the Bible as if they wrote it or know who did. I don't know anyone who has hung out with God, Jesus, Mary, or personally chilled with any disciples. I live by my own faith and spiritual guidance, and no one else's opinion counts. The opinions that I do care about are from the people that I have established great nurturing relationships with and know me for who I am.

It took me a while to get there because people's opinion would be important to me at one point. I put my very all in my work and found that I was being overloaded. One day I was in a coffee shop and was talking with a friend on my cell, and when I completed my call, the friend that I was sharing a cup of coffee with said to me, "All that shit that you are doing is all for someone else." My friend got up and went to the car for something, and a woman at the next table said, "Your friend cares about you, and there is truth in what he was saying." She said, "I get a vibe that you are always doing things for other people and never take time for *you.*"

She introduced herself to me as Barbara. "Would you like your life to change?" she said. And of course, the answer was yes! While trying to build a career, I felt like I was drifting in a large body of water with no oars, just sitting there, waiting for the wind blow any direction just so I can move from that present spot. This woman who had all this energy made me want to listen. She said, "All those people who go to spas do it because they know it is all about them. That is what you call taking a moment for yourself. They are treating themselves from stress like the stress that you were carrying in that phone conversation that I overheard. What you need to do, sweetheart, is do a 'circle theory.' "

"The circle theory? Okay," I said, hesitant.

Barbara continued, "Go home and cut your pager off, telephone ringer off, and don't answer the door." She said, "Do you have a microwave?"

I answered yes I do.

"Well put a bowl of water in it, and set the microwave for two minutes. Draw a circle on a piece of paper, and after that, press start on the microwave. Now put in the middle of that circle all that you need to do, I mean everything—a piece of mail that needs to go out, bills that need to be paid, telephone calls, twenty dollars you owe to anyone, car repair, cleaning out closets, cetera, and when the microwave beeps, put your pen down. Stare hard at the tasks that you have placed in that cirlce. Once you have studied them, you need realize that anything that is *not* in that circle is not important to you. When the circle gets empty as you complete those tasks, do it again. Your circle will always been filled with things that pertain to you and that are for and about *you*. You will begin to understand that everything begins with you."

Barbara stated, "We make other people's problems our problems sometimes just by listening."

When a person calls you for eighty dollars for their phone bill, try telling them that yours is eight hundred dollars, and see how quick they back down. But if you tell them, "Well, I don't have it right now, call me Friday, and I will see what I can do," you have just given that person the solution that they were looking for. Now they won't even seek further because you just gave them the answer they wanted. Try calling back a week later after you told them you couldn't help, and I will guarantee you that they got the money another way.

That very moment I went home I did the circle theory and cleared my life out of things that were no longer important to me. I had to consider if the individuals in my life brought light, was their conversation pleasant? It didn't matter to me how much money they had or what position they held—I got rid of them if they were toxic. In the last six years, it made me focus. It has taught me how to be purely honest and sometimes it comes off brutal, but I would rather live a true me than lie to you. I now realize that it is okay to say no.

My life has changed drastically. Before I became director John Singleton's executive assistant, I was working on movies, managing payroll and accounting. I live in the *now*, which means I stopped procrastinating on so
many things. I have adopted the mantras "Now is the time" and "By any
means necessary." By adopting the ability to say no and "I'm sorry, I don't
know," I have learned that it keeps you out of a verbal binding contract.
Today I have no problem, asking anyone to explain what he or she is talking about. I have goals, and I live and complete them each and every day. I
don't place deadlines on anything I do, because I definitely don't take my
life for granted. I am proud of who I am and of all that I have accomplished
and grateful that God has blessed me.

*Jamaica Carter is an actor, an HIV/AIDS activist in the Los Angeles African-
American community, and the executive assistant to director John Singleton.*

Unnatural
Cris is Bliss

Throughout my life I've heard many arguments about the homosexual act being *unnatural*. I've heard preachers preaching it, I've read writings against it, I've danced to reggae and rap songs condemning it.

I've been repeatedly told in a variety of ways that it is not the "right" way. The hatred for the people who practice it comes from all sources, the same KKK members who hate "niggers" and "kikes" usually hates "faggots," too. But I'm sure that everybody in the KKK ain't straight. Sometimes the otherwise nicest Christian church people have no remorse in using the word *faggot* to condemn homo- and bisexuality and promise that all who practice such "ungodly" acts shall burn in Hell, and some even claim that AIDS is from God to punish the Sodomites, because it (homosexuality) is an unnatural act, and the Bible tells them so.

But then again, good God-fearing Christians have at one time also participated, promoted, practiced, and profited in the if not ungodly then at least inhumane act of slavery and mass genocides. Christians aren't the only ones; the Muslims did also. But no matter what the religion, they were God-fearing people doing ungodly acts, in the name of God or the Bible. And it is these modern-day practitioners of these same old religions who point the finger at what is godly and what is not, because the Bible tells them so. And by the way, lesbian sex (a homosexual act), is the safest sex in regards to AIDS transmission.

So, all our lives we've been bombarded with this message: "Homosexuals are bad, and the act is unnatural." And unfortunately some of us—even though we do it—believe that bullshit.

Yet our attraction to and for the same sex overrides all that shit that we've been taught directly or indirectly. And in the face of all this hostility, we try to be free. Some of us adapt by being in the closet, some adapt by being barely out the closet—you know, on the Low, on the DL. Others say, Fuck the closet, I've got to spread my arms and breathe.

Who is really unnatural?

I say that straight people are the unnatural ones.

Let me make some definitions and clarifications of where I'm coming from when I write.

1. I'm writing from a male perspective.

2. When I say straight or heterosexual, I mean people whose sexual "activity" is 100 percent heterosexual. If you "willingly" mess around with the same sex, no matter what the circumstances ("I was in jail") or what the position ("I only get my dick sucked"), I consider that bisexual.

And, curiosity is a one-time-only excuse, and a weak one at that. If a large number of people started going around stabbing themselves in the leg, curiosity alone would not make you say, "I wonder why they are stabbing themselves in the leg, what are they getting out of it? Umm? I'm *curious;* let me stab myself in the leg and try it."

Or for a more realistic and positive comparison, if a large number of people with similar interest were studying, applying themselves, and becoming successful, curiosity alone would not make you say, Let me study and be focused, and see what this success thing is all about. No, most people observe others, comment or complain about them, but continue to do the bullshit that they've been doing. And I think the same applies to sex. No matter if you are thirteen or thirty-five, curiosity alone is not a motivating factor. There is some physical attraction to the same sex that makes you curious in the first place. Curiosity is a one-time thing.

3. I don't believe that being either 100 percent homosexual or 100 percent heterosexual is natural. I strongly believe that people are bisexual by nature, and given the freedom—freedom from guilt, freedom from punishment, freedom from fear of physical harm, freedom from fear of being rejected by friends and family, freedom from being labeled as weak or wicked, people would be bisexual. Maybe not an equal fifty-fifty, but bisexual to some degree.

Some may say that no one is forced to be gay or straight. It's not that we're forced, but we are not allowed the freedom or given the encouragement to be bi. It's like the child of a mixed marriage, forced to identify with one race and religion or the other, not given the freedom to be both.

And there are plenty of gay people who condemn bisexuals as being confused or fronting, just as the straight people condemn them. Well, if your dick gets hard for both sexes, ain't nothing confusing about that.

Okay, that's where I'm coming from, now back to my theory:

It is the heterosexuals who are the unnatural ones because they are created, not by nature but by the rules of the ruling society. They are heterosexual because they have been *programmed* to be just that.

First of all, if I see a man and he turns me on, and my dick gets hard, because my brain is causing more blood to flow to my dick, there is absolutely—I repeat, *absolutely—nothing unnatural* about *that*. That is "Nature" taking its course. And likewise, if I see a woman and the same thing happens there's nothing unnatural about that either.

So how can nature's response be "unnatural" in one situation and "natural" in another, as the ruling society so claims? Whatever your response to sexual excitement is, whether it's your dick getting hard, your ass getting wet (or what ever an ass can do), your mouth watering, your pussy twitching, your left earlobe heating up, what ever your natural response is—it's natural. No one can put you down about your choice of sex act being unnatural. To my knowledge, it's the straight people who are gulping down Viagra by the pound to keep their shit up, anyway.

So where does this notion of "unnatural" come in? Hello, Organized Religion.

While we are being accused of being unnatural and we've been running for cover from the stones being thrown at us, we have failed to take a good look at heterosexuality and how it is *encouraged, promoted*, and even *enforced*.

Heterosexuality has been *encouraged, promoted*, and *enforced*, while homosexuality has been *discouraged, anti-promoted*, and *punished*. And with the help of television, movies, and radio in setting popular opinion, programming of the mind can now occur on a global level. This is being done in overt and subtle ways every day. From babyhood onward.

With little babies who don't know their hand from their foot, comments are often made like, "Oh, little [boy's name] is so cute. You know he's gonna have all the girls when he grows up." Or when little children of the opposite sex are friends, it's suggested that they are boyfriend and girlfriend. Have you ever made or heard the comments like that? That's heterosexuality being promoted in a subtle way. It is the implanting of the male-female relationship in the young mind.

And some of you are saying, "Oh, yeah, it's natural to say that."

It's the natural thing to say because programming has made it natural.

It's natural because we live in a heterosexual-controlled world, and the heteros are controlling the programming. These are the subtle programmings that take place and are reinforced, right from infancy.

When you were little, did you ever sing the song about Batman? It went something like this:

Batman took her to the movies,
Batman took her to his house,
Batman [something something something—I forgot the lyrics]
Batman laid her on the couch
Batman stuck it in easy
Batman pulled it out greasy
La la la la la la la la Batman

This was just one of the many songs about fucking that the little boys on the block would sing. I guess the little girls knew the songs, too, but we never sang them with the little girls. Maybe because the little girls would say you were singing "nasty" songs, or maybe because after singing the songs we would plot which little girls we were going to hump on while playing Run, Catch, and Kiss or later Run, Catch, and Fuck. I don't remember who taught the songs to us; I just remember singing them in sort of secrecy. Our age was somewhere between five and eight years old. Through these songs and conversations of the "older" guys (ten to fourteen years old), we were already being made heterosexually curious.

I was either four or five years old when I got caught by my grandmother for playing doctor with a little girl of the same age from up the block. The game started out as "Let me see," but I knew the words to the Batman song, and it was my intention to "stick it in easy" and "pull it out greasy," but thanks to Grandma, that didn't happen. Getting caught and punished only made me know that in the future one had to be sneaky with such matters. And it was the little girl who started the game.

When we turn on TV, see a movie, listen to a record, and look at print advertisement, they are all filled with references to heterosexual unions. Even in the video games, in one game, I don't know the name of it, I overheard some guys talking about it, you get rewarded with more health when you fuck some girl.

If you've never thought about it before, take a notice of how often the message of the heterosexual union is put into your brain. And naturally with all of this programming, it generally produces its desired results: heterosexuals.

However, there are those people who don't get programmed, who act upon their natural desires. There are more heterosexuals who have intentionally tucked all their homosexual desires away, and tucked them away so deep that they swear they never even existed, than there are gay people tucking away their heterosexual desires.

If society did not make the homosexual act taboo, more people would be doing it. Period, bottom line, case closed, class is now over, you can all go home! Let me repeat that in all capitals:

IF SOCIETY DID NOT MAKE THE HOMOSEXUAL ACT TABOO, MORE PEOPLE WOULD BE DOING IT.

And this would be a bisexual planet, which eventually it will become anyway. Think about it. You know there are plenty of people who are straight or pretending to be straight because they fear the reaction that they would get if they were otherwise. More women are coming out because it has become more acceptable for lesbians. Unfortunately, the reason it's more acceptable is not because general society is opening up to alternating lifestyles but rather it's because it fits in with straight men's sexual fantasies. But I guess any advance is better than no advance, and every advance leads to bigger victories, because it's hard to keep someone happily chained up once he or she has tasted or seen freedom.

It would be interesting to see straight men's reaction if straight women started saying they fantasized about two men, masculine men, getting it on.

On top of all the pro-heterosexual programming people get, they also receive a healthy dose of anti-homosexual programming. And yet after all the programming that is done for heterosexuality and against homosexuality, still a significant number of people choose to do what comes naturally to them. Still a significant number of people, either out in the open or sneaking in the dark, do what naturally comes to them.

And now I will take some questions. Yes, you, reading this book, what is your question please?

Question: Why was there a need for pro-heterosexual programming?

Only the hetero–sex act could produce more people. I purposely used *could* because now we have artificial insemination and talks of cloning. The sex act itself, whether homo or hetero, is pleasurable in some way, and that is why people do it. If sex didn't feel good, people would *not* be doing it or would just to make babies. It is the pleasure of sex that drives people to do it, not the making of babies.

Question: Why do you need more people?

In the past, you needed more people so that you could have a bigger army to protect yourself or so that you could go out and take over other people. In today's world, with long-range missiles, chemical and biological warfare, and smart planes, you don't need large armies to attack or defend.

You also need more people because people consume, and if you have something to sell, you need people to buy it. Whether you are selling religion or clothing, cell phones, station wagons, or corn seeds, the more people, the more money.

If you had a religion, more of your practitioners having babies meant that in the future, your congregation would be larger. And you would have more people putting money in the cup when it was passed around, making you richer and more powerful.

Not to mention with more followers, the more potential soldiers you have for your army. And with a bigger army—you guessed it—you can over take other people. Kill the men, fuck the women, and make babies who are now part of your religion.

In the days of colonization, the missionaries went in first to win you over with religion, then the armies came in and took you over with force, and the missionaries came back to help ease suffering, and make you realize that for all your pains on earth you will be rewarded in the hereafter.

Question: Why is it promoted that homosexuality is not good for the military?

Well, I think that they had several reasons.

1. Homosexuals can be blackmailed because of their sexuality. But an easy solution to that is not making homosexuality something that one has to hide and therefore if one does not have to hide it, there is nothing to be blackmailed about.

2. If you have two people in the army forming a strong union, like married couples on the same job, their loyalty to each other becomes stronger than their loyalty to the person they serve under or their loyalty to the unit.

3. If you have open sexual relationships between soldiers, it makes for additional tensions, jealousies, rivalries, and favoritism within the unit, which would make unity within a unit more difficult.

4. Going back to the old days (thousands of years ago) when these "rules" were conceived, combat was hand to hand, and you got to see your enemy up close. The standard operating procedure for the attacking army was, you killed the enemy (the men and the opposing soldiers), you raped their women, you looted the town, and claimed the territory.

I think that it becomes more difficult to kill the people who are supposed to be your enemy when you find them sexually attractive. So without the possibility of sexual attraction (no homosexuality allowed in the army), you have an army that can more easily focus on carrying out the attack order. The reward is freedom to rape and pillage.

You may say that is far-fetched, but back in the days when these ideologies were being formed, the people who would be fighting most likely lived in close proximity and looked similar to each other and therefore shared the same values of what they considered beauty.

I imagine myself as a general or soldier two thousand years ago in the mythical army of the Bronx, and planning a surprise attack on Brooklyn for whatever reason. When we would get to Brooklyn, and I would see all the fine-ass niggas there, first of all my dick gonna get hard, and my mind is gonna be more on rape, party, and plunder rather than killing, 'cause you know two thousand years ago, people didn't wear much clothes in Brooklyn, especially in the summertime. Shit—they walk around now wit' their pants hangin' off and their ass showin', so you know two thousand years ago it would be buck naked, come and take it.

But seriously, as a soldier or general, I would find it more difficult to attack and kill (this is what the armies did in the old days) an "enemy" that I found physically attractive. I would be more inclined to want to attack and capture. And capturing was much more dangerous, especially in those days. Keep in mind, I'm talking about being the aggressive attacking army, not defending against an attack. As a defending army, you would kill whoever was trying to take you over, no second thoughts or questions asked. Fuck the sex—maybe you would fuck some captured prisoners, but that would be about it.

In conclusion; I guess that this anti-homosexuality–pro-heterosexuality thing may have—I repeat *may* have—served some purpose in the past. But nowadays with modern technology and overpopulation, the fears and preoccupations of past generations are no longer valid. Human beings are out of control all over the whole planet, polluting the water and air, taking land away from the other creatures of the earth, destroying forests and jungles so we can build more farms and more houses for more humans with no regard to anything else.

But for whatever reasons this anti-homosexuality–pro-heterosexuality thing came into being, it's time for it to come out of being. The human race is still very young, and our total years of being what we call "civilized" are like a grain of sand on a beach compared with the age of the universe, and somewhere in our future, people will look back upon this time and say, "Damn, those people called themselves educated, but they were really stupid and backwards back then, with all their superstitions and inhibitions." And you know what, they will be talking about you and me and the people of our "modern technological age," and they will be 100 percent right. We still have a lot to learn about something as basic as what is natural and unnatural and a person's right to be free.

Cris is Bliss *is a party promoter, producer, and owner of Rough Luxury/Berlin Records, an NYC label specializing in R & B, hip-hop, and house music. Quotation: "Rise, stand up, the third revolution has begun."*

The Final Say

Anthony Dilworth

This essay is dedicated to members of the clergy
You did not say my way would be easy, you did not say that it would be
But if it got dark and I couldn't find my way
You told me to put my trust in thee
That's why I am begging you
Lord, help me to hold out until my change has come
—James Cleveland

My life had been pressing, pushing, swaying me to and fro for what seemed like forever. I was at a retreat in the foothills of Tennessee where seventy-three same-gender-loving, two-spirited men of color had gathered to play, to reflect on the journey, and share their personal histories as well as construct a viable productive community. To love one another in a much more intimate manner. We had come together with a purpose. They were men of vastly different backgrounds and pedigrees. Ministers and preacher's sons, medical doctors and recovering drug addicts, young men trying to find their way and old men who had lost their way. The doubtful. The jaded. The cynical. We had gathered together for a four-day respite from the things that trouble us.

I don't know if it was the flock of mallards gliding across the lake, their heads held high in silent homage to their Creator. It could have been the seven fawns trekking across the footbridge on their Sunday morning stroll. I watched as they observed us, strange two-legged creatures called humans. I wondered if they considered humans armed and dangerous. All of it made me, a thirty-eight-year-old same-gender-loving man living with AIDS, reflect on my life.

I am the good son, the responsible one ever ready to assist Momma or some distant relative with a pending bill. I am the outcast, one forever obligated to love a people who are incapable of loving me back. I am the strangest of strangers. I am the good worker, first to arrive, the last to leave. I am the one some women down South call a "good Judy," who they can call at midnight because their man is in a world of trouble. I am the one who gets the rubbing alcohol for that black eye or that bruised back. I am the one who comforts you. I am the loving father who wonders in the troubled recesses of my mind if my love will be sufficient. Will my daughter still say "Daddy, I love you," or will I become just another faggot mocked by society and cursed by God. I wonder as I wander.

God and love have eluded me like a greased pig at a county rodeo. I believe in love, but love is fickle, sometimey, tends to arrive late and leave early. I believe strongly in the Creator yet sometimes I wonder quite audibly if he believes in me. I have begged, cajoled, and even bartered my life trying to gain His attention. I have searched the Scriptures, meditated to Jesus Christ, Allah, Buddha, and any god who would listen. I have read Matthew, Mark, Luke, and John. I have a collection from Iyanla Vanzant, to T. D. Jakes, to the Harlem Renaissance writers to James Baldwin and the Dalai Lama. No peace anywhere!

My relationship with God is a tempestuous one. We have a family history. It was Easter Sunday 1992, the first one I didn't buy anything new to wear. In fact, I wore black: black shoes, black socks, black slacks, and a black Giorgio Armani jacket I had found at the local Goodwill. The Perry Ellis shirt was royal blue. I guess you could say I was black and blue. Now that time and distance have allowed me to recover, maybe I can explain an irrational situation rationally. Maybe AIDS had come calling like a long-lost relative who had overstayed its welcome. It was not going home today, tomorrow, or forever. It had been six years, and my nerves had gotten real bad. I was singing gospel music twenty-four seven. When I mustered up the nerve to have sex, the gospel station was on high. A lot of death was riding me.

Michael died in August, Mae on Mother's Day. Mae's mother died on Mae's birthday. There was Roy, Eddie, and Michelle. Dominique and La-Toya, real girls with children. Byron was sick, but Bryan was sicker. Marcus lay dying, and I had tested positive. I was on the verge of a nervous breakdown in the middle of one of the preeminent African-American congregations in Memphis, Tennessee. I had a slow-building quiet rage, yet when someone says to you "How are you feeling this morning?" and you reply gleefully, "Oh, I am fine," when you know good and damn well that all is not well. My teeth gritted until I drew blood. My fists clenched and held fast to the bloodred velvet-and-mahogany church pew. I could not stand or sit. My legs had failed me, and my arms were numb. I was all cried out; my strength was gone.

The female minister dripped venom with a fiery baptized tongue. I observed my closeted brothers in the balcony who were totally uncomfortable, dressed in Kenneth Cole and Armani suits like they were coats of armor; the rich ones on the Trustee Board perched precariously on the edge of their seats; the silent ones; the pedigreed ones; my sister friends safe and miserable in the arms of husbands they neither wanted nor desired. I witnessed the down-low brothers with their wives and girlfriends on the left and their male "cousins" on the right; the fat ones, the ones some call ugly, the not so handsome ones who were secretly thanking God that the pretty boys died first. I tried to block out the rousing amen chorus. It looked like the swelling tide of a lynch mob. There I sat, Anthony, the sideshow, the queer, the punk, the fag, the hated one, and the reviled one. I was at once defiant and unrepentant. I was literally dying from an overdose of religion.

I collected myself with all the fortitude that God had given me. I remembered that I was also Clara's boy, Ms. Zula's grandbaby and the grandson of a noted hometown theologian. I considered Anthony, the true Southerner, the fun-lover, the adventure seeker. I recollected apple orchards, pecan pickings, reading about Vashti and Esther, quilt-making and hog killings. I sobbed over Anthony the little colored boy with the big mind; the confident teenager with the strange fast-paced walk and his grandmother's singing voice screaming to be heard. I have always been in a hurry. I also paused to reflect on all of the times I sought solace in the fatal clutches of strangers and would-be assassins who took VCRs, televisions, telephones, and penny jars. I missed the small things, some valuable, some not so valuable, that were mine just the same. Stolen!

My body was racked with the not-so-distant memories of all the times I had sabotaged my dreams, the missed opportunities, the special occasions without an invite. I had a long conversation with the disease ravaging my body with a precision previously not witnessed by the living. I explained to the virus on a daily basis that since we both want to live, we are going to have to peacefully coexist; so far AIDS has not gotten with the program on a consistent basis. I marveled at the fact that I had participated in my own neat crucifixion.

I stood for the benediction—or the verdict, depending on how you look at the situation. Being me was a felonious offense punishable by death and eternal damnation, no chance of heaven, and no communion with God, or so they thought. No one knew what I was feeling or thinking except God and me.

God finally showed up, late as usual, but right on time. This time he was dressed to kill, and to my great surprise, love was with Him. At Easter time, Memphis is awash with the scent of honeysuckle, azaleas, lilies, and just about any kind of colorful plant. It is a beautiful sight. I was riding with my friend Sandy, who took his rightful place in the stressful traffic while I considered how to end my life: Suicide was too public; Valium or Percocet too risky and jail time if you weren't successful; Johnnie Walker Red was out, since my biological father was a mean drunk and I didn't want to be like him. In Sandy's mad dash in traffic, I bumped my head against the window. "Damn!" I screamed. "Watch what the hell you are doing." He looked at me as if to say, I can't wait to get your crazy ass home. I mellowed, the ride home was long. I saw a reflection of myself in the window seemingly for the first time.

The Spirit whispered to me:

I alone am God. I laid the foundations of the universe and placed the stars in the heaven one by one. I even named them. I got lonely so I created you and others like you. The good and the bad, the rich and the poor, the Black, the White, the Jew and the Gentile, the Cherokee, the Navajo, the faceless and the famous—all of you are temporary tenants on a tiny little part of the firmament aptly named Earth. You are needed. You are necessary. You are loved. You are a part of me, created in my image. Did you really think God could be contained within four walls, no matter how grand and tall the edifice? I am the living God. Consider the rose, all glorious with the thorns in her side, the lilies of the field and the tiny mischievous dandelion. The dogwood tree, her growth stunted by a sorrowful journey up Calvary's Hill. The oak proud and strong, her branches carrying the memories of a million Black men hanging, dangling like old Christmas ornaments and her roots watered with the blood, sweat, and tears of an ancient people. The weeping willow tree, her crown bowed in eternal sorrow for every bad word spat at another human being. Look at the evergreens toiling endlessly through seasons, unyielding and unchanging. Each of you will stand in the Judgment according to your own deeds, your own works, and your own lives. I have the final say.

Anthony "Tony" Dilworth *is a thirty-nine-year-old African-American man living with AIDS. He is the proud father of an eighteen-year-old aspiring actress and choreographer. Anthony is a well-known community advocate for same-gender-loving people and persons living with AIDS in the state of Tennessee.*

Misunderstood
Shawn

I wish that you could spend a day in the life of me. It is not what you think. I believe that I probably would smash all of your misconceptions of what a gay man is. I always knew I was gay. However, it took a little time for me to figure it all out.

I can recall that when I was around seven years old, Grandma and I would take early-morning strolls to school, and if ever a couple approached, I would immediately dismiss the girl and pay close attention to her man.

Then when I was a teenager, *everyone* wanted me to act like a boy. So "boy" is what I gave. I began dating girls. That's not who I really was, but hell, I gave it a try. Yet something still wasn't right, but not until my eighteenth birthday did I know what it was. In the pit of my stomach, I always yearned to be with a man, and that night my heart opened to embrace what I'd been missing all along.

I love women for all that they bring to the table, but I am who I am. I choose men and being gay chose me. Regardless of what lifestyle one chooses to live, in life no one ever chooses to be discriminated against.

I often witnessed discrimination and wondered what would my life be like if I didn't look heterosexual. I ask myself, Which is worse, the discrimination that homosexuals receive from heterosexuals or from other homosexuals. Sometimes we can be our own worst enemies.

Aside from being discriminated against, we do have preferences. No, we do not jump at every man we see. Our lifestyle is broken down into different categories. We all have our likes and dislikes. You have some men who date men who look and dress like women. Then there are men who only date men who deal with women. That's why our gay colors are the rainbow—we like it all.

Speaking of rainbows, a lot of us love creativity, and some gay men foster their creative side and will have a setting for four or eight; the apartment or home is well designed. However a straight guy may be creative but was trained not to develop his creativity, so his home or apartment may be more uniform, although they are really starting to loosen up. They're beginning to live out their fantasies. Think about how huge anal sex has become over the last few years. Makes you say *hmmm!*

As crazy as it may seem, we are no different from you. We are judges and doctors, thugs and hustlers. The only difference is whom we choose to sleep with at the end of the day. It took me a lot of years to come out—but child, I'm glad I did. It is the freest and most uplifting feeling one can ever encounter with oneself. But then you have people who just can't afford to ruin everything—they have to be happy. I've dealt with one firsthand, and it would be a tragedy. He would jeopardize his image and possibly lose his family if he were to reveal who he truly is. So he continues to live a lie.

It's sad that society places a stigma on what is considered acceptable. Whatever happened to true love, people? Who gives a damn about sexual genders? If the love is real, then it's right!

However, if the relationship isn't working out, walk through that exit door immediately. That's where I find that women are different from men—they tend to settle for men who are not worthy of their time. Another difference between men and women is that women often think before they act, whereas men usually act before they think. And that is the classic difference that heterosexuals and homosexuals have in common. It's universal.

You see, I am a man, so I think like one; my conversation may entail anything from a V-12 engine to a runway show in Milan. But the key is I listen, and listen carefully while people begin to unveil their deepest darkest secrets. I may not have the physical appeal of a woman, but I have the mental advantage. Men think that they have to be macho and won't confide in their wives, girls, or friends. I come from both sides of the fence, and I permit him to let his guard down. When I connect with a man and touch his soul, he will always be connected to me. After all, I have his heart.

So you see there is no real difference. Our hearts are all the same. We just want to be accepted for who we are, and like you we don't want to be misunderstood. Are you compassionate enough to understand?

Shawn wishes to remain anonymous and continues to live his true self each and every day and has a thriving career.

Temptation

Melvin Taylor

I am a product of an extended family household with my grandmother Maggie Lucille Mckethan and two of my mother's little sisters, Sandra Mckethan and Deborah Mckethan-Gordon. My mother lived with my step-father, Eugene Tyler. I went to live with them from time to time, until we all moved to Rochdale Village.

By this time, I certainly knew that I had homosexual tendencies. In my immediate family, I had no close male influences around me. So I was left open for all to explore. And explore I did. First with cousins during sleep-overs. Then when I went to boarding school in Camden, South Carolina. That is where, I would say, a straight male saw an opportunity to break a fresh boy into "the life," as we call it. I always loved the theater and the music, and dancing. So of course, this world would only encourage that behavior instead of influence you otherwise.

My dreams would always be to be married with a beautiful wife and six children, happily providing for them. Anyone who knows me knows how well I interact with children. Many attempts to captivate the minds of beautiful women who have caught my eye have always been something that I could not go through with. I came close to marrying, but six months shy, I backed out.

By the time I was twenty-seven years of age, I gave my life to the Lord. I knew that I needed to clean up all areas of my life. I started going to church, asking the Lord to clean me up, wash away all my sins. I found that the desire does leave for a season, but then the temptation that's in the Church can be as just as tempting as out in the "world."

Here I am, Lord. Do what you want with me. I would love to bear children and see the Cushite generation live on. Knowing that this will be judged, but struggling with the Holy Spirit to keep you when you can't be kept is the question. Can I trust Him to see me through this temptation that burns in my bones?

Melvin Taylor is an events planner who organizes events across the country.

Your Soul's Journey

I care very little if I am judged by you or by any human court;
indeed, I do not even judge myself.   —1 Corinthians 4:3

When we worked on the very first roundtable in New York, we had over a hundred men in the room openly share what was on their hearts and minds. You could sense the bonding and even camaraderie amongst the men. Then we talked about homosexuality, and the room divided. The straight guys were upset that the brothers they were connecting with were gay. One brother talked about growing up in a group home, where he spent his entire life with men being in charge of his care. He felt a certain maternal love for men that caused him to rethink his sexual preference and to break up an engagement. Others discussed "why do they have be judged by their sexuality," and comments like "the gay guy." The straight guys responded by saying that they are raising their boys to be real men. It became a bit uncomfortable for some in the room, and although the men enjoyed the entire session, they did not want anything to do with one another if they thought that anyone in the group was gay. How unfortunate for them—they were missing out on an opportunity to really get to know a person for who they were in their entirety and bond with other men.

At another roundtable, we were lambasted by both sides when we talked about the love chapter, and a loud discussion erupted. A technology executive snarled at us said "What about the other normal people?" When we brought up the homosexuality issue in Atlanta while we were discussing touch and emotion, Candace happened to mention that men in Africa often hold hands. The men in the room shouted, "This is America and we don't do that here," and "Why are you bringing that up?"

Soul Source

We have a long way to go, but we are beginning to have dialogue that can reeducate brothers. Perhaps we should begin saying "Don't judge me by the color of my skin, creed, or sexuality, but by the content of my character."

- What are some of the challenges that you face as a Black gay man?
- Was there a process involved with telling your family about your sexuality?

- What do you believe are things that you would like to change in the way society views love between two men?
- What types of relationships have you chosen in the past?
- Are you in a committed relationship?
- What do you hope to enhance in your life in the future?

CHAPTER 11

ISMS

I am invisible, understand, simply because people refuse to see me.
—Ralph Ellison

Beginning with the slavery experience, African-American males have been the object of fear and have been perceived as a significant threat to the social order and economic power structure of this country. Today, this discrimination exists in the job market, housing, and the availability of health and social services. Unemployment in the African-American community continues to rise. The *isms* against the Black men are endless: cultural and institutional racism, ageism, capitalism, classism, criticism, and feminism, just to name a few.

Most of the problems in the African-American community are directly related to institutional racism. And this has resulted in psychological scarring, self-destruction, victimization, violence, and Black-on-Black crime. Studies show that Black men, more than any other race and sex, have higher levels of encounters and distress associated with societal racism and oppression. Now here is the prime reason for all the "disappearing acts." This is why Black men's incomes are lower than their White or female counterparts, housing situations tend to be poorer, and purchasing power for food, education, clothing, and health care is low. Yet a question asked by Ralph Ellison is worth a moment to ponder upon: "What would America be without Black men?"

In *The Debt: What America Owes to Blacks*, Randall Robinson expresses that,

> *Yes, racism was used as a basis for justifying the hugely profitable enterprise of slavery. It was used during slavery and since to protect whites from having to accept responsibility for the bitter harvest that we all live with today. Even now, its myriad viruses deploy to protect its group's history and obscure another's, to celebrate one people and disparage another, to advance a majority and hold back a minority.*

Scientists discovered that racism and discrimination result in immediate and significant increases in blood pressure, heart rate, and negative emotional responses, from resentment to anxiety to hostility.

Blacks also perpetuate racism toward other Blacks. The utilization of skin color and economic levels causes a horse race mentality among African Americans. The acquisition of money and stuff is perceived to be the ticket to acquiring status in the Black community.

Thugs Are a Product of Racism

Many young African-American men cope with the anger and hopelessness of dealing with institutional racism by totally disconnecting from the world of work, family, and community. They select the path of rebellion. They choose an alternative lifestyle: the thug life. The modern-day street thug and hustler is part and product of the cultural alienation produced by racism.

The thug mentality has been glamorized for entertainment and economic purposes. Yet it is being adopted as a way of life from disenfranchised young and not-so-young people from the inner city to the suburbs. Thugs don't have to worry about not fitting in, nor do they have to deal with the powerlessness of integrating into White America. The thug's self-esteem and self-worth are seldom violated. And there are many opportunities for advancement in the thug life. There are two major problems in the world of thugism: Thugs go to jail. Thugs die early.

Here are the stories of men who were faced with *isms* and were robbed of self-esteem and self-worth, or who stood up and fought the good fight for all their brothers and sisters. All in all, these men show us how they coped and paved the way, broke ground, and planted the seed of freedom for all Black men all over the world.

Flying while Black

Kevin Walker

I noticed her walking toward me and knew what she was going to say before she could even get it out of her mouth. The whole scenario could be seen as otherwise uneventful. A White woman in a Columbus airport asking a Black man for help. She obviously needed assistance with all the bags that she had to carry. I tried to avert my eyes to avoid an embarrassing situation for either one of us, especially her. She didn't get the hint but persisted.

"Excuse me," she said, getting close to annoyed. Although I was clad in the black top-to-bottom uniform of a Delta employee, it was not my place to help with her bags. My second attempt to help her move in the direction of getting checked was ignored. Even after I gestured toward the airport employees that could provide her assistance, she insisted, "Look, I'm on the next flight to Dallas."

"Miss," I said, "I'm working the Dallas flight, too, but not as a skycap." It seems that she and I would be headed in the same direction, she as a passenger and I as the pilot.

It was a long road that took me from a little boy with flying-high dreams to a career as an airline pilot for one of the largest airlines in the world. Every Christmas that I could recall, I asked for the same thing, a bigger, faster, and more elaborate airplane than the Christmas before. I didn't toggle between fireman, policeman, doctor, and attorney as careers of choice. It seems my decision to be a pilot was hardwired within me from birth. My parents—my mom, Vivian, an artist and homemaker, and my father, Kahn, an army dentist—were supportive of my goal. They never hesitated to provide an encouraging word and later the funds in order for me to realize my dream of flying. However, sheer goodwill and best intentions weren't enough to get me far enough to actually get hired as a pilot.

The process of becoming a pilot is a long arduous one. I had to log countless hours of flight time, and that's in order to qualify to fly. While I studied at Ohio State University, I used every opportunity I could to take to the air. My instructors were helpful, and the other students would later become invaluable resources. However, I remained undeniably alone. As the only African-American in pilot school, I always felt a difference there. I quickly found a support network in the Organization of Black Airline Pilots. The organization was started out of the efforts of the Tuskegee airmen who were instrumental in America's successful flight efforts in World War II.

The Organization of Black Airline Pilots was directly responsible for making sure that I was in a position to obtain a coveted pilot's spot with Delta Airlines in 2000. My dream had finally come true, and in ways that defied basic odds. Just 1 percent of pilots on America's major airlines are African Americans. By working for Delta, I was working toward stabilizing the unbalanced numbers of those that take to the skies. I was proud to step into this position as a representative of my African-American community in general and my mom and dad specifically.

Overall, my experience was positive, and the respect that I expected was given to me. However, there were more instances than I care to count that help to remind you that in many ways, the career that you choose, no matter how elite, doesn't shield you from prejudice. With the cap and the wings that took years to earn, I've still been mistaken for a skycap, flight attendant, or gate agent. When I was younger, I was more idealistic, but it didn't take me long to realize that I shared more similarities with the Tuskegee airmen than just my love of flying. Now, like then, people would see me and see my Blackness first and my pilot wings second. Being Black first can also be a source of pride. I often get knowing looks from airport personnel who take my status as a badge of pride that they can also wear. Those connections help to cancel out some of the other forgettable experiences.

Then, of course, there were times when I felt the same as all my fellow pilots, no matter their birthplace or origin. People often ask me about what things were like for me on the day that life changed for all Americans, September 11. Since I lived in New York City, I knew that my parents had to be worried, and like most people across the country, my first thought was to connect with them. In the days and months that were to follow, I, too, had to grapple with the magnitude of how all our lives had been changed forever. I share that with most people, but very few other people actually had to fly on September 15 out of New York.

My love for flying and trust of the safety procedures that we were trained in helped to provide the foundation for my confidence in flying. Although my first morning flight after the attack was nerve racking, I prayed, holding out faith that things would be fine. Once in the air, I knew not only that things would be all right, but that they were already all right. It was time to move on.

I will always fly. I was born to fly. My love for what I do is so much a part of me that it's difficult to separate who I am from my pilot self. My love for

Hope You're Feelin' Me

Sean Michaels

When people meet me or hear my name, they know something is familiar, but sometimes they don't know from where. When it dawns on them that I have one of the most recognized faces in the adult film industry, I get a range of responses from them. I'm used to it, and I really don't mind what people think about me overall. Some people love me and give my films credit for reviving their love lives. Others tell me that I don't look like the kind of guy who would have sex on screen. They even go so far as to ask me if anything happened to me when I was a child. The only thing that happened to me is that I was raised right.

I wasn't locked in a closet when I was a kid. Nothing traumatic happened to me that forced me to choose a career in adult videos. In fact, I was raised by a caring mother who loved me then and still loves me today. I was a good student, and if I really look back at it, some people might have considered me a nerd. I was a musician who loved jazz, and I performed modern dance while I was growing up in Brooklyn. I played high school football well enough that an athletic scholarship seemed to be part of my future.

My intense education in the world of women came from living with four females. My mother taught me about respect, and through my sisters' experiences, I learned about being sensitive to women's needs. Mind you, I was smart—and in this case, I was smart enough to know when I was outnumbered. I was the oldest son with three sisters who began to fill our home with girl stuff, girl clothes, girl talk, and even girl mood swings. So I moved cross-town to live with my grandmother in Queens to complete my high school education. My relationship with my sisters flourished when I had my own place in which to grow up and be a man. While I was in high school, my sisters were my chief confidantes and not much has changed today.

When I graduated from high school, I moved to California to go to college. My goal was to study at the College of the Desert and prepare to transfer to another college to play football. But a freak accident shattered my dreams of playing ball for a living. Since I was a good student, I put my energy into my studies and became a nurse. My desire to help people and sensitivity in addressing their needs made me good at what I did. Being a nurse is a respected profession that pays good money; however, I felt like something was missing from my life. I needed a way to share my other talents with the world. Modeling was always interesting to me, and I had a sister who worked on the runway. I also loved the idea of acting. So I hung up my scrubs and started my pursuit of Hollywood.

To really get an idea of what it's like to be me, you have to first understand that I wanted to be an adult film star; it was a choice for me. Of course, I'd love to have been discovered by mainstream Hollywood, but the opportunity that was offered allowed me to express my creative side and get my freak on at the same time. Basically, I was getting paid to work with beautiful interesting women whose company I really enjoyed. There's not much difference between my job and anyone else's. Like every one else, I had to master the technical aspects of my craft in order to create a product that people will want to buy. I had to insure that my coworkers were happy by communicating openly with them. And, like everyone else, when I wasn't on my game, it was impossible for me to perform at my absolute best. The main difference between my job and most other jobs is that I knew before the end of my workday, I was going to get laid.

As a college graduate, I got paid to do what a lot of men do daily and some men only get to fantasize about. I had fun, and the pay wasn't bad. I immediately felt that I could add something to the adult film industry. However, like any Black man, I had my concerns about the way that my image was being portrayed. There were things that I absolutely refused to do. In 1989, the industry was not quite ready for an African-American man who would challenge the directors on scenes that called for me to degrade women or act in a stereotypical fashion. It was important to me to make sure that my work was of such good quality that I would be proud of what I put out. My relationship with the women in my life was a very close one. I would have been embarrassed to have to tell them that I was in the movie playing a pimp type whose idea of lovemaking was slapping women around.

I quickly began to realize that there is no profession where a Black man is immune to the impact of racism. I found it ironic that in an industry full of self-exploration and groundbreaking exposure there would be fear about interracial sex scenes. The roles that they wanted to confine me to would have solidified my place as a B-list actor, and I refused to stall my career in that way. So instead of working as a stunt dick and black buck for hire, I looked for an opportunity that would allow me to have the kind of on-screen presence I felt I deserved. Because of this experience, my philosophy of "no color lines" was born, and it would later become a major factor in every movie that I would make.

I left the country on an invitation to work in Europe. There my image and my style were quickly accepted. It was easy to recognize that their idea of a fantasy did not include suppressing a tall Black man and his big Black penis. I had no problem finding scenes working with women of all nationalities. I was never asked to say demeaning things to actresses or act in a way that would embarrass the women who cared for me and raised me. My reputation grew while I was in Europe and allowed me to return to the States as an accomplished actor. Upon my return, people started to give me the roles that I expected, and my philosophy of no color lines was beginning to catch on.

When my career began to take off, it was important for me to have people around me to look out for my best interests. This situation was no different from any other. I had the support of my family when two of my sisters moved from New York to L.A. to do administrative work and manage the books for my company. People would often ask me what does my mother think about the work that I do. For a long time, my response would be that they could go in the kitchen and ask her since she moved to California to help by providing the catering for my staff.

People are surprised to find that I still have such a close relationship with the women in my life. They respect and love me, and I feel the same about all of them. In fact, my feelings about my family and the women who have shaped the man that I am today are a major factor in the way that I treat women on and off the screen. Sure, my on-screen personality is a little more flashy and exudes all the confidence in the world. However, the man who plays the roles, the real me, is very sensitive to the needs of women. I am a hopeless romantic and care about my craft to a fault. I'm proud to say that there are more than two thousand adult film titles with me in the movie; I have won countless awards and have broken down racial barriers with my on-screen work. I have been in this industry for thirteen years and have been the first to do many things, including the first African American to own a manufacturing company of my own videos.

Some people object to the porn industry altogether, and that's fine. There are things that I like and don't like, as well. We all have our limits, and our acceptance of what's cool is different for each person. I know that for me, I draw the line at anything that I wouldn't tell the women in my life that I did. Some people may walk away having read this and feel like they got to know me a little better; other people may have more questions for me—and that's all fine. I am a son, a brother, a boyfriend and I am a proud father. It's in those relationships that others' opinions matter to me most. I don't look for everyone to love me or even like me, but I appreciate respect for the fact that I'm representing as an African-American artist and businessman. But besides my family, who I know has my back, I hope that

A Post-Slavery Pissing Contest

Gino L. Morrow II

Looking to relieve myself of the liquid buildup in my bladder,
I walked into the men's room to find nine unused urinals from which to
    choose.
Which one would I use? (hummm!)
Not a complex decision for it had already been
determined by my subconscious thought,
drawing from a pattern created over time
that taught me to use the first or the last of the nine
and like countless times before I quickly found myself at the last.
Now one might ask,
Why make a big deal of using the rest room?
Understand the logic, my friends!
I am an introvert who enjoys PRIVACY and SPACE
and more often than not, PRIVACY and SPACE
are the first casualties in rest-room warfare.
And so I'm standing there with mini-me in hand,
taking shots at the unsinkable cigarette butt
that I affectionately named Mr. Bigglesworth.
Not a soul in sight who might contest me for my turf.
Then walks in "Mr. Corporate America" himself.
You know the type:
The tall/short, skinny/fat, bearded/shaved, handsome hunk of ugly
    white guy
with a fresh haircut, manicured nails, charcoal-gray wool slacks,
pressed blue button-down and a cell phone
with the *Star Trek* headset connected to his ear.
I peeped him as he walked in.
"Click-clack-click-clack." He passed the first urinal.
For a second I suspected him to be a corporate gumshoe.
Not a certified detective but rather a PRIVATE investigator!
Not to worry though.
He's in neutral territory now.

And besides, every man knows
the first tenet of restroom etiquette, and that is:
Never use a urinal that is in the line of sight of another man's penis.
Violation of this tenet usually triggers an instant red flag.
Then he approached the second urinal.
At a slow strut he passed urinal 2, then 3,
leaving a total of four urinals between us then?
I cut him a sharp glance to warn him of his potential violation.
Not fazed by my warning, he passed urinals 5,
then 6, and 7.
INTRUDER ALERT—INTRUDER ALERT
"Goddamn it! Eight extra urinals and he wants to use the one right next
     to me!"
His aggressive behavior triggered violation sensors within me.
I have ultrasensitive sensors you know!
Can't have another man standing next to me
with his penis in his hand. That kinda behavior is borderline GAY!
And I'm not!
Refusing to have my sexuality misconstrued by a dude,
I jumped on the defensive and did the only thing a man in my position
     could.
Staring over the top of wire-framed glasses,
I glanced him once over, then looked him dead in the eyes and said:
"Wassup,"
while simultaneously twisting my package in the direction opposite my
     assailant.
"What does he want?" I wondered looking away and up toward the ceil-
     ing.
To me, his actions clearly communicated one of two thoughts:
1. That he's homosexual and wants to know if I could be or
2. He's racist!
Okay, You're probably thinking; "How does his behavior make him a
     racist?"
You see racism is just a form of oppression.
And oppression is about
imposing one's will upon another
even when there is no apparent threat to one's existence,
the assertion of one's power to prove his dominance
in the event that the oppressed should even consider retaliation.
Like for instance—a police officer shoving a plunger through an
apprehended man's rectum

or like a woman who blames the kidnapping and drowning of her two
    children
on a fictitious Black man whose profile fits the description
of a third of all Black men,
causing an entire country to fear and pursue the innocent.
But I digress.

As I stood there between the cold restroom wall and perpetrator
who passed up seven other urinals to get cozy with me,
my sense of sound would be violated when at that moment
he released a noise that echoed a torrential downpour.
Turning toward me while nodding his head up and down,
he let out a sigh of relief. "Ahhhhhhh!"
I could smell the garlic of his fettucini leftovers.
He looked down at himself with a smirk about him.
Sensing an urgent need to defend my territory (like an elephant bull),
I released my trunk, placed my hands on waist as if to say, "Let's see you
do that, little man,"
and waited a second or two for his response.
Just about the time he appeared to start and glance my way,
I ripped a fat one, forcing him to guess what I had for lunch.
Baring my pearly whites I gave a sigh of relief as I looked on toward vic-
    tory.
Standing in my full glory, I knew it was over.
He was at the end of his liquid load while I was still goin' strong.
I was praising God for delivering the big "V,"
not realizing I'd begun my victory dance prematurely,
for, in the midst of my celebration and without warning,
my enemy lashed out seeking to inflict a final and critical wound
before he would limp off in defeat.
Sure he was at his road's end with no fuel in his tank.
But he hadn't yet jiggled.
Why, you know the jiggle!
As instinct kicked in, he angrily and violently
jiggled away the residual droplets that collected at the tip of his man-
    hood,
spattering samples of urine upon my pant leg and shoe.
Oooh!
This was unexpected.
But was it enough?
I looked upon my pant leg with disgust.

And then I cut my eyes toward he who was
but half the soldier that challenged me.
Teeth gritted I let out a cry of laughter
that rumbled until it echoed with bass.
His eyes grew large with fear.
He rushed to find his zipper and the exit.
And just as quickly as it began, it was over.
Victory was mine!

And to the victor goes the spoils? Eight additional urinals.
Space? and privacy!

Gino L. Morrow II *is a three-time Midwest Regional Slam Champion. He's the author of a book titled* Spitfire *and founder of Grassroot Literary Movement Press LLC.*

Learning How to Address Racism with White Folks, and Getting Allies

Micah E. Lubensky

A few years ago, I helped organize a racism-awareness seminar for a White audience. Even though there would be very few ethnic and racial minorities present and I would be one of only two Black folks in the room, I wasn't too worried about it. I had just been to a weekend-long anti-racism conference, and I had a lot of discussions in school about racism, so I didn't think anything would surprise me. Damn, was I wrong! This story is about that seminar, and what I learned about discussing racism with White folks who might be motivated to combat it. I thought it was an important lesson, and I think it is worth sharing with others who are also out there, trying to make a better world by addressing racism.

My friend Sam once lived in northern California. The county where he lived had a fairly visible gay/lesbian/bisexual/transgender (GLBT) community. Because Sam is a gay activist, he was happy to find there were some decent GLBT community resources there, too. However, the county was pretty segregated along racial and economic lines. Not surprisingly, most of the GLBT resources were located in the central town, which was also very segregated, and almost all the administrators for these various community resources were White. Few of these resources were located or made available outside of the White town. And if 10 percent of the world's population is GLBT, there must have been some need for them in these other communities.

Sam identifies strongly with his Asian-American heritage, and when he perceived the degree of segregation in his town and county, he got upset. He did some research on the county's demographics, and he had interactions with some of the GLBT resource administrators. Afterwards, Sam concluded that these resource administrators needed to spend some time thinking about racism. Because of the segregation and potential racism from some of the administrators, he was sure that racism was playing a large part in the county's availability and distribution of GLBT community resources, not to mention the county's general segregation. Sam then called me to talk about it for two reasons. He knew I wanted to get more involved in anti-racism activism, and he knew that I care about GLBT resources because I am also bisexual. After a couple of long talks on the phone, we decided that a racism-awareness seminar would be an appropriate effort.

The process of contracting, codesigning, and administering a racism-awareness seminar was pretty long, but I won't go into it here. However, the hardest part was the actual seminar. Early that day, our professional moderators ran into resistance and disapproval from the attendees. Some of these attendees explicitly disagreed. They thought that the seminar was exclusionary and too narrow in its focus; it needed to look at other grand-scale social issues. Others believed that the seminar should have discussed age and physical ability instead, and how folks can often be discriminated against because of those characteristics. A few suggested gender, because sexism is everywhere in the United States. One of the attendees was transgendered; she pointed out that we should have examined negative outcomes because of gender appearance and gender identification. As these dissenters criticized, they came up with more reasons why the seminar was short-sighted and what we, as a group, should be talking about instead of racism awareness.

For a few minutes, I doubted what we had done and felt terrible. Because I helped organize the event and wanted to make sure that it went well, I was totally thrown off guard. But then I started analyzing what was being said. When it came down to it, these dissenters were arguing to change the seminar. It had been clearly laid out to focus on the effects of racism. Instead, they wanted to shift the focus to their own experiences of disadvantage. Whether or not they were aware of it, this attitude communicated a distinct message: They could minimize or dismiss the importance of racism. Within milliseconds, my mind followed the logic: All the pain and anger and frustration I have ever felt because of racism or that anyone else had ever felt because of racism could therefore be minimized or dismissed, as well. After all, if it wasn't worth discussing, why would it be worth caring? Essentially racism didn't matter to them, or at least not as much as what they were going through.

A few milliseconds later, when I hit this, my mind seized. I sat there, no longer fully listening to more criticisms, and became more and more furious until I was actually seeing lights and colors swimming before my eyes. These White folks, criticizing a racism-awareness seminar organized by two people of color, were implying that racism wasn't worth discussing, even when they had been invited to focus on racism! I hadn't felt this insulted in years! I had to express how I was interpreting their criticisms, and I knew that as soon as I opened my mouth, all hell was gonna break loose. But, in that same instant, my urge to explode and yell a dozen nasty things also froze. What if I let go and started to holler? I was afraid that no one would have heard a damned thing I said. . . . *I know too well how angry Black folks are perceived!* Just another angry person of color, who is "too sensitive"! Worse yet, sometimes they try to correct him or her, saying; "No one is racist anymore," or "The Civil Rights Era had accomplished everything," or "I'm not responsible for what other White folks did." And those tired, phony excuses would have pushed me over the edge of frustration. Indeed, I really would have lost my shit. So instead of risking those responses, I sat there, clamped my teeth on my tongue, and let my disbelieving rage burn up my insides until I was back on the brink of the bitterest tears.

Somewhere around this time, one of the moderators addressed the criticisms and got folks to remember what they were there for. I loved what she said. She reminded them that they were there to discuss racism, and that racism deserved a full day's discussion, at the very least. That drastically helped my nerves. After I was able to calm down, I reassessed what happened.

The dissenting reactions shouldn't have been hard to understand. They probably did not mean to piss me off or to imply that racism or anyone's experience with racism didn't matter. I had to remember that we gathered a room full of folks who probably had experiences with discrimination. Given the way that our society treats lesbians, gays, bisexuals, and transgendered folks, I don't doubt that most of them had been disadvantaged because of their sexual orientation, or gender identity. They may have thought that they had a good understanding of the experience of racism. That could have been why some of them were suggesting that we focus instead on other issues that were burning them more. After the seminar, some of the seminar attendees even told me that they had long considered themselves "allies" in the struggle against racism. This suggested to me that some folks had spent time thinking about racism on their own.

However, for those who wanted to switch topics, or just talk about their own *isms* instead, I think they still had a lot to learn. One can't understand racism because one experiences homophobia or sexism or classism or ageism; not all forms of discrimination and prejudice are the same. Yeah, they all hurt like hell, maybe they enrage or depress us, and they can really affect our lives in so many ways. But they are all attacks on people from different angles, attacks on different characteristics, and have different ways of affecting lives.

Because I'm a proud bisexual person of color, I've noticed how discrimination against GLBT people and their communities is very different from the discrimination faced by people of color and their communities. There are ways in which discrimination against women is different from discrimination against low-income folks, and that discrimination is different from discrimination against the elderly, and so on. Even if we think we understand discrimination really well, it doesn't mean that we understand what it feels like to be discriminated against because of a characteristic we don't have. So even if I think I understand what it might be like to face sexism, I still will never feel it because I won't ever be a woman in this society. This is something that White folks need to remember, even if they claim to understand or know what it is like to face racism. They won't ever know what it is like to be Black in the United States. It certainly isn't the same as suddenly finding oneself as the only White person in the room or the neighborhood.

I made this point at the seminar, and it seemed to help the attendees get perspective. After a much longer discussion of racism, how it works in subtle and explicit ways, and how it affects people, the attendees seemed to really get into it. We then discussed the racist nature of the segregation in their county, the importance of their roles as administrators for GLBT resources, and how they needed to consider the possible influence of racism in their organizational practices and policies. By the end of those discussions, I felt like we had raised consciousness for the people in the room. Several of them came up with new plans for community outreach. Others were going to call meetings to analyze their organizational policies. We had made new allies against racism with these White administrators of GLBT county resources.

Since the seminar, I've thought a lot about it, and I have a better idea for how to handle that situation now. When discussing racism with White folks, there are a lot of responses to anticipate. Aside from resistance to the topic ("No one is racist anymore!" or "You're too sensitive!" or other such dismissals, which are a whole different story altogether), I think it is really important to think about *how they think they get it*, especially if they face a different form of prejudice or discrimination. Do they think they get it because they are Jewish and find that they are the target of anti-Semitic violence? Because they receive welfare benefits and know firsthand how Americans tend to punish and hate poor people? Do they think they get it because they are physically disabled and regularly have to figure out alternative forms of accessing public places? The point is to try to understand their perspective, too.

Then, if anyone tries to swing the conversation away from racism, I would openly acknowledge the attempt. Yes, there are so many forms of prejudice and discrimination out there that are debilitating! Yes, we should discuss them. But, I would either offer to discuss how that form of prejudice crosses with racism (for example, just think about how racism combines with sexism—our Black sisters know all about it; or how racism combines with classism—low-income Black folks know all about that!), or ask to make it a separate topic for later. Racism is alive and well, and it still needs to be addressed without being dismissed early. We still need to combat racism regularly; to do so, we have to focus on it and all its permutations.

At the same time, if we hope others will be allies in fighting racism, we need to be sure that we are allies for them against their *ism* enemies, too. When White senior citizens say they are anti-racist allies, but they also complain about ageism, we need to listen to their complaints, and to consider ways to support them. The only way to really establish allies for one's cause is to be an ally in return for a different cause. And if we can truly build stronger alliances between communities, we're more likely to reduce the amount of isms that plague us. Then we can start to beat racism. But in order to whoop racism, we'll need people everywhere, including outside the Black community, to work on it. I guess there are more seminars to plan.

Micah E. Lubensky is a Ph.D. candidate in social psychology at UC Santa Cruz, where his academic research focuses on issues of identity and social justice. Passionate about diversity and pluralism, Micah is also an advocate and activist for increased awareness and inclusion of racial, economic, and political diversity. Much of this work has centered on the diversity within the lesbian/gay/bisexual/transgendered communities.

Separatism

Kwame

As an African-American male you deal with one *ism* or another from day one. You deal with a certain type of classisms when you start school. You take tests that are supposed to determine how smart you are and your potential as a person.

Music has always been a form of escapism from me. Writing, playing, and creating music have been stabilizing forces in my life. Only there is no test early on to measure your musical aptitude. So, I would take these standardized tests, do well, and end up in the smart class. Let me clarify that, end up the *only* Black male in the smart class. This contributed to the perception I had growing up that there was something different about being a Black male. There was always this perception that this Black kid in this top class represented some kind of threat. A troublemaker, maybe not that kind, but still a threat because he shouldn't be in the top class. So, when I was bused to a White school, the perception continued. Only, it became more of an academic separat*ism*.

Most of the black kids were bused, from the ghetto. So, now you have me, among the top echelons of students, and the teacher sits me in the front to draw attention to me and separate me from the other kids. I had not caused trouble, but still I was being penalized and made different. That has a tremendous effect on you when you are six, seven, and eight years old.

So, this is sticking in my mind. Now, I have to prove myself extra. I am not just going to school, I am paving the way for others. And, back at home, my parents know the climate of the school, so they push me extra hard because they know what I'm up against. They know all about separat*ism* so they are going to help see to it that I don't fail. I felt like I lost part of my childhood because I am in the house studying instead of outside, playing with my friends.

As a kid, you can't differentiate between doing extra credit to get an A-plus and playing outside. It made me bitter. I mean, all I wanted to do was watch the *Muppet Show*.

There was also the separat*ism* when it came to doling out justice.

I remember one of my classmates brought in smoke bombs and gave everybody two. One of the kids wanted my two as well as his own. When I refused, he ran to the principal and said, "The Black kid has smoke bombs." I don't want to be a rat, so I end up in the principal's office, and they are threatening to call my mother. So, finally I come clean and say that half the class has smoke bombs. But the principal tells me he didn't catch half the class, just me. It was then I realized that I wasn't playing on an equal field. So, then I started to understand the racism and the double standard of being a Black male.

Catholic school also put another stamp on the fact that this world would be different for me as a Black male.

I was introduced to a sort of ethnicism, where Black kids were treated more harshly than other racial groups. I have never heard a grown-up use such profanity and incite such violence, let alone a teacher. But when I would voice my opinions, I would be harshly disciplined. It was an interesting take on religion—God don't work that way.

But the teacher's patience and ropes were longer when it came to the other ethnic groups. It was like these kids are supposed to achieve and I, being Black, wasn't. I was doing my thing in the arts, designing and performing. But I wasn't encouraged to apply to arts schools. I wasn't told that music was important, or a potential career. They were encouraging me to go to a regular school because they didn't want to see me disappointed. At that point in my life, I began to become aware that the system was being set up for me not to be.

Thank God for music. Thank God for hip-hop! Now, I was always musically inclined—making music and performing. To me, music was an escape, so I never looked at it being my career. I knew people in the music industry. Lionel Hampton gave me a drum set and I taught myself to play. I had relatives who knew Stevie Wonder, and he was a great artist, but I really didn't get it at the time.

But now, hip-hop, that was my music. My parents didn't understand it, but I did, and by the sixth grade, I was a DJ. I had turntables, and I was doing my thing. It was music that provided me with an outlet to escape the isms of being a Black male. It was music that gave me an identity earlier on to get enough space and respect to escape some of the racism, class-ism and separatism.

Talent shows provided the platform for my individualism. Teachers would call on me to put together the school parties. Interestingly, that was the only encouragement that I got from teachers that showed me I was special. It was never you are smart, in the top class. Just the music thing—call Kwame, he can produce that party or talent show for you. It showed me that all they wanted out of Black men was a performance. When it was time for a science project or a spelling bee of a math project, I never got the call, but when it came time for them to be entertained, everything was "let's go." There was a different expectation and exploitationism when it came to entertainment. The romanticism of seeing children of color express their talent and souls on stage mesmerized them.

It still didn't click that this music thing was something I could make a living at. It was while attending the School of Art and Design in Midtown Manhattan that I learned a different kind of ism, hoodism. I was hanging out with the kids from the 'hood, and there was a pressure that Black men put on other Black men to be real and hard. So, when you were hanging out with the cool kids, you were not supposed to go to class. When you cut school, you didn't leave the school, you hung out on another floor.

I found myself caught up. It wasn't a Black or White separatism thing— we were all smart kids—but a part of different cliques, cool, nerd, hood, and straight. In hindsight, I should have been there to get my education, but I fell into the trap of hanging out with my crew, trying to hustle the teacher and find ways to get out of doing what I was supposed to do.

I knew that wasn't me, but I was trying to fit in. The worst ism of all is not being true to yourself.

It got into a situation one day where my crew was beating up one of the nerd kids. And I jumped into it. I could have chosen one of two roads. I could have walked past it and gone to school. But instead, I decided to join in. The other kids fled, but I went to school and got arrested. I couldn't understand why I put myself in that situation, knowing what I did was wrong.

Here I am at sixteen, about to become a part of the statistics. The experience opened me up. When I was in that cell, all I saw was me: other Black men. I didn't see anybody else. Now I am flashing back to high school. I can go left or right. I can take the right road and won't have these problems again. Or I could end up in jail. I got a slap on the wrist, and the charges were dropped.

I made the choice, for lack of a better word, to become one of the nerds. I knew the thugs and I knew the nerds, but I decided to become a "cool" nerd.

My father remarried, and he didn't trust me living in the city. I would learn another important ism living in the suburbs of New Jersey. I started going to one of those upper middle-class high schools that I saw only on television. So now it is either you are rich or poor. Do you take a bus, walk, or drive a BMW? So, here I go again, where do I fit? My father was renting a house, and we didn't have the luxury sedan. So I am reintroduced to classism. The straight hair, blue contacts, the polo shirt—and that was the Black kids. It was like the Black people didn't want to be Black. And the White people didn't want to be White. And the good kids were trying to be hard.

I remember one kid I would hang out with whose father was a big shot in town. He was trying to hang out late and act hard. So, one thing led to another, and the kid and his crew got kicked out of school. Now, I mean, how hard can anyone be wearing Eddie Bauer?

But a funny thing happened. I just got deeper and deeper into the music to escape the various isms. The music provided a uniting force. No matter what clique, crew, economic background or ism, everybody was drawn to Kwame through the music. I ended up back at a New York high school when my father moved to a farm in Virginia. I had a record deal by then. So, now I have recording industry money. So, I don't have to be the cool guy, the nerd, the rich kid. I can be my own man. I have on my designer clothes, my jewelry, my beeper, and I am doing my thing.

The principal and nobody at the school knew what I was about. So, I see guys following me around, undercover cops who think I am a drug dealer. And, then the hoods in the school want to catch me and take my jewelry. My grades are good, so now I have all angles covered. Teachers looking at me as a bad guy, cops are waiting, and the thugs are trying to catch me after school.

This whole feeling was what I put into the album I released at the time. But, I had learned from the isms and the music that it didn't have to be this way. I didn't have to live by an ism. I could be different and be myself. So, I came out publicly as a rapper, and I was a platinum selling artist at age seventeen. But instead of feeding on my positive lyrics, other rappers began hating. So, the "negativism" starts to eat me up.

You can't be rapper and not make thug music. You can't be a real rapper because you play the drums, keyboard, and guitar. But, I couldn't be anybody but myself with the music. So, I sort of lost my way, trying to change my sound. It couldn't work. The music was in me and had to come out. So I lost all direction.

I thought I could go anywhere I wanted, but then nobody wanted me. Is there a played-ism? I had played myself trying to be something I was not. For the first time in my life I had to face being a man.

I am a human again, on the train, walking, collecting little if no royalty checks. Getting a regular job. But, the music is still there inside like a blanket shielding me. And, then a funny thing happens, all the isms I had experienced in my life helped me deal with this new cold world. So, the boxism doesn't work. It was like they were trying to keep me from doing certain things musically that God had given to me. Most Black men experience this feeling; an outdated ism blocking them from growing as a person or making a living.

I started composing and producing music. I loved being a rapper, but I also had more music to give in other areas. It was like the stereotypes holding back Blacks and women. I had to break out of the boxism and go back to the music. So, I used the musicism in my life to break down those barriers to get back into the record industry. Which goes to show, you have to create your own ism so that somebody else's ism doesn't hold you back and stop your dream.

Kwame (a.k.a. K 1 Mil) is a platinum-selling rapper and record producer of such multiplatinum-selling artists as Mary J. Blige, Dru Hill, and LL Cool J.

Your Soul's Journey

May the LORD judge between you and me. And may the LORD
avenge the wrongs you have done to me, but my hand will not
touch you.   —1 Samuel 24:12

While slavery ended in the U.S. more than 138 years ago, many people say we need to forget it and move on. As recently as 1964, in the Supreme Court case of Griffin v. Prince Edward County, Virginia, public schools were ordered to be reopened after being closed for five years to avert the efforts of school integration. Segregated private schools, paid for by tax-deductible contributions, were set up for the county's 1,304 White students while the county's 1,646 African-American students were deprived of an education for five years! A court battle that took place over a hundred years after the abolition of slavery, but still affected the way African Americans were living to that day—and to this day, for that matter. We still face overt and covert racial oppression every day.

Each generation produces individuals like yourself who benefit the next generation by making strides—whether you are Bob Johnson leading the purchase of an expansion team or a fearless political leader who continues to fight for African Americans or a father who is raising his child to be responsible or perhaps a brother building a company from the ground up. Persistence and perseverance are powerful qualities to instill in you. For the women, partners, and family in your life, encourage them to not be part of your battle. The only way you are going to make it is if we work together. A war has been waged on us, but we can't let that stop the show. It is a game and system, and you must learn how to play it. The war is occupying the space where your dreams should be. We all have dreams fulfilled them, work with God and don't let anyone one deter you from your purpose!

Soul Source

For Black men, the journey to equality is an understanding of the dynamics of ignorance and how to effectively combat them. Ignorance is a combination of denial and a lack of knowledge. The journey begins with forgiveness and giving freedom a place inside your head. Although society saddles us with unnecessary baggage, breaking free in your mind is all about perception. It is the distinction between liberties given and taken. Life is unfair for a Black man! Absolutely! Now what are we going to do about it?

- How do we come together as an African-American community and deal with revealing the hidden aspects of institutional racism?
- Are there times when middle-class Blacks use racism to suit their purposes and other African Americans use it as an excuse to not work harder?
- Have you experienced any isms?
- Describe each incident.
- What kind of Black male president would you vote for? What characteristics are you looking for in this candidate?
- Every young Black man or woman born in this country has the potential to be the President of the United States. Have you discussed this fact to your children or younger relatives? Why or why not?
- Do you support Black businesses?
- How do we fix the damages that racism has done to the Black community?
- Have you been able to heal from ism-related incidents that have left a lasting effect on you?

CHAPTER 12

A TIME FOR HEALING

There's definitely a connection between poor health and a lack of employment. Health care falls to the bottom when you're trying to feed your family.
—Dr. Eric Whitaker

He didn't know what he was going to face in the hospital that day. Dr. Dan, as his patients fondly called him, was called in to examine a patient who was stabbed in the chest. At first the stab wound didn't seem that serious, but as the patient grew pale and began coughing violently, Dr. Dan knew that the problem was something more critical. In 1893, without the assistance of X rays and blood transfusions, doctors were almost always unwilling to open a patient's chest due for fear of infection in the chest cavity. Dr. Dan decided to operate. He made a small incision in the patient's chest, enabling him to see into the chest cavity. He saw that the knife had severed a large blood vessel, which he tied off, and it also tore into the sac surrounding his heart. Dr. Dan sewed the sac and then stitched the original incision he made in the patient's chest. Dr. Dan vigilantly watched his patient for the next three days and made sure he successfully recovered. Dr. Daniel Hale Williams became the first Black member of the American College of Surgeons and also the first surgeon to successfully perform open-heart surgery.

We are contributors to medical breakthroughs, but we are not contributors to our own personal health. We have all heard the cliché that Black men are an endangered species. The danger comes from diet, stress, and the bad habit of putting our health last. Often Black men are too busy to find the time to go to the doctor, between working, building a career, finding employment, the stress that can come from managing a family, following their dreams or schoolwork. Quite often, a Black men will find it difficult to find the time to make an appointment and actually go unless pain sets in and a doctor or hospital visit becomes inevitable.

When planning our lives, do we consider our health? We received the news of a wonderful father who worked hard; his wife stayed home to take care of the three children, including an adopted child. The father who took pride in taking care of his family planned well financially and managed over a hundred acres of land out of the state that had been in the family for over a hundred years. He planned to move South to live on the land and enjoy his retirement. He downsized, sold his home, and was awaiting the renovation of the new home down South. He had blueprints and plans, but never counted on being struck down by a stroke. To make matters worse, he had to undergo surgery on both his knees. Instead of the amazing life he planned to have down South, he will be spending a good portion of his time in rehabilitation and therapy. The one thing that was never factored in was how smoking five packs of cigarettes a day would affect his life.

Reuters Health reported that Blacks and the less educated in the United States have life expectancies about six years shorter than their White and better-educated counterparts, respectively. Now a new report suggests that smoking-related diseases are largely to blame.

Cancer affects all populations in the United States, but especially African Americans. It is second only to heart disease as a cause of death. According to the American Cancer Society "Cancer Facts and Figures for African Americans 2000–2001," in general, African Americans with cancer have shorter survival times than Whites at all stages of diagnosis. This difference is believed to be due to poverty, reduced access to medical care, later diagnosis inherently due to less availability of screening and detection. Leading types of cancer for men are lung, bronchus, prostate, colon rectum, and pancreas.

Cardiovascular disease is the leading causes of death for Black males, according to the American Heart Association. The prevalence of high blood pressure in African Americans in the United States is among the highest in the world. The American Lung Association released a report detailing that African Americans represent only 12 percent of the population, but yet represent more than 24 percent of all asthma-related deaths. The asthma attack rate among Blacks was more than 31 percent higher than that of Whites.

The incidence rate of lung cancer for African-American males is more than 54 percent higher than that of White men. The lung cancer mortality rate in African American males is almost 42 percent higher than that of white males. And is the leading cause of death in African Americans aged twenty-five to forty-four.

However bleak the statistics, reports, and news may seem as far as our health, there is a beginning to the healing. It is standing before the Lord and permitting your Creator to begin the healing process that takes place inside. It doesn't mean you shouldn't go to the doctor; it means you should go with the Lord as your guide and partner in your health. The stories here gives brothers the opportunity to share their journey through their health crisis or the health professional who had to endure a health crisis of his own. It is a source of inspiration, bravery, and the opportunity let go of fear and let God in. Share the stories of these men who have downright refused to let anyone steal their opportunity to live free of illness.

My Mother's Blood in My Veins

Jonathan L. Roper

In April of 2002, I lay in a hospital bed, trying to fathom if I would experience the laughter of my unborn child, or see, again, the smiling faces of my three children. I was, for the first time, frightened. I've been in hospitals all my life, but this was the first time I was extremely sick with a pregnant wife and three children. What would my wife do without me? So I prayed to God that I may hold on and stay awhile. So when I got out of the hospital I saw the beauty of walking on this planet. I embraced the love of my wife and children and understood that life does not have to be filled with enormous vicissitudes.

I have spent my entire life living with sickle-cell anemia. Sickle-cell anemia is a genetic mutation that helps the body fight malaria. Though it is considered a good mutation, the effects of the disease cause blood cells to sickle (form a crescent shape) when they lack oxygen, which causes pain in joints and can destroy organs. Its origins are in the western part of Africa and it affects people of African, Middle Eastern, and lower Asian descent. Most who meet me are unaware of my condition, for it is not something I share. I find some people can be extremely truculent and are incapable of understanding sickness until they are ailing. Living with this disease has been self-effacing. The pain can be emasculating, and one learns to adapt and find other means of expression. But dealing with the agonies of this disease makes it apparent to me that many things are not worth the fret. In trying to ascend above the clouds, the blood in my veins brings me down like Icarus. Though I come crashing down, I get up and take off once more. That is the nature of things for me.

I represent many generations who lived with this disease. My grandmother's grandmother's grandmother came to this country in chains to the ports of New Orleans. Martha Hogan would be the first in my family to suffer from sickle cell here in the United States. Martha, however, lived longer than any of her descendants. She reached her late nineties. When I think of my situation sometimes, in dealing with the disease, Martha becomes, for me, an example of courage—how she survived the Middle Passage, years of slavery, and countless years of doctors not knowing her condition. I know her crises were as terrifying to her as lighting was to the first human beings on this planet. This disease robbed my mother of her mother when she was five, and the disease deprived me of my mother when I was twelve.

My mother, Sue Marie Roper, looked so much like her mother, Sarah. My mother inherited not only Sarah's beautiful features and gap tooth, but also her vitality and strong will. From what I'm told, Sarah was very stalwart and cared dearly for her two children. Sarah would die trying to bring a third into the world. Sometimes I wonder how my mother felt not knowing Sarah, not seeing her smile, not being able to touch her face. I recently found out that my grandmother lost her mother when she was twelve, not to sickle cell, but to pneumonia. Because much wasn't known about sickle cell, my mother and grandmother experienced far worse than I. Not only am I assisted by the medical advancement on sickle cell, but I also have the ability to create fetal hemoglobin, which lowers the number of my episodes.

I was four years old when I began having sickle-cell crises. My mother knew when I was born that I had the disease, but the high level of fetal hemoglobin, not just in me, but most infants with sickle cell, prevented me from having a crisis till I was four. In one of her essays, "A Fight For Life," she writes,

> I am a thirty-year-old black woman who since the age of four has suffered very painful crises from sickle-cell anemia. Even though I have been suffering with this disease since I was four years old; it was not diagnosed until I was nine. I have three sons. When my twins were born, the doctors immediately checked for sickle cell. It was found out that they have a trait, which means they won't suffer with the pains, but they can pass it to their children, also my four-year-old son has sickle-cell disease and has had two attacks already. I guess you think I'm a selfish person, since I knew there was a possibility of my children having sickle cell. But I needed someone to make me want to stay alive. Although I didn't want it to be at the expense of one of my children.

My mother was the only person who understood my suffering. Though there have been individuals who witness the pain on my face and who have shared difficult periods with me during those attacks, my mother completely understood because her blood was traveling through my veins. I miss those nights of sleeping in her bed. I miss her hands rubbing my back, my arms and legs. I miss the warm feeling of having her there. She would break her pills in pieces and give me a small piece and I would sleep like a newborn that is full from his mother's milk. When I would sleep, she stayed up. As I write now, tears come to my eyes, not only because my mother was an insomniac, but because she didn't have anyone to take care of her. She writes,

I have problems sleeping at night. Whenever I lay down to sleep, I would soon awaken to terrible pain. There would be many more nights that would turn from a beautiful evening into a horrible nightmare. Which build fear in me in going to sleep. Many nights I would pace the floors or watch T.V. until the wee hours of the morning. This has been one of my most feared experiences.

One must understand most crises happen when you sleep. It's like being in H. G. Wells's *Time Machine.* You feel like the Elois knowing the Morlocks will hunt you while you sleep. You do as much as you can to protect yourself, but like the Elois you know the Morlocks will eventually get you. Nightfall is a hostile enemy you can't endure, but sunrise is a welcomed friend. My mother protected me at night, but unfortunately, when I was sick, no one protected her. Through all her suffering she expressed her regrets in me having the disease. She adds,

I remember one of Jonathan's cruel attacks. He was too sick for me to leave him and for three nights and days, I slept at his bedside. Before long he was back to his regular self. One day I explained to him that I was very sorry for passing him this horrible disease. He immediately answered, "Mommy you couldn't help the way I was born. And if I hadn't been born, who would take care of you when you're sick?" Tears came to my eyes. Here was an eight-year-old child with more understanding than some adults.

My mother died four years later, two days after Thanksgiving, 1982. That morning plays like an unforgettable scene of a movie to me. I have never before or since felt the emptiness, pain, hurt, fear, and confusion of those two hours following my brother's phone call telling me she had died. I was in her room talking to my brother on the phone, and I could still smell her! How tantalizing. I cried and didn't know what the future held. I left our apartment and cried all the way down in the elevator. I had to be around people. I couldn't be alone. That night I stayed at a friend's house in the Bronx and it felt comforting, but that morning, November 28, would be the first day, for the next fifteen years, that I would be alone to face the Morlocks. Now when I think about it, she is resting. She is sleeping and doesn't have to run from the night. She is able to touch her mother, she is able to kiss her grandmother—speak to Martha and ask her how she got over.

Sometimes when I look at my wife and our four children or when my oldest daughter says her name in pride, I think about my mother and how strong she was: living with sickle cell, raising three children alone and being a member of the Black Panther party, which forced her to change her last name to Roper. After being convicted of beating a White man over the head with a two-by-four, she was sent to New York by the Oakland chapter because they felt she would die serving her sentence. So when my daughter says, "Is the Roper clan in the car?" I think about all that my mother endured: her painful crises, her loneliness, her unendurable frustrations with our poverty, her sleepless nights, and her desires to be loved. My mind then travels to Brooklyn during the late 1940s and reflects on what my grandmother experienced. I think about Martha and her voyage in unimaginable circumstances. I know the night followed her continuously for three months as she crossed the Atlantic. I know she screamed out in pain as her captors raped her. But Martha was strong, for had she not been strong, none of us would have been able to take our trips around the sun. And that is all that is important.

None of my children have the disease, but my brother's son has the disease. Though I have the disease, it imbues compassion and forced me to pursue my dreams and aspirations. My mother stated it was selfish for her to bring me into this world, but it is axiomatic that she loved my brothers and me, and I am so thankful she did because her love has allowed me to live a wonderful life—so, yes, Giovanni-Marie, the Roper clan is in the car, and I welcome the night.

Jonathan L. Roper is a graduate of Morehouse College and founder of Banjo Treasures, Inc., a media company based in Stratford, Connecticut. Banjo Treasures is currently producing a motion picture through its subsidiary Banjo Pictures, LLC, based on Mr. Roper's experiences at Morehouse. He is the father of one daughter, Giovanni-Marie, and three sons, Hathaway Baldwin, Cullen McKay, and Ellison Hughes. He is the husband of Elaine Diana.

Weighing In
Lindsey Williams

For some reason, I never took care of myself and I obsessed about my work. I would try to prove myself and everyone, including my family, that in fact I was a strong Black man and that I could be successful. I always took care of work and others before taking care of myself. I worked at EMI as a music executive and developed talent such as Arrested Development, AZ, Gangstar, and any other artist that EMI had at the time. The priority in my mind was to be strong, successful, and a good husband. What happens is you don't get to the gym, and you don't eat right.

I had an addiction—it was and has always been food. At the time that I met my wife at a Valentine's Day event, she had no idea that I had a weight problem. I was small, and I just came from a weight loss center in North Carolina called Structure House. I have been going to Structure House since I was a child, and this last time I kept the weight off for a couple of years. We were dating for six years before we got married. My wife was a good girl, and there is nothing bad I could say about her except at the end she did some things that she really should have not done. My idea of a good husband was buying her off, giving her a nice place to live, and a great car, but that was not enough. I failed at doing the basics: spending quality time with her.

I never really thought my weight was an issue with her because even when I was at 350 to 400 pounds, she was always proud to introduce me to her friends and associates. I was not there for her the way I needed to be there for her. Quality time is always important, and I just didn't do it. That was my downfall, and I know that as men we take advantage of our women. We say to ourselves, "She will be all right." Although I could have gone straight home after my long workday, instead I would stay and talk with producers just to build a relationship, hanging with the boys. I let that take control of our lives, and my relationship at home was suffering. I thought she would be there for me, but of course she has needs and was lonely. How many years could she take of that? It was the traveling between the L.A. and New York offices, and I would tell her that I was coming home for dinner, and I would be really, really, really late. There were many nights that she would wait up for me and be really pissed off.

On New Year's Eve she said that she was permanently leaving and left on New Year's Day. She met someone else and shortly thereafter got married. That was in 1998. I was crushed—I could not believe that she was serious. I laughed it off at first. I told her, "You're not going anywhere." When she walked out the door, I wasn't sure—I tried to tell myself that maybe it would be better for me. But when the shock really wore off, I freaked out. For twelve years, she was there for me every day. I didn't want her to leave because of my weight. I wanted her to leave because I was screwing up.

My weight was always my downfall from the time I was a little kid. I was an addict, and when you have an addiction, it disturbs a lot of parts of your life. Your life becomes completely unmanageable. You don't pay bills on time and you completely mismanage your money. No woman is going to be in your life if her security isn't straight. It is one thing she is completely unhappy with you, but it is another if you don't take care of yourself. Secondly there's the uncertainty of money. Of course, it's not how much money you make, but how much money you keep that matters. When you have all these uncertainties this makes your mate feel uncomfortable.

When my wife left, I decided that it was a time to make a change. I was working on this huge deal with a friend, and it completely fell apart the week after she left. EMI Record division folded, and I depended on this independent label deal. My spiritual side said enough is enough. I felt that God was saying, "I am taking all of this away from you because you are in trouble." I looked at it all: the wife leaving, the business situation completely falling apart, and everything that meant everything was taken away from me. How much could I take?

I fell in this deep, dark depression. I could not get out of the house. My mother called a friend of the family, someone I called my Jewish mother, to go over to the house to see what was going on. When she came in she said, "This is not good and you need to come to a support group with me tonight."

Since I did not have money to go to Structure House, I went to the support group. It was my only hope—I thought I was going to die. That night I felt that God said, "I took all these things away from you so that you could take care of yourself." I knew that I was addicted to flour and sugar, and from then on I started focusing on me. I let my two cars go—they were repossessed. The only thing I cared about was my weight loss. I didn't care if I had only a hundred dollars as long as I had money to eat right.

I attended the support meetings Sunday through Wednesday; I also went to church on Sunday and the rest of the time, I would be at the gym. I did low-impact cardio, because at first I was so heavy I could not run or anything. I focused on my food plan for the day. I looked at my body as a big round sculpture, and I wanted to sculpt it. My day focused on three meals, my cardio and weight workouts, and meetings at night. After a few months of that, maybe nine, I helped my family in the restaurant, Sylvia's Restaurant in Harlem, New York, as much as I could. It was the ultimate test—it would be great because I kept myself busy and got my food plan from the restaurant. I would take my little cousin in the summertime and hang out. I started trying to figure out what I was going to do with my life, and was I going to go back in the music business? Then I began helping my mother with her catering. The catering side of things is where I found my niche. I started doing gospel brunches and began my own catering business.

I have a few chefs that work for me, and I concentrate on the presentation and creative part of marketing, and create the atmosphere and vibe for the event. I love people, and I love the service business. I love to see people happy—it is an incredible experience. Everyone has to eat, even a tough guy who just came from jail eats good food and is content and happy. The catering gives me an opportunity to direct a theater—you sit down and enjoy your food in an atmosphere that I created. I introduce the healthy food spa menu, and will open a healthy soul food restaurant. We are so used to the fact that soul food is not good for you, but I am working on making it healthier.

My journey was tough, and there were many times that I felt like a failure. It comes from my father and my mother preaching about my dad. They always worried that I was going to fail. My mother was seventeen when she had me, and my dad overdosed on heroin. When I was a little kid, my Mom reinforced that I was strong and would not be a failure. My whole life, I was so worried that I would fail. My mother would say, "No matter what, even if you are a janitor, you will be the best darn janitor. No one is better than you are." I am talking about since I was eight or nine years old. Looking back, I think that is why I was so obsessed with my work. I just did not want to fail. The last five years have taught to let go of two hundred pounds of baggage and accept I have to do my best and leave it in God's hands.

Lindsey Williams *is developing a restaurant and has a thriving catering business.*

Out of Focus

Heru Ptah

There was an apple in the mirror. There was a hand holding up the apple in the mirror. From wrist and beyond what the hand was connected to could not to be seen, or at the least was blurred beyond recognizable visibility. But it was there; I knew this because I was there, standing there no more than three feet from the very mirror in which I saw the reflection of the apple, which was held up by the hand, which was connected to what could not be seen, or better put, not seen by me, though it was my hand which held the apple. I was looking directly at myself, and yet I could not see myself: I was going blind.

My blindness was an interesting affliction; interesting in that it affected only my central vision—my peripheral was fine. It wasn't one of the myriad doctors that I had seen who told me this. No, this was something I discovered on my own. One day, I was carefully walking home, looking straight ahead down the block, analyzing the huge mass of blurriness, which blocked my perception, when I recognized a peculiar thing. It was something about the cars driving by the intersection going left to right. While I looked directly ahead, from the corner of my left eye, I saw the cars driving clearly; but then they would disappear as they came into my direct view, and then in a second reappear again to the corner of my right eye. It took me a minute before I realized what was going on. Then it came to me; as long as I didn't focus on it I could see the world around me but the world in front of me was blocked. So I couldn't see myself in the mirror because my central vision was focused directly on myself, however I could see the apple I held out in my hand because that was a function of my peripheral vision. The best way to describe it would be to say that my hand and apple were floating in the air by themselves. It was as if I were a ghost or something. Funny. I was eighteen then, so I thought shit was kinda cool.

I had had perfect vision all my life up until then. It all began around February of that year; for some reason I began to feel a strain or some form of ache around my eyes. Why all this came about, I don't know. I had held all this in for about two weeks before telling my mother. She in turn took me to see a regular eye doctor. Basically he was just a guy who gave you glasses, and that's what he did. I was given a light prescription, which was meant to make me see distances clearer. The strain around my eyes went away, and my vision got better.

I was cool for months. My lenses perfected my vision and were thin enough to give me an air of intellectualism without the stigma of geekdom. Hey, I was in high school, possibly the most materialistic, vanity-driven microcosm in our society; appearances mattered. From late winter until midsummer everything, was all gravy. During this time I had no problems with my vision; but then I started to notice that my glasses weren't helping my sight as much as they once did. Distances became blurred again, things that I used to see clearly became confused, and I was having problems reading. This was all kinda weird; however, I had put it all to needing a higher prescription, though it troubled me that I would be needing another prescription so soon.

I went away to college in late August of that summer. This was my freshman year, and I would be there for exactly two months; and in that two-month span of time, my eyesight deteriorated to such a state that my old frames were virtually useless. I came home from school for a weekend with the sole purpose of getting a higher prescription. (Given the state of my eyesight, I pitied to think what my new frames would look like now.) Who knew that I would not return to campus for a year?

I went back to the same place where I got my old frames. The doctor's assistant took me to the back room, to sit in an old chair, fastening my chin in an erect state, placing before my eyes that mechanical contraption that held a plethora of lenses all for the purpose of testing my vision, as I tried to read the chart—you know the chart—it's the one that starts with the big *E* and descends proportionately into lines of random nonsensical letters; and when asked the question, I was forced to tell the assistant that I couldn't see any of them, "not even the *E*, but I know that it's there," that's what I told her exactly. She, in turn, told the doctor, who then told my mother that I was beyond his scope and that I needed to see a specialist. That was on Sunday. On Monday I went to see the specialist, an ophthalmologist. After waiting two hours to see him, and after him seeing me for half of an hour, he came back to tell me and my mother that it appeared to him that I had popped an optic nerve and if things were to continue, I would eventually go blind. *Blind.* The word sat there like dead weight in the air. It was thirty seconds before anyone else said a word.

My mother and I left with a heaviness on our chest. What was truly going through her mind, I don't know. As for me, I was cool—seriously, I wasn't stressing it. I don't know why, but I was truly very nonchalant about whole thing; I was more like, "Okay, what's the next step?" The next step was to see that same doctor on the upcoming Friday. However that was too far away. Throughout the months, I had been noticing a week-by-week deterioration of my eyesight; however, now it seemed that day-by-day, my vision was getting worse. We couldn't wait for Friday. On that Wednesday, my mother and I went to New York Eye and Ear Infirmary; and on that day I went through the entire hierarchy of doctors: from the resident to the teacher to the guy who had the day off but was told to come in and take a look at this, because it was something they had never seen before. No, I had never received a blow or any trauma to the head. No, my family has no history of blindness or chronic bad vision. No, other than the slight strain I felt around my eyes earlier, I have no headaches. Yes, my vision is going. Why is this?

Then came the tests: a full blood work, a spinal tap (that was a pain: Try being told to stay in one place for, like, four hours after a guy had just stuck a huge needle in your back, with the thought that if you do move, you could possibly be paralyzed or at the least get a really bad headache for a month), a CAT scan, an MRI, an HIV test (hey, you never know), and a slew of others that I can't remember, all for the purpose of hearing: you're fine, you're fine. Okay then, so why the hell am I going blind? After all the tests, they had as much of a clue as I did. But they also had Dr. Cooper-Smith. As was described to me, he was one of the top neuro-ophthalmologists in the world. He's one of those dudes who writes articles in journals and so on. He could be called the Jay-Z of ophthalmology, and he came with his entourage: a parade of students who walked behind him, all fiending to be him; and he came to me with all of the confidence and pomposity that his title afforded. He would know what I had, for if not him, then who else? "Leber's optic neuropathy," that's what he told me. It was an extremely rare hereditary condition. That was his primary inclination, and to prove this I was to take a very expensive DNA blood test. The results of the test would take weeks to come back; in that time, I was left to my own devices.

At this time, the news of my condition had spread throughout my entire family—not everybody, but a lot of people called. All the conversations went the same way, for the first few minutes they were all very sorrowful, by the middle they had forgotten why they had called and that I even had a condition, and by the end they were all happy and cheered up. I don't know, I was going blind but I tried not to let it cripple me. But in a way it was crippling me. I remember when I discovered that I couldn't read and write. I remember vividly opening up the book and having all of the letters appear as blurred nonsense all jumbled together. This was disconcerting. Even worse was not being able to draw anymore. You see I started college as a Fine Arts major; in the beginning drawing and painting were my first artistic love. I had been picking up the pencil and drawing every day since I was about twelve. Back then, one of my two greatest fears were having my hand chopped off and going blind. You see, I had all these images and pictures in my head, and if I was not able to translate them to paper, they would just be trapped in my mind and I believed that I would surely go insane. As an artist, this was the heaviest blow to bear. I couldn't read, I couldn't write, and I couldn't draw—but then the words came. Almost as soon as I had put down the pencil the poetry came to me.

Other than writing love letters to girls, before I would never have considered myself a poet. But during those brief two months that I was on campus, I had seen a talent showcase where I saw other students doing poetry (spoken-word), and I said to myself, "I can do that." I went back to my room, and I started writing that very night. The first piece I wrote was called, "You Cannot Kill Me," which started out as one short piece but would evolve into six other long biographical poems, including poems on Malcolm X, Imhotep, Jesus Christ, and even Michael Jackson. And all of them save for the first piece were written and put together entirely in my head. I couldn't write them down because I couldn't see to write them. So I had to memorize them. At this time, my memory became very sharp; in essence, it had to be. You know what they say about when you lose one sense how the others become heightened. Well, I never got an increased sense of touch or taste, but my memory was on point. The entire piece all together when performed was over twenty minutes, but I was able to perform it straight throughout without a flaw in inflection or timing—no blanks, no nothing. I had developed two new loves: poetry and writing in general. I believe when you write a great poem or a great novel it is like painting a great picture, and I guess that the pictures that were in my head were going to manifest in one form or another.

A few weeks later, I went back to the hospital, the test had come in, and again like all the other tests I had taken, my results came back negative for Leber's. So well if it wasn't Leber's, then what was it? The doctors told me that my condition was still classified as being Leber's optic neuropathy. How can this be? It seems that Leber's is a very rare condition, and of this small percentage of people who the test comes back positive as having it, there is another even more rare 10 percent who when they take the test, it comes back negative for Leber's but they have it anyway. I don't know how they know this, but this is what they told me. They would continue to tell me that my condition could keep deteriorating until total blindness and stay there, or I could go blind and my vision could come all the way back, or it could get worse but not completely blind, stay there or get completely better. Or it could get better from the state that it was at or it could just stay there. Basically anything could happen; basically they didn't know shit and they couldn't help me; but they are doctors, so they couldn't tell me that, especially when you are supposed to be the best in the world. I believe that to some degree *Leber's* is a name that they give to the unknown. Now my mother and I were left to deal with this condition. So here I was, standing in front of the mirror with an apple.

This had taken a great strain on my mother. My grandmother, her mother, and her world had passed on in late winter of that year and here in late fall she was dealing with me, all while working two full-time jobs. Shit wasn't easy. She cried many nights. Once when I had been assigned to a psychiatrist by the state to talk about my condition, I told her to talk to my mother. I believed that she needed it more than I. I am a spiritual person, but I am not religious. I believe in the Creator, but not any particular God. I have faith. It may not be in the way another may perceive it, but I do, and I believed wholeheartedly that I would be all right. Even if I were to go completely blind, I would be all right. I learned to live and adapt to my limitations without always letting the world in on what was going on.

In a few months, my vision got better, far from completely, but enough wherein I was able to read and write again and survive in the world. I can't drive, though. Now when I look in the mirror, I see the whole picture. It's me holding up that apple, it's a blurred me, but me nonetheless.

I don't regret what happened to me. Sometimes I don't regret that I don't have 20/20 vision. I don't know, but I now see the world differently than everyone else. There are things that I see in the world now that I never saw or noticed before. It's hard to explain, but there are literally wavelengths and energies moving all around us that we just don't take notice of. The world and everything around us is alive and filled with spirits, and now I see it. I don't know, but I guess I had to almost lose my first eye in order to gain my third. So I don't regret it, even though in order to write my first novel, *A Hip Hop Story*, I developed severe back pains from sitting hours in front of the computer, my brow six inches from the screen. But I don't regret it, in life all things are meant to be and we see what we are meant to see, and now whenever I see the apple in the mirror, I don't stare at it wondering where I am, I just eat it.

Heru Ptah *is a Jamaican-born writer, poet, and philosopher. His first book,* Love, God and Revolution, *is a collection of searing political and philosophical poetry. His second book,* A Hip Hop Story, *is a timeless novel set in the early days of hip-hop. Learn more about Heru Ptah at www.sunrason.com.*

The Lesson

Calvin Nelson

There are paths in life that one must take to achieve. Some find a path on their own. Some choose a path led by others. I was born in Brooklyn, New York, and raised in Bedford-Stuyvesant and Brownsville. I was the youngest of seven children. My mom had me at age forty.

It was the 1970s, and Mom and Dad played the numbers, and I ran back and forth, putting them in for them. As I got older, I had the business down pat. I was a hustler and grew up in the streets. My brother-in-law let me work in his family's numbers spot, which doubled as a corner convenience store, along with his dad. I was a sponge and watched every transaction and recorded it in my mind. I did the same with my schoolwork. Back then, school is what you did until you grew up and got a job. No one talked about their hopes and dreams; they focused on the now and what was next. My neighborhood is filled with thirty- and forty-year-olds still trying to get their GEDs. I remember my brother-in-law saying, "You are going to be the first boy to graduate from high school." If he had not said that to me, I probably would be joining the older people in my neighborhood attaining their GEDs later on in life.

I never had any real role models, at least no one to point me in the right direction. The only advice that I received was, "Get a job, and work hard." By the time I was nineteen years old, my brother-in-law's father died, and my brother-in-law had issues and other challenges he needed to face, so I became the owner of the spot.

I thought, How hard could this be? After all, I worked after school every day, and it was a breeze. I had no idea how to get up at five in the morning, retrieve the newspapers, and meet the suppliers. Not to mention the bulk of the customers came in around 5:30 A.M. to 8:00 A.M. Now, imagine a young guy like me, with no less that a thousand dollars in his pocket every day. I was a chick magnet. This was the 1980s, and I was all about excess. I always had a different style that was smooth. Some of the stuff I did and wore then is now becoming a fashion trend.

My extracurricular activities included, sex, sex, and more sex. Hotels, motels, and even on the counter at the store. Yes, I was addicted to sex.

Don't be surprised or shocked—many men are. Each and every day, I would bag a girl in the store. When a number came up, people would run to the store to cash in or play the next number. If I had a girl in the store with me when I saw them coming, I would close the overhead gates to the store. It was a game for me, my addiction to the power of fucking. What I was really addicted to was the power that I felt and possessed. Every guy wanted the girls that I had. The guys around the way respected me because I didn't have bodyguards, nor did I feel that I had to prove myself.

Everything certainly does come to an end. When my daughter was two, I chose to close the store. If I had had someone to guide me and teach me about other business opportunities, this might not have happened. The store was located next to a train station with a bus stop out front. It was prime real estate for a business, but numbers was all that I knew. In addition, many of my customers fell victim to the crack epidemic of the eighties and stopped playing their numbers. Instead, they invested in crack. That killed my business. The Puerto Ricans were running numbers up the street, and my mother passed away. All this in three years. I went from having access to thousands of dollars a day to making several hundred dollars a week. I started working a regular job and living with my dad. Although I wasn't making as much money, I still had women. I knew there was more to life, and I wanted to experience it. All that negative shit that went down with the store bugged the hell out of me. Losing didn't sit well with me. Although my baby's mother was and is still a good person, I knew that my life and its priorities needed to change. So, for everyone's sake, I left, and I got the hell up out of New York and landed in Dallas, Texas.

It happened all over again. This time I had a great job after years of education, but I was right back on top of shit. I was the "Don Dada." I promoted parties at Reggae clubs and was part owner of a Reggae record store. I was the man. Nothing went on without me knowing up until the day I left. I ran that town. I had two of everything: two cars, two girls, and double the time. Then, one day at my job, I doubled over in pain. The pain was crazy. I knew something was wrong. My stomach was hard, but for several days I continued to come to work. Finally, I left work after about four days and went to the hospital. My sister Dot really talked me into it, and I trusted her opinion because she is a nurse. I was told that I needed an emergency removal of my appendix. Of course, I didn't want an operation, but the doctor said, "If you don't have this operation, you are going to die."

"Okay, no problem," was my answer. Everything happened so fast that I did not even have time to notify my family. My sister found out which hospital I had been admitted to by searching on the Internet. Scary, huh? Was stress a factor in everything that I was going through, and could I have internalized it in some way and created this illness? I don't know, but I am certain that it played a part in my situation.

Shit, I was thirty-two when I got appendicitis. Luckily one of my girlfriends had my back and came and took care of me. I could barely walk. One day it almost ran through my entire body, grabbed me by the throat, and turned me insides out. I lost a tremendous amount of weight, and I'm already a slim dude. My entire world came crashing in. No longer could I make it happen. Being unable to work for three months taught me a valuable lesson. Going through an operation like that gives you an opportunity to truly reflect about what is important in life. I went through the operation without notifying my family, because it happened so fast. I was doubled over in pain, and next thing you know I was being rushed into an operating room. Shit, that could have been it—lights out!— but God had his hand on my shoulder. Pain really has a way of waking your ass up. Luckily, I had saved up a tremendous amount of money to carry me through; otherwise, I would have been out in the streets. I used to hear older people say save three months of your expenses, just in case. I'm glad it somehow sank in and I listened—and thank God I did. When I filled out the paperwork we all get when we start a new job that asks whether you want disability insurance for three months or six months, I never checked either one. At the time I was more concerned about more money coming out of my check. I thought I was young, and why would I need disability insurance. I needed—no, correction: I wanted—the money. What a mistake! Now I encourage everyone to get disability insurance.

I realized that I needed to connect with my family, and I made an effort to be with them once again. I am glad I did, because my father passed away and my family went through various crises of their own, but we are still standing united. There are more lessons for me to learn, but life is a process. I no longer take life lightly; this is serious, the realization that we are given a body to live in and life to lead. Part of my purpose includes passing on my lessons to other young people, including my many nieces and nephews, even if I get a chance to holler at them for only a minute.

Calvin Nelson is a construction specialist and an entrepreneur.

The Air I Breathe

Coolio

I'm an entertainer; I make money spitting rhymes and using my lungs to rap hard. Because of that, nothing prepared me for the day when I lost all that. The air I breathe seemed all the more precious to me when it was snatched right out of my body. I've had asthma for as long as I can remember, even when I was a little kid. I don't remember not having asthma. Asthma was a stress-induced thing for me. And it was an everyday thing. It was something I lived with, but it wasn't a big deal. I still played sports, but I would just have attacks and have to be hospitalized every now and then. I knew it wasn't normal, but it was normal for me. I know what people think. They make jokes about the image of an asthmatic. People see some nerdy kid running around with an inhaler every time he takes a swing at a bat or runs too hard. I got teased by other kids and constantly found myself having to prove that I could do as much as anyone else.

It wasn't hard for me: I was natural athlete, I could run, I could play hard, and if you give me any ball, I could master that, too. But my family—the women in my life—were protective of me; they understood that asthma was no laughing matter. They tried to restrict my play; they tried to keep me inside and discourage me from roughhousing or anything that might flare up my condition. Even though I loved sports, I spent a lot of time in the house, growing up in Compton; I was really into books. I would read fantasies and comics, and anything that I could get my hands on. If I was going to be indoors, then I was going to make it exciting, and reading books about wild adventures was my outlet. It was hard. I wanted to be active.

People in my family would tell me I couldn't do things, and kids would tease me. When I first started playing sports, coaches didn't want to give me a chance. I had to prove myself twice as much to make the team or get to play. I just ignored the kids who teased me. But of course, that wasn't enough. I had it in me to move around, I needed to be out in the sun and hanging out with the other kids who were getting their bumps and bruises that go along with all the asphalt jungle games. Even though they knew my condition, my family eventually had to let me get out there and do my thing. It didn't make any sense to try to keep holding me back. I was going to do whatever I could to get in the games that the other kids were down with. This required that I manage my asthma even more.

Some people think that asthma is a joke, something that is made up, like a figment of a person's imagination or something. I mean, when you think about it, how does that make sense? How is a person going to have trouble breathing? Breathing is the most basic thing you can do. You breathe while you are walking, talking, and eating. You even breathe while you are sleeping! Getting air into your body is basic, fundamental, and automatic. When I would have an asthmatic episode, I could see that other people would think that all I would need to do is just open my mouth and get the air that I need. But it ain't that easy, and there's nothing funny about needing air. I have found myself gasping for air, feeling the lungs in my body tighten up on me and restrict me from the most primal need of getting a single full breath into my body.

I'm no stranger to crazy situations. I've been around where some stuff has gone down and gunshots have rung through the air. I've snowboarded down some of the craziest slopes ever and been in situations that would cause fear in any man, but nothing prepares you for the fear that you feel when you worry that you may have taken the last good breath of your life. When it happened to me, when I was met with the overwhelming feeling that I might never feel my lungs fully inflate again, I was scared. This happened to me as a grown man.

Nothing that I had done in my life before could prepare me for the experience. About twelve years ago, I was doing really bad, getting sick all the time. I had lost control of the disease and had an episode. I couldn't breathe, and I passed out in the bathroom. I woke up on the floor, went outside, and ended up pulling myself down the street to the hospital. Here I was, a grown man, dragging my body along the street, gasping for air. Luckily, someone saw me low-crawling and knew that the situation was serious. They picked me up, put me in the car, and rushed me to the hospital. The doctors gave me asthma treatments and kept me in the hospital hooked up to those tubes until my body could take over breathing for me again. Like I said, I've seen some stuff, but that was the scariest thing that's ever happened to me. After that, I got superserious about taking care of myself and went to see specialists and started taking medication.

I knew it before, that asthma is real, and you can die from it. But when it was right there, staring me in my face, I knew that I had to make whatever changes I needed to make to get it under control. I mean, How am I going to rap if I can't breathe? was only my second thought. How am I going to live if I can't breathe? was actually the first thing that went through my mind. I didn't think of anything else; I wasn't worried about my career or money, the Grammy that I would win or the people that would love my music. I had to think, How am I going to live if I can't get this disease under control? I stopped taking my asthma casually. I went back to remembering my childhood and being hospitalized for attacks that almost took my life. I started to think of the people who raised me and how important it was to them that they take care of me and then I knew I had to do the same for myself. I don't have a choice. If I want to stay in the rap game or entertain the world on a whole different level, I got to be strong and I got to be healthy. Now I have two of my kids who are teenagers, and they have asthma, and I worry about them, too. I let them know what they need to do to protect themselves because I don't want them ever to go through what I went through. I want them to know that the air they breathe is precious long before something happens that makes them as afraid as I was on that day.

Coolio *is a Grammy Award–winning recording artist and an avid sports enthusiast who loves to play basketball and snowboard. Coolio manages his asthma daily with medications.*

Tumor Theory

Arnold Miller

Most of my adult life I always took pride in my physical fitness. After all, I grew up in an athletic family filled with growing boys. My life for as long as I can remember revolved around sports. I played baseball, football, basketball, and street sports. There was no activity that I wasn't involved with. Physically, I felt I could do it all!

Going to the gym became an everyday thing. It was a great way to relieve the stress of everyday life. Besides getting rid of my stress, I was getting stronger, and my endurance was building up.

One day while I was doing my warm-ups, I completely ran out of gas. I couldn't understand it, so I decided to call it a day. It really troubled me, but I just brushed it off—maybe I was overworking. The best thing I could do was give the gym a break. About a week later, I returned, and the result was the same. I couldn't work out without stopping every other minute. Maybe I should see a doctor? Perhaps I should change gyms? All kinds of shit was going through my head.

I finally made a doctor's appointment. I was sent to take a CAT scan. What the doctor said after my scan blew my mind, "You have a thymus tumor behind your chest cavity. Thymomas are epithelial tumors, which may or may not be extensively infiltrated by lymphocytes. There are tumors that are made of tissue and are extremely rare. Your thymus gland is part of your lymphatic system that helps the body fight infection." I had two questions for him: What the hell was he saying? And why me? I am only thirty-three.

They wanted to do a biopsy immediately, and I was very, very scared. To deal with the situation, I just pretended it did not exist. The doctors were sending letters to my house, and I would get the letters and throw them out. I started overeating. I gained a tremendous amount of weight. I was worried whether or not I had cancer. I was convincing myself that it never happened. I still went and did light gym work. I tried to block it from my mind until that shit started hurting me so bad I would be overcome with pain.

My personal life needed straightening out. My wife and I were not on good terms. I knew I had to do things quickly; we were separated. But I needed her love and support to get me and us through this. A thousand thoughts went through my mind. I worried about my family. I started planning my funeral. I thought about what would life be without me. The tumor was right on my aorta—when I inhaled deeply, I could feel the tumor touch my heart.

I agreed to do a biopsy and told my wife that it was a simple procedure that would take only two hours and to just come with me to the hospital. But during the procedure the surgeons decided to perform the operation right there on the spot because the tumor had tripled in size. This extended the operation from the initial two hours to about six hours. After the operation, which I guarantee you, was an ordeal, I was fucked up for two weeks, just waiting for the results. I was elated when I was told I was cancer free.

My wife was an emotional wreck, and I realized I lied to her, but most of all I lied to myself. One year later, the tumor grew back. The summer of 1999, I started feeling shortness of breath. I said no way, not again. This time I waited five months until I could not take the pain any longer. I was a lot more knowledgeable than the first time. I did some research and talked extensively to the doctors, who were a great team. This time my tumor grew back bigger than the last operation.

"This was rare," the doctors said. All I could think was, "Really, well it needs to go someplace else and be a medical wonder to someone else." I was beginning to think that the doctors did not do a thorough job on the first operation. The procedure for my second operation included my chest being sawed open like open-heart surgery. The first operation was originally done through my rib cage. It was the most painful experience, far worse than the first.

All I can recall was the pain. I felt like I was going to die. I cried and cried; after all, I was just plain scared. What was even more emotional than my own pain and suffering was watching my family suffer, as well. It was then that I realized that what was growing inside me could be a small part of all the frustrations, hurt, and anger I bottled up inside. All the dreams I may have deferred or possibly what I thought was unreachable. I vowed to live the very best life that I possibly could, which included resolving any disputes my wife and I had. I realized before this ordeal that I loved her and didn't want to spend my life without her.

Today I am tumor free! I owe it to myself, God, and my family to be the best that I can be physically, spirituality, and emotionally. I make sure that I take a physical every year as a precautionary measure. If I could share any wisdom from my experience, it would be please don't be afraid to go to the

Your Soul's Journey

*Nevertheless, I will bring health and healing to it; I will heal my
people and will let them enjoy abundant peace and security.*
—Jeremiah 33:6

Stress is the one common ailment that seizes our soul and manifests
into diseases that can destroy our bodies. When compared with other
groups, African-American men are disproportionately affected by many
illnesses and associated complications. These are uplifting stories of Black
men who have taken control of their destinies and faced death—from terminal illnesses such as AIDS to the spontaneous healing of men diagnosed
with blindness. In some cases they may not have found a cure for the illness, but the true spirit of healing shines bright in their journey to well
being.

Your journey to well-being begins with getting to know your body and
tending to it on a regular basis. Look at your family's health history, and
make conscious decisions to eat well and exercise regularly. Creating a life
filled with things that prevent you from taking the time to care for you is a
form of laziness. It is a way to avoid dealing with something that you fear.
Black men work so hard to get to a point that they can breathe easy—maybe
it is that next deal, next promotion, landing a client, or completing an education. The total sum of what you are does not come from money, but is
spiritually complete total health. This allows you to connect with your purpose and provides you to reap your riches.

Changing your diet or bad habits is hard. We won't deny that fact. But
if simply adjusting them would give you an opportunity to be a true participant instead of a bystander of your journey through life, why not begin
today? The Centers for Disease Control and Prevention and the American
College of Sports and Medicine recommended that adults engage in thirty
minutes or more of moderate intensity physical activity on most or all days
of the week. Drinking plenty of water and breathing exercises when you become angry or aggravated are also recommended.

Create a game plan for your life, and keep a log of your appointments,
get to know your doctor, and most definitely never take no for an answer.
Always—and we mean always—get a second opinion. Share your health
challenges with family members and even friends. They could be your life-
savers.

Soul Source

- Describe your health in comparison to just ten years ago.
- What types of food do you eat?
- Do you drink or smoke, and how often?
- Has anyone in your family died from a stroke, heart attack or disease, cancer, or diabetes?
- Describe their experiences and how you felt about it.
- What would you like to change about your health?

CHAPTER 13

❧

YOUR BLUES AIN'T LIKE MINE

Only a man who has felt ultimate despair is capable of feeling ultimate bliss.
—Alexandre Dumas

As little boys you're told not to cry or express emotion. You're told you're not sad, it doesn't hurt, be strong, be a man. Then when we are faced with a Black man, we wonder why he can't show emotion, why he won't talk about how he feels.

Black men are psychologically labeled and misdiagnosed for several mental disorders every day. As young as the age of four, they are directed to take drugs to change their dispositions and alter their moods. Many young African-American boys are sent to special education classes because they're said to be slow and can't function in a "normal" setting. With all the negative labeling, who can blame Black men for their mistrust of the profession of psychology or psychiatry.

More people are being treated for depression than ever before. Studies suggest that the stigma associated with depression may be declining, but in the Black community, it is on the rise. Traditionally, Black men are conditioned to hide their feelings, buck up, and "be a man." The stigma that goes along with schizophrenia or narcissistic personality disorders, post-traumatic stress disorder (PSTD), and nervous breakdowns is often kept hidden, and families are left struggling to maintain a calm exterior while everything is truly in disarray. Where do all their fears, sorrows, disappointments, and feelings of despair go?

Depression is a mental illness characterized by feelings of profound sadness and disinterest in enjoyable activities. It may cause a wide range of symptoms, both physical and emotional. Depression is not the same as a blue mood. It can last for weeks, months, or years. People with depression rarely recover without treatment.

The precise cause of depression is not known. Causes may be mental, physical, or environmental, including,

Stress (family, poverty, work)
Low self-esteem
Chemical imbalances
Feelings of helplessness
Lack of hope (future), despair

There is no definitive cause of depression. Psychosocial stressors, biological issues, genetics, and mental health issues can cause depression. There is no other group in America that faces more psychosocial stressors than Black men. It is not acceptable for Black men to talk about their problems. You are supposed to, "suck it up," and "handle your business like a man." Little boys are taught at an early age what is expected of them. They are taught to disconnect from their feelings. This causes men, Black men in particular, to deal with their problems alone, which creates isolation. Black men begin to think there is something wrong with them! That they're the only one with this problem when in reality they are not. The lack of hope and feelings of helplessness can cause many Black men to choose destructive paths.

Often Black men are told that their problems are self-inflected—they *are* the problem. And often when they seek help they are made to feel that the problems do not truly exist, and are just a figments of their imagination, so they are delusional. Often we don't recognize that we are depressed. We assume feeling continually grim is normal. It isn't!

Your journey to mental peace is beginning to understand that mental health is, if not more important than your physical health, then very closely tied to all aspects of your life. Maintaining positive thoughts and relieving stress and seeking out help when needed are the first steps on the road to peace.

Remixing the Mentals

Damon Bihm

The root of my depression? Wow, it could've been last week or the week before that, but I guess the depression that clearly changed my life was during the fall of 1996.

One year previous I was in the mix like Chex, now I was labeled as being mentally sick. Insane and psychotic, what was crazier than that, I didn't know what was going to happen next. To the outside world, I had everything anyone would want. A great family, nice place to live, a great group of friends, decent luck with women, I had my youth, ambition, and an attainable, foreseeable, lucrative future. "Depression?" you may ask. What's depressing about that? My story is a little different. It was so nondepressing, it created depression. Have you ever experienced a mild streak of everything going for you exactly like you envision? Sort of a surreal feeling, many call this "mania." This is what I was experiencing before depression said, "Uh-uh, no way, big homey, things don't quite work out like that!" All depression has to do is get perception off her road of clarity, and it's on (off for you, though).

You have to view depression as an entity, a being, not just a state. People who visit states are fooled by the weather and other decoys and move right in. Moving out of something is harder than working past, confronting, or ignoring it—whatever the situation may call for. Depression isn't a permanent member of your life, although he would love for you to think so. Well, depression has been around since the beginning! Allow me to give you a bit of genealogy. After glancing at the family tree of *depression*, I came to find out his first cousin was *guilt*. Please don't allow them to double-team you. You see, *depression* has been doing whatever he can to engulf you. Do you know how he affords the luxuries to fool you into hanging around? He receives residuals the longer he keeps you on his frequency. No shit! He has others on payroll. (We'll discuss them later.) Now since you have a somewhat clearer vision of this sad sack known as the "Big D," allow me to continue.

Where was I? Oh, yeah, the fall of 1996 and I had just completed a six-month stay in a facility structured to prepare you for society. One month prior, I was in and out of a few mental institutions. Ward D, Ward E, and Ward F. *Depression* was my best pal throughout those times. Oh, I almost forgot to tell you, *depression* worked sooo hard in recent centuries that about fifty-plus years ago he was given the medical field's answer to a Hollywood star, a self-titled name of a human disease. Manic-depression—yes, folks, he was on his way. Not only did he have medicines created for him, but due to these medicines he would perpetuate his existence. Because now we had a name and a reason why we were feeling down, and on top of that, a solution, to take as prescribed by a physician for the rest of your years. Please have insurance or a good-paying job, because you know our government will recoup on the majority of the profits. And if you don't, you will remain locked up or become a fixture of the streets.

Despite the numerous phone calls I received daily, despite the daily visits by my family—Lord only knows how they did it—despite the great treatment I received from the staff at every level at every facility, my situation and depression worsened. Why? Because every time I was away from my power source, he would capitalize. Part of the program requirement where the doctors and staff deemed you suitable to leave was your attendance in "groups," a class that you took daily. During one group meeting, we had to do an exercise with another group member about your plans for when you were discharged. How did he capitalize? Right when I was looking forward to a solution, a possibility, what I liked, what I wanted, he flew in his sister *doubt*. She was very distracting and convincing. I was convinced I couldn't do anything, and that's when *depression* laid me out. I believed I had no future. I was in such a deep depressive state that my room where I slept was so dark, it made charcoal look like glass.

I was done. I don't know if I was dreaming, in a trance, or what. I like to think of it as a spiritual battle for my soul. But, I will tell you, images and sound started to fuse. I saw why I was in the hospital in the first place. It wasn't for depression; it was for being manic. Really being overexcited about life, if there is such a thing. I apologize I was so looking forward to the next day that I didn't want to go to sleep. I apologize this happened for one week straight. I saw other patients who didn't have family or friends visit them every day, or any day, for that matter. I saw patients who had been through things so harsh, there is nothing to compare to their despair! It wasn't the images that I saw, but what I heard. *Depression* was audiotaping a verbal report on that day's occurrences.

He was thanking his father, *society*, for making his job so easy. *Depression* was already famous and rich. He was merely creating a signature effect to the existence of life in which he called *suicide*. He stated that the more suicides he was responsible for, his signature would not only be perpetually etched, but his offspring (which I learned were *statistics*) would always have a function. I was ambivalent. At first I was like, Wow! I thought this was a vivid dream. "Dammnn" is what I uttered next. Why? Because what I heard *depression* say next changed my life. *Depression* barely lost out to *jealousy!* That woman who shot her husband and dumped his body, I just knew his infidelity would break her! Mental note: *Jealousy* owes me one. Oh, I had that mandatory meeting with the "other side," *faith* and *decision* came in place of *fate* and *perception*. We agreed that this particular situation is left up to Mr. Bihm himself. He's off-limits to both parties. I must say one good thing came out of it. The LIFE committee stated that since I did such a great job clouding his vision, warping his wisdom, gullying his gratefulness, monopolizing his prayer time, reshaping his physical appearance, and best of all having him questioning his future—that because of what *destiny* and *higher perception* had in store for him, if I get this "guy" this "one" guy to commit suicide, I can retire and start a brand new-disease that has yet to be named? (CLICK.)

I admit, I've had suicidal thoughts many times throughout my life. Never before have I desired to take myself out. *Depression* went to Gumption University. He received his master's in the follow-through. Best believe, with retirement on the line, I was going to be the perfect example of a Tiger Woods majestic drive.

The time-out room is a room where you are usually sedated or forced into. A room where you're considered lucky if you're not strapped to the bed and given a shot with a needle the size of a tripod. A room where time stops. A room in which wherever you are or aren't, is magnified. The purpose of this room: Take a breather and relax before you give yourself a stroke or you inflict physical pain on another patient.

I know that after being labeled with a mood disorder known as manic-depression (also called bipolar disorder), I became another statistic, a statistic that is definitely rising in the Black community. But one statistic I refused to become was a young Black man who took his own life and didn't make it to thirty. Life is hard, period, but it is especially hard for a Black man. Considered a threat to other races, a dissension practitioner within his own community, and now they want you to be a threat to yourself. Don't buy into it. For those whose family has a history of mental illness, and their problem is genetic (like me) there is no miracle drug! Yes, take the medicine that helps to stabilize you. But it's more than that. Our Creator. The Higher Power is the only thing that is going to allow you to live with it and function properly. Staying in tune with our higher source will bring about a strength within that's yearning to come out.

It wasn't that my family and friends needed to see a payoff for their time and concern, or to show the doctors and staff the meds were working. Regardless of preserving my self-pride, this was beyond me. I knew there were people out there of all ages and walks of life who were cashing in on their depression investments. I also knew that a lot of those people wouldn't be as strong.

When I opened my eyes, everything around me looked different! Everything was the same but it "looked" different. It wasn't the medicine. I knew for physical reasons I would continue to take it, but I had a self-actualization experience. I saw only the solutions to situations in my life, not "problems." My breath was easier. I could finally breathe. I didn't need or want anything! Everything was right with me. I didn't question the past or fear the future. I saw the beauty in things. Whatever insecurities I had no longer applied to me. I knew how to listen and what to listen for.

I made the right choice. I didn't want to die anymore. I didn't want to execute the millions of ways I could've done it. I was taken to the very bottom only for God to wash me off and bring me up! I knew that experiencing life in an asylum, a time that took nearly one year to get well and almost two years to fully get back in the swing of things, was for me not only to get closer to self, but to be an example for others.

Healing for me probably won't fully happen. I must do my best to deal with fluctuating mood swings daily. Every time I share my story with someone, it gives me a renewed feeling. I won the battle for my soul! The decision I made allowed my perception to change. *Decision* and *perception* were with me the whole time. *Depression* won't get to retire. Too bad he still has a job. I hear these twins called *spoken word* used money from their signing bonus to put their homey *Prozac* in the medical game. I have a feeling *depression* will be a little "perturbed" because his job won't be "as" easy! Before I booted Big D out of my life like an old pair of Timberlands, he said he owed me. Most people get treated for clinical depression; well, it felt good to cynically beat depression! You can, too! Trust me, it's never that bad.

P.S. Depression was right, he did come back for me. The summer of 2000, I relapsed (the lithium I was on no longer worked). I spent the entire summer in the hospital. One month at a halfway house near USC and three months in another halfway house. But you know what? I dug deep again! There I met this old guy called *motivation*. He told me to work with him so I could help others and prevent possible tragedies. *Destiny*, whom I haven't met yet, would allow me to come full circle to work on the "other side" of pediatric, adolescent, and adult units of a psychiatric ward. Once was a patient, now allowed to exercise patience. Those of you who are depressed right now, be impatient! The sooner you get up, the sooner you can kick depression out! Here, you can borrow my boots.

Damon Bihm's *life reads like an adventure filled with suspense, romance, and joy! Not to mention a few chase scenes and intense battles (domestic, civil, and on the field of sport). However, the poet survived and is now converting these experiences into action, books, animations, and performances that will create a long intimate relationship with the public. The world will wear his words. Current projects include "Total B.S." (essays), "?uest-shunners" (animation series), and IdentiTee's (apparel).*

Who Is Tone Boots?

Tone Boots

Who is Tone Boots? A good question, and one I've been asked by several people throughout the years. However, I've only just begun to figure out the answer for myself. A Gemini, my world is rife with duality.

All my life, I knew that there was something wrong—or at least different—about me. I liked girls and had a voracious appetite for sex at an early age. I also seemed to think a few steps ahead of my friends. But, as smart as I appeared to be, my temperamental dysfunction would often undermine any amount of intelligence I possessed. I was constantly in trouble at school and always getting into fights, particularly with older and bigger kids. I was usually merely protecting myself or defending one of my companions, but once confronted, I wouldn't hesitate to escalate matters. I had a strong sense of justice and, as long as I was in the right, I felt little remorse over how badly I hurt another child who was picking on me. My proficiency at fisticuffs, however, had little to do with my size or the fact that I had taken the martial arts. In reality, I was of average height, quiet, and relatively passive. My greatest advantages were my ability to be relentlessly violent at a moment's notice and my almost complete lack of fear of any other human being.

Unfortunately, during editorial meetings, my gallant individualism was interpreted as volatile hubris years later when I was hired as a writer for *Blaze Magazine*. Without my knowledge, they would eavesdrop on my conversations with artists and print them in the front of the book. "That nigga ain't bulletproof, he can die just like me and we can go to Hell together!" is how I was quoted following a heated dispute with one so-called "gangsta' " rapper's manager. Sadly, I meant every word of it, and my reputation for rabblerousing spread throughout the industry—something I regretted after it cost me lucrative consulting contracts and deal extensions with the likes of conservative corporate giants such as the NFL and music-publishing organization BMI. Upon initially meeting me, they'd say, "Oh, what a cavalier and well-spoken professional!" But, following thorough background checks, my aptitude for inadvertently intimidating my employers was discovered, and I was sent packing. I had to get a grip on the fact that some habits and perceptions die hard.

A few years prior, I was in federal prison when I got into an altercation with a couple of inmates over control of the TV. Basically, after I made them turn from a program that wasn't on my schedule, they continued to run their mouths in what I considered a veiled attempt to annoy me during my prescribed entertainment. If you know anything about the penitentiary, then you know that there are certain amenities, particularly the phones and televisions, that are sacred and regulated only by convicts with the most seniority or muscle at the institution. But this wasn't the penitentiary, and although I never actually laid hands on them, I applied enough peripheral pressure to drive these stool pigeons to go and report my actions to the unit counselor. After all, this was Club Fed—a minimum-security federal prison camp replete with an Olympic-sized indoor swimming pool, PTA-quality tennis facilities, and a putt-putt course that'd give Tiger Woods a run for his money. Thus, my dogged and predacious behavior eventually grew intolerable to the staff and the former CEOs, erstwhile politicians, and one-time Wall Street big shots that made up the majority of the population.

As a result, I was forced to attend a succession of weekly anger-management sessions or risk extending my incarceration by about eighteen months. Once sequestered, they then demanded that I take an IQ test and an academic aptitude exam as well as the Minnesota Assessment and the famed Rorschach evaluation—wherein the psychologist shows you a bunch of indistinguishable ink blotches and then asks you what they look like. I scored a respectable 150 on the Intelligence Quotient and displayed at least a collegiate level of proficiency, but I was also diagnosed with a somewhat embarrassing mental condition: antisocial personality disorder (APD). In laymen's terms, their analysis had deemed that I was a psychopath.

Unsatisfied with their assessment, I decided to do my own research into the matter and ultimately found a rather draconian commentary by a noted psychiatrist who indubitably suggested that people like me be corralled and forced to live in colonies. He went on to assert that, because the disorder is highly unresponsive to treatment and since there are no drugs to control the illness, the solution for the dilemma that we pose to the public is to put us in a commune with a coterie of other sociopaths. The problem is, these proposed colonies that the doctor was so partial to already exist by another name, *prison*—and I was already there and scheduled for release in a few short months. Now what?

Once home, I was determined to find help for my condition but was incapable of justifying the exorbitant fees that therapists charge for basic counseling. Being an able-bodied male with a job and not on welfare, it was also virtually impossible to get any of the so-called free psychological services offered by many of the mental health agencies in and around Manhattan. Despondent and without options, I maintained my personal studies but continued to find an array of fatalistic data that essentially labeled me a monster. Corresponding accounts classified those with APD as possessing the most deviant minds in society and that we should be feared more than any other type of human being. Antisocials are severely "emotionally retarded" as a result of a combination of mental infirmities hatched through either heredity, trauma, or a dearth of intellectual development that enables us to do harm without guilt. Moreover, neuropsychiatrists assert that the antisocial's most dangerous attribute is that his overall lack of affect is combined with an inflated sense of self-worth and a fraudulent charm so deceptive that it is extremely hard to recognize. Unfortunately, many of these gruesome characteristics accurately reflected my mindlessness.

Sinking further into despair and void of rehabilitation, my world became a cesspool of larceny. I was a gainfully employed young man with a respectable profession, but thoughts of revenge, extortion, and murder began to consume my mind and eventually my time as I tried in vain to make ends meet on the humble wages of a print journalist. Faced with the prospect of homelessness and living just at the poverty level, I used every ounce of game in my arsenal of criminal skills to get over. Soon thereafter, I was reluctantly committing a swarm of new and lucrative felonies. Yet all I could find along the lines of support was a multitude of pessimistic research that reaffirmed my feelings of helplessness. Ultimately, my redemption came in the realization that the statistical data wasn't resolute and didn't always apply to my circumstances. For one, I wasn't and had never been a substance abuser as held in the clinical analysis of APD. In addition, an untiring pragmatist, I've always taken full ownership of my actions, unlike the reality-ducking sociopaths described throughout the annals of psychology. Those facts, along with the dedication of a few loyal friends, eventually helped me put things in perspective and gain some long overdue self-esteem. However, not every delinquent is as fortunate, and my personal windfall owes a lot more to luck and the undying faith of others than it does to my own ingenuity. With this realization, I dedicate the rendition of my life story as a vituperation of my transgressions in the hope that others can learn from my mistakes as well as from my modest successes. And, although I had to rearrange the particulars of my tale for the impunity of me and my associates, it is still a shrewd reminder of where I'm headed in life and where I don't want to return.

Throughout the course of my book, there'll be an assortment of pedagogical excerpts at the beginning of each chapter delineating the thinking errors of sociopaths as they pertain to my own misdeeds. In an honest effort to inspire constructive dialogue, I share what motivated my character—an alter ego, if you will—to commit many of the reprehensible acts, sexual misadventures, and criminal offenses detailed herein. A thriller that will no doubt challenge the sane reader, *Murder Ink* was written to entertain the fans of pulp fiction as well as the followers of urban griots and true crime authors that have come and gone. Moreover, it provides those at either end of the spectrum, both victims and criminals, with a closer perspective on the sins that tear at the fabric of our society. Hopefully it succeeds. As for me on the other hand, my life's journey took me through several changes before I was able to find a reasonable degree of healing. Neither an introvert nor a social recluse, however, I was confused by the *antisocial* aspect of the ailment's epithet, which I later learned refers only to the subject's pervasive pattern of disregard for the rights of others and overall inability to conform to the rules of society. After extensive research I learned that the diagnostic criteria for the disorder are as such:

ANTISOCIAL PERSONALITY DISORDER (A.P.D.) [Alias "Psychopathic Personality" or "Sociopathic Personality"] : PERSONALITY denotes characteristic ways of thinking and acting. A PERSONALITY DISORDER is said to exist when one chronically applies enduring and maladaptive thoughts and actions to cope with issues. The ANTISOCIAL PERSONALITY displays a temperament that puts one in direct conflict with society due to processes and conduct that are amoral and unethical. This particular disorder involves a history of chronic delinquency that began prior to the age of fifteen and carries over into adulthood. Also known as psychopaths or sociopaths, antisocials have the opposite morals of society. Roughly 3 percent of men and 1 percent of women suffer from APD (with as much as 75 percent of the prison population).

Sociopaths drink heavily, have a history of conflicts, use multiple aliases, are impetuous risk takers, curious, excitable, quick tempered, optimistic and independent. Complications that arise from having this disorder include— frequent imprisonment for unlawful behavior, alcoholism, and drug abuse. The disorder also manifests a pattern of irresponsible and rebellious behavior as indicated by academic failure, poor job performance, illegal activities, recklessness, and impulsive actions. Symptoms may also include dysphoria, an inability to tolerate boredom, feelings of victimization, and a diminished capacity for intimacy. Antisocials can be very charismatic but harbor intrinsic homicidal or suicidal tendencies and at least three (3) of the following diagnostic traits:

A disregard for the safety of self and others
A manipulative and deceitful disposition
A failure to conform to lawful behavior
A lack of stability at home or at work

A hostile or aggressive temperament
A lack of empathy or remorse
A lack of impulse control

The genealogical offspring of alcoholics and schizophrenics, it's safe to assume that I was predisposed to being a maniac. As if that weren't enough, my malevolence was further affected by a criminal svengali who galvanized my adolescent penchant for violence to his own advantage. After all, what crook worth his salt wouldn't pine for a trigger-happy lad blind with rage, loyal to a fault, and too young to know the difference between a mentor and a manipulator? Nonetheless, it made much more sense to be the drug dealer rather than the drug addict, the murderer rather than the murder victim, the motherfucker rather than the bastard son of a bitch. As a result, my iniquitous guru shrewdly instructed me that, when you decide to kill a man, you must also be prepared to die yourself—anger or ostensible righteousness do not guarantee victory in any battle. The realization of my palpable mortality made me own up to my actions, lest I fall victim to the perilous vanity of ignorance. Primordial fear or my lack of it was an essential enzyme in my volatile chemistry and the resulting bravado that gunplay and countless street fights had given me was liberating. Still, my compliance taught me something greater. In contrast, I learned the importance of feigning naiveté; the camouflage of temperance, obscurity and ineptitude make very effective war paint. Consequently, through my criminal prowess and mastery of subterfuge, I recognized the fact that I alone control my destiny and, thus, freed myself of a reliance on excuses and blaming others for my circumstances. I no longer allowed my detractors to define my existence or serve as the chief cause of affect to my life. Likewise, as African Americans and Hispanics—however we define ourselves—we must take full responsibility for our destiny and cease with the pathetic lamenting over the innumerable faults of our oppressors. "The White Man" may or may not ever fully acknowledge or make amends for what their transgressions have cost people of color across the globe for many centuries. Not that we aren't owed a serious debt, but we cant allow their charities and retributions (or, the lack thereof) to be the crux of our redemption. At the end of the day, fate is only 10 percent of what happens and 90 percent how you react to it. I, for one, refuse to be sustained primarily by the limitations of another man's willingness to validate my significance. Thus, I am who I am, due not to the avowal of my enemies and in spite of the neglect of my guardians. I alone have bequeathed myself as the captain of my soul and, therefore, proudly call the shots and take credit for every success or setback that I incur.

Who is Tone Boots? The question is, what is Tone Boots? A sociopathic vampire feeding off the weaknesses of God-fearing folk or a misunderstood victim of society desperately in search of love, sanity, and the American dream? Maybe all of the above. Nonetheless, Tone Boots is merely one of a dozen or so meaningless pseudonyms that I've used over the years to reinvent myself when the trail gets too hot and I need to move on to a new hustle in a new town. Like Clint Eastwood's lonesome cowboy in the spaghetti westerns, Boots is on a perennial run for the border in avoidance of the hangman's noose. Luckily, there is some evidence that suggests that the antisocial's symptoms more often than not decrease after the age of thirty. Thus, I'll be home free if I can just survive long enough past my twenties to achieve mental normalcy or at least confine my indulgences to the foremost sociopathic colony of the world—New York City. *Murder Ink* details a very personal struggle to exorcise my demons and at long last become a conscientious, law abiding and taxpaying citizen. Read on and you'll be able to come to your own conclusions on who or what Tone Boots may be. You never know—you might find that my mind-set isn't much different from yours. Strangely enough, there's an avant-garde concept that is adeptly assessed by author Robert Simon in his book, whose title pretty much says it all: *Bad Men Do What Good Men Dream.*

Tone Boots *is an experienced journalist, quick-witted columnist, and esteemed music critic. Mr. Boots is a regular contributor to publications such as* The Source, XXL, Vibe Online, TV Guide, *SOHH.com*, F.E.D.S., *and* Don Diva. *He is finishing his first book, entitled* Murder Ink, *a novel.*

My Name Is . . . and I Suffer from Depression

Ray Tamarra

For me, depression was my shameful addiction, a secret I kept hidden, especially from myself. It wasn't until after I relocated to New York City and suffered personal as well as professional failures that I began to understand that I was depressed and had been suffering from a chemical imbalance for years.

In 1997, I moved to New York from Los Angeles with my girlfriend at the time. She had landed a promising job, and since I was going nowhere career-wise, I figured that a change of scenery would open up new opportunities.

I severely underestimated how difficult and stressful the transition would be, especially not having a job already lined up. Failing to land a gig after months of searching, I started questioning my self-worth. What was wrong with me?

The difficulties of adjusting to a smaller apartment, unfamiliar neighborhood, no friends, and the brick-cold weather started to bring me down. I gave up looking for work and was jealous that my girlfriend was "makin' it happen" while I couldn't even get it started.

Obviously having no money, whining about NYC, and living off my girlfriend just aggravated an already shaky relationship. Eventually she gave up trying and so did I. I went to a therapist to somehow help the situation. The counselor thought that I was clinically depressed and recommended getting medication, but I denied it. How could a stranger know what was going on with me. Feeling sorry for myself really blinded me from getting help.

This was a very ugly, painful time for me. I was mad at everyone and sad at the same time. I couldn't sleep, I lost my appetite and never left my apartment. I thought about suicide and mentally tortured myself for ruining my life.

I don't know why reading *How to Survive the Loss of a Love* got through to me but the section covering depression really hit home. Rather than seeing depression as a temporary feeling that I could correct by thinking happy thoughts, I found out that certain chemicals not being produced by my brain could be causing me to constantly feel bad.

The funny thing is that the info in the book was the same thing that the therapist and other concerned people were telling me. Rather than denying the obvious, I dedicated myself to getting better. I was fed up with feeling bad, being a victim, so I focused on educating myself about mental illnesses and what I could do to correct my situation. I checked out library books about depression and skimmed more books at Barnes & Noble. Being ignorant of depression was no longer acceptable.

That resolve forced me to reconsider therapy. I read that it was helpful, so I set aside my past uncomfortable experiences and enrolled in a low-cost, sliding-scale program. In the beginning, there were many rocky sessions where I'd just stare at my shrink, wondering what I was going to say next. Eventually I got more comfortable, and through our conversations, I started to understand what was going on inside my head. He'd just listen and chirp in with his observations and recommendations based from talking and listening to so many other people suffering from the same thing.

My therapist pointed out that I'd probably been sick for years, and he was right. I have felt sad since junior high school but assumed that was normal. I remember in high school, I'd go to the Santa Monica Beach at night and cry because I felt so sad and was jealous that everyone else was happy but me.

When my therapist recommended that I get diagnosed by a psychiatrist and get medication, I didn't hesitate. I had already lost so many years to depression, I couldn't continue wasting my life away. Regardless of the stigma that society attaches to people taking Prozac, I was going to do any- and everything possible to get better.

It's been three years since I took Prozac or seen a therapist, and I'm definitely proud of how far I've come. I'm not cured of depression, because I still get bouts of sadness, but I'm ecstatic that I conquered my ignorance of mental illnesses. I don't think people who take medication are weak or losers. I also don't dismiss the signs my body sends me that I'm depressed. I now know what's happening and what I can do to correct it.

But the greatest result of confronting my depression is getting my life back from a chemical imbalance that was crippling me. Now when I get sad, I remind myself of all the progress I've made. I don't beat myself up anymore, and I encourage myself to make the rest of my dreams happen. If I can educate myself about depression and change my life for the better, nothing is beyond reach!

Ray Tamarra *founded and runs TheCrusade.net, an on-line community for people in the urban entertainment industry. The site gives a voice and places a face to the tastemakers and power players on this exciting space. Tamarra is also an actor, photographer, street vendor, and writer.*

Sourced from the Soul

Andrew Perriott

The year was 1995, summer in New York City; I was a consultant for the New York Stock Exchange and the Hair Club for Men. Go figure—it worked for me. The year was going well, and all the business ventures that I had on tap were moving along in a positive and prosperous manner. I still had this sinking feeling that something was missing. One day I was at Grand Central Station, and I saw a young couple around my age, about twenty-something, cuddling. They looked so in love. I realized I didn't have a companion in my life, but that was all going to change. I remember it so clearly, like it was yesterday. On August 10, 1995, I was invited to *Vibe* magazine's third anniversary party with a few of my colleagues. I will never forget that day because that was the first time I saw her. She was like heaven to me. I was passing by a hair salon on Fifty-third Street and Madison, and something made me look into the window of the salon. To this day, she stands as one of the most beautiful women I have ever laid eyes on. As I looked in on her while she worked, she suddenly felt someone staring at her and gazed back. I began to look away, because I wasn't used to staring at people. I continued walking because I had an engagement that I was attending. When I reached my destination, I told my friends about this beautiful girl I saw and how bad I wanted to get to know her.

The anniversary party was good, and everyone had a good time. Quincy Jones and all the heavy hitters were in attendance. I was restless, I still wanted to see this woman again, and I didn't even know her name. Later on that month, I was called to a meeting in the same building where she worked. After I found out that it was there, I began having butterflies. Normally for meetings I would take a taxi, but for some reason I decided to take the train to Midtown. I remember getting to my stop and walking up the steps onto the street hoping that she would be there. It was like she heard everything I said, because there she was, doing what she does best, looking beautiful. Time was of the essence—I had a presentation to make to a client in minutes, so I couldn't gaze for long. I remember walking into the office and closing the deal very quickly.

As I caught the elevator to go back to the main floor of the building, I kept telling myself to approach her. This time as I was leaving the building, she was right there in front of the window, talking to a friend or client. I approached her on impulse and asked for her name. She told me; she then asked for mine and I told her. We both asked each other if we were married with children. We both laughed at that question because neither of us was married. And at that time I had no children. I asked her if I could take her to dinner sometime, she told me she would love to go.

Our first date was at a small romantic restaurant in the Lower Manhattan area of SoHo. I remembered her telling me how bad she wanted to get away from work because she was burned out. I remembered replying that I was planning to go to Miami for a music convention, and I would take her if she wanted to go. She told me that she would think about it. And I told her cool. We began seeing a lot of each other that year, and honestly, neither of us was realized how fast we were moving. In the beginning, I wasn't too into the idea of letting someone in my life. But that was all going to change.

I'll never forget when I began falling in love with her. It was at a get-together for a friend of ours who was leaving the state for a work promotion. We didn't arrive at the function together. As she walked in, all eyes were on her. The whole night while she was there, smart remarks were being exchanged. I suddenly realized that night that some of my friends did not like the idea of interracial relationships, and especially for me. I know she felt uncomfortable, but she did not pay them any mind. It was like the more remarks were said, the more she got into me. It was crazy, I thought. I remembered saying my good-byes and us walking on Broadway for her to catch a cab home. Actually, that was our first kiss—it was magical. That was the beginning of the fall.

Two months later, I gave up my apartment in Queens and moved in with her. At first, it was beautiful. We spent time together, and we lived together, and I honestly thought we were in love. Then the arguments began.

"Where were you?" and "Why didn't you call?" became her commonplace questions. It became a constant battle between her and me. I finally realized that what I was doing in my life was not good for her. What she wanted was a nine-to-five career man. Which I was, but I was still an entrepreneur who worked hard after work to get my own business off the ground. I spoke to a few of my friends who were very close to me at the time and asked them what I should do. All of them eventually said to follow my heart. So I did just that. I told her in the beginning of the fall that I was moving. She felt we could have worked it out, but I told her that was the best thing for us to do. We still spoke to each other every day. I had officially got back into my music stronger than ever. I was focused. The last week of November, my schedule became very busy. I picked a new staff member who had the same vision I did about where we should be taking our music. Believe me, we were ahead of our time. That last week, I didn't have a lot of time to talk to anyone, because I was trying to hold down a nine to five, and finish three projects I was working on at the time. I checked my e-mail and voice messages for a brief moment and heard her messages that she left every hour on the hour. I finally called her back, and that's when she told me she was pregnant.

I truly did not know what to do about this new situation that had arisen. Finally, I decided that I was going to give up my beautiful apartment and move back in with her. We discussed what we should do about the situation and how ready we really were. The decision was made on December 9, 1995. She woke up very early that morning and got dressed and told me she would be out for a little and I should keep sleeping. I felt in me that she had made her decision, but I honestly did not want to accept it. I remember later that evening us going out to a restaurant for dinner, and that's when she told me that she went through with the abortion, and by the way, happy birthday. She also said that she would hate me for the rest of her life. And honestly I believed her.

This was very devastating for me because I honestly did not want her to go through with it. I moved back out and vowed never to see her again, but that was short lived. She never gave up. Months passed, but the calling didn't stop. We met up for dinner at a place that we were known and loved. I got to admit, we really looked good together. I picked her up from work, and she started telling me how much she missed me. When we walked into the restaurant, all eyes were on us. We sat at our usual table and began ordering. A few minutes later, she decided to use the pay phone. For some odd reason, she used the phone several times. I began to take a look around the room, and I saw conversation being held about us. I couldn't believe it. I suddenly decided to make my dinner short, because I truly felt in my heart that something was wrong. I wanted to spend the evening with her, but for some odd reason, she told me it would be better if I went home. The excuse was she knew I had to go to work the next morning. I then walked her down the avenue to catch a train home, and she kissed me like how Jesus was kissed by Judas. I decided to take a cab home. When I got home, I called her to let her know I was home. She picked up the phone and said hello. I said hello, and then she asked, "Who is this?"

I said, "It's me, Andrew."

She then replied, without thinking, "How did you get home safe?"

This was the beginning of the end for me. Everything seemed to be spiraling out of control. The pressure became too much for me. My mother, who saw the good, bad, and ugly of this entire situation, came to New York with my uncle to retrieve me. My soul was broken, and my heart ached, but it was not only the pain of the relationship, but also the years of unresolved aspects of my life. The car accident that almost took my life, my father moving and not really corresponding with me, the physical abuse I witnessed in my home while growing up—it all added up to a severe case of depression, medication, and therapy.

I still did not learn my lesson. I was in and out of relationships all the while trying to gain my mental health. It was not easy—I was trying to please these women without first looking at who I was, what my purpose was, and what my needs were. I didn't trust them. I couldn't, for God's sake—I had a mental breakdown behind my last relationship. This is not so uncommon as you think; some men handle things differently. I internalized it all, and it all combusted; others lash out, and that has other types of repercussions.

Things did not get better for me, because I still had lots of internal work to do. The last person I asked to marry me accused me of being a studio lover.

"What the hell is a studio lover?" I asked.

"Like a studio gangster who writes lyrics of crime from a studio. You write love songs but know absolutely nothing—and may I say again *absolutely nothing*—about love!" she shouted.

She was right, and that ended the relationship.

Eight years later, I have a beautiful son. But honestly, I have moved on, and each day is a struggle. The ironic winner in all this is my music, which was sourced by my pain. Somehow I was able to capture how people feel. I've transformed songs into personal anthems. Doors that were not opened before were swung wide open, and my music is being requested by so many different artists. My Creator, God, who has instilled strength and wisdom has not let me down. Although I have been tested, I have gained victory. Success and the journey to oneself is an everyday choice made one day at a time, regardless of the obstacles

Andrew Perriott is a songwriter and producer. He is also a South American securities analyst for a Tampa, Florida–based bank. Andrew plans on releasing several projects currently in the works.

Your Soul's Journey

For thou, Lord, hast made me glad through thy work: I will
triumph in the works of thy hands.   —Psalm 92:4

Kennth Bancroft Clark, a Black psychologist, conducted several studies on the effects of segregation on the self-image of African-American children. In one experiment Dr. Clark asked African American children to pick the dolls that they thought were "good" and most like themselves. Rather than choosing the brown dolls, the majority of African-American children in the study chose the white doll, and some children actually cried when they were forced to accept the dark-colored dolls as being most like themselves. Dr. Clark's research was used to assist Thurgood Marshall in winning the *Brown v. Board of Education* case outlawing segregation.

How could a Black man be healthy and whole mentally when he is called and listed as an endangered species? Men are conditioned to be tough, quite often there is limited dialogue, everything is held back and suppressed. What tends to build up is anger and aggression. Some Black men choose to walk out on situations, or the wall goes up and the "I am going to hurt you first" instinct sets in. They suffer in silence, angry with all the things that have built up over a period, never giving them an opportunity to heal. The cycle of life has a beginning and an end. Everything is sourced, and when it comes to the end, there must be closure. If you weren't taught how to gain closure in your life you may find yourself going from one situation to the next not fully healed. This "unfinished business" can give stress an opportunity to linger, causing anxiety and loss of sleep, and it is a fertile breeding ground for depression.

There is depression, which can be brought on by psychological ills or a chemical imbalance. One gentleman in our session said that at the age of seventeen, he was called Spot. The reason he gave was at the time his future was bright. He was a graduate from high school with scholarships to three universities. This man was well on his way until he impregnated two young ladies at the same time. He decided to give up his dream and handle his responsibility in the best way he knew how. The stress caused a huge bald spot in the middle of his head, hence the name Spot. One of the mother's friends was so angry with him, she said, "If it was up to me, I would kill you to collect the social security."

Another gentleman called home one day to get some reassurance from his dad. His payroll check bounced, rent was due, and everything was piling up. He could not take the frustration anymore, and he broke down and cried. His father dryly said, "Why are you crying like a girl?" Dad unknowingly added another level of fear and damage.

Soul Source

Life has many cycles. Ask yourself why you are not taking care of care of you. You are a sum total of your experiences. Are you a person who is healthy on the inside and out? The journey to beginning the healing process of mental health begins with a balance of creating peace inside and outside. Stress and people can steal your peace, infringe on your joy, confuse you and have you running in circles. As the song "You've Got a Friend," said twenty years ago, "People will take your soul if you let them," and it still holds true today. When you lose your joy, you lose your strength and ability to strategically work on the problem at hand. Admitting and understanding that right now you are distraught and you must take care of yourself is an empowering revelation. Understand that no man is an island and that help is often a telephone call away. Meeting with a therapist should not be taboo, but is the first step in reclaiming your life. Taking prescribed medication to create balance and harmony is not a sign of weakness, but an affirmation that whatever the challenge is, you will be able to rise to the occasion.

Many great people have been depressed. In the Bible, the prophet Elijah was so depressed, he asked God to die. God loved Elijah and provided him with a nourishing meal and a friend. Talking to God and laying all your burdens down is the first and main source in assisting the treatment of depression.

- What are some of your stress factors?
- Have you ever participated in counseling?
- What was the experience like for you?
- When you are overwhelmed, what do you like to do?
- Do you have any hobbies?
- What physical sport do you enjoy?
- What do you hope or believe will bring the balance that you seek?

CHAPTER 14

ARCHITECTS OF HIS-STORY

A man is born with wisdom that he needs for life.
—Dick Gregory

We are all standing on the shoulders of giants, whether we know it or not. The problem is, too often we don't know it. And, since we don't know it, we think we're the first person ever to deal with the things we deal with—to go through the things that we're going through. When we don't know our own history, we are forced to reinvent the wheel every time with each generation starting from scratch. There's so much we don't know about the greatness of our history that can help us today. So many Black men have made numerous contributions to society and have put their lives on the line for you. We may not know our stories, but it doesn't mean they're not there.

It was great men like Alexander Mills who invented the elevator. Richard Spikes invented the automatic gearshift. Joseph Gammel invented the supercharge system for internal combustion engines. Garrett A. Morgan invented the traffic signal and the electric trolley. Charles Brooks invented the street sweeper. John Love invented the pencil sharpener. William Purvis invented the fountain pen. Lee Burridge invented the typewriting machine. W. A. Lovette invented the advanced printing press. William Purvis invented the hand stamp. Phillip Downing invented the letter drop. Joseph Smith invented the lawn sprinkler. John Burr the lawn mower. Frederick Jones invented the air conditioner. Lewis Latimer invented the electric lamp. Michael Harvey invented the lantern. Granville T. Woods invented the automatic cut-off switch. Thomas W. Steward invented the mop, and Lloyd P. Ray, the dustpan.

So why don't the masses know facts like these as they know who invented the lightbulb? If you were never aware of these men, it is quite simple—a system was put into place during the times of slavery to oppress a race of people by never acknowledging them for the assets they really were and are to America.

Men like Dr. Martin Luther King Jr., Malcolm X, Marcus Garvey, Minister Farrakhan, Muhammad Ali, Booker T. Washington, Randall Robinson, Louis Armstrong, Duke Ellington, Jim Brown, Sidney Poitier, Bill Cosby, Brock Peters, Paul Robeson, A. Philip Randolph, W. E. B. DuBois, Thurgood Marshall, Rev. Wyatt Tee Walker, Jesse Jackson, Congressman Adam Clayton Powell, John Lewis, John Conyers, and Charles Rangel, the Tuskegee airmen, Jackie Robinson, Michael Jordan, Tupac Shakur, Biggie Smalls—these men in their own way revolutionized life and the way that African-American people are perceived throughout the world. They stood up for what they believed and created a legacy through, history, bravery, religion, music, sports, and art, regardless of the circumstances.

Regardless of all the contributions that Black men have made to America, how is it we remain a nation separate and unequal? The great architects of our nation did not wait for their services to be commissioned; they seized every opportunity they had to create their vision even when they were told they had none. They built and designed cities, and created inventions that stood the test of time. Revolutions and movements were started solely on their ideas. Black men endured pain, prejudice, and social injustice and still persevered, understanding that their place in history would advance the African-American race and America on the whole.

We understand the reluctance for anyone to step out on faith and to lead. America has a nasty habit of taking agents for change, celebrating them, then turning on them and destroying them mentally, spiritually, physically, or financially. It has become a national sport. But, are we going to wait for the next Martin Luther King Jr., Malcolm X, Booker T. Washington, Frederick Douglass, or Thurgood Marshall to come along and head the next movement, or will you step up to the plate and do your part?

The truth is, we can use the experiences of our fathers and grandfathers to embrace the present and seize the future. They are truly the architects of their own "*his-story*" that is little known and respected. That's why in this chapter we will hear stories of wise veterans of life that embody the true spirit of invention, exploration, civil rights, and history making.

Power and Politics

Mayor Willie L. Brown Jr.

People might think that I learned everything that I need to know about the politics of people from working in the government. Actually, what's closer to the truth is that I already understood a lot about people before I ever set foot in the state capitol or took up office as the first African-American mayor of San Francisco. Some of my brightest lessons and harshest realities came from my growing up in the cotton-farming town of Mineola, Texas. Though people see me now as a Californian, through and through, I grew up in Mineola at the height of legally supported racial segregation.

My teenage years were spent living in a time when the energy of the civil rights movement was building but the injustices that they sought to fight still prevailed. There were racial discrepancies in everything from economics to housing, and even with education. My family was supportive of my eagerness to learn and encouraged me to read everything that we could obtain. I read a lot, but often I was reading books without covers or backs. It was common for me not to complete a story because the pages that contained the ending were gone. For a young African-American man with big dreams, Mineola was not the place to be.

To date, the best job that I have ever had has been the mayor of San Francisco, but I've held a lot of jobs that weren't nearly so glamorous or powerful. Before becoming a lawyer and a politician, I worked as a janitor, playground director, fry cook, shoeshine boy, and field worker. I picked berries. I picked watermelons. I picked potatoes. I picked beans. I picked cotton. (Berries were the worst. It's hot, you have to put your hand into the brier patch, and it's laced with snakes, and you have to carry your harvest in wooden lugs.) But that was life then. When you are looking for honest work in Mineola, Texas—well, you take what you can get.

I maintained work because that's what you did—helping my family was always important to me. However, I didn't let my education fail. Once I graduated from the all-Black high school with my "separate but equal" education, I left that poor Cotton Curtain town, but I never forgot it. Many times, I have thought that two of the greatest lessons I learned from those experiences were how to survive and how to move on.

The train ride from Mineola to the West was my first indication that things were about to change for me. I can't remember the exact point that it happened, but somewhere along the way the COLORED signs were taken down in the train and I was able to move freely throughout the train. The closer I got to California, the more I began to feel a sense of freedom that went far beyond the symbolism of the signs on the train. My uncle Itsie, who had left Texas some years ago, was there to meet me when I got off the train. He looked at me with my cardboard suitcase and worn clothes and decided that I needed to look the part of a newly emancipated man. Uncle Itsie took me to the Fillmore, carrying more money than I'd ever seen in one place, and selected clothes for me that would further draw a line between me and my Mineola past. Seeing my uncle make his way through the Fillmore district of San Francisco, the cultural hub of the urban Black middle class, made me proud. He made an indelible impact on my sense of style as well as my ideas about people.

From living as a poor African American in a racially segregated and hostile town, I learned to be prepared in my interactions with people. Because of the fact that I had to leave Mineola in order to complete my education and to excel, I learned that sometimes you have to move on from a situation that by its very nature is set up for failure. Having Uncle Itsie take me in and provide me with a foundation to go to school, I gathered a respect for people of all walks of life as being important to forward movement. When I was exposed to the prosperity of African Americans living in San Francisco, I learned that my destiny was now in my own hands.

I have used my survival techniques in every aspect of my political career. Learning to be flexible yet prepared has put me in a position to make allies out of potential enemies. I have even surprised my staunchest supporters with the feats I have been able to accomplish. I worked as a janitor in the same building where I took my classes at Hastings School of Law in San Francisco. Once I passed the bar, I became a criminal defense attorney. I took cases defending pimps, prostitutes, petty thieves, and gamblers—the ones that other attorneys would shy away from. However, many of my clients reminded me of people from my past. Being involved with people on that side of the law taught me how to deal with folks from all walks of life and to recognize their impact on the culture and society of California.

After completing law school, a series of events propelled me into the political scene. I was involved in civil rights protests, especially those involving housing and employment inequities. My name was mentioned as both an up-and-coming politician who could represent the many voices of our community and as a militant whose staunch views and outspoken nature scared many conservatives. I gained fame when I led a sit-in protesting racial discrimination in housing in 1960. I ran for the Assembly in 1962 and lost to the incumbent by six hundred votes. Undeterred, I returned two years later and won the Assembly seat. After that, I would go undefeated for fifteen consecutive terms. In the process, I chaired the influential Ways and Means Committee, and then, in 1980, I won the Speakership. My tenure as the Speaker of the Assembly of California was the longest in the history of the state. I had to broker deals with all sorts of people. I worked together with both Republican and Democratic governors. Under my watch, I saw California grow to become the seventh-largest economy in the world. The irony was not lost on me that I would be responsible for $30 billion of what most people in Mineola might've called "White people's money."

My long run as the Speaker of Assembly ended not because I had failed to serve my state or my district, but because conservatives were eager to see my demise and encouraged California voters to create a ballot initiative limiting the number of terms a person could serve. Although the goal of those who opposed me was clearly to diffuse my power, their strategy was short lived. I reflected on my time in office, and I was proud of the work that had been done and the legacy that I had created. My Mineola roots came back to remind me that it is most important to be prepared for change and be willing to turn adversity into a victory. So it was no surprise to people who knew me back in Texas that I would move from holding one of the most powerful positions in California government to become the first African-American mayor of San Francisco, one of America's most beautiful and diverse cities.

Mayor Willie L. Brown Jr., as the city's first African-American mayor, continues to represent the past, present, and future of civil rights and the cultural and intellectual diversity that symbolize San Francisco's history of acceptance.

Don't Let the Wagon Roll Down the Hill

Imar Lyman Hutchins

Maybe my grandfather realized he was getting near the end of the line. Or maybe he had been telling the story all along but I just hadn't had ears to hear it. Whatever the case, in the last few years of his life, Papa, (as we called him), began telling a story I'd never heard before but that has been passed down orally in my family for over 150 years.

The story begins in the dark days of slavery.

I always hear Black people say, "I couldn't have been no slave," but if you had actually lived in those times, it's almost certain that, yes, you would have been a slave. If your parents, your grandparents, your great-grandparents and every person you'd ever seen or heard of who looked like you was a slave, how would you even be able to envision anything different? It's hard for us to wrap our minds around slavery today because the depravity of the institution of slavery is by its very nature almost unimaginable.

Having said that, in the 1830s and '40s my great-great-grandfather, Dyer Johnson, was a slave in Tennessee. He was fortunate as slaves went in that he was a very skilled carpenter. He was so valuable that his master would often rent him out to other people in town to do various carpentry jobs such as building houses. Sometimes his master would let him keep a few pennies of what he'd "earned" even though technically a slave couldn't own property because the slave himself *was* property.

Dyer couldn't read or write, but he was obviously intelligent and could "figure" well enough to build a flawless house from scratch by himself in short order.

One day Dyer came to his master and said, "Massa, would you ever sell me?"

I guess Master Johnson figured that Dyer should be pretty happy living on the top of the slave-hierarchy on the plantation and wanted to make sure that he wouldn't sell him "down the river" to some "hard" master. But nevertheless, the master was in business to make money and said, "Dyer, I'm not gonna lie to you. If someone comes to me with the right amount of money, I've got to sell you."

Unbeknownst to his master, Dyer was religiously saving—burying his pennies in the ground in multiple hiding places.

As the months and years passed, Dyer returned to his master and said, "There's a man in town who said he wants to buy me. He told me to ask you how much you would sell me for?".

Master Johnson thought about it for a second and said, "Thirteen hundred dollars. Tell that man to come see me and give me thirteen hundred dollars, and you'll be his problem and not mine."

Dyer went back to working and secretly saving his money.

Eventually, he returned to his master and said, " I saw that man in town again who said he wants to buy me—"

"I told you to tell the man to come talk to me," his master interjected.

"Well, he gave me the money and told me to give it to you," Dyer replied.

At this, Master Johnson launched into long a speech to the effect that "a deal's a deal" and culminated with saying, "Once I get that money in my pocket I'm never giving it back to *anybody*. You're gonna be his problem not mine, understand?"

Dyer acknowledged and gave Master Johnson the thirteen hundred dollars at which point, Master said, "Okay, get outta here, you're not my problem anymore. Go to your new master."

"Oh, Massa, one more thing, the man said he needed a receipt," Dyer added as he prepared to leave.

The master got a piece of paper and wrote out a receipt and as he got to the bottom he asked, "To whom should I make out this receipt?"

Master Johnson's mouth must have hit the floor when Dyer replied with his own name, "Dyer Johnson." Master Johnson realized that Dyer had tricked him and that really there never was a man in town who wanted to buy him but rather that he wanted to buy *himself*. At first the master got furious, but then he calmed down. After all he was in business to make money so why did it matter where the money came from? He could have just taken the money and returned Dyer back to his status as chattel for a life of eternal servitude. Dyer was his property and he could do whatever he wanted to with him. He did not under any circumstances *have* to allow him to buy his freedom. Slaves weren't even allowed to own property, much less thirteen hundred dollars, which was a fortune in those days.

But on the other hand, he thought about his diatribe and said, "Well I did tell you a deal's a deal and once I take this money you're somebody else's problem. So here you go old boy," he said as he made the receipt out to Dyer Johnson and signed it. "Good luck my boy," he said to Dyer as he handed him the receipt. "You're a free man now!"

The year was 1842 and once free, my great-great-grandfather kept working day and night in the hopes of buying his wife, Elizabeth's, freedom from a neighboring plantation owner. But her mistress said she wouldn't sell Elizabeth only to have her living in the woods somewhere like an animal. If Dyer wanted to buy his wife, he would have to build a house for her to live in first.

So Dyer bought some rocky, undesirable land—the only land that anyone would sell to a Black person—and set about building a house on that land.

He eventually finished the house and was able to buy his wife's freedom for just three hundred dollars because her health had always been fragile and it wasn't expected that she would live long.

They had three children together who were born free, as they were born to two free Negroes. In about 1849, when my great-great-grandfather was on his deathbed, he gathered his two sons and daughter around his bedside and told them the story of his life.

He told of his travails.

He told of his dreams.

He told his children, "I leave you with three things: First, this house, when it rains it doesn't leak, when the wind blows it doesn't rattle. You'll always have a place to live and you don't have to worry about that. Second, I leave you this land. You can raise animals on this land to support and feed yourself, and if you take care of this land, you should be always be able to take care of yourself. And third and most important, I leave you your *freedom*. Don't take it for granted. I've given the best years of my life as a slave. I was no better than a donkey. I've lived it, and believe me *slavery is hell*."

Remember this was still fifteen years before the end of slavery, and no one had any way of knowing *if* or *when* the deplorable institution would ever end.

Dyer next gave his children a charge: "I've done a lot of pulling to get the wagon this far up the hill. All the work that's been done can be lost in a second. If you stumble or fall, that wagon will go rolling right back down the bottom of the hill. If you feel yourself getting weak, or you think you might not be up to the task, just put a brick behind the wheel of the wagon, and maybe someone else coming on up behind you will have the strength to take it up higher from here. But whatever you do . . . *don't let the wagon roll down the hill*."

In this way, he implored his children not to simply be content with their own personal advancement and comfort, but rather to give themselves to trying to uplift their people. He essentially said, "You're set financially for life, now *what are you going to do with your life?*"

My great-grandfather, Robert Graves Johnson, and his brother, William "Uncle Will" Johnson, I must say, heeded the call and devoted their lives to efforts to uplift their race, their efforts occurring in the days of Reconstruction. They had the good fortune of being "adopted" or sponsored by the family of an abolitionist named Lyman Beecher Tefft, the brother of Harriet Beecher Stowe, the author of *Uncle Tom's Cabin*. Through this relationship, they were able to receive unheard of educational opportunities including degrees from northern universities such as Brown. The two brothers then returned to the South, where they both became educators and built and operated universities and schools. They also helped to start churches, businesses, and every manner of institution possible, giving themselves selflessly to the work of pulling the metaphoric wagon up the hill.

When my great-grandfather was old and was on his deathbed, he gathered his children around the bedside as his father before him had done. This time there were nine children assembled. He recounted his life's work and likewise passed on the challenge to his children: *"Don't let the wagon roll down the hill!"*

My grandfather, Lyman Tefft Johnson (named for his father's benefactor) was the youngest of those nine children gathered around that bed. Apparently, the story of the wagon planted firmly in his young mind, as he grew up to become a fiery civil rights leader in Louisville, Kentucky, known for his fearlessness in the face of danger. His biggest battle came in 1948 and '49 when he, along with Thurgood Marshall of the NAACP, brought the case that ultimately desegregated the schools in the State of Kentucky. It was one of the cases that led up to *Brown* in 1954. Because my grandfather had advanced degrees from such institutions as the University of Michigan and otherwise impeccable educational credentials, he was the most indisputably *qualified* Negro to be admitted to the University of Kentucky. But perhaps more important, he was the only Negro *crazy* enough to try. So he became the plaintiff in a case that successfully challenged segregation in Kentucky schools. But you see, a victory in the courts was one thing; a victory in the streets was something entirely different. When he attended classes for the first day, at least seventeen crosses were burned on the campus. Many a night he stayed up all night on the front porch of his house with a shotgun on his lap to protect himself and his family, prepared to pay the ultimate price if necessary in the face of the innumerable death threats he constantly received.

I remember my grandfather telling me, when I was about to go to law school, about how Thurgood and the other pioneering civil rights attorneys would have to stay up all night and type briefs (on manual typewriters) by flashlight in the backseat of a car because Blacks couldn't stay in hotels in those days. They'd stay up all night working in the backseat of a car and go straight to court and argue their motions in the morning. I think there's no way we can ever really know the sacrifices that our ancestors made in our behalf.

In retrospect, it's easy to look at the civil rights movement as a foregone conclusion—something that was going to happen anyway. Some say it was just a matter of time. This is arguable. It hadn't happened in the hundred years since slavery. The status of the Negro and race relations had fluctuated wildly during this time, sometimes better, sometimes worse, with Reconstruction being a better time for blacks than the Jim Crow pre–civil rights era that followed it. Things were not necessarily going to get better. And clearly there was no way of knowing when or if anything was going to change, nor whether part of the price of change would be your own life.

When I think about those soldiers who came along in the thirties, forties and early fifties, I think of them as real revolutionaries. These were people who were really risking *everything*. In the 1960s it became clear that, as the song says, "times they are a-changin'" and that the world would soon be different. It was safer to hop on the bandwagon. But back in those dark days, there were no guarantees whatsoever. Most of those people who struggled in those early days are names that history has failed to record. Their legacy lives in us, their descendants, and in the world they helped to create

Having been born in 1906, my grandfather used to say that he'd lived his life in two halves. Half of his life, forty-five years, in the darkness behind a veil; and the second half in the light. He lived long enough to literally see the same people who were trying to kill him decades earlier bestow rooms full of plaques and accolades upon him. Those awards made him happy, but they were simply gratuities after the fact and were almost unimaginable when the sacrifices themselves were made.

Now I find myself with my own hand on the wagon's handle and charged not to let it roll down the hill. I feel so blessed that I was able to hear the story of the wagon, in particular when I did. It has literally helped me to know my place in the world. I know that no matter what the appearances, I am never alone. I'm not the first person to face the struggles I'm facing. I imagine the hardships that my ancestors must have endured, and it gives me the strength to press on and not complain, especially when I consider that anything I might complain about undoubtedly pales in comparison.

Knowing the *wagon* gives me a feeling of connectedness with my past and my future. It has also led me to start reading books that were written by people who lived long before me, through slavery and other hardships that we can only imagine, and to draw strength from their lives, even though I am not related by blood to the authors. I've made up my mind that—knowing how much work has gone into getting us where we are today and how much farther we still have to go—no matter what, the wagon is not rolling down the hill on my watch! And if it rolls down after me, then I haven't done my job of teaching the next generation about how important the wagon is and how it got this far up the hill.

If you'd had the opportunity to meet my grandfather, he would have recounted all his life's struggles to you, as he would to any young person who would listen. He would remind us that the battles that we have to fight today and tomorrow are at least as important as the ones he fought yesterday. He would tell you, "Now, look, it's on you. My days here are numbered. I've done all the pulling I can do. Now it's up to you. Whatever you do . . . *don't let the wagon roll down the hill!*"

Imar Lyman Hutchins *is an author and a lawyer.*

Another Sunday

Keenan McCardell

On the eve of the Super Bowl XXXVII, on Saturday, January 26, 2003, I am sitting on the edge of my bed in my hotel room and thinking about what is my winning formula. It took a lot of hard work, persistence, never giving up, never believing that you can't do anything, always saying you can, and never letting anyone tell you that you can't do anything. It's just one of those things where you've been through a lot, and now you're at the climax of a football player's year, which is playing in the Super Bowl. And you look back at all the times people said you weren't fast enough, you weren't big enough, you didn't play at a big-time college, and you look at them and say, "Hey, I'm here!" I must have been doing something right. I look back at the times I didn't have my opportunities right away, like some of the first-round guys. I was a twelfth-round pick to the Washington Redskins from the University of Nevada of Las Vegas. I've beaten the odds, and the only reason is because I've been persistent. You know that hard worker who goes out and makes himself into what he wants to be, or what other people said he couldn't be.

I had six remarkable years in Jacksonville, career totals of 579 receptions for 7,526 yards (13.0 average) and 38 TDs. With the Jaguars, I snagged 499 passes over the past six years, sixth-most in the NFL over that span. My running mate, Smith, had 562 receptions in that same duration, making us probably the most dangerous receiving duo in the league. I was blessed to have led Jacksonville in receiving on three different occasions, with 85 receptions each in 1996 and 1997 and a career high of 94 in 2000. In addition, I racked up more than 1,000 receiving yards in four of my six seasons with the Jaguars.

Stats are great, but this game of football is a little different because if you don't have the right size and speed, a lot of times they overlook you. When I was a kid, I was probably one of the better athletes, but I wasn't blessed with a lot of size. Being that guy that's six feet four inches, 210 to 220 pounds and being a receiver. I'm sitting here six feet one inch, 190 pounds, playing receiver. I wasn't that prototype football specimen. They've always said, "You need to be bigger," and I've gone to the weight room and got bigger. You need to be faster, I went out and got faster, and one thing they couldn't take away from me was my ability to play this game and my love for the game. And I think that's what kept me going being persistent at what I do, the love for the game.

I was a big Houston Oilers fan coming up, and I'd always said I wanted to play football. It's like a dream. I know you might say that everybody says that's every kid's dream—to play football—but it's my dream that I would play football and play at this level. I told myself from a very young age that I wouldn't let anyone stop me from seeing my dream. I worked hard at it. I played football, baseball, and basketball when I was little. I started when I was seven, playing contact football. That was the first sport I ever played and the first sport I loved. I love basketball, but I truly, truly love football. I love the competition and the contact. Lots of people say, "But you're smart—why do you like the contact and all that?" It's a part of the game, and I just love to play the game. It's a strategic game, if it gets into that type of game. The thing that most football players love is to wake up in the morning, knowing they have to beat the guy across from them for each and every down for at least sixty to seventy plays a game. I think that's what ex-players miss, you know, that competition—that man-on-man competition, that gladiator-type competition.

I always remembered my college coach and high school coach telling me not to do anything to embarrass the team or the program. It's, like, if you go out and do something, you feel like you let some guys down who's been in the battle with you. And I try my hardest not to bring that into my lifestyle for my family and for my other family—my teammates. You know, if you think of them as a family, you don't want to hurt your family. And that's the one thing I try to do; I try to think first. I mean people make you mad to the point that you want to do something, but you gotta think rationally and say this is not right. I'm usually the one with the cooler head in the situation. I've been with some guys where it's been very close, and I've probably had that cool head, like, Let's think first. Think about how you're going to explain that to your children. And vice versa, how are you gonna explain that to your mom.

I am looking forward to what's next, but for me, first off is to win the Super Bowl. The next level is to create a dynasty in Tampa. Because they say nowadays in football there can't be a dynasty. Then why not start one? My thing is to start something. To start something that they say can't be done. It's kind of like my career; people said that you can't do it—well, why not? Why not make the Tampa Bay Buccaneers the next dynasty. That's how you have to think, and I just need to continue to be the best receiver I can be. And so far, it's been pretty good in the National Football League. I think personally you look at what a lot of guys have accomplished, and you try to set your goals. Look at J. L. Rice—you may not ever catch J. Rice, but what's wrong with trying to catch him? What's wrong with setting your goals that high? I think that's why he's so good, and I'm a big believer in J. Rice.

When I talk to young kids, I tell them never let anyone tell you you can't be whatever you want to be. Whatever you dream, you can do it. You dream it, you believe it, you do it. If you believe in your dream and you go out and put forth the effort to make your dream come true, nobody can stop you. You have to put forth the effort. You might say I can't do this, but think about it, you can always do something about it.

You know when you dream something and you believe it in your heart, nothing should stop you from getting to your accomplishment, your goal, your dream. I mean, if you say you're going to be the world's greatest basketball player, you have to go out and work at it each and every day. If you want to be the best doctor in the world, you've got to go out and prepare yourself. You have to mentally and physically prepare yourself to be the best. I'm not saying don't have any fun, but you've got to get to your goal first before you can have fun.

I want to keep Super Bowl Sunday as a regular Sunday. I think a person who keeps his calm, his cool, while all the hoopla is going on is going to be the guy who's going to go out and concentrate and play his best type of football. I'm not saying be so calm that you don't have any emotions—you're going to have emotions—but you have to try to keep them bottled up until you step on the field. I'm going to be excited—believe me, I probably won't sleep much tonight—but when I wake up, I've just got to go about business as if it's another Sunday in the National Football League. And when the kickoff goes, it's going to be unbelievable. I get goose bumps now just talking about what's going on; what's going to go on. That's the kind of stuff you try to keep to yourself. I'm Keenan first as a person, before I'm a football player. I'm just blessed to have one of those famous jobs.

I have a couple of things I want to do, but I know I'm going to have to narrow it down if I'm going to go to that next level, which is what I want to do. I would love to be a GM in the National Football League. There are not that many minority GMs in the NFL. Or one of those personnel guys, you know like an Ozzy Newsome for the Baltimore Ravens. That's something that I would enjoy because it keeps me around football. If that doesn't work, I want to be a broker or a financial adviser, because I know a couple of guys in this league, and I want to see guys leave this league comfortable. I want them to be able to enjoy life after football. I mean after they've come out and put their bodies on the line, they need someone to look out for their well-being after football. They need to be able to enjoy themselves and enjoy the fruits of what they've accomplished and enjoy the fruits of how hard they've been working.

This is not an easy job; if it were, anybody could do it. You have to have a certain mind-set and a certain pain tolerance. That's one reason I said a financial guy, because I see a lot of guys when it's over, and they're just sitting there looking like, Now what? You play this thing long enough, it's a job that lets you sit back and watch your kids grow up. That's my thing—I want to sit back and watch my kids grow up.

Super Bowl Champion **Keenan McCardell** *is an avid golfer and admitted video game junkie and the PlayStation 2 Champ of the Super Bowl. Keenan has several interests outside of football that help keep him young at heart, including playing basketball, gourmet cooking, and surfing the Internet. He and his wife of ten years, Nicole, who reside in Sugarland, Texas, during the off-season, have three beautiful daughters: Keandra, age 6, and twin girls Nia and Nakeeya.*

The Soul of My Grandfather

Adolfo García Montesino

For me, each day is a challenge due to many facts—sometimes economic facts, sometimes political facts, sometimes even spiritual facts. However, I have had to defy each fact and to raise my head up high in order to face them all. The person who taught me to meet all these obstacles head-on and to overcome them is my grandfather. He has inspired me and been a light deep inside my heart and soul—even though death took him away from me before I was born.

The lessons he has taught me, primarily through his son, my father, are especially important for me because I live in Cuba, a country that is always under siege, but is still surviving nonetheless.

For kids, having a grandfather or a grandmother is something really great. They stand by us since the beginning of our lives. They watch us, take care of us, teach us, and talk to us when Mom and Dad are busy at home or work. They always have time for us, and we also feel the need of having them close to us anytime, anywhere. Sometimes, we inherit some skills from them, even when we never have met them. I did not meet my grandfather (he died two years before I was born), but my father has taught me everything about my grandfather's ideals, thoughts, and feelings. Throughout my life, I have felt my grandfather's presence in almost everything I've done.

I remember when I was a kid, I began drawing and painting by myself. It was something great, because there was a hidden skill that I developed and that I still keep. When I realized what I could do with my hands and personal creativity, I started taking classes at an art school until I was fourteen years old.

I always had my parents' support with my artwork, but it wasn't until later that I realized that my grandfather had been something of an artist himself. He used to paint and also make little sculptures, some of which I had the opportunity to look at. I knew then that his eyes were looking down on me and he was smiling every time he saw a painting or drawing that I did.

I learned to be careful with my creations, to be patient, persevering, and always to listen to my conscience. My grandfather used to say that conscience is that secret voice that reveals itself to our reason and tells us whether or not we have done right or wrong in any circumstance of our lives. That revelation is made in two different ways. In one hand, when our behavior is reproached by the reason's judgment, the soul goes through a painful sadness known as regret, which follows us like a weird vision, taking away happiness and rest. On the other hand, when our behavior is approved by the reason's judgment, the soul feels a secret pleasure, which makes all the sufferings melt away.

As the time went on, I became a lawyer, perhaps inspired by the strong feeling of justice I carry inside me. I agree with my grandfather when he defined reason as "a faculty that human beings are equipped with in order to distinguish between good and evil, useful from harmful." The light of the reason is faith, this celestial voice never deceives us. We can't silence or persuade this inner voice, because it is higher than any human force.

I remember the hard times when I was at law school, but each difficulty was really just a challenge for me to overcome. I faced every obstacle with courage and pride, that is what I have learned from my ancestors. Sometimes I've been forced to be my own adviser, so I cannot really feel sorry about most of the decisions I have made in my life. I've drawn upon the spirit of those departed anscestors, and it has given me the strength to go on and to conquer what lies ahead. I understood the importance of having courage and its meaning when my grandfather defined it as "the fortress of nerve that gives us energy to defend our rights and to fulfill our duties, even though when we have to face sorrows, bitterness, and dangers." The courage recommended by the moral ideas isn't the imprudent one that consists of going through life recklessly, but rather it's the serene and restrained courage that allows us to suffer adversities and misfortunes, but to come out on top.

My grandfather taught me that a hero is a person who defies danger, risking his own life to save someone else's honor, life, or fortune. Some heroes put themselves on the line for the general welfare of mankind, and they deserve the highest esteem and respect of all humanity. But to do this, it is necessary to have a great spirit of justice in order to hold up our behavior to the laws of equity and reason.

It is curious how much we learn once we start working and realizing by ourselves the different ways we are able to choose in order to determine the best paths to follow in our lives. It is like a riddle or game in which your fate is uncertain and each event or move makes you analyze what move is the best one at the end. It could sound a little bit philosophical, but indeed, we can't deny the lesson we get every time we open your eyes and see through all these memories we keep deep inside ourselves.

I'm sure my grandfather, wherever he is, will be proud to know that I don't forget him. His ideals and thoughts are like a flag for me. I'm sorry I was not able to physically meet him, but he is always on my mind.

These are some of the qualities that he has taught me to live by:

To stand firmly on your values and beliefs even when everybody is against you, without folding in the presence of the pressure that is almost breaking your resistance—that is courage.

To have always a smile on your face, no matter if you feel you're dying inside yourself, just to help and motivate the ones close to you—that is strength.

To not stop before anything, and always to do what your heart knows is right—that is determination.

To do what people expect from you and to make others' lives more pleasant without complaining—that is passion.

To help a friend if necessary, to do your best no matter how long it takes or what you have to do—that is loyalty.

To give always what you got and never expect anything for it—that is devotion.

To always keep your head up and be the best that you can be, no matter what is against you. To face each difficulty with the certainty of a better tomorrow—that is trust in yourself.

He taught me that it is very important that we have solid ideals and that we always be conscious of what we should or should not do. We always will have difficulties, but on the other hand, we have the strength we need to avoiding to falling down.

I can never give up on myself. I will always be fighting and fighting until the end. The solid ideals that my grandfather gave me are a fortress for me, and I know that I will always come out on top.

Adolfo García Montesino was born on September 26, 1974, in Havana, Cuba, where he still lives. He works as a lawyer handling commercial transactions. This is his first work of expository writing, but he looks forward to continuing to write in the future. This essay is dedicated to the memory of his grandfather.

Whateva Happened to the Music?

Daddy O

From the first time in 1979, when I heard a "Yes, yes, y'all" from Melle Mel on a Flash tape, I was hooked. The sound of the funk machine (old school echo chamber) was like the best thing I heard since Mandrill.

I was born on February 20, 1961, in the East New York–Brownsville section of Brooklyn. The ENY–Brownsville I was born in was very different from today. We had vendors of all kinds and nationalities, and very seldom did my mom take me to the market on Belmont Avenue without returning with a free toy of some kind. The ensuing years of my love for music involved everything from dancing in front of the record shop on Ralph and Saint John's for quarters to a James Brown 45, to singing in groups imitating Blue Magic, to seeing this little guy named Michael and his brothers open for the Temptations at the Apollo and all but steal the show.

Me and Bushon played disco in Alabama Park with power from the community center years after, and danced to the hustle and webo till our legs hurt. Not long after that, I heard the "Yes, yes, y'all." To me, it sounded like *all* the music I ever heard making love. There was melody, there was rhythm, and what's that, Mel? Rap? Wow!

My brother Kedar had a friend of a mutual DJ friend of ours who did this "rap" thing. I already had experience in writing poetry, so I asked if I could write a rhyme or two for him to perform. Kedar got the okay, I wrote the rhyme, gave it to dude, went to the performance, and he absolutely *stank*. Needless to say, I started MC'ing myself.

My influences kicked in, and growing up liking Mandrill; Sly; Earth, Wind & Fire; and James, I formed a six-man alliance called Stetsasonic. Rap, drums, turntables, human percussion, and keyboardist. We made three LPs, sold records, traveled the world, and defended an art-form we naturally accepted as a continuum of the traditional Black music we were raised on.

Fast forward, and in 2003, the same art-form we once defended finds me in forums at forty-two years of age, screaming about lyrical poison. I ask by my title . . . whateva happened to the music? The long answer is what we *all* do to preserve tradition and educate our youth. The short answer is that my generation did a poor job communicating with our elders while we were creating this new art-form. If we had communicated, Mandrill would have been singing the hooks (chorus parts) on Stetsasonic records.

"Yes, yes, y'all." This is a boldface confession. Whateva happened to the music? We dropped the ball. Can you forgive us?

Daddy O *is a writer and an executive producer.*

Free by '63

Rev. Amos Brown

I was a young man once. And when I was a young man, there were things that I worried about just like the men of today. I worried about someone perpetrating violence against me or my family. I worried about how I was going to make a way in a society that didn't fully embrace my optimism for my future as a Black man. There are a whole lot of things that are different now, a lot of evils that the average young Black man faces that I didn't have to worry about it. However, there are a lot of things that are still the same, they have just taken on a different face.

When I was growing up in Mississippi at the height of everything that was wrong with this country in terms of race relations, I did my best not to let my spirit be broken. Back in those days, there was only one of two ways that you could go. You could either succumb to the idea that you were less than a man. Or you could choose to defy that and try to be the man that you were destined to become, get a good education, follow God's path, and try to bring your people with you. I decided very early on that I would follow the path that God had decided for me and attack civil injustices where they happen. Now in making that very bold decision, I had to quickly grow in ways that I wasn't fully prepared. It was up to me to remain hopeful when there was little hope. I had to stay strong when I felt weak. And most of all I had to believe when I looked around me and found that there was very little to believe in.

Like many people involved in the energy that would become known as the civil rights movement, it was an event that hit to close to home that made me feel compelled to act at a very early age. Early in 1945, my older brother Clarence was walking home from a study session at his friend's house. He picked a shortcut that would end up being an unfortunate route for him to take on that night. While walking home, he was met with a team of White police officers who immediately accused Clarence of being in the neighborhood for some reason related to the pursuit of White women. In those days, it was commonplace to be detained by the police without provocation. Just as common was the reality that my brother was in grave danger the minute that he was spotted by those Mississippi police officers.

My brother made it home, but he had been severely beaten by the police. My family immediately rushed to aid my brother, praising God for the fact that he had been returned alive. He was just sixteen years old, and his life had changed forever. Although my family was enraged and worried, they had very little options for recourse in those days. As was the case with many Southern families, my parents decided to find a safer place for my brother to continue to grow in his manhood. Clarence was sent to Detroit, Michigan, on the invitation of our aunt. I have a picture of my entire family at a Jackson reunion. All three of my sisters were there, and there are four sons present along with our parents. However, there is one person who is missing, a stark reminder of the civil liberties that we were denied. Clarence was not in that picture, nor would we eight Brown children ever be in the same room again. Clarence left home in 1945, and he never looked back. He was so scarred by the events that it would take decades of time and the death of our beloved father to cause him ever to step in the state of Mississippi again.

Although I was only four, my family made sure that I was aware of the incident involving my brother. Back then, being honest was a matter of protection for young Black men, to warn them about the potential dangers of living in a racist and segregated world. However, my parents could try to protect me from immediate danger, the stark reality of growing up in the 1950s and '60s required that I be part of the action or sit on the sidelines and wait for something to happen. Because of what happened to my brother, I was determined to fight racism and social injustices as soon as I came of age to do so. I was inspired by the work of Thurgood Marshall, Medgar Evers, Martin Luther King Jr., and Benjamin Mays. The movement that was coming to the surface at that time governed my world. I gravitated toward a place where I could actually do something about the world that we lived in.

It was an expectation that I would go to college, but I didn't wait until I was away from home to become a part of the movement. In fact, by the time I was a senior in high school, I was already part of the NAACP's youth movement that had just made it to Jackson in the late 1950s. A young Medgar Evers, who was instrumental in culling the energy of disenfranchised but activated youth, mentored me. My sister Gloria had attended a NAACP conference in Dallas, Texas, and I'll never forget her excitement when she came back and told me that "Free by '63" was the slogan for the youth movement stirring the nation. I wanted to be Free by '63, so I knew that I had to act immediately.

In 1958 the *Cleveland Plain Dealer* interviewed me as a part of the NAACP youth movement. I was offering my position on the desegregation victory of the Little Rock Nine. My words weren't only heard in Ohio. The interview got back to Mississippi by way of an anonymous letter sent to the Black Superintendent of Jackson schools. Without warning or opportunity for reply, I was immediately expelled from school. Medgar Evers quickly came to my aid and brought the now growing influence of the NAACP with him. A court notice was filed that we intended to have me admitted into the White high school to complete my senior year. Obviously, this was a battle that they did not want to face, so I was immediately readmitted to school. However, there would be more battles for me to face. I had previously been elected as president of student government. To censor my impact on the other students, the total student council was disbanded for that year. My classmates showed their confidence and support by electing me as the president of the senior class. The high school administrators did not mask their contempt for me and openly forbade the senior class adviser from allowing me to take the office for which I had been elected.

Although "Free by '63" would be many years off, the civil rights movement was in full swing by then, and I was an active part in it. Because of my family (and most especially the injustice handed down to my brother) I felt compelled to move forward. As a young person, I recognize that sometimes we can feel powerless. We often imagine that we have to achieve a certain age or get a particular number of accomplishments under our belt before we can truly get involved. I would remain active in the struggle past my high school graduation and matriculation through Morehouse College. The struggle would remain a part of my life as I pursued my degrees and experience to allow me to become a reverend, move to San Francisco, and lead a politically progressive congregation through a pivotal time in American history. I didn't know the power that I would later wield when I would be elected as a city official or work directly with the heroes from my past. However, I now know that the power held in the days of my youth was so strong that it was intimidating to others.

The Mississippi State Sovereignty Commission was a secret government group that obtained information and kept files on Blacks involved in the civil rights movement. I was a middle-aged man when I found out about the impact that I must have had on the political scene before I was even eighteen. In recent years, one of my parishioners was in Jackson when the sealed files of this secret committee were ordered open to the public. He brought back a copy of the file that had been made on me. It was an eerie feeling to know that I had been watched closely, that my words were being scrutinized and my steps were being recorded. There were articles, pictures, and copies of programs where I had spoken. I chose not to harp on the feelings of having my privacy invaded. However, I reflected on the fact that the experi-

Your Soul's Journey

For I do not want you to be ignorant of the fact, brothers, that our
forefathers were all under the cloud and that they all passed
through the sea. —1 Corinthians 10:1

Your journey through time will help you recognize the gems in our historical tapestry and glean wonderful knowledge from the elders who came before us. We don't know who we are until we find out about our ancestors. Begin spending time with the older and wiser folks in your family. If you stop long enough, you will see the patterns that have developed over generations. Learn from the past, and don't wait for someone else to create your future. Whether you are young or old, you need to take stock of your life.

Adopt-a-Hero

Black families have had to adapt and adopt and be expansive, elastic, and flexible—or else we wouldn't be here today. Adopt a hero—just because a person isn't related to you doesn't mean that they can't inspire you. Just because somebody isn't related to you doesn't mean they aren't family to you. Who really knows who is related to whom? Chances are that adopted hero could be related to you. How many of us can name their eight great-grandparents much less know something about them? That's why African society had ancestor worship. It's not that they're worshiping dead people, but they're paying honor and respect to the people who gave them life. They are the architects of our collective history.

Elijah McCoy's machinery inventions were so innovative that they saved the machine industry millions of dollars and were in use around the world. Many tried to duplicate his work, but their copies were refused, and that's where the well-known universal phrase "the real McCoy" originated. You're the real "McCoy," and you need to realize it. We are the inventors and the creators of tomorrow's future. You, too, can make a difference with your purpose. Your contribution, regardless of how big or small, will make this world a better place.

Soul Source

- Do you know your own family's history?
- Describe your greatest challenges.

- Do you have any regrets in your life?
- What would you like to change?
- Reflect on the greatest moments in your life.
- What would you like to accomplish?

CHAPTER 15

❦

GOING HOME

Death is not the end for someone who has faith.
—Desmond Tutu

A dear friend of ours, Maria Davis, was asked to care for a man she never met. She was asked to care for him by his manager because he was in the advanced stages of AIDS. He was alone and in a hospital with his family hundreds of miles away and unable to be with him. Maria cared for him up until the very moment that he took his last breath. He didn't die alone, and he was surrounded with love. Kenneth Green was a producer, songwriter, and the lead singer of the musical group Intro. He wrote beautiful songs and brought joy to the lives of many. He worked with many musicians like the Winans, Will Smith, Ashanti, LL Cool J, and Mary J. Blige, to name a few. While many people were devastated by his passing, they knew he contributed a great deal to the lives of others. We know Kenny merely went home to his new studio in heaven to make beautiful music with God.

Death is a passage of spirit from one realm to the next, though preparation for this final rite of passage is painful for those of us left behind. It becomes infinitely harder to mourn the death of a loved one when you are the one left to break the news to family and friends, handle the details of the arrangements, and make sure other loved ones are able to cope. Needless to say, if you have been caring for someone with a long-term illness, you may not have the emotional strength to care for yourself.

We met so many Black men who were accustomed to death to the point that they were almost numb to the occurrence. It didn't matter what station in life these men were in, they knew someone they grew up with who had died a violent death. Death is always right around the corner for the Black man in a way that it simply isn't for the average American.

We are conditioned to look at death as the end of one's existence. These stories will help change that perception of death and help us to see that the person's spirit continues to live and grow inside us. The journey's end is finding the peace in the passing of a loved one or ourselves and being able to look at the totality of the value of the journey and the lessons learned along the way. Black men who have experienced saying good-bye to that special someone—and have grown because of it—share their insights.

Mama's Boy

Karu F. Daniels

I've always prided myself with being my mother's promised child.

Not only were we born on the same day, but we had identical mole birthmarks on our right biceps. Interesting.

Early on in my life, my mother groomed me into becoming a full-bodied, self-respecting and caring person. She encouraged me to be all that I can be and live my life to the fullest. My mother wanted me to live the life she never did, to reach my highest potential, see things that weren't attainable for her and her eleven siblings who came up during the turn of the civil rights era.

Because of my closeness to my mother, I knew that I was different from others early in my life. And that was okay by her. Like any real nurturing parent, she allowed me to be me. And that's a gift that has proved to be invaluable to this very day.

I'm the middle son of three boys born to both my mother and father in the early 1970s. Before any of us were ten years old, our father was slain on a hot summer night around the corner from where we lived in East New York, Brooklyn. Without much thought, my young mother and some neighbors took us along with them as they ran to the site of the bloody murder. It's an image that will stick with me for the rest of my life. Seeing your father's body covered by a blood-soaked white sheet is traumatic by any standards. It took us years to heal from that, even with therapy. I honestly believe, even to this very day, that my father's murder may have had even more damaging effects on my two other siblings.

Because of my closeness to my mother, I never used my father's death as a crutch. It actually strengthened me. Mom told her boys that we should always be prepared for life's unexpected twists and turns. With a very warning tone, she would tell us to pull ourselves up by our bootstraps and be ready in life. "If I were to die tomorrow, would you be prepared to go on in life?" I remembered her always asking us as teens. "Would you be ready to stand on your own feet and take responsibility into your own hands?" she'd ask.

Her words rang true in the spring of 1995, when she died suddenly from a terminal illness that I and quite a few family members didn't even know she had.

Winter 1994 was celebration mode for my family. I was accepted back into college after a two-year disqualification period. Timing couldn't have been more perfect. When I originally got booted out of school in January 1993, my mother did not disown me for my fall from grace. As her only child who sought higher education, I did make her proud, and I knew she was disappointed, but she never ever uttered a word about it. Instead, she encouraged me to pick up the pieces and chalk up the experience as a lesson learned.

And that's exactly what I did.

In the interim—a two-year period to "exonerate" myself (New York State Universities have some of the silliest "rehabilitation rules," in my own humble opinion), I forged ahead with my freelance writing career, writing for a host of national entertainment magazines, and even embarking on new career pursuits in media relations consulting. I made professional relationships and associations that I am proud of to this very day.

So without any hesitation I was ready to head back upstate—six long hours away from the home I knew—that January. But before I made the trek in my uncle's dilapidated van, I had to make one very important stop to visit my mom in the hospital. Two weeks before, she talked of back pain. And then she went into the hospital so they could run routine "tests." I made several trips to the hospital to be by her side, and she seemed fine and assured me that everything was fine.

The day I was leaving to go to college, we stopped at the hospital. I asked mother if she wanted me to stay at home. "I've already been gone for two years, I can go a few more. Can I stay?" I asked.

"No, you need to go back to school. It's a dream of yours, and it's a dream of mine. There's nothing to worry about. They're just running tests. Let them. I'll be fine."

I remember leaving her in the hospital with a smile on her face. Everything did seem to be fine.

So off to college I went. And I went back armed with a new sense of awareness and was taking no prisoners. I did not get immersed with extracurricular campus activities like before, and I hit the books—hard. I was determined to bring home the gold—or the degree.

By spring break, I was looking at a 3.7 grade-point average, and ready to get back to Brooklyn to see how things were going with the family.

When I got home, everything was cool. It was April. Spring. And mom was home. She seemed great. She was never a big woman. Slender all her life. I didn't notice anything different. We had our Sunday Soul brunch as usual. (After cleaning our huge apartment on Saturday, we would find solace the next morning by getting up and cooking hominy grits, sage sausages, home-style home fries, and omelettes while listening to the sounds of Patti LaBelle and the Blue Belles, Jennifer Holiday, Dr. Charles G. Hayes, and The Cosmopolitan Church of Prayer Choir, and the like.) We got fat and fussy. The week I spent home was one of the best I've ever experienced.

Who knew that it would be the last time I would see my mother the way I knew her.

A month later, I was frantically packing up my dorm room. The brilliance of the college residence life and housing department forced us to take every creature comfort we knew out of the room, and transport it to wherever we were headed when the semester ended. I remember that my best friend's brother, David, slept over the night before and helped me load up his car. He was going to school at a nearby Ivy League university—where he was completing his master's degree in engineering.

So after saying my good-byes to my college pals, I was looking forward to saying my hellos and spending the summer with my loved ones back in Brooklyn.

The darkest day of my life started to occur six hours later, after I arrived in front of my building on that balmy May afternoon. Because it was warm out, Black people, naturally, were sitting on the stoop and loitering in the front of the building—damn conditioning!

As I started to unload my goods on the pavement to walk it up the two flights, I bumped into one of my old running buddies, Freda. Freda was this burlesque, high-yellow woman-child who always strove for the finer things in life—even as a "bruising" youth. Although she was known to be a loudmouth daughter of a bitch who fought her way through life, she went to college to study nursing. As an adult, Freda became a paramedic.

I hadn't seen her in years. And it was kind of odd to see her out there with the stoop dwellers. But as she told me, she wasn't just hanging around—she was taking care of business.

While in conversation and catching up, she mentioned to me, "Your mother is in the last stages of cancer, but she's handling it well." Naturally, I wasn't fazed because I didn't know anything about cancer. Last stage usually means you're nearly finished with something. So, I reacted very cavalierly with, "Last stages of cancer? Oh, that's what the tests determined. She didn't tell me that. Oh, well, everything can get back to normal, now that I'm back home."

Freda took her two big arms and pulled me closer to her. "You don't understand. Your mother is in the last stages of cancer. The final stages of cancer. The cancer is metastatic, and it's at the point of no return."

Still naïve, I wasn't too clear at the fact that my childhood friend was telling me that my mother was going to die—and die very soon.

I'll never forget that day.

I ran upstairs. We lived in a long apartment. I ran through the bedrooms looking for my mom. No signs. And then I ran into the living room. Her sisters and some of my cousins were there. They were expecting me, and they seemed relieved to see me. But I was really focusing on finding my mother. I'm looking all through the apartment. And everyone's looking at me like I'm a chicken with my head cut off.

No one could've prepared me for what I was about to see next.

My mother was before me, lying on the couch. She was ashen and skeletal. I saw bones in her face that I didn't even know the lady had.

She was just a shadow of the image I saw only six weeks before.

Tears welled in my eyes. The wind was literally knocked out of me. I could not let her see me break down. So I stepped backwards down the hall and into my bedroom. It was there that I broke down, and cried, and cried, and cried. I never remember crying the way I did that afternoon.

I had so many questions. So much to say.

Darkness started to consume me.

My mother's baby sister came in the bedroom about a half hour later to console me. To comfort me. But to no avail. The only thing that I could murmur was "Why?"

She explained to me that the family members—even the ones I was in close contact with—knew for quite some time that she had pancreatic cancer, but my mother forbade them to tell me under any circumstances. My aunt Barbara didn't have many more answers for me, but she wanted me to understand that my mother was very forthright with her decision to keep me in the dark about her illness. She explained to me that if the cancer didn't spread as rapidly as it did, they may have not found out when they did just a few weeks before.

Things were just the way they were. No one could control it.

This was the day before Mother's Day 1995.

The living room was set up as a hospice of some sort. Fragrant with rubbing alcohol and white sheets everywhere. It was where she accepted her visitors.

I sucked up this travesty and put on a happy face to appease her. To appease myself. But I wasn't fooling anyone. I was torn. But I did not want to leave her side, so I set up sleeping arrangements next to the sofa on which she lay, bedridden and deathly ill.

On Mother's Day, one of my relatives who haven't seen my mom in months was so stunned by her physical appearance, she went crying and screaming as she ran out of the apartment after having one look at her as she entered the living room.

I felt my mother's heartbreak that afternoon. What a way to spend Mother's Day.

Looking back at it, I don't know how I got through it. It's something that I wouldn't wish on my worst foe.

The day after Mother's Day, mom was rushed into the hospital. She had stopped breathing that morning. We were the only ones home. I panicked. The paramedics came shortly after, and she was later admitted into the nearby hospital, one of the worst in the city. The family assembled later that afternoon. I did not leave her side. The doctors that were on duty were the most nonchalant people I've ever encountered in the health care industry. Still I demanded answers. I learned that pancreatic cancer or any cancer dealing with the intestine was the worst kind a person can get—for the fact that by the time it is discovered, it has spread so much that it is inoperable.

While she and I shared moments of quiet time in the hospital ward, I had so many questions to ask. I was nearly overcome by rage, but I bottled it in. Aside from the fact that I was kept in the dark about her and her fatal disease, I just had some real deep sorrow for one of the only angels on earth that I knew.

We men tend to always have high regard for our mamas, but anyone who came into contact with my beloved mother knew that she really was a nice and decent woman. No matter how much some of us want to say that about our parents, we know that in some cases, we really can't.

So to sit there and see her in this emaciated form, I couldn't ask the questions that I wanted answers to, like, Why didn't she tell me? How long did she know? How long does she have to live? What will I do without her?

Two days later, my beloved mother succumbed. That was twelve days before her forty-seventh birthday. Three days after Mother's Day.

I was alone in this world and didn't know what to do with myself. As the last person to see her alive in the hospital, I was too drained to go identify her body at the morgue the next day. But I pulled myself together enough to organize her business affairs and arrange all the memorial within a week of her death.

I was in a haze after that. Everyone tried to reach out to me, get through to me to no avail. I was slipping into darkness. I was going down real slow. I was at the dark end of the street.

I gave away most of her worldly possessions to any family member who asked for them.

I felt so alone. In my heart, I believed that I was betrayed by my mother and my Father God.

"What did I do to deserve such horrible fate?" I would continally ask. My mother was the only angel I knew. She cared for me. Nurtured me. Encouraged me and helped develop me into the young man that I was proud to be. She kept me on a straight and narrow path and deterred me from despair. When I overcame my alcohol addiction, she was there, too, through the darkness and the light, the good times and the bad times. And even when our father, her husband, was killed, she wholeheartedly held her family together like so many single women are forced to, due to whatever circumstances.

Such an open heart she had. Although she had eleven siblings who were alive and well, she took her invalid mother into our home and cared for her until her death.

And now she was gone.

One close friend tried to take my mind off my loss and help me garner full-time employment at an entertainment company. That lasted two weeks.

A month later, some other close friends invited me out to sunny Los Angeles, California to get some fresh air. And so I went.

Manhattan Beach was the last place I needed to be. It was there that I walked in the water, and kept walking, and walking, and walking into it—not knowing how to swim.

That's right. I wanted to end it all. I wanted to be where the ones who, I believed, truly loved me were.

But as fate would have it, my suicide attempt was just that—an attempt. I was talked out of it. And was told that I have so much to live for.

So here I am today—stronger, better, and more aware of what life and love is all about.

My mother selflessly gave me a timeless gift of time. Her holding on and letting me finish my first successful semester away at college enabled me to not lose any ground in my higher education pursuits. It was as if she saw everything before it happened and planned it.

Or as I own up to, it was divine order.

It took a while for me to realize that. I was angry for so long. Angry and disappointed. When people say knowledge is everything, I know what they mean. It's due to therapy and the support of my closest and dearest friends being there by my side that I made it through. But it's still a struggle. I miss my mother immensely. For years I dreamed about her day in and day out. Now she crosses my mind daily. She watches over me in my day-to-day walk toward grace and peace.

And I wear the title mama's boy, loud and proud.

And I'm a living testimony that before we judge a young man for being so close to that female parent of his, we must really take the time to think about the reason why it is so.

Karu F. Daniels is a nationally renowned entertainment journalist and author of the best-selling biography Brandy: An Intimate Look. *Born and raised in Brooklyn, New York, and a graduate of the State University of New York, College at Oswego, he is working on his debut novel, in between traveling and making a new home in rural northeast Pennsylvania.*

The Question

Jamez Williams

"**W**hat is it you want to tell me, man?" was the last full sentence that I heard my father utter. It probably was the last sentence that he articulated before his death. I don't know. I remember how it came out—slow cadenced, deep voiced, and slightly grainy—as he looked up with his brown eyes and locked his with those of his eldest son, me. The blank stare that was present moments before was replaced by one that commanded clarity. He knew who I was, which in recent days had become a rarity. Not bad for a man who had been diagnosed with limited brain activity stemming from a stroke. He did this just before the pain medication took effect and he slowly closed his eyes and started snoring.

He lay there, on that stale, mechanical hospital bed, clearly suffering. The pain that existed within him was something that I could not comprehend, but I am beginning to understand it now. Being a double amputee had taken the once street-mobile person and converted him into someone else. Plus the stroke that he suffered along with the infection in his heart didn't help any. He was no longer the fearless person who walked effortlessly through New York City's underground, sometimes causing trepidation in many of its dwellers. He was now a person who feared the loneliness that he felt consumed by all the hours of his remaining life.

The antiseptic room and those like it in which he spent this last year and a half were a far cry from the back alleys and the hustle dens where he had spent his time—his life's existence. *Existence* is a word that he chose because he claimed never to have lived, so he merely *existed*. "Living" he often said, was "reserved for those who had surpassed the struggle and had something to show for it. Most squares go to work all day long for all those years and have absolutely nothing to show for it. They are not living; they exist; just as I do." His philosophy, although fragmented and somewhat harsh, held major legitimacy.

In that very moment, we both existed—I as a testament to him and a person far from finding himself, and he as one who never accomplished the life that he had designed.

In an ironic twist, I looked down at him in awe as he did me when I was as a child. Surveying all his features and noting every nuance. From his brushed-back freshly cut silver mane to his cleanly shaven face, his skin texture, cheekbones, and dimples, I took in everything. I wondered if this was how he looked when he was sleeping as a baby; that answer I will never know, for no pictures of his earlier years exist, almost as though *he* didn't exist back then. I felt embittered and content at the same time, knowing that I was experiencing what he may have experienced thirty-four years prior. I often reflect back to childhood stories that he told about me—how I wouldn't eat until he came home from running the streets—no matter how late it was. My mother wouldn't know what to do to make me eat, so she just set my bowl alongside his plate and waited. Pop tried to make it his business to come home early so that I wouldn't starve. Once he did arrive, we ate together, and then I promptly went to sleep in his lap. Those stories always made him smile, and he loved telling them. For a moment, I became him and I smiled.

That smile quickly faded away when I looked at his velvety dark brown skin and pondered what had transpired between us in recent weeks. What had estranged this union, one that was conceived in blood? What had taken the son from the father? What had brought us to the point where he had to ask me this question? This question that sat in a compartment housed in the recesses of his now fragile, splintered mind. One that I didn't want to ignore, but didn't have the fortitude to answer.

The arguments and the fights that came from the demon that I held in my heart all these years came to surface, and I attacked him when he needed me most. The sharp, piercing words that I exchanged with the man who sparked my existence caused me pain as I reflected on them. I was ashamed. How did I get to that point? I don't know. I ache and wince at how low I had stooped. "You are too good to stoop," he used to say. "You are my boy!" A statement usually said to deter me from running the streets. But it meant nothing to me at the time because I had gone to a darker place, one that I had no business going. I cursed my father and went against all that I believed.

Each word that spewed from my mouth toward him cut deeper into my being, eliminating whatever comfort that I felt moments before. I looked for comfort around the room, but no one was there, just as he looked for me prior to his stroke.

I released my hands from the twisted knots that they have become and placed my left hand on his forehead and the other on his hand, cupping it gently. His eyes opened.

"Pop," I said in a shaky voice that struggled to remain confident and strong. He looked in my direction with a blank stare, searching for the face that the voice belonged to. "Pop," I said again, "it's me. I came to see you and help you get better." His head turned more toward my direction, his eyes squinted, and a distorted smile twisted onto his face. He puckered his lips, bit his lower lip and grunted as he enunciated, "Yeah."

My eyes watered, and I rubbed his head as I looked around his room; one that clearly was for the dying. Nothing in it took away from the all-encompassing sterility except for pictures my sister Ronell had left him of her and her daughters. Four separate pictures in total, giving each person her own identity and character. Just the way that he liked it.

His head rolled back, and he closed his eyes seconds before he began to snore; the medication once again showed its influence. I watched him for a few moments before I began to speak.

I started to talk to him about everything, from the family, both his and mine, to what antics his grandkids had gotten themselves into lately—the whole gambit. Things that he needed to know and possibly some that he didn't care to acknowledge. I spoke to him about everything. I spoke and spoke until I could not delay the inevitable any longer. I had to answer his question!

I didn't know where to start. My mind raced, looking for how to begin. I darted in, out, and through the passages of my psyche, trying to find the right answer; reaching under and over scattered remnants of the past, convoluted and confused emotions of my present that affected so much of my future.

Should I start with how much I was upset with him for choosing the streets over us, thrusting me into the seat of being the man of the house? His abandonment? Maybe I should tell him how much his unorthodox knowledge and sense of humor aided me throughout life? Should I tell how much I missed and needed him to be my superhero when he was locked up for all those years? Or how much it meant to me that he kept the promise that he made to his oldest grandchild? The promise that he would never go back to jail. Should I talk about how I despised him when he almost killed Mommy by beating her unconscious and put her into the hospital for weeks? Or, how he made me become accountable for all my actions? How he was responsible for helping me become the father that I am? Or how much I appreciated the phone calls from prison, just so he could help us with our homework? Should I talk about how much all his funny little off-beat stories actually livened up my life? Or how he provided us with the best Christmas that we ever had when he came out of jail for a short while when I was ten? No! I won't talk about any of those things. Everything that I had to say to my father over the course of the last seventeen years has been said among two men. Seventeen years is how long I had him on a consistent basis, and we cleared the air on major issues that plagued us. Some things still lingered and hurt, but they were all said.

In light of all my thoughts, no matter how disjointed they were, I needed to discuss something more pertinent, more meaningful! Something more personal.

Once again, I looked at him and watched his chest rise and subside with each breath. He looked content, while his eyelids struggled to open. Once again I recalled how bad I felt things had gotten.

My heart rate increased, and sweat started to form on my brow as I remembered the conversation that led to the argument. I bit my bottom lip in abhorrence at how things snowballed from there, at how I let my emotions consume me. My emotions were the one thing that betrayed me. He always warned my mother that I was the one with his anger still inside me, that I should never release it and for her to watch over me to make sure it stayed in check. I was just like him as he was in his youth, and he didn't want me to become the embittered person who led him to do the things that he had done. The details of the conversation are now irrelevant; who said what and why is meaningless. I was standing over the man I had abandoned, just as I had accused him of abandoning me in my youth. I had abandoned him when he needed me most. The irony is not even funny.

My stomach was sick and in knots while I tried to find the composure to tell him what I needed to tell him. My voice cracked, and my face was streaked with tears, as I looked down at my father, whose smile I possess, whose eyes mine mimic. At that moment, I said the most profound words that I have ever said to him in my life, "I'm sorry, Daddy, I want to take you home. I'm sorry."

His eyes, still closed, forced a tear through the eyelid. He heard me, and he was sorry, too.

Jamez Williams was born in Bedford-Stuyvesant, Brooklyn, on April 24, 1968. He holds a BA in business from Audrey Cohen College and an MBA in general management and an MS in multimedia industry and e-commerce from Metropolitan College of New York. He started writing short stories at the request of a few professors who encouraged his artistic ability and is now working on a few titles, including "My Father's Eyes," "And Just Like That," and a compilation book of short stories entitled One Day. *He is a father of three daughters and is a single parent. He resides in Brooklyn, New York, where he raises his middle child.*

Sister

Conrad R. Pegues

The evolution of change began with my mother showing me the knot on her shoulder blade. I touched it, having rarely touched my mother, not coming from a hugs-and-kisses kind of family. The fleshy little knot moved around at my fingertip. "Mama, that's just a cyst," I assured her. She had this shocked innocence in her eyes when she said, "I think I got the same thing as Virgie Lee." Her sister had died in 1998 of lymphoma, throat and lung cancer peculiar to smokers, although she never smoked a day in her life.

"Naw," I said, "it's just a cyst."

I accompanied my mother to the doctor and sat in the room while he excised the cyst to send to the lab for tests. It was my sister who went back to the doctor with her to find out she had cancer. The doctor told her to talk with her family, and he needed to start her immediately on chemotherapy and radiation.

My mother had always vowed that if she ever "got cancer," she wouldn't take chemotherapy. As a matter of fact, she and my aunt Virgie made that vow many times, years before they had to face the reality of cancer. Aunt Virgie agreed to take the radiation treatment, and when being prepped to take her first dose, she changed her mind. The administering physician was pissed off and told the family she would die—as if he'd made some earth-shattering revelation. She didn't change her mind. She died weeks later in a not very peaceful manner, striving to be free of her body at the last, claiming to see a room full of girls and heaving as if she would tear her essence out of her dying shell. It was a disturbing scene.

When the cyst first appeared on my mother's shoulder blade, she intuitively knew she had the same disease as her sister before her. One day, while I was bringing her home from the doctor, she asked me about taking chemotherapy and radiation. I told her that her body belonged to her and the decision was hers to make and we would support her whatever she decided.

After talking with one of my coworkers at the time, a cancer survivor herself, my mother decided to try chemotherapy and radiation, going against the vow she'd made years earlier.

The treatment didn't work.

The doctor told us that my mother's cancer, like Aunt Virgie's, had spread faster than any he'd ever seen before. They couldn't keep up with it. They gave her six months to live. My family adjusted as best they could under the circumstances, realizing that someone we love and have seen as the hub of our reality was not going to be here much longer.

The doctors may have given her six months. It was me who told her she'd live about seven days beyond her seventy-seventh birthday. I got the number seven one day while sitting alone by myself, thinking. I saw a seven pop up in my head in a big bold figures and instinctively knew what it meant. She accepted my word without question, having already said "they" had shown her a nice white room where she'd be going.

On her hospital bed, which the hospice had moved into my old bedroom at our family home, she told my sister she wanted to wear her dark green dress, her necklace my sister had given her some years before, and her brown pumps—all earth tones, I noted. The rest of the funeral arrangements she would leave up to us. I remember asking her that day was there anything she wished she'd done in her life. Thoughtfully and with the steeliness of someone who has accepted her fate, she said, "No, I've done everything I wanted to, and don't regret anything." I looked at her lying there and thought to myself, this is the way I want to go, too.

I would be lying if I said navigating those eight months from diagnosis to death were easy. They were trying but at the same time, they were a veritable stream of knowledge of what it really means to be a human being in this world.

I came in from work one evening and asked her without thinking, "How you doin' sister?"

She answered back, "Fine, brother."

I called her *sister* from then on, watching her as I fed her milk and Jell-O mixed together, about the only thing that she would really eat. Anyone who has had the experience of dealing with someone struggling with cancer knows how the appetite can come and go in a minute. She had cravings for everything from homemade dumplings to a piece of chicken fried hard, to cabbage and corn bread. She might taste it and leave the rest alone, the craving having passed as quickly as it had come.

What she really anguished over was using the bathroom. I, along with other family members, had to move into her private space of helping her to the portable pot and emptying it when she was finished. That was the one thing that really bothered her the most.

Seeing my mother in need of help moved me to stop calling her *mama* and start calling her *sister*. She needed a friend and brother at that time more than she needed a son. I realized as much feeding her spoon for spoon waiting for her to gesture with a turn of her hand for the next spoonful. Our eyes met as I stood there, amazed at the profound turn of events to make us change roles, both of us adults, me feeding her like the child I once was. There was just no room to be a son at this moment. It was a role I stepped out of unconsciously, without consideration of how to be—no map, without sentiment.

In this new role, I found myself jockeying to know what to do, because I wasn't sure. When those helping women—nurses, sister, cousins, friends, and neighbors—came to change her bed linen, change her adult diapers, or give her sponge baths, they closed the door, and I was shut out of the world of her body from which I'd been born. I found myself in a peculiar nexus of son and friend who would have no trouble helping her wherever needed and looking upon the wasting breasts from which I'd once fed or the gray at the crossroads of her body through which I'd emerged into the world. I felt I owed it to her to cleanse her, change her, or do whatever to make her comfortable. I was not asked. I wasn't sure a man should ask. The door just closed in my face. I noticed the nurses who came always sought out my sister to ask questions or advise in administering medicine. My sister would then tell them to ask me. Looking back, those women weren't being insensitive. They did not know me, had no record that Black men like myself even existed, so it did not enter the realm of their imagination, and I was too new to myself.

I was an emergent species of Black male in the dark hour of my mother's dwindling time on earth. She was the waning moon as I was a new moon arriving, not yet full. They had not seen a man caught between how to be to a woman who was no longer just his mother. That role was fast moving to a twilight because the imminence of death and the infirmities of its coming had altered our relationship. I was brother and friend now and a stranger to myself, not comfortable in my newfound way of being in the world. Certainly not willing to imitate my father, who had become an angry ghost of a man lurking in the background. My two brothers helped where they thought they should.

My mother passed on the eighth day after her seventy-seventh birthday instead of the seventh day. It was a Sunday. That Saturday on her deathbed, my niece called from Australia to tell my sister and brother-in-law that she was lost in the Sydney airport, not knowing who would pick her up. She was upset, and I told my sister this while standing over my mother as we thought she was passing and not fully cognizant of our conversation. My mother opened her eyes, moaned, and turned herself to the side as if to say, "What?" I knew immediately I had disrupted the process of her passing. She would stay another day. That Sunday morning, somehow sensing she was lingering unnecessarily, I went into her room and said to her, "Sister, move on now."

My niece called to say she had reached her destination. I told my niece, Ebony, that I would put the phone to her grandmother's ear so she could tell her she was fine. My mother seemed to rest easier. I remember asking her, "Are you afraid?" She moaned something; whether she was saying yes or no, I can't say. I told her while others were absent from the room that I would do what I could with those left behind, but that her work here was done.

It's a strange feeling to be altered by death into roles and ruminations of mind no one taught you to know in life. In addition to friend and brother, I found myself playing the role of psychologist and guide with no instruction book or elder and feeling a certain amount of guilt if I didn't quite serve her well in that capacity; this would worry me months after her death. As she lay dying, I told a cousin that she was not quite ready yet. "They" were synchronizing her weakening heartbeat rhythm with the next plane of existence. Just who "they" were that both my mother and I spoke of, I couldn't say and still can't.

In my mind I saw a tunnel that reminded me of a womb and ghostly, unformed beings coming to wait for her. Whether or not it was my imagination, it allowed me to sense the very point of her passing and tell her that it would be all right, that "they" were coming to meet her. That everything continued on, nothing was ever really lost, and we would meet again. I often spoke to her alone not wanting to fight with those in her midst who believed differently from the way I do, in their heavens and hells, their sins and redemptions. In response to her dying, I was more and more the stranger with the very people I had known all my life. All I knew was what I felt and saw in my mind's eye, and it was our secret. She died a few hours later.

Still after her death, I've not developed a clear sense of the kind of man I am now. I have been altered in ways for which I have no models amongst men. I feel blessed and terribly alone. I sense that who I have become reflects some long-lost role, natural to someone like me, a name, before our ancestors were torn from Africa and our spiritual knowledge gutted and cast away like so much offal to survive on American soil.

I may never fully grasp the way I have come to exist in this moment in time. But I do know that I'm a better human being for what I experienced of Sister's dying.

Our lives had become much larger than a mother's and son's. Being a man or woman is not an isolated thing, not a gender role, not something we attach money, status, and power to robbing ourselves of an intrinsic human value we rarely call upon. In the midst of dying, Sister helped me find and begin trusting a whole new part of myself.

Conrad R. Pegues *is a writer who has been published in several anthologies. He believes writing should be a means to help and heal in our lives.*

Unplanned Estates Never End Pleasantly

Chris B. Bennett

I found out at a relatively young age that few things can affect a person more than the death of a loved one who is very close to them. Given the circumstances, the untimely death of a mother, brother, sister, father, son, or daughter can change a person's outlook on life. Though it took some time to set in, the experience that I encountered gave me a new outlook on life.

As my sophomore year in college was about to end, I was hit with the heartbreaking news that my mother had died from a seizure. It was a week before finals, and now I found myself on a plane headed from Atlanta to Seattle in disbelief because I had not a clue that my mother, who had turned forty-three just one month earlier, was sick.

When I arrived at my mother's house, it was already full of friends and relatives going through my mother's belongings and taking things for themselves and throwing out everything else that they deemed as trash or junk. It was a difficult thing for me to watch, especially since the funeral was still a few days away. Friends and family going through her wardrobe like an after-Christmas sale, valuables being taken from the house for so-called safe keeping never to be seen again.

After the funeral, I headed back to Atlanta to take my final exams.

Could I pass them? Will I pass them? At that point in time, I really didn't care one way or the other.

I knew that my mother would rather have had me stay in Seattle and attend the University of Washington, and she thought that I was influenced by my father to attend school in Atlanta. But indeed, I was at the school of my dreams, and had you asked me a few years ago in my wildest dreams if I thought I'd ever attend Morehouse College, both you and I would have laughed at that idea over and over again.

But now, I was second-guessing my decision to leave Seattle and go to school down South.

I remember thinking about how things could have been different if I had stayed in Seattle and gone to school. I remember blaming myself for not being there for her, like she had been there for me for so many years. If I had been there, she'd still be alive.

I completed my finals and said good-bye to all of my friends on campus as if it'd be the last time I would see them in my life. I was headed back to Seattle full of mixed emotions and had no idea of what life had in store for me, but I certainly wasn't going to let life pass me by. I was going to live life to the fullest because the one thing that I was sure of was the fact that in life tomorrow is not guaranteed.

However, I took this fact of life the wrong way. I wanted to have a kid to replace the life that had been lost. I wanted to have material things right now, regardless of how I got them. I wanted to do all the things that eventually led to the downfall of so many Black men.

But then as always, my path was set for me, and all I could do was survive the ride.

I learned very quickly that people will take advantage of you, if you don't stand up and put your foot down.

A few weeks after I got back into town, I got a call from a relative telling me that my aunt was moving back to Seattle and she had told everyone that she had a conversation with me and that I said it was okay for her to move into my mother's house and help take care of the mortgage payments.

Well, the truth of the matter was that we did have a conversation at the house the same day that everyone was picking through things and throwing things out of the house right before the funeral. At that point in time she stated that she was *thinking* about moving back to Seattle and that she was thinking that she could move into the house and help take care of the mortgage, so that I wouldn't have to worry about it.

My response at the time to her was that we'd have to talk about it later after I got back into Seattle from taking my finals. Needless to say, that was neither the time nor the place to have such a conversation. With so much going on and people coming at me from every which way, I was an emotional mess, and to make a commitment like that to someone was nothing I was prepared to deal with.

I talked to my uncle, who was supposed to be executor of the estate but had yet to file the papers, and he was saying that she had quit her job in Texas and was headed to Seattle, and that she needed a place to stay.

This, in my opinion, was not my problem, and nothing I had to deal with. I told everyone I was against her moving into the house and gave my reasons for making that decision. Besides, she hadn't even talked to me. She talked to everyone else about her packing up, heading to Seattle, and moving into the house, but she hadn't contacted me at all.

I had the keys to the house, and I was not going to let her move in. Given the way that things were coming down, I made the decision to file the paperwork with the court to become administrator of the estate. I had come to the conclusion that in order to look out for the best interests of my younger brother and sister (and myself) was for me to take control of the estate. Especially given the fact that I was the only sibling who was not a minor. I called my uncle and informed him of my decision, and he wished me luck.

Was I ready to take on such a task? I didn't know. But what I did know is that I wasn't going to have people make decisions for me and not include me in the process. No, I was either going to sink or swim, but whatever was going to happen, I was going to do it my way.

A few days later, I got a call from one of my other uncles. My aunt was coming into town in a few days, and he wanted to know if it would be okay for her to store some of her things in the house until she got settled into town. I was reluctant at first, but I finally agreed to let her store some of her things in the house for about a week or two until she got settled. My keys to the house were supposed to be returned to me the same day.

A week and a half went by, and I hadn't heard back from anyone yet or gotten my keys back. So I decided to drive by my mother's house. I got out of the car, walked up to the front porch and knocked on the door. My aunt opens the door and acts as though nothing was wrong. She was entertaining, and had rearranged my mother's furniture in the house to her liking.

I was very upset—not only had she moved into the house, but she was also making herself very comfortable, and no one had the decency to tell me that she was living in the house, or how she planned on paying for the bills that she was accumulating by living there. I didn't want to make a scene in front of her company, so I simply told her that we needed to talk and to call me the next day.

I called my uncle as soon as I got home. I asked him why my aunt was staying in the house and why no one had returned my keys. He replied by saying that they were moving her stuff into the house and she had no other place to go, so he didn't see anything wrong with here staying in the house.

The next day my aunt called me, and I told her that she needed to move out of the house and return my keys to me. There were just too many things going on with the estate, and I needed to get everything under control. She said she didn't have any place to go, but we eventually agreed that she'd move out in two weeks.

Needless to say, two weeks later she still had not moved out of the house. So I called her and told her that she needed to be out of the house by the end of the week or else I was going to have to take drastic measures to get her out of the house.

I didn't know who I could trust. Everyone was coming at me from all angles, and my brother and sister's dad, whom no one really trusted, was silent but lurking in the wings. He was a real estate agent and had always wanted my mother to sell the house, and the first thing he said to my uncle after her death was that we could get a lot of money for the house. My uncle told him that they were not going to sell the house. I always knew that my mother was adamant about not selling her house. Regardless of the circumstances the one thing that she was not going to do was sell her house.

Another week passed, and I was forced to play my hand. So with the help of a friend, I went to the house and changed the locks on the doors. It was a very hard decision to make, but in my opinion, no one respected me or what I had to say, and people were taking advantage of the situation that I was in.

The move needed to be made, and it was a clear lesson for me to distinguish between personal decisions and business decisions. While the initial thought process behind the decision was based on a personal level of disrespect, the bottom line was that this was not personal, it was business. I knew that I would not be popular with my family, but being popular and taking care of business in this case, were two entirely different things.

After changing the locks on the door, I thought to myself how much easier this whole situation would be had my mother had a will. Supposedly she had one, but no one had been able to find it. So I decided to start going through the house myself in an attempt to find it, if it existed. I didn't find a will, but what I did find was one of my mother's pay stubs, and as it turned out, she didn't make quite as much money as I thought she did. She made a good living, but it definitely made me realize how creative she must have been in order to provide for us the way that she did, and how much she must have sacrificed. She always was willing to help others, and she loved to cook extravagant meals for other people.

I realized then, quite a few things. Number one, you don't live for yourself, but you live for others, and money does not constitute happiness. I realized that the only difference between myself and many other people I grew up with is that I was able to take advantage of opportunities that were available to me. But I also realized that in order to take advantage of opportunities, you had to be prepared for them, because timing is everything and if you miss the boat, the opportunity may never present itself to you again. I realized that the opportunities were not really about me, but it was about how I can turn these opportunities into something positive for someone who may not have been afforded the same opportunity. One person's individual success means nothing, if that person's actions do nothing to improve the well-being of the masses.

About a week after the changing of the locks, I received a call from my aunt at work. She informed me that some of her silk dresses were locked up in the house and that she needed to get them. I told her that I hadn't seen any dresses in the house.

Before my mother passed away, I was stubborn, spoiled, selfish, and my ambitions were driven by greed. But the biggest thing I learned is that as a Black man, you have to be able to stand your ground and make decisions that you can stand by. You're not going to make everyone happy all the time, but as long as you are firm, fair, and objective, you can always look yourself in the mirror and be happy with anything that you've done. Because at the end of the day, all the people full of advice are nowhere to be found, and you're left there all alone without anyone to hold your hand.

This was the first of many situations associated with the death of my mother that helped me grow as a person. I wouldn't say that I grew up, because the dynamics of a young man becoming a strong Black man is a life-long journey.

Eventually, because of all the infighting, I was taken to court over the estate, and a court decree ordered the sale of the house, and I had the right of first refusal to match any offers on the house. Eventually, I lost the bidding war over the house and the house left our family for good. The bad thing about the whole situation is that nobody gained anything in the process of settling the estate. After all the lawyers, the accountant, and the people associated with the sale of the house took their share out of the sale price, there was very little to split among my siblings and myself. And more than anything else, there are tarnished relationships that can never be fully mended.

Am I hurt by some of the experiences? Of course. But I wouldn't change anything that has happened, because without them, at this point in my life I would still be struggling to learn the lessons that have helped sculpt me into who I am today. All things happened for a reason, for what reason you'll never know until much later in life. Many say that I'm an old soul, but I have fun, I enjoy life. And I cherish the opportunity to have a positive impact on the lives of others.

Chris B. Bennett is associate publisher of the Seattle Medium Newspaper Group and cohost of the Rhythm & News Radio Show on KRIZ/KYIZ in Seattle. He is currently working on his upcoming novel, Undeniable Fate.

Ten Years of Mourning Jean

Marcus Reeves

I remember sitting in the living room when my mother, while walking into the room from the kitchen, started turning into a demon. Literally. Her eyes transformed into ominous red marbles. She walked slowly with a zombie pace. Her teeth began to fang slightly. And the only thing on her mind, at that point, was to kill . . . me. Horrified at the sight of my mother and the thought of what she might do, I jumped from my chair, bolted out the front door, down the stairs, and into the street. I ran past three houses when I felt safe enough to turn around, only to see my mother and the apartment I grew up in explode into a fiery, orange ball of flames. Then, immediately, that image would disappear, and I'd wake up, sweating and breathing furiously.

Almost ten years had passed since my mother's death, and I was still having the same reoccurring dream about her. And with all the intellectual power I could muster, I couldn't figure out what the nightmare meant especially the part about her becoming a monster. Jean (my older siblings and I called my mother by her first name) died in August 1991, the summer I was entering my senior year of college. She was getting her dialysis treatment when she had an allergic reaction, causing her air passages to swell and suffocate her to death. Jean's sudden departure rocked me—the youngest of her three children. But surprisingly, I was hurt mostly by the painful and scary way in which she died, not by the fact that I wouldn't see my mother again. I loved my mother, but I had been preparing for her death emotionally when she began dialysis several months prior. Nevertheless, even while she was alive, I hadn't thought much about Jean or my life growing up with her.

When I left our apartment in Newark, New Jersey, four years earlier to attend Rutgers University in New Brunswick, I'd put much of my past—especially my home life—on the outskirts of my mind. After Jean's funeral and a brief grieving period at home, I was off to finish school again to complete the most crucial year of my academic career—senior year. But I was also subconsciously beginning the process of totally putting Jean out of my mind. Four months into the senior year of my semester is when I started to have the recurring nightmare.

I initially interpreted the dream as the trauma of seeing my mother dead, and I was unconsciously mixing her up with a creature feature. But after a decade of the exact same vision, I became extremely concerned that at age thirty-two that I was still having the same dream I first had at twenty-two. But the big difference was I was two years into a marriage, and felt I now needed to begin revisiting life with my mother.

Besides, my wife always asked me about Jean. "Do I remind you of her?" she'd ask. But I would skate over the topic, responding jokingly that my mother was a simpleminded woman who was hot tempered and an alcoholic. I'd always finish by saying I made it a point to never date or marry someone like my mother. Not much was said afterwards. At that point in my adult life, I'd removed Jean so far from my thoughts, except for an occasional joke about her with my older brother and sister, that I had no idea of what I thought of Jean as a mother, a woman, or even as a human being. The only sure thing about Jean I did recall was I knew that I loved her. After all, she was my mother. There wasn't much beyond that. So at my wife's behest, I began a mental journey, a cathartic self-therapy project to remember and evaluate life with Jean.

The project was a journal where I'd write down past anecdotes involving Jean and my thoughts about her. Since I didn't have too close a relationship with my mother, and my memory of her was blurred a little by suppression, I'd have to piece back the past through scenes. At first, the task was a bit intimidating because I was used to pushing forward and leaving my personal history slightly buried. And initially I didn't know where to start. So I began with the first memory that hit my brain and proceeded to write them down spontaneously.

I carried a journal with me at all times, kept my mind searching for any recollections of Jean and began writing madly whenever and wherever the thought hit me. A substantial bulk of the process took roughly a month before I was able to start making sense of my mother or begin to form a true opinion of her. Honesty was important for this journey because folks, especially men, can be extra protective of their mothers (alive or deceased) and remembering them in ill light can seem disrespectful. But this task wasn't to glorify or crucify Jean, it was to complete my mourning process by remembering my mother—the good and bad of my mother—and become a better man because of it.

After several weeks of writing, the stories and thoughts began to yield a candid portrait of Jean, one that was painful and sometimes embarrassing. I started to recognize a few of Jean's traits that were a great source of dysfunctionality for me as a child. The first thing, though minute, was her great vanity. Call it narcissism, but at times her concern for looking good and guarding her possessions took precedence over her kids. The first anecdote I remembered occurred when I was eleven and my mother insulted and refused to wear the first gift I ever bought her—a gaudy, silver flower brooch. One day I asked why she never wore it, and she replied, "I'm not wearing that ugly thing." Enraged by her remark, I immediately took the brooch in the backyard and crushed it with a pair of pliers.

Another time, a year after the gift incident, I was taking Jean's clothes to the dry cleaners and was robbed of her purple corduroy pants. The guy who robbed me threatened to kill me if I told on him. (Mind you, his threat came six months after his own throat was severely cut in a fight.) But I told my mother anyway. Surprisingly I wasn't asked if I was okay, but instead I was loudly insulted because I didn't put up a fight for her pants.

Another matter of home life, which was the theme of several journal entries, was my mother's serial dating. Jean was single, having only married and divorced my sister's father (my brother and I also had different fathers). So living in a house devoid of a father figure left a hole that was filled, off and on, by the various boyfriends she would date over the years. Only most of these relationships wouldn't last long enough for me to really get to know any of the men. Or when a boyfriend did stick around and if the idea of marriage was seriously considered, he turned out to be an afflicted, domineering asshole who made me and my siblings sick.

I really grew fond of her boyfriend Chester. He was the first boyfriend to set aside time whenever he could to play catch with me. Plus he was funny as all hell and talked to me often. And the fact that he was a yellow dude with an Afro (just like me) didn't hurt either. But when he and my mother talked of marriage and he moved in, everything went south. He started dictating new rules about what time I should come home, when I went to bed, and even how I should eat my breakfast—all without consulting my mother or me. Jean did nothing and said nothing when I questioned his rules. She just said, "That's what Chester wants." Also it seemed like every other night Chester would come home drunk, fall out on Jean's bed, and start snoring as loud as a jet engine. Needless to say, that quelled me of my strong desire for a father in the home. I was glad when that relationship ended. But I did understand that my mother needed love and companionship, too.

The mammoth issue and the common thread running through many of my memories was Jean's alcoholism. My mother was a functioning addict whose sole afterwork activity was stopping at our neighborhood bar. This ritual became the root of many turbulent moments in both my childhood and teenage years. Because whether tipsy or flat drunk, a different Jean from the one who left for work in the morning would enter our front door at the end of a day. And no matter which Jean came in, all of them eventually turned embarrassing and confrontational. Numerous fights between her and my older sister ensued, resulting in my sister being kicked out the house. And there were times when a stone-drunk Jean would become delusional and begin talking gibberish from her own subconscious. She'd say stuff like, "I'm going home and get something to eat," which filled me with occasional fears of abandonment as a child. Since she was already home, our home, I felt she was tired of her kids and about to run off, leave me, and find a new home. Or there were times when Jean would misplace rage. When I was twelve, and told her of an argument I had with another student at school, she slapped me in the back with a force I'd never felt before from her. Her heated reaction came on the heels of an argument she had with her current boyfriend. After watching her go get an aluminum ruler to finish my beating, I ran out the house in my socks and bathrobe. During my high school years, Jean's intoxication would mostly result in episodes of her own silent nostalgia. I would see her listening to my brother's Edith Piaf records, quietly reflecting on the past and sometimes crying. But by that point, I had developed my own coping mechanisms to deal with my mother's drinking problem. One was avoidance, and the other was developing a wry and biting sense of humor that would keep me psychologically afloat and aloof until I graduated high school and could escape to college.

Despite her problems, Jean still dished the nuts and bolts of motherhood, raising my siblings and me with love and some guidance. When I joined the Avenues (one of the largest gangs in Newark) in the fifth grade, my mother's calm words convinced me to quit. And when I began to perform below par academically in public junior high, Jean transferred me to a private school, where I improved dramatically. I was recalling the positive moments along with the negative in my journal entries. But unfortunately, I would eventually discover that life with Jean was filled with a lot of the latter. That's why as I moved on in life, I did less thinking or even talking about her.

Nevertheless, through my writing, I was getting a clearer understanding of my mother and how I felt about her. I was constantly dialoguing about it with my wife. Also, through discussions with my brother and sister about Jean, I was made to realize that my mother had a rocky childhood and felt unfulfilled in her own adult life. Jean drowned unresolved issues in alcohol and the need for affirmation through looking fly and having boyfriends. I had pretty much filled my journal and was finally able to put my mother and our lives growing up with her into perspective. It was the proper way to mourn my loss. Once in a comfortable mental place, I finally sat my wife down and explained Jean. She was a mother who loved her children, but

Your Soul's Journey

*And if I go and prepare a place for you, I will come back and take
you to be with me that you also may be where I am.*
—John 14:3

*Those who are dead are never gone,
they are there in the thickening shadow.
The dead are not under the earth;
they are in the tree that rustles. . . .*
—Unknown African Poet

Saying good-bye to the ones you love is never easy. Suffering is the comparison of what we have and what we wished we had received. As we age, our physical and mental abilities are diminished. Death comes to everyone and everything. Life is fragile, and the body that you received at birth is not yours to keep. In your own life, you have had close calls with death. The kind that gets your armpits hot and your heart racing. A quick turn of the car, a missed accident two minutes sooner or two minutes later. How many times have you said, That could have been it for me? Life is just unpredictable. Do you know how long you really have to live?

The pain really begins when we grieve for our loved ones who pass, parents, other family members, friends. Rarely do we celebrate their lives when they're here, but we truly grieve for their physical body when their soul has passed on. We want to reach out and touch them one more time. Tell them how much they may have meant. Apologize for not sticking around to see the last few days of their lives because the pain was too great to bear.

Why not begin preparing for death today? You can give everyone the love they deserve as if it's the last time you may see them. Prepare your will and talk to your friends and family about preparing their wills. Buy life insurance, so you can have peace of mind and know that your family can be taken care of in their time of need. The honor is giving your family the comfort of being prepared so that they can truly celebrate the service and commitment that you have given the Lord!

Soul Source

Today you have a brand-new chance to add new memories and foster love within your family. If you're busy, just stop! The simple things bring happiness to the people who truly love you. Dinner, time at the park, or a special note that says "I love you." Although you can never ward off death, you can enjoy the days that are left and create a source of peace and inner joy for yourself.

- What are your fears about death?
- Describe the life that you have led.
- Have you lived or attempted to fulfill your purpose?
- Have you contributed to the pain and suffering of others?
- What is your next plan of action to help any loved ones who may need to die with grace?

SOUL RESOURCES

Here are a few resources to help you on your journey to peace, wholeness, and joy.

Educational

United Negro College Fund

www.uncf.org

Having supported the postsecondary studies of over three hundred thousand African-American students, the UNCF is doing valuable work every day. The UNCF is widely known for its popular tag line, "A mind is a terrible thing to waste." If you are a student, contact the UNCF about ways they can assist you in your education. If you're not a student, a tax-deductible contribution would be a concrete way for you to assist in the UNCF's valiant mission.

United Negro College Fund
8260 Willow Oaks Corporate Drive
Fairfax, VA 22031
(800) 331-2244

Kaplan

www.kaptest.com

For more than sixty years, Kaplan has helped over three million students pursue their educational goals. Through its Web site, you have access to SAT and other test-prep courses, tutoring services, admissions consulting, and financial-aid guidance. A service such as Kaplan is highly useful to those thinking about college or graduate school.

www.africana.com

This Web site focuses on African and African-American interests, in particular news, history, culture, and other educational content. In part, the site is based on Microsoft's Encarta African-American Encyclopedia.

Elder Care (and Child Care)

www.careguide.net

This on-line "personal care giving resource" provides directories, articles, newsletters, and more about issues concerning dealing with older loved ones. There is also another channel that deals with child care concerns.

www.hospicenet.org

A site for patients and families facing life-threatening illness. The site offers a great deal of assistance for patients and caregivers. It covers everything from resolving pain without medication to talking to children about death to preparing for approaching death.

Health

American Cancer Society

www.cancer.org

The ACS is the foremost group in education and information on all types of cancer. The organization conducts a wide range of programs.
(800) ACS-2345

American Heart Association

www.americanheart.org

The AHA is dedicated to providing education and information on fighting heart disease and stroke. Its Web site is a valuable resource for women.
American Heart Association, National Center
7272 Greenville Avenue
Dallas, Texas 75231
The organization is affiliated with the following hot lines:

Customer Heart and Stroke Information
(800) AHA-USA1

ECC Information
(877) AHA-4-CPR

Stroke Information
(888) 4-STROKE

Women's Health Information
(888) MY HEART

Office of Minority Health

www.omhrc.gov

The Office of Minority Health provides a wealth of information about health issues affecting minorities. It provides information about current health reports and resources of health services nationwide. In addition to its Web site, the department offers free communication on various health topics specific to ethnic minorities.

Office of Minority Health Resource Center
P.O. Box 37337
Washington, DC 20013-7337
(800) 444-6472

Magic Johnson Foundation

www.magicjohnson.org

The Magic Johnson Foundation is "dedicated to serve the educational, social, and health needs of our community" by disseminating information, funding community-based programs and health-related services specifically geared at enhancing the lives of African Americans.

Planned Parenthood

www.plannedparenthood.org

Planned Parenthood Federation of America, Inc., is the world's largest and most trusted voluntary reproductive-health-care organization. Its Web site provides an nearly exhaustive list of resources on family planning and sex-related concerns.

Sickle Cell Disease Foundation of California

www.scdrf.org

The Sickle Cell Disease Foundation of California has committed itself to "education and life-enhancing programs and services to individuals with sickle cell disease" to broadening public awareness about sickle-cell disease and to promoting medical research and education to ultimately find a cure.

5110 W. Goldleaf Circle, Suite 150
Los Angeles, CA 90056
(323) 299-3600, (877) 288-CURE
Fax: (323) 299-3605

www.unspeakable.com

According to unspeakable.com, one out of every five Americans carries a sexually transmitted disease. This site is designed to be a "frank, accurate, and unembarrassed guide to the prevention and treatment of sexually transmitted diseases." The site aims to dispel common misconceptions about STDs and to encourage people to get routinely tested for STDs.

Internet Resources (General)

www.about.com

The African-American culture section of About.com offers expert-guided Internet resources of interest to African Americans.

www.africanbynature.com/kingdom.html

The aim of this site is to "blend progressive attention to the study of history and professional service with special items to encourage your social, emotional, and intellectual growth."

www.toptags.com/aama/

The Afro-American Almanac is an on-line presentation of the African in America. A historical perspective of a nation, its people, and its cultural evolution. From the beginning of the slave trade through the civil rights movement, to the present. Information that will give you a better understanding of the problems we face today as a nation. This site provides a virtually unlimited number of links of everything related to the African-American experience from shopping to educational needs to health and wellness resources.

www.blackplanet.com

Simply the best Black on-line community on the Web. With hundreds of thousands of members, you'll find lively discussions on just about any subject you can imagine.

www.blackwebsites.com

A somewhat comprehensive collection of links to African-American Web sites on every subject.

www.agoodblackman.com

A 100 percent Black-owned Web site dedicated to loving, honoring, uplifting, and celebrating men of African descent and men of color by providing a place of information and inspiration.

www.melanet.com

Melanet.com is the platform for intellectual, economic, and spiritual expression of peoples throughout the African diaspora. Provides information on various life projects including wedding planning, Kwanzaa celebrations, chat rooms, shopping, business resources, and an Afrocentric calendar.

www.netnoir.com

Netnoir is a very popular Black Web site of general interest that boasts half a million visitors every month. Its channels include news, music, virtual communities, shopping, chat rooms, personal e-mail accounts, and much more. (As of this writing, Netnoir's Web site is under construction.)

www.SoulsOfMySisters.com

What started out as this book has became an exciting movement of sisters. SoulsofMySisters.com is a community of sisters working together toward peace and healing. By sisters, we mean women of color who share a kindred spirit that gives us strength and faith. The community is like a second home for its members. It is a community where women of color can come together for an intimate sharing of information and heart-filled support. It's like sharing secrets over a cup of coffee or having a late night phone chat with one of your closest friends.

At SoulsOfMySisters.com, you can do the following: Get the latest information on your spiritual health and well-being. Find out if you're truly in love. Enter contests to win fabulous prizes like trips and spa days! Meet sisters like yourself who aren't afraid to tell their personal stories to aid in the healing of women of color—and much, much more. SoulsOfMySisters.com can start a spiritual journey toward healing yourself and your sisters.

Membership Organizations

National Association for the Advancement of Colored People

www.naacp.org

Founded by W.E.B. DuBois, Ida B. Wells, and others, today the NAACP boasts over 2,200 branches in all fifty states and internationally. The NAACP sponsors scores of educational and political programs from voter-registration initiatives to college counseling, placement, and scholarships.

NAACP, Washington Bureau
1025 Vermont Avenue, NW, Suite 1120
Washington, DC 20005
(202) 638-2269

National Urban League

www.nul.org

Founded in 1910, the National Urban League is the premier social service and civil rights organization in America. The League is a nonprofit community-based organization headquartered in New York City, with 115 affiliates in thirty-four states and the District of Columbia.

120 Wall Street
New York, NY, 10005
(212) 558-5300
Fax: (212) 558-5332
E-mail: info@nul.org

Money Resources

www.blackenterprise.com

Black Enterprise magazine's Web page serves as a good financial homepage. It offers such information and market tools as stock quotes, tickers, and financial news. It also offers general news of importance to African Americans.

Debtors Anonymous

www.debtorsanonymous.org

The focus of Debtors Anonymous is to help people "recover from compulsive debting." The only membership requirement is that you want to stop incurring unsecured debt. There are no dues, and DA is not affiliated with any sect, denomination, or political viewpoint.

Political

Congressional Black Caucus Foundation, Inc.

www.cbcfonline.org

Established in 1976, the CBCF is a nonprofit research and educational institute that seeks to assist African American political leaders of today and prepare those of tomorrow.

1004 Pennsylvania Avenue, SE
Washington, DC 20003
Phone: (800) 784-2577 or (202) 675-6730
Fax: (202) 547-3806

Professional Organizations

Association of Black Psychologists

www.abpsi.org

ABPsi is the national organization of African-American psychologists. In addition to providing resources for its members, the organization also offers a psychologist locator search on its Web site. ABPsi helps to maintain the focus on African-American mental health.

P.O. Box 55999
Washington, DC 20040-5999
(202) 722-0808

National Bar Association

www.nationalbar.org

The NBA is the national organization of African-American lawyers. Its mission is "to advance the science of jurisprudence, uphold the honor of the legal profession, promote social intercourse among the members of the bar, and protect the civil and political rights of all citizens of the several states of the United States."

1225 Eleventh Street, NW
Washington, DC 20001
(202) 842-3900
Fax: (202) 289-6170

National Association of Black Journalists

www.nabj.org

The National Association of Black Journalists (NABJ) is an organization of "journalists, students, and media-related professionals that provides quality programs and services to benefit Black journalists worldwide." Foremost among the goals of the NABJ is increasing numbers of Blacks in the media, especially in management positions. The NABJ also sponsors numerous informational and educational programs.

8701A Adelphi Road
Adelphi, MD 20783-1716
(301) 445-7100
Fax: (301) 445-7101

National Society of Black Engineers

www.nsbe.org/

NSBE's mission is to increase the number of culturally responsible Black engineers who excel academically, succeed professionally, and positively impact the community. With more than ten thousand members, NSBE is the largest student-managed organization in the country.

National Society of Black Engineers
World Headquarters
1454 Duke Street
Alexandria, Virginia 22314
(703) 549-2207
Fax: (703) 683-5312
E-mail: info@nsbe.org

National Black MBA Association

www.nbmbaa.org

Association of African-American professionals who have obtained their master's of business administration. Their vision is to be an "organization that leads in the creation of economic and intellectual wealth for Blacks."

NBMBAA National Headquarters
National Black MBA Association, Inc.
180 N. Michigan Avenue
Suite 1400
Chicago, IL 60601
(312) 236-BMBA (2622)
Fax: (312) 236-4131

National Medical Association

www.nmanet.org

The NMA is the national organization of African-American physicians committed to the welfare of its members and patients. They provide physician-locator services, on-line resources, health reports, and public information videos on health issues that affect the African-American community.

National Medical Association
1012 Tenth Street, NW
Washington, DC 20001
(202) 204-1223

Fraternities

Alpha Phi Alpha Fraternity, Inc.

www.alphaphialpha.net
2313 Saint Paul Street
Baltimore, MD 21218-5234
(410) 554-0040
Fax: (410) 554-0054

Omega Psi Phi Fraternity, Inc.

www.omegapsiphifraternity.org
3951 Snapfinger Parkway
Decatur, GA 30035
(404) 284-5533

Kappa Alpha Psi Fraternity, Inc.

www.kappaalphapsi.com
2322-24 North Broad Street
Philadelphia, PA 19132-4590
(215) 228-7184

Phi Beta Sigma Fraternity, Inc.

www.pbs1914.org
  145 Kennedy Street, NW
  Washington, DC 20011
  (202) 726-5434
  Fax (202) 882-1681